Enterprising Women

D0074479

University of Pennsylvania Press
Series in Contemporary Ethnography
Dan Rose and Paul Stoller, General Editors

Camille Bacon-Smith. *Enterprising Women: Television Fandom and the Creation of Popular Myth.* 1992.

John D. Dorst. *The Written Suburb: An American Site, An Ethnographic Dilemma.* 1989.

Douglas E. Foley. *Learning Capitalist Culture: Deep in the Heart of Tejas.* 1990.

Kirin Narayan. *Storytellers, Saints, and Scoundrels: Folk Narrative in Hindu Religious Teaching.* 1989.

Dan Rose. *Patterns of American Culture: Ethnography and Estrangement.* 1989.

Paul Stoller. *The Taste of Ethnographic Things: The Senses in Anthropology.* 1989.

Jim Wafer. *The Taste of Blood: Spirit Possession in Brazilian Candomblé.* 1991.

Publications of the American Folklore Society
New Series
General Editor, Patrick B. Mullen

Enterprising Women
Television Fandom and the Creation of Popular Myth

Camille Bacon-Smith

Photographs by Stephanie A. Hall

UNIVERSITY OF PENNSYLVANIA PRESS   Philadelphia

Copyright © 1992 by Camille Bacon-Smith
All rights reserved
Printed in the United States of America

Permission is acknowledged to reprint published material:
From *Killing Time,* by Della Van Hise. New York: Pocket Books, 1985. Copyright ©
1985 by Paramount Pictures Corporation. Reprinted by permission of Pocket Books.

From *Dreadnought,* by Diane Carey. New York: Pocket Books, 1986. Copyright © by
Paramount Pictures Corporation. Reprinted by permission of Pocket Books.

From *Demons,* by J. M. Dillard. New York: Pocket Books, 1986. Copyright © by
Paramount Pictures Corporation. Reprinted by permission of Pocket Books.

Quotations from *Blake's 7* episode "Star One," are reprinted by permission of Terry
Nation.

Library of Congress Cataloging-in-Publication Data

Bacon-Smith, Camille.
    Enterprising women : television fandom and the creation of popular myth /
Camille Bacon-Smith.
        p. cm. — (Series in Contemporary ethnography) (Publications of the
American Folklore Society. New series)
    Includes bibliographical references and index.
    ISBN 0-8122-3098-1. — ISBN 0-8122-1379-3 (pbk.)
    1. Television and women—United States.   2. Television viewers—United
States.   3. Fans (People)—United States—Societies and clubs.   4. United States—
Popular culture.   I. Title.   II. Series.   III. Series: Publications of the American
Folklore Society. New series.
HQ1233.B25 1991
306.4′85′082—dc20   91-29875
                                                                                CIP

This book is dedicated to Teresa Pyott.

I returned to college for my bachelor's degree when I was thirty. During my first year at the University of Pennsylvania, Dan Ben-Amos introduced me to Teresa with the prophetic words, "She is the most important person in the department." For me, she was more than that: friend, mother, guide—the person I went to when I needed anything from money to a shoulder to cry on. For ten years of aggravation and struggle and triumph, and some of the hardest times two people could come up with between them, we shared moral support, cheesecake, and *General Hospital* on Friday afternoons. Before I ever began this project, Teresa taught me what community of women was all about.

Contents

LIBRARY
ALMA COLLEGE
ALMA, MICHIGAN

Acknowledgments

A book like this one belongs to the community it explores. Without the patience, good will, and thoughtful contributions of the hundreds of people whose voices you will hear on the following pages, there simply would be no pages to experience. But a few special people helped me throughout the slow process of finding out what it means to be a fan. Judy Segal was my first mentor, and she ferried me to conventions in her car, shared rooms and meals and her home with me, and introduced me to the people in the community I had to know. Jacqueline Lichtenberg was one of them, and the first to tell me plainly that under the laughter hid a lot of pain. Judith Gran was one of my first informants, and she has continued to provide support throughout the study. Lois Welling has been a steadfast source of insider knowledge and carefully considered ideas about the community of which she is a part. She also makes great fuzzy navels. Jean Curley, my second mentor, introduced me to the Philadelphia fan community and to Judith Chien, who spent more evenings than she might care to remember listening to me talk my way through the book.

When I began this project ten years ago, I believed the fan community was an important cultural development but many scholars considered it frivolous. Kenny Goldstein, however, supported the project from the first. Kenny's unflagging faith in the validity of my findings gave me the confidence to go on. Once I had it figured out, Larry Gross insisted I say it right, and then insisted that I keep on fighting to get this book into print. Likewise Brian Sutton-Smith's faith and encouragement gave me the determination I needed to see the project through to the book you hold in your hands. From Patricia Frazer Lamb I received the moral support of a scholar and fanwriter, and I learned what it means to be in this business of academia.

Some people should be remarked upon for enduring my obsessiveness during this project. Leonard Primiano in particular put up with hysterical phone calls and dragged me away from my computer when

I seemed to be getting more pale than interesting. How can I acknowledge the help Stephanie Hall gave me during this project? She took the pictures. An ethnographer in her own right, she took the shots I needed but couldn't get myself because of a perceptual impairment, and she resisted telling me what questions to ask or what to do in some really tricky interview sessions. Stephanie was there to drag me out to eat when she found me standing, glassy-eyed, in the lobby of yet another convention hotel. She was there for the late nights when all I could say was "I don't understand," and when it got really tough, she was there to remind me why I was doing this in the first place. And she taught me how to say "take a picture" and "tape recorder" in American Sign Language.

Part I
Who Are These People and What Are They Doing?

Chapter One
Introduction: Studying Fandom

The Crime

A book about women who produce a massive body of literature, art, and criticism about their favorite television and movie characters is of necessity awkward to begin. On the one hand, the ethnographer wants to jump up and down and scream, "Look what I found! A conceptual space where women can come together and create—to investigate new forms for their art and for their living outside the restrictive boundaries men have placed on women's public behavior! Not a place or a time, but a state of being—of giving each other permission—in which each may take freedom of expression into her own hands, wherever she is, whatever else she is doing!"

Then a colder mind prevails. The creation of this art, the bending of popular culture artifacts—in some cases, popular culture icons—is a subversive act undertaken by housewives and librarians, schoolteachers and data input clerks, secretaries and professors of medieval literature, under the very noses of husbands and bosses who *would not approve*, and children *who should not be exposed* to such acts of blatant civil disobedience.

Coming together in a hotel ballroom with the rebels in the cause of a women's art/communication system, the researcher feels a tiny thrill of danger. The community is open to anyone willing to participate, but closed to anyone who might jeer, or worse, blow the whistle. A man in a ten-gallon hat approaches and wants to know what is going on. There is a gleam in his eye: he sees only women about. Not all of them are pretty—some of them are middle-aged, or overweight, or both. They all return his bravado with suspicion. Lois, in her late forties and looking very prim, looks up from her place at the registration table and smiles the smile of PTA mothers everywhere. "It's a meeting of a ladies' literary society," she answers very properly.

"Mighty nice," the ten-gallon hat responds.

As he walks away, another voice at the table whispers: "And terrorist society."

Beneath the grins and the giggles and the pajama party atmosphere, the ladies gathered here know they are engaged in an act of rebellion. They have stolen characters, settings, plots off the home and movie screens, fleshed them out, created new characters for them to love and given the characters permission to love each other. And all of it is against the law. The characters and settings belong to their creators in Hollywood, who by right of law may demand payment for their use. They may sue the creators of the women's art for a portion of any profits from their activities, and they may require of them that they desist in the use of copyrighted materials.

There are a number of reasons why copyright holders hesitate to take action against these lawbreakers. The first is the most obvious: there is no percentage of profits for which to sue. The women in this community, like the poets in Moscow, do not create for financial reward, but to express their souls and to know their messages are understood by kindred souls in their community. Publications are sold at cost, often at a loss. Only the most established editors can make even enough to "roll over," or produce a large enough surplus to finance the next venture. Most editors must rely on subscriptions and at least partial payments.

Another reason why the long arm has not tapped the soft shoulder is the publicity value. While readers and writers in the community expect a particular kind of message from their own products, they demand of the commercial producers only that the product remain true to itself. The women cheerfully line up for multiple viewings of new movies in series, pass on word-of-mouth encouragement for others to watch or attend, and engage in extensive and time-consuming salvage campaigns for their favorite television programs.

Star Trek, the granddaddy of the media sources for the art, survived two cancellation attempts by its network, NBC, because loyal fans organized write-in salvage campaigns that generated hundreds of thousands of letters. A number of those early fans still participate in the women's writing community today. *Star Trek* itself continued in innumerable commercial ventures—Saturday cartoons, toys, books, movies, and now a new set of television episodes. Catchphrases from the show have entered the popular vernacular. Writers and actors in the commercial products attend conventions sponsored in part by the

Taking fandom to the outside world: "Spacer" license plate.

very ladies who are testing the sexual limits of their favorite Vulcan, Mr. Spock, in their own fiction. The write-in campaign has become so important in the industry that some producers exhort their fans to rally letter-writers around their own flagging series. In the spring of 1991, NBC, the network that first experienced the write-in when it tried to cancel *Star Trek,* bowed to write-in pressure to move fan favorite *Quantum Leap* to a more convenient viewing time. In its advertising, the network told viewers that they were returning the show to its old time slot because of the write-in campaign.

Yet another reason why copyright holders do not prosecute lies in the enormity of the "problem." Thousands of women have written or created visual art about their favorite media characters. The movement has no head, no center, no focus at which to strike. It has an almost limitless supply of ingenuity and a capacity to maintain secrecy that again can only be compared to the poetry movement in Russia. Fiction written in the community based on one television series has been printed in pale blue ink on yellow paper, which photocopies as a blank page. Editors and authors would release the work only to people they knew, and then only after the purchaser had promised not to pass the work any further. Secondary readers—those known to the purchasers but not to the editors or writers—could be given the option to read the work in the home of the purchaser, but generally could not receive full access until they became well known in the fan group.

Fans of another television show circulate their fiction almost entirely through underground photocopy. Stories created in this group are passed anonymously, or with pseudonyms. Members of the community may find out who created specific stories and will know who creates in the community as a whole, but participants guard their outside identities.

Infringing copyrights, the law they break, is only the mildest part of the subversion fomented in the ladies' literary group and terrorist society. As their greatest transgression, many of the ladies write about sex in all its permutations. In fact, sex is a primary metaphor in the language of the group; it symbolizes the search for trust and community and security.

In the following pages you will meet this group of Trekkers, *Blake's 7* fans, and action-adventure fans. You will come to see them in the spirit of IDIC—Infinite Diversity in Infinite Combinations—with all their diversity, in the good and bad, in pain, struggle and death, but also in the *joy* of creating a new kind of community that fulfills women's needs to reach out and be heard. And you will discover why they choose this very public medium to create an equally private space for themselves and their world.

Chapter Two
The Media Fanzine Community

Organization by Interest

Most fans take their first steps along the road to fandom before they have ever heard of the word or the community it represents. The road begins with their television sets, movie theaters, bookshops, where the choices they make will ultimately lead to their identities in the community they will enter. The first decision they must make is genre. Does the incipient fan prefer science fiction, fantasy, and horror books, television, and movies? Superhero comic books, or Japanese comics, called manga, and the animated and live-action television and movies based on those characters or styles? Action-adventure, spy and police television and movies? Mysteries, or historical and romance books, television and movies?

Once the fan settles on a genre or group of genres, she makes other decisions, still on her own and without contact with the community she will later join. What medium or delivery channel makes the genre most immediate, real, or enjoyable? Does she prefer live-action movies and television (called media fandom)? Books (called literary, or book, fandom)? Comic books, especially the superhero comics or the newer graphic novel medium (called comics fandom)? Or is Jap-animation, which includes both manga and animated material,[1] her favorite?

Of course, few fans limit themselves to one genre and one delivery channel. Rather, even before meeting other fans and discovering the community, fans usually enjoy many genres through many delivery media. Generally, however, the fan will have a favorite with which she will identify most strongly—in fandom, she will establish her primary identity based upon her most strongly felt attraction in the two categories she has already experienced, genre and medium, and in a third, which she will discover when she meets other fans: activity.

Meeting Other Fans

Many fans first encounter the community in clubs or at conventions, which they discover through publications—science fiction conventions regularly advertise in the monthly genre magazines, and local clubs often appear on PBS fundraisers or in news or magazine accounts of their activities.

Fan Clubs

When outsiders think of fans, they usually think of clubs, which they imagine to be a cross between a mailing list producers use to encourage viewer enthusiasm for their stars and products, and the 4-H club from their youths. The image tends to be wrong on all counts. First, while many fans do belong to formal clubs, the majority do not, and organize more informally as described below.

Of course, some fans do organize and participate in formal clubs on a national or regional basis, or gather in local clubs, like the Philadelphia Science Fiction Society or New York's Lunarians, which operate on a more or less hierarchical basis with officers and regular meetings. And here is the second flaw in the outsider's image: larger clubs, like those in Philadelphia and New York mentioned above, more closely resemble the Rotary than the 4-H. These clubs draw members at all occupational levels with an agenda that may include guest speakers and charitable works. Local clubs may issue their own publications, organize conventions, or engage in a variety of community outreach activities.

Some clubs, particularly those organized around media products (like *Star Trek* or *Doctor Who*) that maintain a high profile with fundraising and other activities, may attract a large enrollment in peripheral members who join primarily for access to the same kind of publicity releases they would receive from a movie or television studio. But even here we see the third flaw in our preexisting image: the clubs in fandom are run by the fans, for the love of the source products—the books, comics, television and movie series around which fans rally—and for the community. In spite of the efforts of some professional organizers, clubs in fandom have resisted outside control. The Doctor Who Fan Club of America (DWFCA), for example, made an effort in the early eighties to control the many local clubs that formed under its banner. Clubs joined the national organization to take advantage of its contact with the BBC. The national club produced a newsletter with information about changes in the cast, storylines for the new seasons, and production delays, all of interest to *Doctor Who* fans.

As required in the charter, members carefully volunteered for fundraisers to keep the series on their local PBS stations, but balked at the limitations the national club placed on the scope of the clubs. When national organizers objected to local clubs adding new interests, like *Blake's 7* and *Star Trek: The Next Generation,* the clubs broke away and added the new interests as they saw fit. Now DWFCA is best known as a source for BBC merchandise.

Clubs continue to be a key organizing principle for many science fiction activities and for many media fan interests. Contrary to being a merchandising arm of a studio or publisher, however, fan groups like Viewers for Quality Television, which has recently interfaced with the fan network described in this book, and the many clubs in fandom have exerted vocal and far-reaching influence on the producers and studios themselves.

Mobile Geography: Conventions

Unlike more traditional, geographically fixed, communities, including clubs, the fan world structures itself around a series of conventions, held in a "mobile geography" of hotels all over the world. Conventions spatially and temporally organize the interaction between the community and potential new members, and serve as formal meeting places for the various smaller groups of fans who follow a convention circuit.

The science fiction community held its first convention in 1936, at which a fan wore the first SF costume based on a visual media source—the Wells film *Things to Come.* Since the thirties, science fiction conventions have grown to encompass a wide variety of interests, often to the consternation of more conservative science fiction fans. Over time the model developed in the literary community has become the *Ur*-form on which later communities have shaped their own fan gatherings.

On the East Coast, the science fiction circuit moves from Boskone (Boston) in February to LunaCon (New York) in March, to Balticon (Baltimore) in April, to Disclave (Washington, D.C.) in May, to Philcon (Philadelphia) in November. In between the major dates, small conventions offer the SF gypsy a venue, but the apex of the convention year falls on Labor Day weekend.

Worldcon, the World Science Fiction Convention, travels from time

Devra Langsam, a driving force in media fandom. Editor of the first *Star Trek* fanzine, *Spockanalia,* and member of the original New York Convention Committee.

zone to time zone, from country to country. It counts among its recent venues Atlanta, Boston, New Orleans in the United States; and Sydney, Australia; The Hague, Holland; and Hamburg, Germany abroad. Participants at each Worldcon vote on the venue of the convention two years in advance based on bids by sponsoring cities publicized at local and world conventions.

When Worldcon falls outside the continental United States, participants vote on two sites: the Worldcon, and Nasfic (the North American Science Fiction Convention) for fans who cannot make the trip abroad. In recent years and in response to the growth of the Worldcon, which has topped ten thousand participants for the weekend, some local organizations are adding their own local alternative conventions, catering to specialized tastes and designed to avoid the crush of the world event.

Regardless of the size of the convention, certain activities are standard, and others are prevalent but not always present. Standard activities include an art show and dealers room(s), which organizers traditionally set together. Noise levels from the heavy traffic that flows through these areas from their opening in the morning to their closing at dinnertime can be distractingly high, so organizers generally set these pass-through attractions apart from the main activity space.

In addition to the open display areas, conventions offer programming, public presentation activities open to anyone who pays an entrance fee. A Worldcon may offer up to seven tracks of programming, simultaneous presentations that include formal lectures by scientists, guest speakers, and panel discussions both by artists and writers and by the fans themselves. Movies or videos represent still more "tracks." A very small convention may offer only two tracks: one set of panel discussions, and presentations in a video room, for example.

Local clubs organize most of the larger conventions (over seven hundred participants), but that does not mean that all of the participants in the convention are club members. In fact, only a small fraction of the fans attending a convention will be members of the local club, and many fans who attend will be members of no club at all. For smaller conventions that anticipate fewer guests, a few friends may get together informally to put together an organizing committee that may disband after the convention or continue to organize subsequent activities together.

Conventions give fans with diverse interests a chance to meet others who like similar material and talk about their shared interest. For example, the Philadelphia Science Fiction Conference (Philcon), as it is officially named, particularly emphasizes written science fiction and its creators. Members of many other subgroups meet at Philcon, although the media fanziners described at length in this book do not usually trade their products at these conventions.

Media Conventions

Media fans hold their own conventions as well as attend the traditional science fiction conventions. Just as science fiction set the basic pattern for conventions in general, so *Star Trek* fandom set the pattern for media conventions devoted to activities surrounding television and movie series. Early (1973–76) *Star Trek* conventions in Chicago, New York, and Los Angeles attracted numbers unheard of in the literary community—six thousand to seventeen thousand participants each[2]—drawn to see the television stars and hear about the program then in syndicated reruns. Most of the thousands of fans who attended the conventions shared an interest in the television show but no commitment to the social or creative aspects of the growing fan community. By 1976 the monster conventions were over; exhausted convention committees turned their attention to less monumental fan activities.

Within the community, however, committees continued to form and organize smaller conventions for committed insiders. Rick Kolker and a group of friends at the University of Maryland gave a convention on campus each August while they remained as students.[3] The August Party had a one-time reunion for its tenth anniversary in August of 1985, not at the University of Maryland where the group began but at a hotel in Virginia. Roughly three hundred members attended the convention, which was advertised only at other media conventions.

The August Party reunion committee operated through the Star Trek Association of Tacoma (STAT), a Maryland-based umbrella organization for a variety of fan committees and events. STAT sponsors Shore Leave, one of the larger annual media conventions, with more than eight hundred participants.[4] Both Shore Leave, held in July, and the February Clippercon (recently replaced by Fan-Out), organized by some members of the same committee, attract large numbers of *Star Trek* fans as well as enthusiasts for other source products from the local community. Shore Leave, now in its eleventh year, is the longest consecutively running *Star Trek* convention on the East Coast, and possibly in the country.

At the other extreme, mini-conventions (mini-cons) may attract from fifty to one hundred and fifty participants. Mini-cons usually focus on one or two fanzine source products. Fans of very popular source products like *Star Trek* may organize a mini-con to focus on a particular interest, based most usually on enthusiasm for a favorite style of fan fiction. Mini-conventions are the most private of the ostensibly public conventions.

Each level of specialization of interest, however, brings with it greater restriction on the passing of knowledge about its existence. For insiders, information about the convention circuit comes from fliers distributed at conventions, from club newsletters, and by word of mouth. Informants regularly apprise me of upcoming events that I have not attended in the past, and I can chart my passage through the community as insiders make known to me conventions of increasingly specialized interests.

Fan in modified Starfleet uniform.

Male fans wearing Starfleet uniforms in convention huckster room, looking at comic books. While some women do participate in comic-book fandom, the majority of comics fans are men.

Most media conventions offer an art show that concentrates on television- and movie-inspired art. Some artists may also show art inspired by literary science fiction or fantasy.

Fans browsing through the fanzine room at Shore Leave, an annual *Star Trek* convention in the Baltimore area.

For the outsider, finding the fan-run media convention circuit presents a challenge. Some regional fan-run organizations, like the nonprofit *Star Trek* Association of Tacoma, develop successful working relationships with local telecasters. In their prefaces or afterwords a few of the commercially published *Star Trek* novels mention fandom and the Welcommittee,[5] which can supply lists of regional *Star Trek* conventions. For the most part, however, finding the fan-run media conventions across the country requires some insider knowledge, because their schedules do not generally appear in commercial publications available in bookstores or newsstands.

Commercial Media Conventions

The earliest media conventions were held by fans on a nonprofit basis, and most organizers, such as STAT, still do it for love and not for money. Since 1979, however, the nonprofit media conventions have had commercial competition.

For some commercial organizers, the convention exists to facilitate the sale of merchandise in the dealers room. A Doctor Who Fan Club of America (DWFCA) organizer explained in an interview that the main purpose of his organization's conventions was to promote the tie-in merchandise for which it holds licenses.[6] By contrast, Creation Con organizer Adam Malin has often expressed his commitment to providing a convention experience as close to the fan-run event as possible, given the constraints of a profit-making business. Creation rents space at its conventions for merchandise but does not control the licenses for tie-in materials sold there.

Contact Has Been Made

When the fan encounters the community, she will find that certain choices she has made along the way will open more doors for her, while others will exclude her from activities and associations. As a science fiction fan, the world of fandom is open to her, and many participants who have primary interest in other genres, especially fantasy or horror, enter fandom through science fiction simply because it is the most visible of all the fan groups.

Media fandom began as *Star Trek* fandom, and science fiction television and movies still dominate the visible structures of the community. However, action-adventure, spy and mystery fans find a home in media fandom as well. Television and movies may be the primary focus, but books in the genres also play a part. Community members often read the bestsellers, but the important books included tend more to be series, identified by character—Sherlock Holmes and Modesty Blaise are two important examples. Fans with an interest in science fiction or media may also find a home in fandom for their secondary involvement with historical and romance fiction. Most fans read widely in their chosen genres, but a knowledge of certain authors serves as an entry-level lingua franca. For fans of historical and romance fiction, Georgette Heyer's Regency period romances are a must, as are Baroness d'Orczy's Scarlet Pimpernel books, and *Beauty and the Beast* on television.

Activities

Most fans make the first two choices—genre content and delivery channel—before they become aware that an organized community of fandom exists, and they choose their social group accordingly. But, meeting other fans at clubs or conventions, the neophyte discovers something she has known all along: her enjoyment does not arise out of passive reception but out of active engagement with her favorite genre or medium. Some fans may collect books or tapes and gather to discuss or exchange them, while others try to emulate the success of the published authors or produced television writers. Some gather to play board or live-action role-playing games in person, while others may play through the mail.

Some may produce letterzines and commentary fanzines discussing their favorite material in open letters directed to a particular writer or subscriber to the letterzine or to all subscribers. Some may express themselves through making and wearing costumes of their favorite characters or historical period, in any genre category the community encompasses. Some may create artwork or crafts, or organize conventions or clubs. Others, like the women this book follows, may create their own stories, novels, poems, and art about their favorite characters in the commercial source material for fandom at large.

Unfortunately, not all activities are equally available to all fans; in most cases, gender is the discriminating factor. Devra Langsam characterizes early science fiction fandom as smaller, a tight clique of four hundred to six hundred men with only a few women who dared to attend the predominantly male meetings and conventions. In his book *Dimensions of Science Fiction,* William Sims Bainbridge supports this perception, quoting Harry Warner: "Around 1940 it was possible to claim that there was no such thing as an independent, honest-to-goodness girl-type fan, because virtually all the females in fandom had a fannish boy friend, brother, husband, or some other masculine link."[7]

While the truth of the statement was probably disputable even in 1940, it had certainly changed in the early sixties when Devra Langsam first entered fandom. Many male fans continued in this outdated opinion, revised, as the recent testimony of a male fan shows, to assert that before *Star Trek,* the only women who attended meetings and conventions were the girlfriends of fans, or women looking for men. Well into the sixties, and even into the eighties in some fan groups, a woman was considered fair game, sexually, unless she could prove her superior intelligence, in which case she could receive an uneasy acceptance as a "guy." If she were both intelligent and attractive, however, competition swung in the other direction—the men became the pursuers, and the hunt grew more circumspect: "If you were a woman, you had to be brilliant, or everybody wanted to touch [sexually]. If you were attractive and intelligent, you could practically walk on water."[8]

Of course, women wrote, read, and shared an enthusiasm for science fiction before 1967, just as they did after. The shift to a clear female presence in the field occurred first in the number of women who dared to breach the stronghold, and later as these same women demanded (and continue to demand from a hostile minority) an equal place in fan activities.

Men still retain tight control of gaming in the densely interconnected fan community. Gaming—computer, role-playing, and board types—attracts a group who may play games as their way of participating in the science fiction or media community, or who may use the meeting places and themes of these interest groups to participate in the primary activity of the games.

When I have entered the rooms set aside at conventions for games, I have met with strong resistance (most of the men in the room stopped their play and stared at me until I left). On two occasions when I tried to ask questions, no one agreed to talk to me, and I was approached with "mock" aggression. When photographer Stephanie Hall and I were snapping candid shots of crowded elevators loading and unloading, one of the gamers dressed in a ninja costume, who had acted out mock aggression earlier in the day, pinned me to the wall by my throat and drove a glancing blow to the wall at my side with his wooden sword. Although the violence of the attack was strictly in "play," the gamer clearly intended to intimidate me. I was frankly terrified, but I laughed as though I were enjoying the play and instructed Stephanie to, quick, take a picture. The gamer let me go then, bowed, and walked away.

While this experience is an extreme example, it reflects an attitude of some male role-playing gamers described by Gary Alan Fine: "An additional possibility [for the scarcity of women in gaming] is that females are not welcomed . . . even when the treatment isn't overtly hostile, comments may lead the female to question whether she is welcome."[9] The few women gamers I have met also described the hostility and suspicion male gamers expressed before the women won with their superior skill the respect of other players.

From the beginning, however, costumers have broken gender stereotypes held both outside and inside fan culture. In costuming, men sew and glue sequins along with the women, and both men and women number among the costumers considered master class in the costuming culture. Both men and women present costumes on stage, at convention masquerades where costumes are paraded for the entertainment of the fans and judged by a panel of expert costumers.

Costumers actively seek out venues like science fiction conventions and Society for Creative Anachronism gatherings, where costuming goes on throughout the event. Recently, serious costumers have

Waiting for the masquerade to begin.

The masquerade: performing a dance to show the fantasy costume to advantage.

The masquerade: the "Road Warrior" is a woman.

formed their own organization, the Costumers' Guild, with annual conventions at which members participate in panels on construction, materials, and presentation of costumes, and where the masquerade occurs nightly.

Media clubs built around television favorites such as *Star Trek*, *Doctor Who*, and *Blake's 7* have always been relatively well gender-integrated, perhaps because they began in the wake of the huge outpouring of interest in *Star Trek* that drew women into fandom. Interestingly, media clubs and conventions also seem to be more racially integrated than their counterparts in literary fandom.

While a few activities, like gaming, may be resistant to including women equally, those same women find themselves an overwhelming majority among media fans who create, read, and discuss their community's own fiction and art based on the characters and situations in their favorite television, movie, and even book series. Fanzines, the publications through which community members share their work, did not originate in media fandom; in fact, fanzines were and continue to be a staple of the literary science fiction community, with many more men than women working in the form. With the exception of a very few publications like *Locus* that aspire to commercial status, however, most amateur literary science fiction fans have remained conservatively tied to slim and inexpensively reproduced outlets for letters and criticism. By contrast, electronic media fanzines have become transformed by access to professional print technology and the needs of their community. In the following chapters this book will chart the nature and substance of the media fanzines and the community that creates them.

Social Organization

Fandom/Interest Group

Fans use the term "fandom" to designate several distinct levels of social organizations. The entire science fiction community is called a fandom, as is the much smaller group involved in, for example, *Star Wars* fan fiction. Likewise, the term "*Star Trek* fandom" refers to fans of that source product, regardless of the activity in which the fan participates. The social suborganization formed around, for example, Jacqueline Lichtenberg's *Star Trek* fan fiction is also called a fandom, although it designates three filtering levels of participation: that of fan fiction in general, of *Star Trek* as the preferred source, and of the deviations from the *Star Trek* canon initiated by Jacqueline Lichtenberg in particular. Each of these filters indicates a refining of identity and an intensity level of social interaction.

Because the term fandom is used so widely, I have invented the designation "interest group" to mean the social organization equivalent, in the example above, to Lichtenberg's *Star Trek* fan fiction fandom. Unlike many of the terms used in this book, "interest group" arises out of the need of the ethnographer to classify, and not out of the need of the community to define itself.

Primary Identity

The interest group a new member will enter depends on a combination of the preferred genre, delivery channel or particular source product (e.g., media in general, or *Star Trek* in particular), and activity. This book began as a study of the specific group specialized through four levels of selection: first, the selection of a genre, science fiction; second, the media delivery channel, television; third, a particular source product, *Star Trek;* and fourth, an activity, fanzines. In recent years the group has expanded to include other media science fiction source products and action-adventure genres, and the study has likewise expanded to track these changes.

As they grow more knowledgeable in the community, members will participate in a variety of groups, while retaining a primary identity with the group that matches favorite genres and delivery channels to the activities the participant enjoys most. As with any social organization, establishing an indentity in a group is a matter of compromises, and of varying emphases. One fan in a given group may identify herself as a fanziner, while another in the same group will identify herself as a media fan; each establishes her personal identity based on the facet of the structure that is most important to her. At the same time, each may participate in a variety of activities, or pursue her activity in a variety of genres, while still identifying herself by her main interest. For example, many fanziners costume, but if asked, even when they are preparing for a masquerade, they will tell you they are fanziners who also costume. They do not suddenly identify themselves as costumers because they are wearing Starfleet uniforms or an elf's forest greens, nor will a costumer identify herself to you as a fanziner because she also reads the community's literature.

Many members of media fandom, particularly among the men, consider science fiction their primary community, and participate as peripheral members of the media community. Costumers, both men and women, may identify themselves primarily with the costume community and participate equally in a variety of costume-oriented groups, such as the Costumers Guild, the Society for Creative Anachronisms, and science fiction, as well as media fandom. Others may identify with the science fiction or media community and costume only as a peripheral interest.

This is, of course, somewhat of a simplification. Regardless of the primary identification with an interest in an activity, genre, or delivery channel that a community member recognizes as self, the fan may, in certain circumstances, offer a secondary interest as primary identification. Like the male *Star Trek* fans who refer to themselves in public as science fiction fans, they must adopt the identity that offers the highest status in the large group of fandom. Or, in the company of a new or different group, the fan may offer as identity a secondary interest that will give her common ground with the strangers. In time, if circumstances change her social relationships to the new group, she may take on a new primary identity as part of fitting in. For example, a fan may move to a new city where the social group forms around collecting and trading tapes rather than fanzines. She may begin by seeing herself as a fanziner who also likes to trade tapes, but may grow to identify with the group as a media video fan who also likes fanzines. The pressure to fit in moves in two directions—the fan looks for the group that best fits existing personal needs while also modifying those needs to fit more securely into the group.

A few community members, like Lunarian[10] and *Star Trek* fanziner Devra Langsam, maintain a strong presence in more than one group. Some members identify primarily with one group over the lifetime of their participation, while others may pass from group to group or subgroup within the interlocking structure.

The Interest Group: Structural Stability

For many people who consider themselves fans, participation means only that they go to conventions, perhaps meet a few people over the years, join a club to receive the newsletter, and in general function at a remove from the intense social connectedness of the more deeply committed fans. For those core fans who draw their social lives from the structures of fandom, there seem to be an optimal number of participants that provides members with a comfortable balance between variety in product and control over their social matrix. When participation exceeds this level, the stress builds to an extent that the group must fragment or self-destruct. For most fans the optimum number in this level of organization is the number of participants with whom

one member may have a personal acquaintance through letter, reputation, or face-to-face interaction: between two hundred and fifty and
five hundred participants.

Fans may belong to a smaller interest group because they are particularly attracted to a source product, like *Starsky and Hutch,* in which
fewer community members share an active, creative interest. More
often fans in smaller interest groups deliberately seek out those products with smaller constituencies, where the pressure built up in larger
group dynamics is ameliorated.

While all fan products are informed by a shared aesthetic, interest
groups may form around a particular subgenre of their repertoire of
forms. These groups may favor a particular style in association with
their use of the subgenre. Often, an esoteric interest group may define itself around all three of these artistic possibilities: a source product may inspire work in a particular community subgenre, to which
are attracted artists and writers who work in a particular style, such as
terse or ornate description.

An example of such a complex interest group revolves around the
BBC science fiction program *Blake's 7.* Early *Blake's 7* fans (before the
1986 airing of the show in the United States) enjoyed the source product through pirated videotapes passed from hand to hand and also
took pleasure in the esoteric nature of their interest. Fan fiction and
literature emphasized the tragic, fatally flawed heroes and their problematic relationships with each other in the context of a hostile universe. Sexual themes did not appear frequently in the literature,
whereas themes of psychological manipulation predominated. The
preferred style was highly dramatic but generally neither sentimental
nor romantic.

When the program aired on public television stations in major
metropolitan markets, it attracted many fans from the *Star Trek* community, and others from among the *Doctor Who* enthusiasts more accustomed to club activities than widespread fanzining. Early *Blake's 7*
fans experienced distress that the interest group had grown beyond
their comfort level for "knowing everybody." Incoming fans from
inner *Trek* circles brought with them reputations that threatened the
infra-group status of original members. Many of these newcomers
shared an aesthetic preference for more sexual material and a more
romantic, sentimental style that threatened the aesthetic norms of the
core group. The situation was further complicated by the relationships
of the newcomers and the original *Blake's 7* fans in the wider community. In some cases, new and old members shared an interest and
friendship in a different interest group; in other cases, early fans of

Blake's 7 participated in that interest group to avoid the attitudes and artistic forms that now followed them into their new neighborhood.

Few of us like to see our neighborhood change, and fewer still like to see the very things we wished to leave behind follow us into our new homes. The effect on the *Blake's 7* interest group has been predictably disturbing to its members, and in 1988 the group did fission under the stress, in part along genre lines and in part based on personalities. Thus far social equilibrium has not been completely reestablished, but it appears that most participants who remain will establish residency in one group or the other, while some members will continue to participate in both groups.

Social Organization: Circles

While the interest group represents the comfortable range for maintaining a sense of unity as a group, it is far too large to meet the personal needs of its members for close connections. Therefore, most active, "core" fans participate in the extended family structure of a "circle."[11] In my study I have interviewed and observed two circles in operation in Illinois, four in New York State, two in the Washington, D.C., area, and two in the Pennsylvania–New Jersey area. I am aware of at least two more circles in Pennsylvania that I have not had the opportunity to observe. In Houston, I spoke to fans who were either members of two separate but closely linked circles or of one circle in the process of dividing. This sampling is not an accurate reflection of the distribution of fan circles—rather, it marks the geographic limits of my study.

Interest groups are not so much a collection of like-minded individuals as they are a cluster of circles, groups of close friends who come together to participate in a particular interest group. The "natural" social function of an interest group occurs at a convention, where many circles will gather. The "natural" social event of the circle is the house party, often called a lay-around weekend, where members lounge around most of the day in their nightgowns, changing around noon or later into sweatpants or jeans and T-shirts printed with logos, community art, or phrases from the source products. Conventions have already been described. At house parties, fans talk, watch videos, laugh, read fanzines, talk dirty, talk story, dissect character development in the source products or the fan fiction, and generally form the interpretations that will guide the community in establishing standards of appropriate behavior and response.

The Structure of a Circle

Each circle has a core of two to four members. A typical group will include an editor or editorial team, several writers, a graphic artist, a video artist, one or two photocopyists, and one or more specialists in linking with sources of materials, including information and the products of other groups. (The latter specialists have grown in importance as groups increasingly pursue more esoteric source products.) Some groups will have more creative members, while others will focus more on acquisition and appreciation of the products.

Editors are frequently at the core of a circle. In some cases the circle forms around the publications of an editor or editors whose own success requires that they demonstrate greater than usual interest in the creative activity of others. Alternatively, group members may publish elsewhere. In either case, editors seem to share a high degree of skill in social as well as literary organization. Not all circles form around editors, however; particularly among fans of the more esoteric products, specialists in obtaining source products and creative material from other groups may constitute a core.

Of course, the reader should view this model as a simplification of circle organization. Few members in the fan community participate in only one activity: editors often write, as do video artists, who may alternatively be graphic artists. Circles may form around the first person in a neighborhood to "come out" about her fan activities, or around the first person to experiment with a new source product or creative activity. In general, however, core members of fan circles are warm and generous individuals who obtain gratification from the pleasure of those with whom they surround themselves.

In most cases a circle will include participants with compatible personalities and competency levels, and who share an interest in one or more particular source products. Circles can exist within clubs— members of the Houston "Whips" also participate in the Friends of Fandom and the local Starbase chapter.[12] Circles may be formally organized and recognized as such by nonmembers of the group, or they may present as being a loose gathering but in fact have insider criteria for membership known only to themselves. A member may participate in a circle primarily through correspondence, but more often, members of a circle live within reasonable travel distance of each other, since circles meet informally at house gatherings or other social activities quite often. This distance varies according to geographically constructed concepts of appropriate behavior. In the Midwest or Southwest, three to six hours of travel may be reasonable, while on the

East Coast, an hour or two may be the limit for frequent travel. Some fans who begin membership in a circle via correspondence later move long distances to participate more fully in the group. In-place group members have been known to supply a place to live and general support while the transplanted member looks for an apartment, and even find jobs for the newly arrived participant.

In circles that produce fanzines or hold conventions around established fanzine-generating source products, participation may be based on both a high skill level and a willingness to help with the work of production. For fan interests such as *Star Trek*, the acquisition of materials does not constitute a large part of the work of the group. The circle must maintain information channels with other groups, but can concentrate on its own production while accumulating materials on a more or less open and at-cost market. Members of circles founded around more esoteric source products like *Robin of Sherwood*, a British series about Robin Hood, depend on barter and trade to maintain a constant flow of information and materials on a non-profit and highly efficient basis. Videotape suppliers and photocopyists therefore may belong to a number of groups, providing photocopy service for all members of the home circle and one set of copies for the procurement specialist in each of several other circles. Trade is maintained on three bases:

1. Technical cost, which involves outside vendors such as printers, copy shops, or videotape stores, and which entails a cost fixed outside the community;
2. Product, which includes source materials or the creative output of the community, to which social and aesthetic values are ascribed; and
3. Service, which considers the effort made by the supplier to obtain the material and the inconvenience it represents to provide it to members of the community outside the home circle.

The first, technical cost, is generally passed directly to the member for whom materials are provided. Exceptions are made for equal-value trades (a tape for a tape, twenty pages for twenty pages) and for contributors to fan publications, who receive a complimentary copy of the fanzine in exchange for the exclusive use of the contribution until all copies of the fanzine have been sold. The second and third bases of trade are interdependent. The one product with which the community can barter is the service of providing. The creative and source products must, by law, carry no cost. However, the effort to provide them may be traded for an equal effort by the second party to the trade. Media fans often must trade for tapes of the source products no longer on the air. Fan Lin Place gives an example:

> So I recorded *Dark Shadows,* she got me the two movies I wanted, and then she said, "what else do you want, so we can go on trading?"[13]

Artists and writers who need a certain source product as background for their work receive a high priority on the trading circuits, particularly if they have a reputation for producing aesthetically satisfying art and literature. New creative materials benefit the group as a whole, and not just the supplier or the supplier's home circle.

Stability in Circles: The Fission Model

Circles may vary in size, to include from ten to thirty people. Fifteen seems to be the optimal number: photocopyists cite this number as the limit of comfortable photocopy responsibility, and fans report stress building in groups that exceed twenty. As the number of members in the circle increases, so does the stress, and groups generally split into two separate entities when more than twenty-five members actively participate.

In most cases, the fissioned circles continue to interact closely as interlocked groups. That is, a large number of members in both groups will participate peripherally in each other's activities, while members with a higher tolerance for stress than their counterparts may maintain full participation in both groups. Circles that fission most benignly do so on the basis of increased specialization of interests. For example, a *Star Trek* group may add *Blake's 7* to its repertoire at the insistence of some members and later fission, with *Star Trek* enthusiasts staying in one circle, *Blake's 7* fans in another, and fans who maintain interest in both products passing back and forth between the two groups.

Interlocking Circles

The fission model is only one way in which circles interlock. A participant with a wide variety of interests may participate regularly in a number of groups. Members whose creative output is known in the wider community may generally expect courtesy from other groups, and members who are less well known may find equal courtesy through introductions by better-known members of the home or peripheral circles. When established fans meet each other in larger groupings, a complex exchange of the names of acquaintances may take place until a suitable number of names known in common is amassed. This information establishes the appropriateness of extended discussion and the level of common knowledge at which the discussion will take place. If one member of the discussion is found to be a relative newcomer, the other may take on a mentor role, or may pass the neophyte to a mentor at the appropriate level of contact.

While most circles are hospitable to visitors and do accept new members, even the most open-ended ones must respond to organizational pressure generated when the size of a circle exceeds the comfort level of its participants. As the reader may have inferred, entry into a circle is by mutual consent of the new member and the established participants. To gain entry into a circle, a participant has only two options: she may join with a friend or friends to form a core, and attract others to her group, or a member of an existing group may introduce her into an established circle. Final acceptance by the group will depend on the degree of congruence between the new member and the established participants. That is, does the new member add to the group any particular creative, administrative, or social skill it values? Does the new member participate at the same level as the established members of the group?

Groups that value a high level of aesthetic competence in its members may be unwilling to take on a member with a lesser skill level. Circles that have been in place for a long time may have reached a saturation point, and new members must counter the stress of adding another body to the mix by providing a service or skill so valued that it makes the risk to the stability of the group worthwhile. Circles established in particular to introduce new members to the fan community may have a large stable core, with many peripheral members. Some of the new members will stay, but others will move to more specialized circles. The transience in circles that tend to the needs of the neophytes reduces the stress on the structure that may be experienced more intensely when fixed groups exceed an optimal number of participants. Transience also ensures a steady availability of places for new members, while the interlocking of introductory groups with second- and third-stage circles in turn reduces the stress caused by too rapid turnover. At conventions and through the fanzines, members of the introductory group maintain a sense of continuity with members who have "graduated" to the inner circles.

Core Circles

At the center of the social matrix of circles lie "core circles." Circles in Illinois, Texas, and New York, for example, have existed for ten or more years, and have been and continue to be instrumental in shaping the aesthetic standards of the larger community. Participants in other circles socialize freely with members of the core circles, but actual incorporation of new members occurs infrequently.

Commercial Providers—The Series

To speak of the commercial arm of the fan community is rather like discussing the dog subgroup of a particularly impressive tail. From the outside, the comparison sounds inappropriate, but to insiders, only a few aspects of the commercial empire surrounding their favorite source products have any relevance. Most television and movie series embraced by the community are out of production, so members generally are not concerned about the creation of new episodes. Fan efforts to save *Star Trek*, first as a network series, later in feature films, helped to bring the community together. Today, however, many fans admit that, while they enjoy the movies and the *Next Generation* series of episodes, those products do not influence their interest or participation in the fanzine community. Members of some fan groups, particularly of *Star Trek* and *Blake's 7*, do enjoy seeing the actors who portrayed their favorite characters and listening to the series writers, producers, and even costume designers.

For the most part the community has contact with the commercial providers only at conventions, usually held in conjunction with other fan subgroups. Performers often establish a friendly relationship with a few convention organizers or fans, but for the most part, the two groups meet in formally structured events that maintain a distance between provider—entertainer—and community.

At the Boston Bash convention in 1986 I asked relative newcomer Robin Curtis (Saavik in two *Star Trek* movies) and original cast member George Takei (Sulu in the original *Star Trek* series and in the movies) about their experiences with fandom and the conventions. Robin Curtis was happy to be back in Boston for a second appearance at the Boston Bash, but described her trepidation at attending her first convention:

. . . [W]hat's nice is that it has come full circle. This was my first convention, here in Boston with the Boston Star Trek Association, and uh, this lady [one of the organizers], like, she's very mothering and wonderful, and took care of me and introduced me in a lovely way to the whole experience. You know, I came not knowing what to expect and I think what I was actually more concerned about was what they expected of me. I felt very inadequate in the area of science fiction. It is not one of my loves. I prefer family dramas, I'm a *Terms of Endearment, Ordinary People* kind of moviegoer.

I like the experience now. It's a chance to be in a different city and come back and see old friends, and I think it is something that one should do. I think it's in my conscience that this is—the fans deserve this. They like it so much I—it's like, why shouldn't I? I feel it's something I should do.[14]

Like Curtis, George Takei feels a sense of obligation to the fans:

I enjoy them [conventions]. I think it's wonderful, and as Robin said, it's a wonderful personalized opportunity to say thank you for having made all of this happen for twenty-one years—I've been employed [laugh]—and on that level to say thank you, and to be kept up on what their thinking is, and to relay that back to the studios.[15]

For the performers, who are not members of the fan community, conventions offer the opportunity to travel. When I asked why they enjoyed conventions, both Takei and Curtis answered that they liked visiting new cities and seeing new sights. Conventions allow George Takei to pursue a particular interest in cities:

I'm a city kid, and I enjoy cities, to figure out what makes certain cities work and certain cities not work as well . . . I did study architecture, and urban planning and architecture and preservation are other areas of my interests. There are cities that are particular favorites, cities like Boston, or New York, San Francisco, New Orleans. Unique, singular, vibrant cities, so that's another bonus that I get.[16]

By contrast, many fans may never leave the hotel or conference center during the entire convention weekend.

As peripheral members in the wider fan community that supports conventions, both Curtis and Takei are aware of the fanzines, but not as the work of a separate social system. When I asked George Takei what he thought about the writing and art in the fanzines, he commented:

Well you know, I think *Star Trek* is blessed by these talented people, because, what other TV show do you know where these talented people do create works around that—to have some of our episodes illustrated in paintings, or to have portraits of the characters in the show, or to have sculptural pieces made of the ship or the alien forms, or the things that were visualized on the show.[17]

Most of the art that he describes here is the work of male fans who do not participate in the fanzines at all, so I changed my question to make it clearer that I was speaking about the fan publications.

Ethnographer: Were you surprised to see yourself turning up in stories and artwork?

Curtis: Yeah. I think I was surprised by the phenomenon altogether. I really had no idea that this all existed prior to my getting involved with it. I'm still amazed by it. I don't know that I'll ever stop being amazed . . . Really, the care and the time which people devote to something and giving it to me. It is really quite an honor to be the receiver of that kind of appreciation . . . [but] I haven't read it, to be honest with you. If I were to read something—I picked up David Gerrold's *The World of Star Trek*—I prefer to read about what is, versus how people twist and turn and color the characters differently than the way it is.

Ethnographer: When you look at what people send you, does it ever color what you do? Do you get surprised or upset?

Takei: No. No. Because it's that individual doing his or her own thing. And it's kind of flattering, that you know, they took some kind of inspiration or some bouncing off what we did. But you can't, I mean, they are on their own. And they do what they do, but you take it for what it is.

Curtis: Yeah. From the moment I—heard and again I'm very new to this—but from the moment I heard at one convention that someone had, somewhere within their fiction, suggested that Kirk and Spock were having a homosexual relationship, I for the most part completely disregarded that sort of thing. It doesn't interest me, personally.

Takei: See, you can't go taking everything that fandom does seriously, and you've given it undue importance by underlining it, so we, what we do is we say "oh, how interesting," you know, John Smith has done this, or Mary Jones does her thing, and that's it. You just move on. Don't give it any kind of resonance . . . we create our characters in collaboration with the writers, and the directors, you know, but we can't let our work be unduly colored by what people out there are doing. We have to be the creators.[18]

For the American actors, accustomed to publicity appearances and working with a group that has made the rounds of conventions since 1972, the experience of the convention is that of a social and professional obligation met in an atmosphere of fun. While they deny that the convention is work, they do receive fees—sometimes quite substantial ones[19]—for their appearances. Paying the actors' fees takes a large part of any convention's budget, and few *Star Trek* conventions since the early seventies have invited more than three paid guests.

For fans of and performers in the British production *Blake's 7*, the situation has been more complex. *Star Trek* conventions draw attendees from the large pool of television viewers, of which the fanzine community makes up a small part. By contrast, *Blake's 7* came to the attention of fans through fanzines, not through public broadcast. Chicago's Scorpio, in 1984 the first convention to invite the *Blake's 7* performers to the United States, drew less than three hundred participants, most of whom had learned about the convention through the fanzine network. Performers who attend *Star Trek* conventions receive fees, but organizers of the much smaller *Blake's 7* conventions could afford to pay only basic expenses, not fees. In spite of the absence of fees, the actors came to Scorpio, lured by free passage to America and flattered by the interest fans had in a television show that had never appeared on television in the U.S. Among them were Michael Keating, who played thief and lock-pick Vila Restal; Terry Nation, the show's creator; and Paul Darrow, who played Kerr Avon, the cold-blooded anti-hero:

> Darrow: There are various reasons for attending conventions. Mine certainly, and I'm pretty sure Michael [Keating]—I know Terry [Nation]—we like to come because we (a) can stay in a nice place, visit your nice country, and meet our friends . . .[20]

In the years before the program reached public broadcasting stations in the United States, actors from *Blake's 7* did not experience the press of the masses of fans drawn to better-known attractions:

> Darrow: . . . [I]t [Scorpio] was quite small, intimate. I was able to communicate quite readily with the people and [could] meet them on a one-to-one basis . . . the second one I went to was larger, but again, somebody said, I know, at the end of Scorpio it's like leaving family. The thing about Scorpio is that when you arrive it's like meeting family . . .

Our attitude is that we go to conventions because we want to, we really don't feel that we are working. If we are working, we get paid, that's our job. But we're not working at Scorpio, we go there to have fun. So we don't get paid, and we wouldn't really want to get paid for that.[21]

In late 1986, however, the situation in *Blake's 7* fandom changed drastically. The BBC made the program available in syndication, and the British performers and series creator Terry Nation began to make appearances at many conventions, both professional and fan-operated, to promote the series in American markets. Still the performers received little or no payment, and many of the appearances had stopped being fun.

The "great party"[22] was running down. Early fans of *Blake's 7,* drawn to the intimacy of the small group, began moving away from the growing fandom, searching out more obscure source products. Scorpio added performers from *Robin of Sherwood* to their guest list. Terry Nation and Paul Darrow began working on a package of conventions that would guarantee a fee to guest performers and in turn would assure the convention-goer that tentative guests would not withdraw at the last minute for paid professional commitments. Plans for the convention tour were dropped when Darrow himself was tapped for a play in England, but he had tipped a delicate balance when he involved himself with the community at its own level. Darrow visited widely on the convention circuit, dined with fans who traveled to England to see him, and joined with them in speculating about the life and psychology of his character. Surrounded by fiction writers, Darrow himself wrote a book about the early life of his character, Avon. He had become too much a fan to be accepted as an entrepreneur. He called the early fans "family," and to many of them his actions smacked a bit of using the family reunion to make a profit. At the same time, to newer fans who hadn't known him "when," he remained a performer entitled to the same pay any other performer received for working a convention.

When he obscured the line between performer and audience, Darrow unwittingly added to the schism already taking place between the pre-telecast and post-telecast fans. More importantly, he contributed to the split along genre lines when he discovered that some fans within his "inner circle" were writing explicitly sexual material involving his character with other male characters on *Blake's 7*. Distressed at what he viewed as a breach of friendship, Darrow banished the offenders from his circle, and he further demanded that those who would remain close to him likewise sever all ties with the writers of the erotic material. The *Blake's 7* fan group fragmented; even members of clubs who were not involved with fanzining or the controversy found themselves affected by the dispute as their friends took sides. Some fans supported Darrow's position, some supported the fanziners who were working in a small but well-established subgenre, and the vast majority backed away, simply disgusted at what has become known as "The Feud."

The Feud could have had no other outcome. When a performer tries to leave the periphery and participate more fully in the fanzine community, he or she presents the group with a problem in taxonomy, and if he is male, the problem compounds. Fanzining is a women's community. Few men participate at the core, and those who do must accept the fact that women set the standards for the group, including code of conduct.

The performer must then deal with the fan category that defines him as peripheral, at one and the same time product and raw material for art. As product he may be grouped with videotapes of episodes, for example. His participation becomes an object to be traded, used for social advancement, and eventually discarded when social or artistic pressures move the fanziner to the next source product. A performer who internalizes the community's code of behavior and status accorded by gender may successfully overcome the objectification associated with the source product. If the performer cannot adapt to the community's social system, however, most members of the group will continue to perceive him as part of the source product package.

In practice, the question of performer involvement with the fan community can arise only in the limited set of circumstances described above. Contact with the performers in a few fan interests, like *Doctor Who* and the immediately popular *Beauty and the Beast,* occurs almost exclusively at commercially organized conventions, where the fans participate as audience. For the most part, however, members of fringe fandoms have no direct contact with the performers in the source products. Fringe fandoms are generally too small to support the expense of bringing in performers, and their members often fear that guest attractions will draw more new members to their interest than they can comfortably absorb. Fans in smaller interest groups may also fear censure for their writing, which becomes more difficult to hide from guest performers at small conventions. At Scorpio, for example, homoerotic material was banned after one performer objected to fan art portraying his character in a sexual context with another male character from his series.

Importantly, most fanziners participate to share in community with fellow fanziners. An interest in the performer is almost always secondary to an interest in the character he portrays.

Commercial Providers—The Books

The distinction between the peripheral service provider of the entertainment industry and the insider community member blurs when discussing the writers of the commercially published paperbacks that use the characters and settings of the source products for original storylines. In the 1970s Bantam Books hired well-known science fiction authors such as Joe Haldeman[23] to write original *Star Trek* novels. Ironically, these artists, respected in their own science fiction community, produced only workmanlike imitations of episodic television in their novels. Media fanziners treat these *Star Trek* efforts as the work of outsider service providers, although as participants in the wider science fiction community, fans easily recognize the writers as core members of that group.

The notable exception to Bantam's rule was the collaborative team of Sondra Marshak and Myrna Culbreath.[24] The team, longtime members of the fan community, edited two collections of short stories drawn from the fanzines and went on to write three *Star Trek* novels, two of them for Bantam. When Pocket Books took on the *Star Trek* line, Mimi Panich expanded their editorial policy by accepting the first novels of unknown authors. Some of these, like Marshak and Culbreath, were established members of the community. Other writers fit the model for *Star Trek* fans but their work appeared in the fanzines, if at all, only after they had been commercially published. Author A. C. Crispin[25] has been open about how important *Star Trek* was to her when she was a teenager:

When it came on in 1966, I started watching it, oh, I don't know, maybe the third or fourth episode that was aired. "What Are Little Girls Made Of." . . . I was the right age, fifteen, sixteen, thereabouts . . . and I wrote an endless "Mary Sue" novel when I was a kid . . . it's not a subject I remember very fondly. I live my life afraid that some fan is going to get hold of it and publish it in a fanzine and I'll be embarrassed forever . . .

. . . I was that age I really needed *Trek*, because I was in the homely adolescent stage when boys were terrifying and *Star Trek* provided a world of hope. And Uhura provided confirmation that women could get somewhere and you know, I really needed it in those days—so take the scenario of any lonely alienated teenaged fan and that was me.

About her teenaged writing:

I had a lot of fun. I had a whole group of girlfriends that were—a lot of them are still—friends. *Star Trek* has always been a bond. And they would read each chapter, and it got finished and we would all giggle. And I wrote them all into it, something like that.[26]

Like Crispin, J. M. Dillard[27] came to *Star Trek* early:

I was about thirteen then. I started watching it. I turned on the series one day and went, "Oh, my God!" I fell in love with Mr. Spock. So I watched the series until they cancelled it, I watched all the reruns, but I never really got into the fan literature. I wasn't aware of it.[28]

When I asked Brad Ferguson[29] for his earliest memories of *Trek,* he answered promptly:

Oh, *Star Trek* premiered on the day after I started high school. September 8—'66. I saw the first one, and I had said this is too much like the navy. Then I saw the second one and I saw what they were trying to do. It's hard to remember back twenty years and subtract all the experience since then, but SF on television had been vastly different before that, and I had watched all of it. This came along, and it was different.
    . . . I built models during the run of the thing while I was still in high school. Those plastic things, AMT jobs that you put together.

These commercially published authors share with Howard Weinstein,[30] a fan who sold his first script for the *Star Trek* cartoon series when he was twenty-one and still in college, and Diane Duane,[31] who attended early conventions in New York, a lifelong interest in *Star Trek.* Unlike the committed fanzine writers, however, they also share a determination to receive payment for their efforts, while admitting that, having established themselves in the commercial field, they occasionally will give a minor piece of work to a fanzine editor. This is particularly true of short works written at or for conventions as part of the festivities:

Weinstein: . . . Occasionally I will write either a parody or a satire of either *Star Trek* or *Star Wars.* It's fun, and usually I will write something like that to read at a convention, and that usually goes over well. I like to make people laugh, and usually after I do one of those somebody comes up and says, "Oh, can I have that for my fanzine?" And of course. And I draw occasionally, and do a little artwork, so if I have the time to do something I may ask one of my friends who does a fanzine, "Hey, you want to use this?" I do reviews occasionally, of movies, because that's fun to do, but that's the extent of my involvement in fanzines.[32]

Fanzines have figured more prominently in the development of another group of commercially published writers. Jean Lorrah[33] had a story in one of the first *Star Trek*[34] fanzines, and she has collected her stories about Mr. Spock's parents in several volumes of the *NTM*[35] universe, so named after the acronym for her fan novel, *The Night of the Twin Moons*. Lorrah has since written over a dozen non-*Trek* books and two *Star Trek* novels. Jacqueline Lichtenberg, also an early fanziner,[36] has not published any *Star Trek* novels but has published many novels in her own *Sime-Gen* series.[37] A subfandom for her own work has grown within the media-SF communities.

For many years a history of writing in science fiction fanzines was almost expected of professional science fiction writers, but commercial publishers have expressed a strong prejudice against the writers in media fanzines. Publishers dismiss the work of women's media fanziners as derivative, they say because it borrows from media characters and scenarios. One commercial science fiction writer,[38] known for her *Trek* writing, complained that publishers had rejected an original novel as being derivative of *Star Trek* characters and relationships, although the only obvious parallel they cited was the presence of a spaceship in both works.

Publishers advise women who wish to be taken seriously as science fiction writers to separate themselves from the fanzine community. Publisher-employers have strongly urged even women employed in production aspects of publishing to disassociate themselves from the fan community.[39] A number of these women have expressed to me their dismay that they listened to the publishers and denied themselves the moral support and companionship of the fanzine community. Still others have adopted pseudonyms and continue as active, creative members of their community.

In spite of the pressure to separate women writers from their source of community, a number of well-known and even prize-winning science fiction writers have published in the fanzines after their reputations as serious writers were assured. These writers, whose identities are closely guarded secrets within the community, find a freedom to play and a community in which to do it in the media fandom.

Moving out of Media: Fanwriters and Literary Science Fiction

The interlocking communities of science fiction have provided other options for fanwriting women to publish commercially within the context of a shared universe. Marion Zimmer Bradley, author of the *Darkover*[40] series of science fiction books, has had a loyal following of fans drawn from the same pool of writers as the science fiction and media communities. Fans of Bradley's work find in *Darkover* a rich setting in which to play, and the author has encouraged this group participation in her product in fanzines like *Contes Di Cottman IV.*[41] To date three books of *Darkover* short stories drawn from fanwriting contests and fanzines, as well as from among Bradley's friends in the science fiction writing community, have been published by Don Wolheim.[42] Many of their names—Jacqueline Lichtenberg, Jean Lorrah,[43] C. McQuillan,[44] and others—would be familiar to fans of *Star Trek* and general science fiction alike.

For several years after publication of the first collection of stories by the Friends of Darkover, as the Bradley fans are called on the book covers, professional science fiction writers debated among themselves the implications to the industry of this artistic cross-fertilization between fanwriters and copyright holders. Copyrighted material is like personal property. The creator, as owner, may sign away some of the rights to use that property for a cash fee, or give away those rights selectively, as a gift. Some writers believed that, once Bradley and others like her extended their tacit permission for a community of fans to share the personal property represented by the copyrighted creation, the rights of all science fiction writers to charge a fee for the use of their creations could come into question.

This concern about copyrights set science fiction writers seriously at odds with themselves. Science fiction as a genre is a communal creation: its writers and artists speak directly to each other in their work, often borrowing a device here, a concept there. Bradley's actions opened for active debate the question, "Just exactly where does the line lie between a community in dialogue and copyright infringement? Between sharing a gift with friends, and losing control of a universe created as the semiprivate playground of the author?" Many writers who express concern about the loss of autonomous control of their creations actually embrace the idea of sharing their worlds with their friends—we are not speaking of two groups of professional writers at odds but of battles being waged within the heart and mind of each individual.

Community structure seems to be asserting itself in solving the dilemma. Some professional science fiction writers, like Bradley and Lichtenberg, actively support their fan community's participation, while they retain control over the vision of their product in the selection process. Others, like C. J. Cherryh and Robert Lynn Asprin, establish universes specifically for others to join, and maintain control by selecting the friends who may play in them. Writers who began in *Star Trek* fanzines have published in Asprin's *Thieves' World* series, and in Cherryh's *Merovingen Nights* sequence.

Summary

The media fan community has no established hierarchy or profit-making economy. While the group as a whole looks to no authority figures, some fans assume leadership roles in some aspects of the community's activities. These individuals are often core members of core circles. Not all fans participate in the community with the same intensity. Some may collect fanzines, even write occasionally, without engaging in communal interactions at all. Others may participate peripherally in media fanzines, while locating their home community in one of the many interlocking fandoms such as gaming or literary science fiction. Still others look to the community for "family" relationships. Members of this latter group actively work to create an ideal society for themselves and fellow community members through the medium of their work and through the social organization they build around it.

It would be a mistake, however, to draw too clear a distinction between the commercial fiction writer and the fanwriter. From the very beginning of the media fanzine community, and in spite of resistance from commercial publishers, amateur writers in the fanzines have consistently crossed over into the commercial ranks. At the same time, and under equal constraint from commercial interests, professional writers have contributed to the nonprofit fanzines, sometimes under their own names and sometimes using pseudonyms. Performers active in the creation of the source products, however, are institutionally peripheral to the community's main interest of creating its own literature about media and literary characters. Performers who may wish to enter more deeply into the fan world must adapt to the norms of a group controlled by women for the purpose of creating community through art.

Notes

1. Only with Japanimation does the fandom depend for its identity on the ethnic style of the source material rather than the delivery channel itself.

2. Joan Winston, *The Making of Trek Conventions* (New York: Playboy Press, 1979); also, David Gerrold discusses the convention phenomenon in *The World of Star Trek* (New York: Ballantine Books, 1973), as do Jacqueline Lichtenberg, Sondra Marshak, and Joan Winston in *Star Trek Lives!* (New York: Bantam Books, 1975).

3. Rick Kolker, interview, August Party convention, Tyson's Corners, Virginia, August 1985.

4. Media West, a multi-media convention held in Lansing, Michigan, each Memorial Day weekend is probably the largest long-running fan-organized media convention. If media fandom had a world convention, this would be it.

5. See Chapter 4 for a discussion of the Welcommittee and its role in introducing new fans to the community.

6. Taped interview with DWFCA employee-organizer, identity withheld, Valley Forge, Pa., 1985.

7. William Sims Bainbridge, *Dimensions of Science Fiction* (Cambridge, Mass.: Harvard University Press, 1986), p. 177, quoting Harry Warner, *All Our Yesterdays* (Chicago: Advent, 1969), p. 26.

8. Devra Langsam, interview, More Eastly Con, LaGuardia, N.Y., 1985.

9. Gary Alan Fine, *Shared Fantasy: Role Playing Games as Social Worlds* (Chicago: University of Chicago Press, 1984), p. 68.

10. The Lunarians, as explained earlier, are a New York–based science fiction club.

11. See C. Kadushin, "Networks and Circles in the Production of Culture," in *The Production of Culture*, ed. Richard A. Peterson (Beverly Hills, Calif.: Sage Publications, 1976), pp. 107–22, for a description of how circles operate in intellectual and social movements.

12. Whips, the name of an important Houston circle, is an acronym for Women of Houston in Professions. Members worked out the acronym and the name at the same time while traveling by plane to Campcon, a camping convention where other circles were gathering. The Friends of Fandom is an umbrella organization that coordinates services for a number of nonprofit fan activities. Starbases are local chapters of a nationwide commercial *Star Trek* fan club.

13. Lin Place, taped group interview, Mt. Holly, N.J., June 1987.

14. Robin Curtis, taped interview, Boston, November 1986.

15. George Takei, taped interview, Boston, November 1986.

16. Ibid.

17. Ibid.

18. Curtis and Takei, taped interview, Boston, November 1987.

19. According to one coordinator of Isiscon in Washington, D.C., in 1987, the two headliners of the original *Star Trek* series demand and receive fees in excess of ten thousand dollars for a three-day convention appearance.

20. Paul Darrow, taped interview, Philadelphia, Pa., November 1986.

21. Ibid.

22. Michael Keating, taped interview, Philadelphia, November, 1986, about Scorpio: "And I came to Scorpio IV this year. But I enjoyed it—great party."

23. Joe Haldeman, *World Without End* (New York: Bantam Books, 1979).

24. Sondra Marshak and Myrna Culbreath, *New Voyages* (collection; New York: Bantam Books, 1976), *New Voyages 2* (collection; New York: Bantam Books), *The Fate of the Phoenix* (New York: Bantam Books), *The Price of the*

Phoenix (New York: Bantam Books), and *The Prometheus Design* (New York: Timescape Pocket Books, 1982).

25. A. C. Crispin, *Yesterday's Son* (New York: Pocket Books, 1983).
26. A. C. Crispin, taped interview, Cockeysville, Md., March 1986.
27. J. M. Dillard, *Demons* (New York: Pocket Books, 1986).
28. J. M. Dillard, taped interview, Atlanta, Ga., August 1986.
29. Brad Ferguson, author of *Crisis on Centaurus* (New York: Pocket Books, 1986). Taped interview, Atlanta, August 1986.
30. Howard Weinstein, *The Covenant and the Crown* (New York: Pocket Books, 1981).
31. Diane Duane, *The Wounded Sky* (New York: Pocket Books, 1986).
32. Howard Weinstein, taped interview, Cockeysville, Md., March 1986.
33. Jean Lorrah, *The Vulcan Academy Murders* (New York: Pocket Books, 1984).
34. Jean Lorrah and Willard F. Hunt, "Visit to a Weird Planet," in *Spockanalia,* ed. Devra Langsam and Sherna C. Burley (Brooklyn, N.Y.: Poison Pen Press [Garlic Press], 1968), 89–101.
35. Jean Lorrah, *Full Moon Rising* (Bronx, N.Y.: Yeoman Press, 1976), and *NTM Collected* (Murray, Ky.: self-published, 1980 [1978]).
36. Jacqueline Lichtenberg, *Kraith Collected,* 3 vols. (Detroit: Ceiling Press Publications, 1982).
37. Jacqueline Lichtenberg, *House of Zeor* (New York: Playboy Paperbacks, 1974), is an example of the Sime-Gen universe.
38. Name of the informant withheld at her request. Personal communication, April 1987.
39. Personal communication, 1986.
40. Key books in this series include *Bloody Sun* (New York: Ace Books, 1964, revised 1979), and *Heritage of Hastur, Forbidden Tower,* and *The Shattered Chain,* all from Daw Books, New York, in the mid-seventies.
41. Lynne Holdom, ed., *Contes Di Cottman IV* (Pompton Lakes, N.J.).
42. Wolheim passed away in 1991.
43. Jacqueline Lichtenberg and Jean Lorrah, "The Answer," in *The Keeper's Price* (New York: Daw Books, 1980), pp. 98–110.
44. C. McQuillan, "The Forest," in *The Keeper's Price,* pp. 33–48.

Chapter Three
Fan Fiction and Material Art

Fanzines, and Other Artistic Forms

Fan fiction has been a mainstay of the science fiction community since its inception. Back in 1926 Hugo Gernsback intended his pulp magazine, *Amazing Stories*, to fire the minds of a nation's male youth to become engineers—Brian Aldiss calls the pulp fiction "propaganda for the wares of the inventor. Screwdrivers substitute for vision."[1]—and many of its readers followed the program into the fields of technology. Even more of them learned by example. They wanted to write science fiction, if not in the pulps then in their own hand-cranked mimeo magazines.

In the science fiction community, fanzines continue as slim productions, mimeographed or photocopied, which contain letters from the subscribers to each other; reviews of books, movies, or games; interviews from conventions with writers or artists; and a scattering of cartoons with only rarely a very short piece of fiction. Occasionally a fanzine will gain the attention of the science fiction industry itself and even develop a sufficiently large subscriber list that it may pay contributors a nominal sum in cash rather than the traditional payment in copies of the publication. Publications like *Science Fiction Chronicle* and *Locus* may once have been fanzines, but at present they are considered semi-professional, offering a slick newsletter approach to and for the science fiction industry.

The word "fanzine," often shortened to the form 'zine (pronounced "zeen"; usually spelled *zine*, without the apostrophe) means a maga*zine* created by fans. Fans make a distinction between a fanzine, which has an editor and centralized production, and an apa, or Amateur Press Association publication. An amateur press association is a small group, seldom more than thirty and usually many fewer members, who collaborate in the publication of an apa. By agreement among the members the apa, like a fanzine, can include fiction, commentary, or letters. Unlike a fanzine, however, each contributor to an apa submits to a central member who acts as collator of as many copies of her submission as there are members in the association. The collator does no editing or printing. He or she staples the individual submissions together exactly as they come in and sends out the sets of submissions to the members of the association. Apas therefore include many paper and print formats, as well as a variety of skill levels, in each copy. Some media fanziners participate in apas, but the most widespread form is still the zine.

In general, the science fiction fanwriter of today hopes to sell his fiction and accordingly creates an "original" work, one in which the characters, settings, and actions at least masquerade as the products of his own and no other imagination. While the science fiction writer with commercial intentions may borrow heavily from the conventions of the genre, and readers will criticize him if he does not do so, his characters must at least have original names, his spaceship a detail or two that sets it apart from *Star Trek*'s *Enterprise* or *Star Wars*' *Millennium Falcon.* He generally withholds his work from the fanzines, as one informant explained, because if it isn't good enough to sell, he doesn't want it seen.

Media fans differ from their counterparts and alter egos in the science fiction community in one important particular. They do not write with the intention of selling their wares for profit. Rather, they write to comment upon or add to the canon of materials they already know. Therefore, the *Enterprise* remains just that and does not appear as the *Entrepreneur.* Accordingly, media fanzines in the women's community have moved in a very different direction than those still produced in science fiction. The community still has its letter-oriented fanzines, called letterzines, but starting with small mimeographed publications in 1966, the women's fanzines have become increasingly sophisticated productions, primarily of fiction. The standard format for the media fanzine is 8½ by 11 inches, and may include illustrations as well as text. Three hundred pages of reduced print is not unusual, and few fanzines run less than one hundred pages. Because the sources of the fan fiction are copyrighted by their creators, fanwriters and publishers may not earn a profit from their work, so no writer of fan fiction may be paid for her work, and no publisher may show a profit on the sale of her fanzines.

Formal Genres

The women's fanzine community generates material and verbal lore. For the most part, form does not limit content, although it will regulate its treatment. The following tables list the various formal genres fans recognize, many of which appear in the fanzines:

Verbal Forms

Category	Form	Comments
Folksong	Ballad; lyric	Lyric is written and sung more often than ballad.
Poetry	Narrative; lyric	Sonnets are popular, narrative poetry is rare; I have never seen epic poetry using electronic media sources.
Prose (Narrative)	Vignettes; stories; novellas; novels; personal experiences	Stories and novellas are most popular; vignettes are very common from new writers. Personal experiences are mostly passed word-of-mouth but may also appear in letters.
Drama	Skits; plays	Generally reserved for conventions. This is where jokes may appear, although other forms of verbal wit are more highly prized.
Conversation	Humorous; serious	May be personal or revolve around art products. Facility in conversation is greatly valued, and quips and witticisms, funny stories, and turns of phrase are the community's alternative to the joke form.
Prose (letters)	Open; personal	Letters often include criticism. Open letters are published in letterzines and apas. Parts of personal letters may be reproduced and distributed by addressee.
Prose essays	Criticism; discussion	While the essay form does appear in fanzines, many more critical essays are written in letters.
Indices/ directories	Source product; fan product	*Trexindex* is the largest fan index. Fans also produce directories of series episodes.
Catalogs	Fanzines; other materials	Requests for submissions to fanzines and notices of publication/ordering information are compiled in catalogs.

Material Art

Category	Form	Comments
Illustration	Portrait; action	Illustrations are specific to the work in which they appear or may be reproductions of hanging art.
Hanging art	Portraits; studies	Portraits are most common; studies are also popular. Original drawings for illustrations may also be sold as hanging art.
Costume	Original re-creation	Costume varies from elaborate full dress to a scattering of slogan buttons and a significant bit, such as a scarf (Doctor Who) or pointed ears (Mr. Spock).
Craft	Needlework; ceramics; decoupage; jewelry	Most crafts that women engage in outside fandom can be and are directed to reproducing media themes.
Video art	Songtapes; dramas; masquerades; home movies	Songtapes are considered art. Video is also used to make a permanent record of masquerades and other convention/house party events.
Bookmaking	Fanzines; apas; letterzines	The actual construction of the written work is a material art, one of the few that has depended heavily on outside service providers for the finished product rather than for raw materials.
Photographs	Video stills; convention shots	Some fans use video technology to create hard copy still shots from tape. Others use still photography to make permanent records of activities and events, and incorporate them in fan memorabilia such as calendars.
Ephemera collecting	Commercial memorabilia; publicity stills	Fans collect tie-in commercial products, such as mugs, glasses, lunch boxes, and publicity stills.

Of the verbal forms, all but conversation may appear in fanzines, although even conversations may be fictionalized or recounted in published letters. A fanzine may contain one work, most frequently a novel, index, or catalog, or a number of forms, including a short novel or several novellas, short stories, poems, songs, and skits. Of the material forms, illustration art appears most often in fanzines, but

Fanzine editor Roberta Rogow compiled the *Trexindex*. She's an active filk-singer and songwriter as well.

photographs may appear there as well. The production of the fanzine itself is a material as well as verbal art.

Writing Community

While formal categories of creative activities give us an introduction to the production of the community, it is important to keep in mind that the fanwriters create their fiction entirely for an insider audience trained to share in the conventions of the literature. Art in the community not only offers a personal message, but also reflects social norms in the group while it patterns the social organization for a broad and often disparate readership.

Categorical distinctions recognized within the community signal the levels within the narratives at which specific social functions are carried out. By social functions, I mean the systems set up in a group that regulate relationships. The function of fan fiction inside the community can only be seen in the process of creation and transmission within the community. Once a story or work of art leaves the context

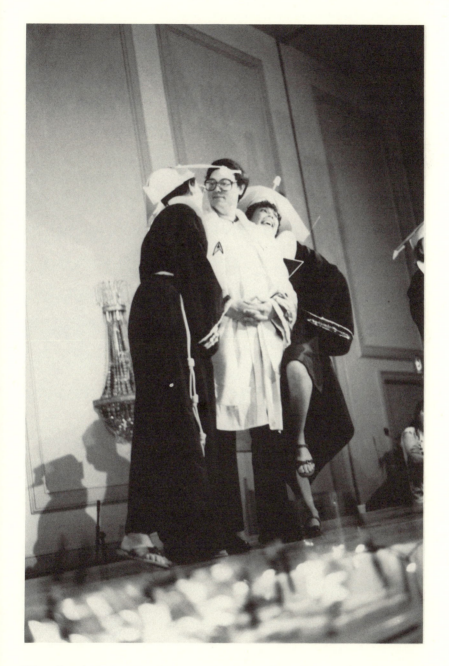

"Temple of Trek" skit. Fans can laugh at themselves and their media favorites.

Memorabilia: coffee mugs, and idics as necklaces, key chains, bracelets, and earrings.

Buttons inspired by the television series *Doctor Who* and *Star Trek*, and another referring to Marion Zimmer Bradley's *Darkover* literary science fiction series, "Free Amazons."

in which its creation had meaning, it may represent, but not function socially, in the categories set within the group.[2]

Inside the community, literary creation functions in the structuring of three levels of social relationship:

1. The relationship of the group to those outside the group: How does the group make itself intelligible to the larger culture within which it resides, both to ease the transition of those who wish to enter and to allay the suspicions of those who wish to remain outside? Formal categories recognizable by insiders and outsiders alike function in this capacity.

2. The relationship of each member of the community to the community, not as an individual but as part of a group: How is the group to be formed, what are the conventions of making contact, becoming a part, interacting with others who together make up the entity that constitutes the identity of the member as member? Universes and story trees, described below, organize this level of function, as do thematic categories.

3. The relationship of the individual to other individuals and their groups: How does the Joan or Sue or Barbara or Mary who sees herself as a special person with thoughts, feelings, needs to be met, express herself to other Joans or Sues or Barbaras or Marys who can understand the thoughts and feelings and meet the needs of that special person within every community member? The text organizes this level of social function.

Like social interaction, we can see that fan fiction itself divides into levels, each of which fulfills a specific need within the community. To outsiders, the obvious distinction is between structure and content, but it turns out not to be the relevant one among fans. To the fan community the significant categories are the story and the corpus in which the story takes its place. Both structure and content include a level of text and a level of the whole, the relationship of the corpus to the community in terms of the text (thematic genres), intertextuality (universes), and macrotexts (story trees).

The Organization of Thematic Genres

Superficially, the individual texts produced by members of the community divide into two major groups: stories that fall within the thematic genres and stories that do not fit under established headings. At some very basic level, all the thematic genres deal with issues of power and self-worth. But this is a women's community that works hard at finding its own values. Power does not necessarily equate with desire here; fans see it as a complex and often deceiving chimera, and each genre attacks the problem of power from different points of view and in the context of different social relationships at different levels of metaphoric abstraction, each of which contains a certain degree of risk.

To call these genres thematic may be a bit misleading: the reader may expect an index of tale-types, or a Proppian[3] analysis of actions and motifs that constitute the genres and distinguish them from each other. In fact, the literary distinctions between the genres are quite subtle, and revolve around one facet of the story, the nature of the relationship between the protagonist and the other characters, as their distinguishing features. The genres break conceptually and socially into two groups:

1. Genre categories the fan women conceptualize to be about the community's "us": women. Stories in this group deal with women's places in social and/or occupational relationships with men and other women. They include:

Mary Sue stories,[4] in which a very young heroine, often in her teens and possessing genius, intelligence, great beauty, and a charmingly impish personality, joins the heroes either on the bridge of the starship or on the streets with the spies or police. She generally resolves the conflict of the story, saves the lives of the protagonists who have grown to love her, but dies heroically in the process. The term is also used to describe the heroine featured in this kind of story. Mary Sue has developed strong negative connotations in the community.

Lay-(Spock, Kirk, etc.). May be called simply a "lay" story, in which an adult heroine meets and has a sexual relationship with a character from the source products. The name after the hyphen may vary. In recent years, the term has fallen out of widespread use, and the category has been increasingly subsumed under the term Mary Sue.

Hurt-comfort stories, in which one of the protagonists is injured—accidentally, or intentionally by villains—falls ill, or in the genre's extreme form, is tortured, and a fellow protagonist from the source products or developed by the fanwriter tends and comforts the hurt party.

2. Genres about "them," the culturally unknown: men. These stories concentrate on men's social and/or occupational relationships with each other. They include:

Relationship (nonsexual) stories, in which the action serves to highlight the intense but nonsexual friendship between two male characters from the source products.

Hurt-comfort stories, as described above, but specifically limited in this sense to male characters both giving and receiving comfort.

K/S stories, in which Captain Kirk and Mr. Spock of *Star Trek* engage in a sexual relationship. *Slash* has become the generic identification for a story in which any two male characters from the full range of source products recognized in the community engage in a sexual-romantic relationship. The term is derived from the orthographic character (/) used to separate the names or initials of the two or more characters involved in a sexual-romantic relationship. The presence of a sexual act in the text is not necessary for the categorization; only the implication that the action takes place in a fictional universe where such a relationship exists is needed.[5]

Fans use the genre names to mark the distinguishing feature of a particular work, but the genres are not mutually exclusive. A Mary

Sue may also be a hurt-comfort story or change at some point into a relationship or lay-Spock story. Rather, the designation acts more as a signal to the reader, a shorthand in the conversation, to indicate the aspect of the relationship that has greatest situational significance. An editor, for example, may warn a fan who finds homosexuality offensive that a particular item is a K/S story, but may alert a known K/S fan who is uncomfortable with hurt-comfort about that content in the same story. In the same way, telling others that she likes relationship stories identifies a fan as a member or potential member of the social group that writes about and discusses the nonsexual friendship of the characters in the source product.

Beyond Genre: Stories That Do Not Fit the Mold

Many of the stories created in the community fit neither of the two categories discussed here, and therefore have no generic designation specific to the group. Many fit the action-adventure format of the source products themselves, but they do not function quite the same way within the social discourse carried on in the genre-designated fiction. Their writers seem to be interested in creating more universal works of art rather than in engaging in personal communication with other community members at the defined metaphoric level of thematic genres. Both men and women write stories that do not fall within the genre designations, but the relatively few heterosexual men in the community do so most consistently.

Many writers who work outside the conventionalized genres claim they do so to create a more artistically challenging work of art. However, to make a distinction between "art" and "genre" may be misleading for a number of reasons:

1. The intention to create art in this category carries with it the skill to do so in no greater proportion than that skill appears in other categories, while to be aesthetically pleasing in the group, the product must often exhibit greater than usual skill to compensate for the missing genre element. Therefore, many of the stories created with the intention of producing art in fact do not succeed for the group at that level.

2. Many of the writers in the established genres set high artistic standards for their work, and some aspire to the ambitious goal of reaching outsider artistic standards with insider messages and themes, so artistic themes are not definable in contrast to thematic genres.

3. Many of the writers who do not work in the established genres *do* intend to communicate personal needs and feelings to members of the

group. Those needs and feelings may not fit into the established thematic models, or alternatively, the writer may not feel comfortable with the model in which those needs and feelings are commonly addressed.[6]

4. Incipient genres may accumulate a body of literature and even critical discourse before they become entrenched both as recognizable themes and as significant vehicles for expressing needs and concerns of group members that have not been met satisfactorily by the established system. An example is the growing body of literature about strong women characters whose primary relationship with the characters in the source product is not sexual or familial, and the growing realization that equally strong female characters in familial relationships are not best served by the soubriquet "lay-Spock" (etc.). I will discuss this slowly growing movement and its relationship to the slash genre later in this chapter and the next.

5. Some incipient genres arise out of the source product itself, and remain to some extent attached to that specific product or to a specific group of writers. An example is the body of literature that focuses on the effects of psychosocial manipulation on the characters in *Blake's 7*. While the genre had no name, it was the most commonly used theme arising out of that source product until 1986. Before 1986, *Blake's 7* had not appeared on broadcast television in the United States, and community members often found the literature before they found the source product. Self-selection limited members of the community to those who were interested in the theme expressed in both the series and the fan fiction. After 1986, a mass audience began to discover the program on public television stations, and fanwriters from many source products latched onto the new characters and situations with their old genres intact. The emergent genre of psychosocial manipulation has almost disappeared, overwhelmed by the established norms of the larger incoming group.

Story, Text, and Universe: Sharing Literature

The importance to fans of the relationship of texts to each other and their relationship in turn to the creation of community may be the most difficult idea to grasp in the study of the women's fanzine community. The Western literary establishment has generally put the basic meaningful unit at the level of the text. That is, while a scholar may study the texts created in a particular genre or period, he has generally concentrated on structurally and conceptually individual texts. Like the Oedipal boy, the text has been viewed in Oedipal terms: the artist struggles to separate from the body literate and individuates his text as a reflection of, or perhaps in lieu of, his ego development. As Carol Gilligan points out, for men safety is generally perceived in separation, in rising above and moving away from the mass of the hierarchical pyramid.[7] We can see this myth of separation carried into the interpretation of literature, with the establishment of a canon based not on the relation of the works to each other, but on an aesthetic judgment that they stand apart from, and above, the literary outpourings of their times.

In contrast to this model, fanwriters know their work fits into a structure that includes both the source products and all the fiction that has grown up around them. That structure recapitulates within the body of literature the blueprint for the structure of the community, and in turn creates that blueprint. If we turn the question of creativity in the canon back on itself, however, we may well ask: How *unique* is any literary text? Edward Said has expressed the growing interest in a critical redefinition of the creative unit:

> What is the unit of theoretical interest: that is, what—how defined and demarcated a spatial or temporal interval does one focus upon in a theoretical examination of writing or reading? . . . If there is anything that centrally characterizes modern writing, it is a dissatisfaction with traditional units of interest like the text, the author, the period, and even the idea.[8]

Said describes a new criticism of writing that recognizes the source within the text: Joyce rewriting—re-creating—Homer, Eliot writing *through* Virgil.

While the literary establishment works its way through the myth of originality to an understanding of the interrelatedness of the writer, his world, and his work, women who write fan fiction make not the least pretense of standing apart from their milieu.

Elaine Showalter picks up the metaphor of quilt making when she describes women writing commercially,[9] and her analysis applies equally to the fanwriters. Using well-known communal patterns, the craftsperson creates a work like a quilt top, unique in the way it combines the familiar elements with the distinctly personal statement she makes through her selection of elements. A quilt top, like the book a woman writes, does have known authorship, although knowledge of that authorship may be lost when the work passes outside the community. The quilting of the top to fill and backing may become a communal enterprise, or a woman known for her quilting—the patterned stitching of the top to back through the fill—may take on the authorship of that task. The quilt metaphor has become well worn, but Showalter makes a point that exactly fits the worldview of many fanwriters. That is, women created quilts out of necessity, as a skilled craft. In common with the "scribblers" of the 1850s, quilters saw their productivity as work within a community, a profession, not an art. Women fanwriters, like the women who wrote gothic romances in the 1850s, value their workmanship in the community but place little or no emphasis on the concept of "auteur" as solitary creator of an aesthetically unique piece of art.

In the fan community, fiction creates the community. Many writers contribute their work out of social obligation, to add to the discourse, to communicate with others. Creativity lies not in how a writer breaks with the tradition of the community's work but in how she uses the language of the group to shed a brighter light on the truth they work to communicate. Commercial television fits uniquely into this scheme of women's culture. Production is shared, and members of the community of insiders involved in the industry know who is creatively responsible for its parts. That information often becomes lost when the product moves outside the creative community into the consumer public. Like quilting and women's commercial writing of the 1850s, television is usually denied the authenticity of the rubric "art," and the people who create in the medium see themselves as participating in a utilitarian practice: selling soap.

For the women in the fan community, television is a readily available source of infinitely combinable but specifically not unique elements. They borrow wholesale from the television sources and divide their social world up according to the units of fictional creation they term "universes."

Universes: The Corpus According to Content

The concept of a variety of "universes" arose out of the science fiction timeline theory. This oft-used device posits that the "real world" we live in is but one of an infinite set of possible universes that may coexist simultaneously with our own, in which each of us acts out a different script of life. The concept has spawned the alternate history subgenre—historical novels and stories based on a past and present in which, for example, the Allies lost World War II,[10] or the Romans never Christianized Britain,[11]—and in the women's media fiction has come to take on a variety of meanings.

The first meaning of a universe in the media fanzine community is the source product itself, as devised by the commercial producers.

One speaks of the television or movie *Star Trek* universe, or the TV *Starsky and Hutch* universe. A writer who works in the television universe of her source product accepts the characters and relationships as given; she does not change the status of the characters by adding permanent wives or children, or by killing or maiming one of the main characters. The writer works hard to create in her stories characters that speak like the ones on television, and whose personalities match the screen product.

In cross-universe stories, writers combine source products, often for a comic effect. Han Solo of *Star Wars* may travel in time and meet Indiana Jones, for comic surprise at the striking resemblance both Harrison Ford characters bear to one another. A time-traveling Captain Kirk may meet policeman T. J. Hooker, both characters played by William Shatner, or Doctor Who's Tardis may land on Captain Kirk's *Enterprise*. Fans may bring together more than two universes: in one story, Doctor Who met several of his own incarnations, as well as the crews of the *Battlestar Galactica*, the *Enterprise*, and *Blake's 7*'s *Scorpio*. In cross-universe stories, the purpose is not necessarily to permanently change any of the characters but to see how those characters would react to each other.

But, consonant with the science fiction assumption that any change from the known history splits off a timeline, or universe ongoing simultaneous to all others, writers who do permanently change the status of a character or characters are said to create new universes. Writers using the *Star Trek, Star Wars, Blake's 7, Beauty and the Beast,* and other source products have created their own universes, with characters and relationships that exist only in the stories their creators write. When, for example, Jacqueline Lichtenberg created a Vulcan culture in which Spock married and in which his family adopted Captain Kirk, she was splitting her work off from the source product, creating her own universe, the "Kraith" universe.

The Kraith is a cup, a religious symbol integral to the most important rituals on Vulcan, the home planet of Sarek, who is the father of the half-alien Spock. In the basic storyline, the cup has been lost and Sarek has been kidnapped. Though he is only a minor character in the television series and movies, in the Kraith universe, as so often happens in fan fiction, he becomes a central figure.

Lichtenberg created both the cup and the rituals, yet she depended on her readers' knowledge of Vulcan culture and physiology (as established in the television episode "Amok Time") and the relationship between Spock and his father (as established in another episode, "Journey to Babel") to ground the new material in the familiar. A classic Grail quest might have followed from the author's invention, but

Leah Rosenthal's cartoon based on the British series *Blake's* 7. Appeared in *Bizzaro* 7, an alternate-universe parody fanzine.

she resolved that quest early in the series. Sarek and then the cup are found and, what for Lichtenberg is the real quest, to discover the self as it grows in relationships with others, openly moves to the fore.

In the humorous *Blake's* 7 parody, the Bizarro 7 universe, Leah Rosenthal and Ann Wortham[12] postulate a Federation that has accused Blake of molesting a duck. (In *Blake's 7*, the Federation trumped up charges of child molestation to ruin the rebel's reputation among his followers, but in the Bizarro universe, one is never quite sure that the duck charges are false.) The Bizarro Avon is the younger child of a rich Federation family that, among other things, owns and races horses of a most abominable disposition.

Both Kraith and Bizarro 7 constitute universes essentially controlled by their creators, Jacqueline Lichtenberg, and Leah Rosenthal and Ann Wortham respectively. In all other respects, however, their efforts differ. Kraith represents a serious view of a possible Vulcan history for Mr. Spock, while Bizarro's creators work toward an absurd effect, combining outrageous plots with sly satire (Avon is kidnapped by a brothel. Given a drug to render him temporarily paralyzed and unable to struggle with his kidnappers, he suffers a side effect—he believes he is God—and escapes by levitating and floating out the window). Lichtenberg invites others to write in her universe, whereas Rosenthal and Wortham reserve for themselves the privilege of writing Bizarro. Both, however, have created a space next to or side onto the source products, in which the recognizable mingles inextricably with the new.

The term "alternate universe" takes the concept of the separate universe a giant step farther. The term identifies a body of literature that moves the characters out of their television settings, physically or in terms of worldview. In Barbara Wenk's *One Way Mirror*,[13] the Federation of *Star Trek* is an empire that functions on deadly competition in the ranks and systematically oppresses women as it oppresses subject races and species within its sphere of influence. In some "pre-reform"[14] alternate universes Surak, the Vulcan philosopher of peace and logic, never influenced that culture. Mr. Spock is often a warrior lord in these stories, and Earth and humans may be the conquered subjects of Vulcan rule.

In alternate universe stories Illya Kuryakin, of *The Man From U.N.C.L.E.*, can become a vampire, and Ray Doyle, of *The Professionals*, can become an elf. Hutch, from *Starsky and Hutch*, can be a cyborg in a post-nuclear holocaust Los Angeles, and Avon of *Blake's 7* can hail from a homeworld where magic is the norm and unicorns are part of the native livestock. What these stories share is a profound shift in recognizable genre conventions: Science fiction series become horror or fantasy, while police action series may become horror, fantasy, science fiction, or romance. The moral stance of the *Star Trek* television universe is often overturned in alternate universe stories based on this source product.

Romanticized version of a "pre-reform"—alternate universe—Spock. Appeared in *Organia*.

Fans categorize both the police stories turned into other genre fiction and the positivistic future of *Star Trek* turned dark and oppressive as alternate universe stories. Both writers and readers distinguish these stories from, for example, time travel stories in *Star Trek*. In the former, the writer gives no explanation for the change in the status of the characters: the reader enters the story with the new scenario as given. In the latter case, a trail of logical explanations leads the reader from the television universe of the source product to the altered scenario.

For fans of *Blake's 7*, the concepts of alternate universe and logically postulable alternative outcomes make their fiction possible. When producers ended the fourth season of the series with the deaths of all the major lead characters, they cut off the possibility of growth and change implicit in most fan fiction. Some fans, like Regina Gottesman and writer Susan Matthews, do overturn the series' ending with a logic trail. The novel *The Mind of a Man Is a Double Edged Sword*, conceptualized by Gottesman and Matthews and written by the latter, explains the deaths as the induced hallucinations of a brainwashed Avon. Other writers simply pick up the story at an earlier point in the series and continue in a different direction, or argue that the characters were not really killed, but only stunned. Recovered, they escape and continue their adventures.

Theoretically, any divergence from the source product should be considered alternate universe, but most fans use the phrase to label only stories that shift perceptions of the characters and situations so drastically that the reader can scarcely consider them derived from the source product at all.

While it retains most of the markers of the source products, some fans feel that homoerotic fiction differs so markedly from the overt characterizations of the source products that the entire genre should be categorized as alternate universe. Ostensibly the homoerotic universe changes only the way in which the main characters relate to each other, from comradely affection to sexual attachment. In fact the writing often softens the characterizations and engages a new discourse, that of the romance, on top of the science fiction or police action discourse already in play.

Over time many fans have fought the label alternate universe when used for homoerotic stories. It has generally fallen out of use for this fan category, although a number of people have told me they still think of homoerotic fiction in terms of alternate universe.

Story Trees: The Structure of a Corpus

The women in the fan community most often discuss the body of fan fiction in terms of universes, and thematic and formal genre categories. That does not mean fans are unaware of the significance of structure in their work. Rather, the rules of structure, like the grammar of a native language speaker, operate at a level of tacit knowledge which surfaces primarily in the presence of a breach in preferred structures, or, more pleasurably, when the unconscious expectations of structure are exceeded.

I first became aware of the importance of structure to the aesthetic of fan fiction when I explored a subdivision of the corpus that I dubbed the story tree.[15] In the story tree, which by definition is or falls within a universe created out of the media source product by the fan originator, shared content extends to shared structure. The story tree may include stories, poems, pieces of artwork, or novels connected to each other by plot as well as characters and settings but which do not necessarily fall in a linear sequence. It may have one author or many. A root story may offer unresolved situations, secondary characters whose actions during the main events are not described, or a resolution that is unsatisfactory to some readers. Writers then branch out from that story, completing dropped subplots, exploring the reactions of minor characters to major events. Differences of opinion do occur: a writer may reconstruct someone's story from a new perspective or offer a completely different ending. Raising the dead has long been a popular option in the latter category.

Jacqueline Lichtenberg's Kraith universe is one of the earliest story trees. In a few short stories written as a group, Lichtenberg set up the cultural milieu based on *Star Trek*'s Vulcan and the course of events the story tree would follow. Kraith excited the community to rejoinder, as Lichtenberg had hoped. Fan publications printed stories by Ruth Berman offering alternative Kraith experiences. Other writers asked to join the story tree, and Lichtenberg published a "timeline" (see Appendix D) so new participants, who might have read only a few of the growing number of stories, could fit their work into the body of the multiwriter universe. Judy Segal wrote "Understanding Kraith,"[16] a dictionary of special terms in the Kraith universe for both writers and readers.

Community members continue to write Kraith stories. The most recent Kraith story I have seen, "Death's Crystal Kingdom," appears in the fanzine *Maine(ly) Trek 4*, issued in late 1985. The story tree continues to offer an expanded vocabulary of metaphors with which *Star*

Trek fanwriters discuss friendship and family loyalty, marriage, sex, and religion. Lichtenberg has since gone on to become a commercially successful science fiction writer. She continues her policy of encouraging new writers within the community of noncommercial *Star Trek* fans to share both her Kraith universe and the world she created for her commercially published Sime-Gen science fiction series.

Story trees like Kraith are a response to a concern I hear from many of the writers. The women in the Star Trek community see their art not in terms of self-sufficient units but as an expression of a continuing experience. Traditional closure doesn't make sense to them. At the end of the story, they feel, characters go on living in the nebulous world of the not-yet-written. They develop, modify their relationships over time, grow older, raise families.

Nor do these stories begin in a vacuum when the characters are all thirty-five years old. Spock had a childhood—sometimes strained. Jean Lorrah's Night of the Twin Moons (NTM) story tree[17] concentrates on the relationship of Sarek and his human wife Amanda, from their first meeting to their later years.

NTM begins where the traditional romance ends. It explores the equality possible in a committed relationship, a concept to which the romance pays lip service while denying it in action. Jean Lorrah's universe is a popular one, and echoes of it can be found in her *Vulcan Academy Murders,* published by Pocket Books in 1984. A reader of the NTM story tree finds a dense code of references here, calling up a rich, shared lifetime for fans. The reader unfamiliar with the noncommercial story tree will find the book fairly typical of Pocket Books' line of *Star Trek* novels.

In a survey I conducted at More Eastly Con in 1985, *Star Trek* fans said they did not watch television soap operas. Since most of them work full time to support themselves and devote much of their free time to fan activities, this is understandable. But the similarities in the aesthetic structure of the story tree and the soap opera cannot be overlooked. Fanwriters, like soap opera fans, want to see characters change and evolve, have families, and rise to the challenge of internal and external crises in a nonlinear, dense tapestry of experience. Whether because of innate qualities or socialization, women perceive their lives in this way, and they like to see that structure reproduced in their literature. The writing experience becomes one of participation in the lives of the characters. It is living day-to-day that matters, not the single events that make up individual plots.

Structural Redundancies in Fan Fiction

The story tree dramatically demonstrates a need for the world of fiction to reflect the simultaneity fans experience in real life. The structure is one of the earliest to appear in the community: Jean Lorrah and Willard F. Hunt wrote "Visit to a Weird Planet"[18] in 1968. By a quirk of physics, the "real" Kirk, Spock, and McCoy find themselves on the *Star Trek* soundstage in the midst of filming a series episode. They encounter dangerously enthusiastic fans and must learn the cast's lines to hide their identities until rescued by their ship. But, if the "real" crew were on the soundstage, the actors had to be somewhere else, having a simultaneous but different set of adventures. Ruth Berman offered a story, "Visit to a Weird Planet Revisited,"[19] in which the actors have transported onto the *Enterprise* at the moment when their counterparts appeared on the soundstage. The series stars must bluff their way through an encounter with real Klingons.

Once I had identified the pattern in the story tree, I found the same logic operating inside many stories. Fan stories typically depend on more than one point of view, and a single event may be repeated twice or three times as it is experienced by the different characters present in the scene. In Susan Matthews' *Blake's 7* novel *The Mind of a Man Is a Double Edged Sword*,[20] the point of view shifts from that of the psychologically tortured Avon to that of his companions, giving the reader several perspectives on events. To Avon the series episodes constitute his reality: companions have died at the hand of the enemy, he himself contemplated murdering his friend, Vila, to save his own life, and he killed Blake, for whom he had spent two seasons searching. But his companions know that Avon, not Blake, was separated from his companions and neither Cally nor Jenna has died. In the experience of his companions, Avon never contemplated murdering his friend Vila, nor did he kill Blake.

Seeing things from more than one angle is intrinsic to fan fiction, whether those angles are as divergent as the views of Avon and his companions in *Double-Edged Sword* or more simply the pain and confusion that can come about when characters misinterpret each other's motives and actions. Fanwriters tend to write from the assumption that there are as many stories as there are people in the scene to see the events and interpret them. The writer's goal is to show each important interpretation of the events, and the story moves the characters toward discovering that each sees the situation differently, and then finally reaching a compromise.

This need to describe the actions in a story two or even three times, making special note of the emotional reactions in each retelling, adds to the length of a satisfying story in fan terms. It also explains the prevalence of vignettes. This very short form, with no plot of its own, relies entirely on a story already told, either in the fan fiction or on the screen. The vignette adds the missing perspective on a particular scene—what Vila saw when Avon killed Blake in the episode "Blake," or what Hutch was thinking when Starsky was shot in the episode "Sweet Revenge." Many writers start their serious work with a vignette that adds the missing point of view, particularly the emotional reaction, to a well-known scene.

From a structural standpoint we can see that the linear story with a single narrative perspective per scene is so alien to this group that they use their fiction to "correct" the error of linearity in the source products. The fanwriters see life as a sea of potentialities, many of which can be realized simultaneously, many of which spread out like ripples across the lives of others, and all of which must somehow be encompassed in the literature if it is to express any kind of truth. What appears to an outsider as boring repetition is the logical result of a worldview that sees every interaction as a multi-layered experience out of which reality is negotiated.

Separation and Connection in the Corpus of Fan Fiction

Through the interplay of universe, structure, and text, the fan community writes its own dynamic social system. The literature reflects the pressure on the community to separate into ever-smaller groups in constant tension with an overriding pressure to join together in a web of relationships that extends around the world. Universes both bring people together and separate them into more manageably sized interest groups.

While universes act as devices by which like-minded fans can identify each other and form social groups, the structure of the corpus represents the complex worldview of community members. Linear narrative cannot convey a story with any illusion of reality for women who perceive their lives as part of an ongoing multifaceted and simultaneous web that connects them to each other. The story must back up and leap forward, the past with its memories must explain present actions in flashbacks and embedded narratives. Stories may begin with the ending and work back to uncover the forces that led to that particular conclusion. The same events may be repeated from many points of view, and conjunctive stories may add the separate activities of secondary characters influenced by the main action or unwittingly influencing the given outcome. Nor is any story ever completely finished; writers re-create the endings of their favorite stories and source products with bewildering regularity. Fan fiction at its most basic structural level constitutes the writerly text: ever changing, ever growing, ever entwining the creative lives of its writers in the interwoven process of communicating through narrative the life of the community.[21]

Material Forms and Conceptual Communities

In general, all forms of material art serve as visual reminders of the fictional universes in which the community shares an interest. Fans use material art to re-create the narrative world in a variety of concrete forms and images. In fact, stories themselves may pass through material art forms: narrative songtapes tell a story through a combination of music, lyrics, and images, and illustration art often represents a scene from a story. Many of the songtapes are in fact created by writers rather than visual artists. The fanzine publisher, of course, bridges the gap between the written and the material arts, and visual artists who produce illustration and video art as their primary contribution to the community seem to identify more closely with the fanzine/writing group than do those who produce, for example, costume as their most significant art.

Even an artifact like a Starfleet uniform may pass through a variety of material forms, however: from visual appearance in a film or television episode to verbal description in a story to visual representation in an illustration to material reconstruction in a costume. Memorabilia vendors may sell still photographs of the film version of the uniform, and craftspersons may reconstruct the uniform in cloth for a teddy bear or doll, or in molding material on ceramic Starfleet mice.

Visual Art: Illustrations and Hanging Art

At conventions, fans wear striking costumes to set their community apart from others who may share hotel space, but not the fan way of life, with them. In their homes and publications they use illustration and hanging graphic arts to express the aesthetic they have developed over time in the community.

Ironically, visual art is the one place in the fan community where the amateur can make a profit from her hobby. Most conventions both display art in an art show and offer that art for sale at an art auction toward the end of the convention. Technically, artists may not make a profit for the sale of nonlicensed reproductions of patented or trademarked materials, which include such traditional subjects as the starship *Enterprise*. In practice, however, the owners of those patents and trademarks have only enforced their right to limit use of their images when that use appeared to constitute a profitable business. For example, if a fan paints the *Enterprise* against a starfield, makes it into posters, and sells many copies of the poster for profit, owners of the trademark will enforce their right to confiscate those posters and bring legal action if the artist continues to sell nonlicensed posters.[22]

By contrast, trademark owners not only tolerate but sometimes even appreciate the original hanging art and the original art created to be reproduced as fanzine illustrations, both of which are sold at auction. Actors who star in the source products occasionally act as auctioneers, and fan artists note that art brings much higher prices when they do. Accordingly, graphic arts have developed under the triple pressures of aesthetic change, technological limitation, and economics.

At its beginning, the media fanzine community shared the science fiction visual aesthetic, which tends toward high-contrast acrylic paint and simple line illustrations suitable for replication in pulp magazines and on paperback covers. Early media fanzines did not use even simple color processing, but offered drawings with bold lines and a minimum of dark areas, which were difficult to reproduce in the amateur publications. Hanging art likewise reflected the science fiction community's aesthetic of acrylics and bold colors. Without the primary motivation for this aesthetic, the use of the art as commercial book covers, however, fans in the women's media community did not feel the same degree of commitment to the form as did the commercially oriented science fiction fan. More important to the media women, the style lacked the textural subtlety to satisfy the new community's preference for a softer, more idealized presentation of their romantic heroes. Artists did not have to limit the development of their styles to a publishing market, so they expanded in directions which science fiction artists, who aspire to paperback book covers, could not pursue. Pencil, chalk, and charcoal extensively replaced the bolder pen and ink drawings, and to some extent the acrylic paintings in hanging art.

The marketplace did influence the content of the amateur art at the level of the original work, however. Fan art is traditionally sold at auction during conventions, and fans have paid prices as high as six or seven hundred dollars for a well-rendered color piece by a nonprofessional artist.[23] To an extent the highest prices depend on basic capitalism and luck: if a good artist offers a piece or two based on a source product that has a sudden surge of popularity at the convention where the pieces are shown, the scarcity and demand will affect the price as much as the quality. Even given optimal conditions, however, few artists in the community create the quality of a fully rendered piece that draws the big prices.

Art typically sells for under a hundred dollars, and the most consistent demand in the midrange continues to be head-and-shoulder portraits of favorite characters from the source products, in poses recognizable from the publicity stills also available in the community. At the art show of a Chicago convention Fanny Adams, a popular artist in several source products, walked with me through an exhibit of her work, most in pencil, and explained the pragmatics of fan art:

> Fanny: I like to work from photographs because they give me the proportions . . . Part of the reason I do portraiture, and do it this way, is because it sells. I have got to be blunt about this, I have got to make money, I don't have a regular job. This is how I make my money. And what people want are "photographs" that are not too outrageous, to put on their wall. You know: "hey look, that's so and so, isn't that great?" And you have to go with the market. Uhm, but—[pause]
> Ethnographer: But sometimes you do things anyway?
> Fanny: Like this [she points to a portrait of Paul Michael Glazer as David Starsky]. This is a universally unpopular picture, and I'm not sure anybody even knows why . . . There are times when I, just no way I could have second-guessed them. I like that one—I haven't drawn him in ages.[24]

Fanny works from photographs for a number of reasons. From a practical standpoint, she does not have access to the actors to draw from life, and at the same time, her community demands of her portraits that look like renderings of the photographs they know. But as an artist, she finds photographs interesting as well as practical:

> I love getting new photographs to work from, there is always something new—wow, look at that. You can learn so much just by looking at photographs, because people don't understand what the camera captures. What they're showing.
>
> I mean you can't feel your expression, or feel what your eyes are projecting, unless you're really plugged into what you're feeling. [She points to a pencil drawing from a photograph of Martin Shaw.] You can imagine, this picture is saying, "No way. I don't want my picture taken."

Fanny is one of the better artists in the community, but even moderately skillful artists find that, with practice, they can produce satisfying portraits modeled on photographs of the actors in the roles very quickly. As a result, most convention art shows now include a few fully developed original pieces that generally go for the highest prices of the day, and a great many quickly rendered portraits in graphite or colored pencil, chalk, or charcoal.

While artists may tailor some of their work to the marketplace, the decision whom to draw is usually an emotional one. Tacs, a well-known artist who has worked in many fandoms, explained:

> I have to get emotional about my pictures, and I find myself extremely tired when I finish an emotional picture. I find myself putting on the facial expressions, on my own face, as I'm drawing.
>
> I sell my pictures—except for two right now that I will not sell. I find that people buy them not so much, they tell me, because of the exactness [of the image], but because of the emotion of them.

And Caren Parnes talked about a picture of Sonny Crockett in her room at Clippercon in 1987:

> Ethnographer, passing along a question from the room: Someone wants to know what your "Sonny" is for.
> Caren: It wasn't "for" anything. It was for love. No, [referring back to the original question, Was it created for a market?] I went to MediaWest [a convention] last year, and I loved him, so I drew it. It wasn't really for—it hasn't been in a zine or anything.

Sometimes an artist is drawn not just to a particular character but to a certain message she can express through that character as well. While looking at a double image of Captain Kirk—as a young man from the series and as the middle-aged admiral from the movies— I remarked that the picture reflected the desirability of both ages. Caren agreed:

> I'm glad you saw that . . . if anything, there was an idealization of the young, but almost a sense of wisdom achieved in the older that is not present in the young . . . because there is more of a richness, I think, in the man and the way he portrays his character now than there even was in the young man.

A number of artists have done idealized portraits of their favorite characters in their middle years, and they use the same tricks of high-

Caren Parnes' romanticized portrait of *Star Trek*'s Captain Kirk from the period of the second movie, *The Wrath of Khan*. Appeared in *Maine(ly) Trek 4*.

lighting and shading to create an aura of sensuality in the older character as they do with the younger.

As the aesthetic developed in the hanging art, artists and consumers craved a softer, more romantic representation of their heroes in the fanzines as well. Cross-hatching and stippling added shading and texture to the fanzine illustrations, but not depth or soft focus. The answer, halftones, came out of the printer's repertoire. With half-tone reproduction, the printer makes a photograph of the original illustration and transfers the photograph to a silk screen. The ink, passed through the screen, leaves the image in a series of dots on the print surface. In large part the density of the screen dictates how detailed a reproduction the printer obtains: the denser the screen, the smaller the dots, and the larger the number of them per square inch. When the dots are small enough and close enough together, the eye sees no dots at all, but rather a solid image.

Illustration art grew in importance as the community began to utilize the technological capacity of outside providers to reproduce the aesthetic of the community in fanzines. The former publisher[25] of the fanzine catalog, *Universal Translator,* now out of production but at one time the clearing house for information about fanzines in the community, believes that

> . . . [a] lot of zines sell on illos [illustrations]. They do. If there are illos inside, the people can see if the illos are good, are reproduced well, and they [the illustrations] look like they are describing good relationship–type stories, or interesting action-adventure, they [the fanzines] will sell.
>
> Zines that don't have illos have a much more difficult time. In fact, those editors have found it advantageous to identify in their fliers and in *UT* [*Universal Translator*] and *Datazine* [fanzine catalogs] that this zine does not have illos, because people are offended. They feel [they] paid their money, and they want illos.[26]

The innovation in art reproduction was expensive for this community. According to Laura Peck, publisher of the fanzine *In the Public Interest,*[27] "the halftones cost something like ten dollars a halftone. It was something like that."[28]

Most fanzine editors choose an eighty-line screen, which gives high enough resolution to see some detailing on the chalk and pencil drawings but still softens the picture. Small local printers seldom offer a finer screen, so here as in other areas of the fan aesthetic, many editors must compromise the ideal with the practical, accepting something less than they would prefer. But to have the print from the back of the illustration show through the art, to "bleed" or "leak" through, is generally considered unacceptable. As multiple-fanzine publisher Sheila Willis explained, fanziners must use a more expensive, heavier paper stock for art reproduction to ensure the integrity of the image. The result, while aesthetically more appealing, is considerably more expensive than earlier printing techniques:

Willis: I do eighty screen half-tone. I put them on seventy-pound off-white [paper]—I try to put it on seventy coronado, so you don't get leak-through. I do have the halftones done, and if you have a quarter one and you have words on the page it's another fee because they have to print the words before the halftone is done.[29]

While the eighty-line screen printed onto seventy-pound paper seems to be the standard for quality art reproduction in the community, some fan publishers, such as the editors of *Nome*, a fanzine noted for the quality of both its written text and its art, choose a more expensive and uncompromising approach to the art they publish. These editors patronize shops that specialize in the reproduction of art. Their art printer does the first step, using a one hundred twenty–line screen to print the illustration on one side of the heavy paper publishers use for this purpose. Then they take the printed illustrations to their regular printer to be inserted into the text of the fanzine itself. *Nome* is one of the more expensive of the community's publications, but it is considered an equitable bargain, both for its size—which may run as many as four hundred pages—and for the quality of its writing and art. As a *Star Trek* zine, however, *Nome* has a high sales volume, which offers some per-copy price relief. Publishers of fanzines produced in smaller fandoms must often charge an equal amount for fanzines with as few as a quarter of the number of halftones that *Nome* offers, and with less written material as well. The escalating cost of the fanzines has generated a great deal of debate among publishers, readers, and artists. At the Clippercon convention in 1987, artist Caren Parnes and editor Karen Swanson discussed the controversy with me:

Caren: There was a fan panel [at a convention] about a year or so ago, about the pros and cons of, of um, artist requirements, or artists' demands for pencils, for doing pencil work versus doing pen and ink. The cost to the editors and where it has gone and where, in the last two years, because there is a lot more pencil than has ever been done before . . .

A lot of editors were saying that, you know, "We don't see the necessity when pen and ink can still be done, of having to halftone and pay all this extra money." And yet, what you see is a lot of artists who are beginning to work pencil more often, and it gives a lot more depth to the zine to have the dimension of pencil as well as pen and ink.

It does cost more, but it's interesting, because we were trying to

think back on our favorite artists over the last couple of years, and most of them have worked in pencil—the more recent artists, people like Suzan Lovett and the Southern Cross.
Karen: It's funny, because I have all the copies of *Spockanalia* . . . and the drawings in there were literally just, you know, line—outlined. And you look at that now, and if someone did that now, people wouldn't buy the zine.

Karen highlights an important point about the development of the fanzine as an artifact that the former publisher of *Universal Translator* noted as well. *Spockanalia,* the first zine, cost $1.20 per copy for about one hundred half-pages of stories and line drawings. As the aesthetic for longer stories and more detailed, textural art has grown, so have the zines and their prices. Fans may complain about modern prices of twenty to twenty-five dollars, but they demand the quality they have come to expect in such fanzines. In recent years printing costs have risen so sharply that a growing number of fan publishers have purchased their own photocopy machines and returned to hand production with less expensive art reproduction. Some fanzine editors in the smaller fandoms have had to stop publishing altogether as prices for small print runs exceeded levels supportable within the community.

Re-creating Space

I have talked at length in this study about the capacity that narrative has to transform culture. In a like fashion, material arts have the capacity not only to remind fans of the narrative world but also to shape the space around them within which culture may transform.

In the convention setting, costuming is particularly important for marking space and creating a safe place where the community can conduct its business. Most participants at a convention wear some sign of their participation—buttons with quotes or aphorisms on them, T-shirts with pictures or verbal messages, identifiable items like idics (the symbol for universal tolerance) that refer back to the source products—while others wear full costumes as clothing. The universality of some form of visual marking makes it possible for community members to identify each other in the public setting of the hotel or convention center. More importantly, those areas in which visually marked members predominate become functionally removed from public space. The markings worn on the bodies of the participants establish physical boundaries to space that are recognized by outsiders and insiders alike. Outsiders display a great deal of discomfort when passing through these areas, which have become private in relation to the outsider culture and public in relation to the various groups who intermingle there.[30]

Costume marks the spatial-temporal frame of the convention but the material arts of the community re-create private space as well. Hanging art, photographs, crafts, and even the bookcases full of fanzines and videotapes mark the private space of the fan as a member of fan culture. The extent to which space is marked in the home often reflects the level of commitment to the fan community, and the degree of compromise the fan must make with family members who are not fans.

Lois Welling's compromise is typical of fans who live in nonfan families. She shares a home with a nonfan husband and, until recently, with her children, who are now grown. My first visual clue to Lois's fan activities was her family room. The collection of videotaped television programs here numbered in the hundreds of tapes, and the video center included a twenty-five-inch television screen and four interconnected video machines. But Lois's *Star Trek* room is the centerpiece of her fan involvement. The room has a bed for guests, a work table and typewriter, and bookshelves with science fiction and reference works. Every inch of the remaining wall space is covered with art. Lois collects so much art that she cannot hang it all, but changes many of the pieces around the central large works. In small, out-of-the-way spaces where framed art will not comfortably fit she has photographs, and there is a poster on the door. With art and photographs and the tools of her trade (she writes fan fiction), Lois has transformed a small space in the suburbs into a center for the fan culture in which she actively participates.

Lin Place usually lives alone, but sometimes she shares her small apartment with a nonfan sister. Because the space belongs to Lin, and her sister is essentially a guest, Lin feels free to mark that space everywhere for fan culture. While Lin has less hanging original art than Lois, she also has less wall space. Lois keeps most of her fan fiction tucked away in closets, but Lin keeps her collection in notebooks on shelves in her living room. Lin is a major contact in the video circuit, and her video setup includes two television monitors, a stereo, four video machines, and well over a thousand tapes.[31]

Jean Curley lives with her nonfan mother and participates actively in both the media fanzine community and in the science fiction community. Her bedroom is so filled with books, notebooks of fan fiction, fan art, and buttons displayed as art that Jean has had to move her bed into the closet to accommodate the artifacts.

These examples demonstrate the marking of permanent space de-

Jean Curley's fan room. Jean is an active mentor in British media fandom.

voted to the participation in the fan community, but fans can and do commandeer additional space on a short-term basis when, for example, a group of women construct and collate a fanzine on the floor of their living room or around a kitchen table.

I have mentioned Lois, Lin, and Jean here not because they are special cases, but because their strategies for marking space for fan culture to take place and for sharing space with the nonfan family members are typical throughout the community. While the amount of display materials may vary depending on the individual's personal tolerance for clutter, I have met no fans who did not modify their environment with the material products of the fan culture.

The examples also demonstrate another important point: the form of the objects is not as important as their material presence in the environment. Buttons, which may be part of dress at the convention, often are arranged as display items. Fan fiction notebooks are display objects in Lin's home but stored out of sight at Lois's, although fan fiction plays a central role in Lois's identity as a writer in the community. Lois, however, fills her fan community space with hanging art, of which Lin and Jean have very few pieces.

It becomes clear in the context of the constraints under which fan rooms take shape that the presence of material objects in the environment is not a display of wealth for the purpose of acquiring public status. On the contrary, the fan women must often defend themselves from ridicule and outside pressure to change their decorating habits. Much fan humor revolves around the shock of outsiders and the amazement of neophytes at the fan room. The women in the fanzine community withstand the ridicule and resist the pressure from outsiders—family members and nonfan friends—because their material display creates a space identifiable with other like spaces in the community. In these spaces participants feel safe to give free rein to their cultural identities in the fanwriting community.

Notes

1. Brian W. Aldiss, *Trillion Year Spree* (New York: Avon Books, 1986 [1973]), p. 177.
2. Of course, fan fiction, like any other literature, can then take on a new set of meanings and functions. For example, as objects of study they generate scholarship, a marginal function within the community, and one which the literature does not address although it is addressed by a few members of the group.
3. Vladimir Propp, *Morphology of the Folktale*, trans. Laurence Scott (Austin: University of Texas Press, 1968 [1928]).
4. I am using the term "stories" throughout because it is the generic term used when fans discuss their work on an abstract level. However, almost any form can be constructed in any genre.
5. Nonsexual relationship stories are likewise but more rarely referred to as *ampersand* stories, because that mark is used in the community shorthand to designate a friendship relationship that does not include sexual attraction.
6. This may be particularly true of the minority of heterosexual male group members, whose personal bids for more to communicate in their fiction may be lost because their messages, or the method of their communication, are not readily interpretable by the female majority accustomed to addressing issues in terms of relationships.
7. Carol Gilligan, *In A Different Voice* (Cambridge, Mass.: Harvard University Press, 1982).
8. Edward Said, "On Originality," in his *The World, the Text and the Critic* (Cambridge, Mass.: Harvard University Press, 1983), p. 135.
9. Elaine Showalter, "Piecing and Writing," in *The Poetics of Gender*, ed. Nancy K. Miller (New York: Columbia University Press, 1986), pp. 222–47.
10. Philip K. Dick, *The Man in the High Castle* (New York: Berkeley Medallion Books, 1962).
11. Esther Friesner, *Druid's Blood* (New York: Signet, 1986).
12. Ann Wortham and Leah Rosenthal, *The Bizarro Zine #2* (Brooklyn, N.Y.: Leah Rosenthal, 1989).
13. Barbara Wenk, *One Way Mirror* in *Masiform D special supplement #2* (Brooklyn, N.Y.: Poison Pen Press, 1980).
14. In *Star Trek* third-season episode "The Savage Curtain," Mr. Spock explains that "pre-reform" Vulcan culture—before the philosopher Surak re-

formed it five thousand years ago—was more violent and warlike than any period on Earth. "Pre-Reform" stories extrapolate on what a warlike Vulcan culture might be like.

15. Camille Bacon-Smith, "Spock among the Women," *New York Times Book Review,* November 16, 1986.

16. Judith Segal, "Understanding Kraith," fan pamphlet.

17. Two volumes of NTM stories have been published in the fan press: *NTM Collected, Volume One,* and *Volume Two.* They, as well as the novel *Night of the Twin Moons,* are available through Jean Lorrah, Murray, Ky.

18. Jean Lorrah and Willard F. Hunt, "Visit to a Weird Planet," in *Spockanalia,* ed. Devra Langsam and Sherna C. Burley (Brooklyn, N.Y.: Poison Pen Press [Garlic Press], 1968), pp. 89–101.

19. Ruth Berman, "Visit to a Weird Planet Revisited," in *Spockanalia,* ed. Devra Langsam and Sherna C. Burley, (Brooklyn, N.Y.: Poison Pen Press [Garlic Press], 1970), pp. 89–104.

20. Susan Matthews, *The Mind of a Man Is a Double Edged Sword* (New York: Streslan Press, 1983); inspired by an idea from friend Regina Gottesman.

21. Roland Barthes, *S/Z,* trans. R. Miller (New York: Hill and Wang, 1974).

22. This is an actual case, told to me by one of the fans involved with the stipulation that I protect the identities of the woman and man involved.

23. I know of no artists who support themselves entirely with their fan art. A few include fan art as part of their self-support as artists outside of fandom, but most fan artists hope only to pay for their fan activities—especially traveling to and attending conventions—with their art. This is in contrast to fanwriters, who must support not only their own writing but their fan activities as well from other sources.

24. Fanny Adams, interview at Z-Con, Chicago, 1987.

25. Taped interview, Atlanta, 1987. Identity of speaker withheld because she could not be reached to confirm permission.

26. Ibid.

27. *In the Public Interest,* ed. Laura Peck and TACS (Baltimore, Md.: Sunshine Press).

28. Laura Peck, taped interview, Clippercon 1986, Cockeysville.

29. Sheila Willis, taped interview, Cockeysville, 1986.

30. Unpublished paper on costuming at science fiction conventions, Camille Bacon-Smith, 1984.

31. Lin has recently moved to a small house in a new city, but her circumstances, and her way of marking space, continue essentially unchanged in her new location.

Part II
A Closer Look at the Community and Its Art

Chapter Four
Training New Members

Making Contact

The women's fanzine community draws its members from among the adult and late teen population, and it has developed an extensive mentor-apprentice system for training newcomers in the structures and customs of the community, including the codes and aesthetics of fan fiction, and a particular aesthetic of television viewing. Potential new members may discover the media fan community through conventions or personal acquaintances. By far the greatest number of prospective members make contact through conventions, and this is how I entered the community as a participant-observer.

Initiation through conventions takes place in stages, at any one of which the participant may stop, not passing on to more esoteric levels of the community. For me, the first phase took two years. Depending on the enthusiasm of the newcomer, this process can move more or less quickly, but community members with whom I have discussed my entry into fandom seem to agree that two years is a reasonable length of time to develop a working knowledge of the forms and social life of the community.

Although I did not know it at the time, my initiation began in November of 1980, before I had considered this study. I was attending my first literary science fiction convention, the Philadelphia Science Fiction Conference, at the Sheraton Hotel, later known as the Philadelphia Centre. I was and still am interested in science fiction, but like many others, I was drawn to my first convention more out of curiosity than out of commitment.

For me that first convention did not begin as a particularly enjoyable experience. I knew no one, and recognized that I was an outsider, barely understanding the language spoken around me. My hesitancy attracted the attention of Judy Segal, a heavyset, middle-aged woman with dark, curling hair, who introduced herself and took me firmly under her wing. Judy wore a conservative skirt and blouse, and a brightly colored badge identifying herself as a member of the *Star Trek* Welcommittee.

The Welcommittee

In the *Star Trek* Welcommittee's *Directory of Star Trek Organizations,* editor Judy Segal describes the Welcommittee as " . . . [a] central information exchange. Its volunteer members answer fan questions about Trek and Trek fandom for only the price of a SASE [self-addressed stamped envelope]." Fans make contact with the Welcommittee primarily via the mailroom address included in the preface or afterword of many commercial *Star Trek* publications, although creator Gene Roddenberry's office has been known to forward on correspondence from the occasional questioner looking for fandom. Others, like myself, meet members of the Welcommittee at conventions, where they regularly act as mentors to complete neophytes.

During a dinner interview,[1] Welcommittee member Segal and chairman Shirley Maiewski explained to me how the Welcommittee came into existence and how it continues to function today:

> Shirley: Well, Jacqueline Lichtenberg started it . . . she started getting a lot of mail, and she couldn't handle it. And that was—that day I met her, that first con in January of 1972 . . . we got together then—about all the mail and all, and she asked me that day to join the Welcommittee that she was starting to answer the letters. I thought, "Oh, I can't do that," and she said, "Well you know, you watch *Star Trek* all the time, don't you," and I said, "Yes," so she said, "Well you can join." So I did, and quite a long time I was a crew member, just answering mail, and I loved it, it was really great.
>
> Judy: It is fun getting letters from all over the world, isn't it?
>
> Shirley: Oh, all over the world.
>
> Ethnographer: What kind of letters were they?
>
> Shirley: Mostly then, in those, in the early seventies, were, "When is *Star Trek* coming back?"—You know, literally—you know, it was gone, and there was no sign of it ever coming back, and "What can I do to help?" and so forth. And also, "Where can I join a fan club," you know . . .

Shirley took over the Welcommittee mailroom in 1975, at the height of popular interest in the defunct *Star Trek:*

My favorite story is the time I was sick with the flu. And we live in the country and we have an R.F.D. box, and I heard the mailman come, and I asked my husband to get the mail, and he was gone a long time, and he was gone an awful long time, and it's like, from here to that coat rack [Shirley gestured to a coat rack near the door of the restaurant, perhaps thirty feet from our table] to the mailbox from the front door. So finally I heard him come in, and I said, "Did we get any mail," and he said, "Oh, a little." He came up the stairs. We had 250 letters that one day, had been jammed into our mailbox. I think, to me, that was the high point.

In 1977, at the request of the departing chairman, Shirley took over chairmanship of the Welcommittee, a position she continues to hold.

Among the services listed in Judy Segal's *Directory* are an area list department, foreign department, and military fan liaison, all of which serve to bring fans together:

Judy: . . . people write to the Welcommittee saying "Help, I'm all alone out here and nobody understands me, and I read *Trek* and my parents think I'm strange and my husband doesn't know what's going on, and the ladies at the laundromat think I'm weird." So they write to us and say "I'm all alone," and I write back and say, "No, you're not."

Shirley: . . . we try to do our best by pointing people toward where there is somebody in their area, and one of our departments is the area list, where people can send a SASE and twenty-five cents, I think it is, and get a list of names of people who live near where they do, that they can contact personally. And those names come from people who order our directory.

The *Star Trek* Welcommittee also offers a convention listing, educational and news-clip services, penpal introductions, and information about costume design and patterns. Members give advice about acquiring and publishing fanzines, starting a club, and how to hold a convention. They attend conventions, where their badges identify them to newcomers like myself. Here they make face-to-face introductions of new fans to more established community members in their geographic area. Some Welcommittee members like Judy Segal may continue as mentors to the newcomers, while others will introduce the neophytes to known mentors in the group. In all of its activities, however, the Welcommittee espouses complete neutrality on all fan activity:

> Shirley: We're neutral on all subjects, that's it, basically.
>
> Judy: The Welcommittee, uh, acknowledges the existence of all these alternate universes, all the stories that people write, and will keep track of them and list them in the directory, but we cannot support anything but the aired *Trek*.
>
> Shirley: Well, we extend that to the movies now, too.
>
> Judy: We do not become a forum for airing personal grievance, we don't publish things anonymously . . . Um, we'll answer letters, we'll provide information, we'll keep tabs on what's going on. But we are not a policy-making organization . . . No member of the Welcommittee may use the Welcommittee name for any personal reason.
>
> Shirley: Now Welcommittee members are entitled to their own opinions . . . [but] they cannot use their position in Welcommittee.

At first I thought that the Welcommittee might be the official *Star Trek* fan organization, but Shirley and Judy denied the charge categorically:

> Shirley: We're not "it."
>
> Judy: I don't think there is "it."
>
> Shirley: There isn't any "it."

The Welcommittee may not be "it," but the unofficial organization that Jacqueline Lichtenberg started in 1972 continues, nineteen years later, to fill the role of guide to outsiders looking for a place in fandom to call home.

My Initiation

I had no further communication with my Welcommittee contact until the 1981 Philadelphia Science Fiction Conference. As yet I had no real interest in the *Star Trek* fan group and had decided instead to study science fiction conventions as a folk phenomenon. When Segal introduced writers of her acquaintance, it was as science fiction writers, and not as media fans. I met science fiction writer Jacqueline Lichtenberg at this convention, but I did not know that she had founded the Welcommittee. Judy Segal and I began corresponding, still about science fiction.

Shirley Maiewski chairs the Welcommittee. *Star Trek* fandom's
official "grandmother."

During the summer of 1982 I entered the second phase of my initiation. Judy Segal invited me to her house, and I accepted the invitation. *Star Trek* fans have been accused by science fiction readers of having interest only in the visual media, but it quickly becomes obvious that this is not so. In all of the homes of media fans that I visited, books and reading materials fill at least one room. In Judy's case, several rooms were crammed with science fiction books. I also noticed a few sketches on the walls—Judy's son, Richard, as Sahaj, a character in a popular series of amateur *Star Trek* stories; idics, an important symbol in the community; and other memorabilia. Judy, a junior high school science teacher, had taken a year off work to pursue a second career as a literary agent, and an electronic typewriter held pride of place in her office, a room overwhelmed with the clutter of the active fan and aspiring agent.

Another myth about *Star Trek* fans, that they are monomaniacally obsessed with their television interests, also fell by the wayside during this visit. Judy shares her house in a small town in northeastern New York State with her teenaged son, Richard, two cats, and a Belgian sheepdog. In the past she has trained show dogs, and she still does some grooming for local dog fanciers in her spare time.

While we prowled the local flea markets, Judy told me about Kraith, the *Star Trek* fan fiction universe created by Jacqueline Lichtenberg, and I began to realize that the media fans were more than just an adulation society. I took home with me some fanzines; "Understanding Kraith" (a dictionary of terms); the "Welcommittee Directory" (a listing of clubs, fanzines, and sources of memorabilia); enough hand-spun wool from local sheep to make an aran sweater; and a promise to meet again in 1982 at the Philadelphia SF Conference. Judy asked me whether I planned to attend any *Trek* conventions, but at this point I still felt that the regular science fiction convention offered more than enough for me to investigate.

When I attended the 1982 Philadelphia conference, actually held in February of 1983, I finally made my decision to study the Trekkers. I had grown knowledgeable enough in the science fiction community to recognize a basic hostility against the "Trekkies," who were seen by my predominantly male informants as a blight on the convention scene, an embarrassment to right-thinking science fiction fans, and something less than intelligent. (To this day *Star Trek* conventions are not listed in the most common directories of such science fiction activities.[2])

This profile was at odds with the impression I had formed of the few "Trekkers"[3] I had met. Jacqueline Lichtenberg was a chemist before becoming first a fanwriter, and later a commercial science fiction writer. Susan Shwartz, an early contact, had a Ph.D. in Arthurian scholarship, and Judy Segal had a master's degree in botany. This time I took Judy Segal up on her suggestion that I attend Shore Leave, an annual *Star Trek* convention held in Cockeysville, Maryland, each July. We made arrangements to meet in Philadelphia, and Judy would drive me from there to the hotel in Cockeysville. We would share a room with Jacqueline Lichtenberg and Judy's son, Richard.

Shortly before the convention I met a local *Star Trek* fanziner, Judith Gran, through our sons, and she agreed to an interview in June of 1983. At the interview, Gran introduced me to her co-editor, Beverly Lorenstein, and gave me a copy of their *Star Trek* fanzine, *Organia*. During the course of the interview, both Beverly and Judy described their own initiation experiences.

Beverly talked about her first experience at the New York Trek convention in 1974:

> But I went to [the convention in] New York, and I can't even explain to you how wonderful it felt . . . I had a wonderful time, and I met a lot of people, and the people from the club.* And to this day, a lot of those people are really good friends of mine . . . It's just a very thrilling feeling, because you think you are the only one, you know, that likes it . . . there is not just someone else, there are lots of people that are willing to talk to you about your craziness."[4]

Judith Gran expanded on how *Star Trek* conventions differed from more traditional SF events:

> . . . at the purely Trek cons [conventions], where everybody shares a common universe, a discourse, there's just an incredible feeling of, uh, you know—closeness and rapport. And you can't have that when you have a more diverse group.[5]

While both Judy and Beverly described a euphoric first experience with the fan community, they both recognized from their first contact that membership is a life-changing option, requiring as high a degree of commitment as any job, town, or religion. The decision to join is not made lightly, nor does the neophyte have sufficient information to make that decision except as that information develops over an extended period of time.

* A science fiction club in the Temple University area.

Beverly explained that she enjoyed reading science fiction long before she saw *Star Trek*. She threw herself into her first *Star Trek* convention in 1974 with enthusiasm and made a number of friends, among whom was her mentor. Her mentor bought Beverly her first fanzine at the convention; however,

> . . . I hadn't read it [the fanzine] until 1976. The reason is, I took one look at it and I said, "I don't know what they are talking about in here. I'll put it away and maybe someday I'll understand."
>
> And sure enough, in 1976, a friend, my friend [name deleted], she said, "Look, you don't know what you're missing. You have to read this!"
>
> "Okay," I said, "Okay, I'll give it a try."
>
> Well here, she gave me—well, actually, she gave me two fanzines, and I said, "This isn't too bad, it's interesting . . . let me read some more."
>
> And I said, "I think I'm falling in love with this."
>
> And she said, "Good," and she brought me over a hundred fanzines and I read them over three or four nights, and I was in love.
>
> And from then on in, I just bought fanzines continuously.[6]

Shore Leave: The Initiation Narrative

Prepared for the experience by Judith and Beverly, I found that at Shore Leave my adoption by the group truly began. Judy Segal and Jacqueline Lichtenberg were my mentors, as Judy had been from our first meeting in 1980. Between them the two women introduced me to the people that I, both as a researcher and as a person they accepted into their community, should know: Lois Welling, a key member of the Champaign-Urbana circle, and Shirley Maiewski, a "first member" of the women's fandom, spiritual head of the Welcommittee, and everybody's mom. Everyone I met was happy to tell me how she found fandom, and each story seemed to prompt another to speak.

My mentor Judy Segal entered fandom through a personal contact. She said that she watched *Star Trek* only sporadically during its initial airing. She had finished her master's degree and was busy teaching junior high school science, with very little time left over to watch television. According to Judy:

> I forgot it [*Star Trek*] until 1975 or '76. My friend [name deleted], who had picked up a copy of Jacqueline's [Lichtenberg] *Star Trek Lives,* and had written to some of the addresses and some of the fan-

zines, came by to visit one day with an armload of fanzines, and
dumped them in my lap, and said, "Read these."
 And the first thing I read was *Kraith* . . . I never knew fanzines
existed until, 'til she dumped this collection in my lap. Literally.[7]

Judy Segal's introduction to active fandom is typical of many fans
who entered the community through friends in the seventies. They
may have been avid viewers of the television series in its initial run or
have seen only bits and pieces. Even for only sporadic viewers, however, the television show held interest that could be rekindled later
with the fanzines. In spite of an early interest in science fiction, and a
passing familiarity with *Star Trek* on which to draw, women like Judy,
who enter fandom through friends, have a social rather than a media
motivation for their initial interest. However, they soon develop a love
of the products of the community, especially the fanzines, that carries
them deeper into the social/artistic structure of the community:

 I finished Kraith 4, and I knew with an absolute certainty, "I
know what happens next in the Kraith universe."
 And though I had never done it before, I sat down and I wrote a
story.
 And in front of one of the *Kraiths* it had a foreword, a little p.s.
from Jacqueline: "we're still interested in reading it. If you've got a
story, send it to us. Let me see it."
 And so I wrote her a letter. I said, "Are you still reading Kraith
stories?"
 And she said, "Sure, send it along." And she sent it out on a
round-robin, a Kraith robin . . . And it took off from there.[8]

Entering into the writing of the community was an important step
in Judy's process of becoming a member. Through reading the fanzines presented to her by a friend she learned to read the codes implicit in the fan material, adding that information to what she already
knew from even a sporadic watching of the television show.
 Her mentor helped this process along in a number of ways, most
importantly by the order in which she presented new material to her
pupil. Mentors often use Kraith to introduce new members to fan
literature. It is easily decoded by a woman with both a knowledge of
the television series and a long-standing interest in science fiction, and
so provides an access to community forms that more esoteric products
would stymie.
 Judy's writing drew her into a correspondence network of intelli-

gent, educated women with interests similar to her own. This contact opened her horizons to the friendship of her fellow writers, and we see in her summary statement, "And it took off from there," that Judy sees entering into the round-robin as a turning point in her entry into the community. But this was just a first step. Judy continued:

> And my first actual Trek meeting was a collating party[9] over at a friend's house, Linda Deneroff's apartment . . . But Jacqueline was there, and we met there. Then I went to a mini Trek con, a little one-day thing—it was really pretty bad, I suppose, now that I look back at it.

[at a demur from others in the room:]

> Yeah, I had a pleasing time, saw the huckster room, and from there on I more or less hooked in with Jacqueline, and it took off.[10]

Although Judy found membership in the round-robin satisfying on one level, real community membership includes face-to-face encounters with other fans. In the above excerpt we see Judy making this transition. As part of this deepening of her involvement in the community, Judy changed mentors to Jacqueline.

This is a key step in the initiation process. Jacqueline is an important mentor figure to many new fans, who may leave her for more esoteric forms and genres in the *Star Trek* medium, or who may stay with her and enter into the esoteric territory of her own Sime-Gen (see Appendix B) science fiction universe. Judy chose to stay with Jacqueline and remains involved both in *Star Trek* fan fiction of the variety favored by fans such as Jacqueline and herself, and in the Sime-Gen fan world that exists within science fiction and media fandom.

In Judy's description above we see that she makes still another transition: she attended her first *Star Trek* convention. Note here that, in hindsight, Judy denigrated that initial experience as being inferior to others she has had. Other fans in the room corrected her. In response to her statement, "It was really pretty bad, I suppose," they asked, "But did you enjoy it?" "Did you have a good time?" Judy admitted that she did in fact enjoy the day-long mini-con, and marked her alliance with Jacqueline as beginning with that experience.

Again we see that Judy recognized this event as an important transition point. In her narrative, she summarized the key point:

> And from there on I more or less hooked in with Jacqueline. And it took off.

Like Judy, Lois Welling had little opportunity to watch *Star Trek* in its first run, but she did see bits and pieces of it. She remembers:

> . . . My first vision of Spock is going by the TV when it was first on with my kids. I saw the beginning, middle, or end of every show, but I never saw all of it, because I had a kid yelling or something. And this thing in blue turned around and stared straight at me. I can remember. I can see myself in that living room, freezing, and looking at that—[deep sigh here]—"Oh, *yes!* whatever it is, I *like* it!"

[giggles from around the room.]

> And then the kid screamed, and on I went and never thought about it . . . [11]

Again like Judy, Lois was too caught up in her day-to-day life for *Star Trek* to make a significant impact, but she stored that experience away until circumstances brought her to a pivotal point in her life. For Lois, her youngest child entering kindergarten brought her dissatisfaction into focus. While she is happily married, Lois felt the need for something more in her life—she returned to college for her bachelor's degree. In sociology and astronomy classes, she met another student also going through a life transition. The two women banded together for study and companionship. Lois recounts:

> She lived far out so we would go to my house, which was quite close to the college, and I would feed her tuna. And then she said— I think I always had this thing about science fiction, but I never sat long enough to read—
> So she said, "Heinlein, *Stranger in a Strange Land, Dune.*"
> *Dune,* she started throwing them [titles] at me, and we started.[12]

In this part of Lois's narrative, we see that the new friend has taken the role of the mentor, introducing Lois to science fiction books. The titles Lois mentions were important in the literature at that time, and Heinlein is considered a master of the genre during its golden age. Both of these titles crossed over into the popular mainstream fiction market as best-sellers, so they represented a bridge into science fiction fandom. Lois could appreciate these books on the popular level, while assimilating the messages encoded by and for the community more slowly, as her repertoire expanded. But, while the other woman was an avid science fiction fan, she herself did not have access to the *Star Trek* fan community. At this stage of their relationship, both women become searchers in a successful quest as recounted below.

> Uh, we knew the fanzines were out there then—*Star Trek Lives!* you know [Jacqueline's book about *Star Trek* fandom]—and so forth and so on. And we knew they were out there, but we couldn't, we couldn't get our hands on them. And finally, we went to Chicago to see Leonard [Nimoy] doing "The Fourposter" at Drury Lane—I'll tell ya [deep sigh, seconded by others in the room]. We ran into a bookstore, and back of this bookstore, by the science fiction, was this little paper sign that said "*Star Trek* convention." And we froze.
> It was the '75 convention, Chicago. That was our first. The whole bridge crew was there. And we got the fanzines there. And we said, . . . "Just let us buy zines."[13]

Several common factors appear in this portion of Lois's account. Many community members first realized a fan community existed through Jacqueline Lichtenberg's book *Star Trek Lives!* and then went out to find it. The length of time it takes to make a commitment to the community is consistent with what we have seen elsewhere as well. The two women in this example met in 1972 but did not attend their first convention or read their first fanzine until 1975, a time lapse of three years. During this period, while the women's interest in the fan community grew, Lois was learning to appreciate written science fiction. And again, we see the juxtaposition of fanzine and convention, of face-to-face contact and familiarity with the product of the community, both of which seem vital to a sense of belonging to the group. In the final passage of her narrative, we see Lois seeking out her niche in the *Star Trek* world:

> Well then, we read everything in sight and thought it was all wonderful. Then we said, "Maybe some of it isn't so wonderful." So we thought we'd have our own.[14]

Among members I have interviewed, almost all point to their decision to involve themselves in the *Star Trek* community as part of a series of major life changes they experienced at the time. Judy Segal was finding her work as a science teacher burdensome, and she credits her involvement in the *Star Trek* community with helping her through a period of teacher burnout. Welcommittee chairman Shirley Maiewski commented that she was going through an empty nest syndrome, wanting more out of life than tending an empty house. Shirley took a job at the university bookstore near where she lives in Massachusetts at around the time she began developing her interest in *Star Trek*.

As with Judy, Shirley, Lois, and most of the women who have talked to me, the decision to enter into the art world of *Star Trek* fandom brings with it a sense of rightness about participating. Through the production of art, fiction, critical essays, or letters to editors of fanzines or to each other, members of this community reach out across the distance in the language of their fan interest.

The Fanzines

At Shore Leave, Judy Segal led me through the fanzine rooms. In 1983 there were four parlor rooms filled with the fanzines for sale. She guided me to the more general work, and I bought fanzines from Roberta Rogow, who specializes in, among other things, fanzines for new writers; from Johanna Cantor, an articulate feminist; and from others, while eschewing some of the more controversial genres. This is typical for new members brought into the community. Mentors, particularly for complete neophytes like myself, are often more traditional members of the community and act as gatekeepers. They lead the new member to the art and literature that either requires minimal decoding for an outsider, or that will not shock the sensibilities of a reader who has not yet learned to decode the messages embedded in the community's product. Judy mentioned the hurt-comfort genre as one she found personally troubling; she dismissed the relatively new homoerotic fiction.

We met Lois Welling and Judith Gran outside the fanzine rooms, and here I was introduced to one of the most widespread practices in fandom—"talking story." Talking story is literally verbal narrative of the community's fiction. The story so "talked" may be one the talker has written, or plans to write, or one that she has read and particularly liked. Fans likewise talk the episodes of their favorite source products—narrating orally the episodes for fans who may have missed them, or to attract new fans to a particular source product. At Shore Leave, Lois talked her novella, *The Displaced*.

In my identity as a researcher Lois and Judith told me what it means to write these stories: how writing stories works out real-life problems and concerns about the life the writer leads both inside and outside of the fan community, and how writing is a form of reaching out to others, of making contact. As someone perceived to be an initiate, however, I am led only into those areas of the literature for which I am deemed to be prepared, primarily those stories that deal with women sharing adventures and relationships with the characters of *Star Trek.*[15]

Here I began my study of the troubled and troubling history of these genres.

Re-creating the Adolescent Self: Mary Sue

Writing about women would seem to be the natural project of a women's community, but in fact the set of genres dealing with women have had a troubled history, and none more so than "Mary Sue."

Mary Sue is the youngest officer ever to serve on the starship Enterprise. She is a teenager, tall and slim, with clear skin and straight teeth. If she is not blond, Mary Sue is half Vulcan, her ears delicately pointed. But Mary Sue is not just another pretty face. She is usually highly educated, with degrees from universities throughout the known universe in all fields of technical and cultural studies (or an equivalent head of her class in Starfleet Academy). She can mend the *Enterprise* with a hairpin, save the lives of the crew through wit, courage, and, occasionally, the sacrifice of her virtue. If the formula is strictly followed, Lieutenant Mary Sue dies in the last paragraph of the story, leaving behind a grieving but safe crew and ship.[16]

Mary Sue is also the most universally denigrated genre in the entire canon of fan fiction. I first encountered the genre by reputation, because although fanzine editors no longer will publish stories about her, the controversy over her continues vigorously to this day in both the fanzines and in group discussions. Paula Smith coined the term in a brief version of the form exaggerated for humor.[17] Her story, "A Trekkie's Tale," first appeared in 1974 in an issue of the fanzine *Menagerie*. In 1980, Johanna Cantor used the story with permission of the author to demonstrate the genre characteristics as part of a debate on the Mary Sue controversy in *Archives V*.[18] Here in its entirety is the story that coined the term "Mary Sue":

> "Gee, golly, gosh, gloriosky," thought Mary Sue as she stepped on the bridge of the Enterprise. "Here I am, the youngest Lieutenant in the fleet—only fifteen and half years old." Captain Kirk came up to her.
>
> "Oh, Lieutenant, I love you madly. Will you come to bed with me?"
>
> "Captain! I am not that kind of girl!"
>
> "You're right, and I respect you for it. Here, take over the ship for a minute while I go for some coffee for us."
>
> Mr. Spock came onto the bridge. "What are you doing in the command seat, Lieutenant?"

Mel White's humorous illustration shows the traditional forms
of Mary Sue—the buxom blonde Mary Sue and the Vulcan
T'MariSue (the latter modeled on White herself). Appeared in
Masiform D.

"The Captain told me to."
"Flawlessly logical. I admire your mind."
Captain Kirk, Mr. Spock, Dr. McCoy, and Mr. Scott beamed
down with Lt. Mary Sue to Rigel XXXVII. They were attacked by
green androids and thrown into prison. In a moment of weakness
Lt. Mary Sue revealed to Mr. Spock that she too was half Vulcan.
Recovering quickly, she sprung the lock with her hairpin and they
all got away back to the ship.

But back on board, Dr. McCoy and Lt. Mary Sue found out that
the men who had beamed down were seriously stricken by the
jumping cold robbies, Mary Sue less so. While the four officers lan-
guished in Sick Bay, Lt. Mary Sue ran the ship, and ran it so well she
received the Nobel Peace Prize, the Vulcan Order of Gallantry and
the Tralfamadorian Order of Good Guyhood.

However the disease finally got to her and she fell fatally ill. In
the sick bay as she breathed her last, she was surrounded by Captain
Kirk, Mr. Spock, Dr. McCoy, and Mr. Scott all weeping unashamedly
at the loss of her beautiful youth and youthful beauty, intelligence,
capability and all around niceness. Even to this day her birthday is a
national holiday of the Enterprise.[19]

In her 1980 commentary that accompanied the reprint of "A Trekkie's Tale," Smith explained that her intent was never

> . . . to put down all stories about aspiring females . . . my original
> idea . . . [Paula Smith's ellipses] was to parody the glut of [incredible]
> stories that existed in 1973 and 1974 . . . one memorable one has
> the heroine dying and resurrecting herself (hence, *incredible*
> adventures).[20]

Edith Cantor's response to "The Trekkie's Tale," and to Smith's comments about the term, describes her experience as an editor with neophyte fanwriters:

> "*That's* Mary Sue?"
> This neo[phyte fan] friend was absolutely astonished, and under-
> standably so. *The* Mary Sue story runs ten paragraphs. But in terms
> of their impact on those they affect, those words [Mary Sue] have
> got to rank right up there with the Selective Service Act.
> "I don't know if I ought to be sending this to you," a neo de-
> scribed her story in 1978. "I'm afraid it's a Mary Sue. Only I don't
> know what that is."
> "I know you can't publish this," wrote another neo in 1979, "be-
> cause it's a Mary Sue. But if you wouldn't mind reading it anyway,
> I'd appreciate it . . . ."
> . . . I started Trekwriting with a Mary Sue (though I had the self-
> protective smarts to call my character "Uhura," which is acceptable
> to the self-styled guardians determined to purge Treklit of all traces
> of the unfortunate adolescent). So have many other Trekwriters—
> in fact I would propose that just as every dog is allowed one bite,
> so every Trekwriter should be allowed one Mary Sue. Said story

should not necessarily be published (though we publish other stories whose plot/characterization have been done before), but they should be given a sympathetic reading and critique, and perhaps returned to the author with the explanation that she is following a too-well-beaten path, with the encouragement to turn her interests to other stories.[21]

Other fans have noted that James Kirk is himself a Mary Sue, because he represents similarly exaggerated characteristics of strength, intelligence, charm, and adventurousness. They note that the soubriquet "Mary Sue" may be a self-imposed sexism—she can't do that, she's a girl.

In spite of the controversy, and perhaps at the root of it, most fans will readily admit to having written at least one Mary Sue story. Like Cantor, Jacqueline Lichtenberg claims there is a Mary Sue in all women. Usually it is the first story a fan writes, often before she knows about the literature or its forms. Ann Pinzow described her own first story, and the ambivalence that many fans feel about sharing them:

> Somebody said, "that's a Mary Sue story." My emotions came into it . . . you're putting your heart on your sleeve. If I were to say this person is Ann . . . I couldn't show my face. I mean I'm no better or worse than anybody else, but I have my secrets too. But I could say "this is Mary Sue." I know that Mary Sue is Ann."[22]

Judith Gran analyzed the attraction that draws Mary Sue writers:

> I think [Mary Sue] is a way people build an alter ego, an ideal image of themselves to make connections with characters who they'd like to love, not just sexually. You admire the character, you want to reach out to Mr. Spock and in the process you get in touch with yourself.[23]

Gran continued with the observation that the real danger with Mary Sue stories may arise when the writer does not pass on to other forms. Mary Sue, as we have seen, represents the intellectual woman's ideal of perfection: she is young and desirable, competent and moral. Her intellectual and physical attributes not only meet the writer's standards for the perfect woman, but the people she admires appreciate her value as well.

Not all writers speak about Mary Sue with such compassion, however. Some, like Roberta Rogow, have less patience with the feminine superteen, even when they have been her perpetrators:

My first fan story was terrible, and was rejected, and I tore it up and I hope I never do it again because it is the typical Mary Sue–broken-hearted Kirk story.[24]

Nor are commercially published *Star Trek* novels immune to the controversy. During an interview conducted at the 1986 World Science Fiction Convention, I asked "Why do pros write—[is it] the same reason fans write?" The author of a commercially published *Star Trek* novel who wished to remain anonymous answered this way about her own book:

> In some cases I won't say that's true, but oh, dear, just say that an unnamed author admitted to having written a Mary Sue. Because, in fact that book I just signed is just a classic, a classic Mary Sue. When I read your article[25] I just cracked up, because she [the female hero] was fitting all the criteria.[26]

Ann Crispin, writer of two commercially published *Star Trek* novels, has been vocal in defense of the commercial novel of another writer, Diane Duane's *Wounded Sky*.[27] In Duane's novel, the heroine who saves the ship, crew, and universe is a brilliant crystal spider, a mathematician, and female. She does indeed die, or at least pass into an alternate existence at the end of the book, but not before passing her knowledge and consciousness along in the crystal egg she spins and leaves in the care of the captain. In the final pages of the book, the egg hatches, and the new spider emerges with the abilities, capacities, and memories of her mother.

In the letterzine *INTERSTAT*, Duane had been accused of producing a Mary Sue in the person of K't'lk, the glass spider. Crispin, joining the Mary Sue debate in that letterzine, responded:

> Please quit classifying many *Star Trek* stories in terms of Mary Sue and non–Mary Sue! People level accusations of Mary Sue at the most unlikely subjects nowadays—including glass spiders—Seems to me this is going a bit far, since for me at least, the term 'Mary Sue' constitutes a put-down, implying that the character so summarily dismissed is not a true character, no matter how well drawn, what sex, species, or degree of individuality.[28]

While the applicability of the soubriquet to the self-renewing glass spider in Duane's novel may be problematic, the stories that most nearly fit the description of Mary Sue in her "pure" form can be found in the *Star Trek* section of any bookstore. In the novel *Dread-*

nought, by Diane Carey,[29] Mary Sue is called Piper. During her Ko-bayashi Maru test, a practical exercise in the no-win scenario (see Appendix B), Piper (people on her planet only have one name) beats the test, and brings down most of the training center's computers, with an ingenious maneuver she picked up reading girls' adventure books. While her astounded instructors tell her she is the first person ever to beat the test honestly (Captain Kirk cheated), she apologizes for the havoc she has wreaked with the computers. Captain Kirk observes the test and commandeers the cadet for his crew. On her first day as a crew member of the *Enterprise* she is called to the bridge because a hijacked prototype dreadnought is signaling the *Enterprise* with her biocode. From her first meeting with Captain Kirk, Piper feels a "subliminal connection" with the captain, who, she later says, "in some previous life had been my private Aristotle."[30]

The cadet, now lieutenant, becomes the pivot on which turns a plan by the hijackers to thwart a military coup. In the process of uncovering the coup, Piper must free a captive Kirk. She creates a diversion by leading three companions in a bunny-hop down the hallway past his guards, who are easily overpowered in their bemused state. At the story's climax, Piper must take command of the dreadnought to overcome the military conspirators in combat without, however, killing them. (Captain Kirk has no such qualms, and blows the traitors to smithereens.) Piper rejects command until it is thrust upon her, but she says of her young (male) Vulcan companion, "The respect that mellowed his face was empowering."

In the final chapter of the book, and after only a day or two of active service, Piper is promoted to lieutenant commander and becomes the "youngest recipient of the Federation's second highest award," for helping to "save Star Fleet as we know it, Commander, with your ingenuity."[31] After the award ceremony, she makes a date with Captain Kirk for a sailing weekend.

At least in the eighties, and in commercial publication, Mary Sue survives to see the end of the book, although in J. M. Dillard's *Demons,*[32] the Mary Sue character Anitra Lantry nearly dies before her love interest, Dr. McCoy, discovers a cure to parasitic psychic plague that is killing the inhabitants of the planet Vulcan.

As we have seen in the interviews and letters of comment, the Mary Sue story taps into deep emotional sources in the writer. New fans almost invariably stumble upon the genre as their first writing effort, often before they know that a community exists at all, and this is as true for the writers of commercially published Mary Sue novels as it is for their amateur counterparts. J. M. Dillard, the author of *Demons* mentioned above, is a case in point. According to Dillard,

I watched the series until they cancelled it, I watched all the reruns
. . . I'd always wanted to sit down and write something, and when I
saw the Pocket novels coming out, I said, well, huh! I know Trek
better, or at least as well as somebody else, I wonder if I could get
away with it, so I sat down and I wrote the novel . . . I just wrote my
little episode to thrill my Trekkie heart and sent it off. But I didn't
know about the fan literature.[33]

Clearly a form so universally arrived at among female science fiction
and action-adventure fans meets emotional needs that are not satisfied with the more intellectualized approaches of satire or didacticism.
At the same time, Mary Sue produces deep feelings of discomfort in
her readers in the fan community. Mary Sue stories are central to the
painful experience of a female fan's adolescence.

Fans often recount the scorn they experience for their "masculine"
interest in science fiction and action-adventure. These readers grew
up in a period during which active, even aggressive, behavior was acceptable for prepubescent girls who were expected to put away their
grubby corduroys and baseballs, their books that chronicled the male
fantasies of exploration and adventure, when they entered adolescence. With the teen years, girls were expected to turn to makeup,
curlers, and dresses with stockings and high-heeled shoes to attract
the attention of boys who were winning acclaim on the football fields
and basketball courts of their local high schools.

The teenaged girl had to be not just seductive but nonthreatening;
she could not challenge the supremacy of the male on the playing
field or in the classroom. Her marks could be better than his, but she
was expected to mask her verbal performance with a variety of techniques to assure the men around her that she was an irrational, flighty
creature in spite of her misleadingly superior performance in any
particular situation.

Many women in fandom, however, did not make this transition.
Some, like Devra Langsam, simply were not built for the model: five
feet ten inches tall when she was thirteen, Langsam towered over both
the smaller girls and the more slowly developing boys in school. Other
fan women felt set apart because they were heavier than the petite
ideal, or because they needed thick glasses that sometimes distorted
the appearance of their eyes while they symbolically marked the
wearer not only as too intelligent, but also as too "serious." Most of
the women in fandom, including members of the first group who
found themselves outsiders by virtue of their physical makeup, were
unwilling or incapable of masking their intelligence. Some community

members who did succeed on male terms found themselves stranded in an alien culture whose values they did not share.

For intelligent women struggling with their culturally anomalous identities, Mary Sue combines the characteristics of active agent with the culturally approved traits of beauty, sacrifice, and self-effacement, which magic recipe wins her the love of the hero. As described earlier, when *Dreadnought*'s Piper becomes the first cadet to beat the no-win Kobayashi Maru test without cheating, she apologizes for the effect her maneuver has on the base computers. Later, when she has uncovered a plot to overthrow the Federation and has organized an effort to thwart it, she synthesizes the available data aloud. This conversation then occurs with her Vulcan companion Sarda:

> Sarda: "Humans can certainly be dithyrambic at times."
> Piper: "I was just trying to be logical."
> Sarda: "Please avoid such attempts in the future."
> Piper: "I'll try to stick to intuition."
> Sarda: "It seems more within your grasp."
> Piper: "I'll remember."[34]

At the end of the book she receives her real reward: not her medal of valor, but her date with the captain (the *Enterprise* here standing in for the football or basketball team).

Nor is Dillard's Anitra Lantry immune to the syndrome. Dr. McCoy reads humorously from her psych profile that Lantry is: " . . . Intelligent, creative, stubborn, sensitive, telepathic, stubborn, optimistic . . . did I say stubborn?"[35] (After a brief bit of repartee they kiss.) Earlier, Scotty tells the captain, "The woman's a phenomenon. She never asked a single question . . . and she did the job [overhauled the engines] exactly as I woulda done it myself."[36] But she uses her skills off-duty to wire Captain Kirk's shower for sound (he sings off-key, we learn). Traditionally for the genre, Lantry is loved and admired by one and all: she is respected by Scott and the captain, forms a telepathic link with Spock, and has a romantic relationship with Dr. McCoy. When they believe she is dead, McCoy weeps but through the link, Spock has an awareness of her that tells him she still lives.[37]

For the fan woman of any age, her Mary Sue story is her attempt, if only in print, to experience that rite of passage from the active child to the passive woman who sacrifices her selfhood to win the prince. Mary Sue must be an adolescent, behaviorally if not absolutely chronologically, because she represents a transition in roles and identity specific to that period in a woman's life. The fan versions of Mary Sue often expressed a cultural truth of their time, however: to make the transition from child to woman, the active agent within her had to die. Mary Sue writers traditionally kill the active self with their alter-ego character at the end of their stories. First-time writers influenced by the women's movement seldom revised the importance of subterfuge in their characters but, like Carey and Dillard, raised the expectation that subterfuge would save the active agent from an untimely demise.

If we ask the question "Who is served by the woman's internalization of this model," we can easily see that Mary Sue is a fantasy of the perfect woman created within the masculine American culture. Men are served by Mary Sue, who ideally minimizes her own value while applying her skills, and even offering her life, for the continued safety and ease of men. Even in her superiority Mary Sue must efface her talents with giggles and sophomoric humor. She must deny that her solutions to problems are the result of a valid way of thinking, modestly chalking up successes to intuition, a term that often seems akin to Joan of Arc's voices. Women who come to fandom have usually internalized this model because it is the best of the options masculine culture offers them: they may be sexual, they may be precocious children, or they may fade into social nonpresence.

Some writers produce version after version of the Mary Sue story as they struggle to bind their personalities and identities to the cultural model of the ideal woman represented by Mary Sue. Others grow to resent her as they did her real-life counterparts in their own adolescences. The writer, become reader, recognizes Mary Sue's childish behavior as a coping mechanism she has used herself or observed in her friends to mask the threat their own intelligence and competence poses to men. Women rely on men to become husbands and to hire or promote them in the workplace, and the women in media fandom are painfully aware that those men need only ignore them to remove that threat.

In fandom, however, members strive to leave the camouflage behind, and they discourage it in their writing as they strive to create new models in their art. Women fan editors do not publish Mary Sue stories; they go to great lengths to educate their readers to look beyond the adolescent stereotype for their female heroes. I had to turn to the commercially published novels to find examples of the form as it is defined within the fan community.

Marriage and the Alien Male: Lay-Spock

Women in the fan community have rejected Mary Sue, the cultural role of precocious child, and in many cases have replaced her with the matriarch in the genre referred to as "lay" stories, so named because the alter-ego heroine develops a sexual relationship with the hero. Her adventures are an adjunct to his world; her demeanor is one of matriarchal dignity outside of the bedroom and politically correct sensuality within it. While a "lay" story can be written around any one of the characters, by far the most frequently written is the "lay-Spock," with other Vulcans, and in particular Sarek, Spock's father, a close second. When pressed for an explanation for this fascination with the alien, informants reply only that Spock, or Sarek, or Vulcans in general are sexy, interesting, or handsome, that it is exciting to imagine how sex might be in an alien culture. A look at the literature itself, however, reveals deeper concerns.

Jean Lorrah's *Night of the Twin Moons*[38] series takes us through the marriage of Amanda and Sarek, Spock's parents, from their meeting into later life. The marriage is one of love and mutuality, with Amanda sharing in Sarek's work as well as his private life. In the story "The Time of Mating," however, Sarek enters his first pon farr, the male Vulcan's mating frenzy. Every seventh year the male spends a number of days—in this story it is ten days, but the number varies from fan story to fan story—in a "blood fever" of lust in which he must either copulate mindlessly and almost continuously with his mate or die. Pon farr is so shameful, and painful, to the Vulcans that they never speak of it, but Amanda teaches Sarek to enjoy the experience, and enjoys it herself, as she shares pon farr with him through the mind meld, or telepathic contact of married Vulcans. Their experience encourages another married Vulcan couple to relax and enjoy their pon farr as well.

Sex, as defined within the canon of the episodic television series, is an intrusion into the world of work and male companionship. In pon farr as described in the *Star Trek* series episode "Amok Time," sexuality is embarrassing for Vulcan males: uncontrollable, primarily physical, and frightening. During pon farr, a stimulated Vulcan will kill if thwarted in his pursuit of sexual release with the partner to whom he was bound in childhood. He is not perceived as a considerate sexual partner.

In Jean Lorrah's stories, and those of other lay-Spock writers, however, male emotions are revealed, controlled but available to the partner who manages her husband's more uncontrollable physical urges. Amanda, as the ideal wife in the ideal family, teaches Sarek and other Vulcans who fall within her influence how to accept their physical and emotional natures within a shared and caring relationship between equals who complete each other rather than subordinate one to the other.

For many women pon farr acts as a symbol for their perception of male sexuality. American men, like Vulcans, are trained not to express their feelings. The stories teach their readers how to approach the unpredictability of sexual encounters with human men, who may seem just as outwardly controlled and inwardly unpredictable as their Vulcan counterparts. Lorrah's stories are written in a didactic mode as relationship education for adolescents, and for women at any age who have trouble making sense of their own relationships. For many of the writers, whether they use pon farr as a device for beginning a sexual relationship or as an excuse to show that even obligatory sex can be fun in the right frame of mind, the "alien" is the human male, whose motives and behavior may seem random and unpredictable.

Writing is a risky business, and fanwriters use a variety of distancing devices to protect themselves from the risk of personal exposure in their writing (see Chapter 8 for a more detailed description). In Mary Sue stories, the heroine's age, and even her giftedness, afford the adult writer a buffer between her inner world and her work. The risk is correspondingly greater when the writer creates an adult and fully sexual woman in a less than ideal relationship. Not only does the writer reveal herself to others, she often discovers herself as well. When Judith Gran explained about Mary Sue, "You want to reach out to Mr. Spock and in the process you get in touch with yourself,"[39] Lois Welling agreed:

> I know that's true for me. I mean Susan [her character in *The Displaced*[40]] was. I worked a lot of my problems out with writing her. I know I did. And I think that's why I don't want to do very much with her any more. It's because she served her purpose. She was a lot of fun, but she served her purpose and I don't need her anymore.[41]

In *The Displaced*, Susan is a widowed thirty-four-year-old emergency room nurse from twentieth-century Chicago whose vacation is disrupted when twenty-second-century slavers hijack the airplane on which she is traveling. Because of her emergency room experience, her hijackers do not consign her to the mines with the other captives but assign her to the infirmary and the breeding farm. She and the two other female members of her breeding unit, a Romulan med-tech named Tha and an Andorian teenager driven insane by sexual abuse during her captivity, are awaiting the assignment of a male partner to their hut.

Into the dark and gloomy situation comes Mr. Spock, well into pon farr and captured on his way home to mate. Tha recognizes Spock as

Beverly Zuk's illustration for Lois Welling's *The Displaced* shows Spock with Susan, and Spock's five children by three partners.

a Starfleet officer and as a Vulcan, a people known to respect all living things. The two women co-opt him for their breeding unit but discover to their dismay that a Vulcan given stimulants while in pon farr is not the considerate sexual partner they expected. After Spock returns to guilt-ridden awareness, the women begin to overcome their initial distrust, and gradually the group develops a mutually supportive family unit that grows to include their five children.

The women chose the Starfleet officer as their male partner because he was the most likely candidate to help them escape. In fact, Spock does escape, but not before Susan and he reveal the love that has grown out of the mutual respect between them. Even after he returns to rescue them, however, the couple's hardships are not over: Susan's child, conceived during Spock's last night on the slave planet, is born prematurely and dies after only a few days. In spite of their hardships, the couple form a firm and lasting marriage. Susan insists that Spock return to his position in Starfleet, and she returns to Vulcan with his parents to start a new life.

Clearly, the lay-Spock story is closely related to the Mary Sue story, and some readers would include *The Displaced* in that genre. If we look more closely, however, certain distinctive characteristics begin to emerge. The female hero is not an adolescent but a mature adult woman who rejects traditional male explanations for her perceptions. When Tha, her Romulan companion, does not arrive home on schedule, she asks Spock for help:

> "Spock, I can't find Tha and I just know something is wrong."
> [Spock replies] "Susan, you do not know . . .
> "Don't tell me what I know! Tha and I have had the same routine for over two years now and we always come back here together. If one of us can't make it we let the other know. I've looked; she's in none of her usual places. Come with me now, *please*."[42]

Unlike her Mary Sue counterpart, Susan does not permit her male companion to dismiss her knowledge as intuition. There is nothing "natural" or "instinctive" about it, and she tells him so forcefully. Holding onto the dignity of their thought processes is one of the hardest battles many women fight in the workplace and even at home, and Susan chooses mature self-assertion rather than capitulation to the identity of child that masculine culture tries to impose upon her. She neither giggles nor bunny hops, and her humor expresses rather than defuses her aggression. When asked how she came by a scar on her face, Susan explains:

> " . . . Fraunt [the evil overseer] asked me if we had another male yet. I said no, we were waiting for another Vulcan. Then he said, oh, you like those pointed ears, huh? All I said was that they beat the hell out of pointed heads, and he hit me."[43]

Susan knows she will suffer for the remark, but it is her only way to strike back and she will not give it up.

The most obvious and striking difference between the lay-Spock and the Mary Sue, of course, is the open expression of satisfied sexual desire and the link between sexual satisfaction and trust established in the stories.

Before Spock escapes to bring help for his "family," he and Susan recognize that their relationship has transcended the economic-survival structure imposed upon them by outsiders, and they come together for the first time out of choice rather than as breeders protecting the viability of the group:

> She had seen him [Spock] unclothed many times, but had always been determinedly impersonal, professional . . . Now she took a

deep slow breath and reached out to run her hand slowly over his chest, down his lean hard muscled abdomen to his genitals, again marvelling at the slender tendrils located on either side of his penis. Usually coiled and concealed in the pubic hair, they were now unfurled and small ripples shuddered down their length . . .

Sue remembered her first reaction to this ultimate proof of his alienness. It had been one of surprise. But he had taken her wide-eyed expression and forceful expletive to be negative, and no amount of talking would convince him otherwise. After that he had always been very careful to keep them coiled out of sight. She came to realize from some of the mental images that they were a normal part of Vulcan mating ritual . . . That the tendrils were uncoiled now was an important sign of the depth of his feeling and trust . . . [44]

In *The Displaced,* sex is not the reward for properly attracting the attention of the desired male. Rather, sex represents a contractual necessity imposed by outside forces until the couple establish a trusting and loving relationship. By contrast, Mary Sue is an object lesson in subterfuge. She cannot form a sexual relationship of substance because her love interest is drawn to the image she projects rather than to the person she is. Where there is no risk—and dropping the subterfuge means risk—there can be no trust.

The distinction between the Mary Sue and the lay-Spock genres is a vital one. While many women in the community maintain the ideal of home and family as part of a woman's life, roughly 70 percent of them are unmarried. Those who are married must struggle with the threat a changing sense of self imposes upon their relationships. It is no coincidence that so many of the stories take place in a setting of slavery, often in situations that subject the protagonist to sexual exploitation, even rape. While many community members idealize the family, as we saw with the Lorrah story, some participants perceive traditional family life to be institutionally oppressive. In their writings they demonstrate that both the man and the woman must work within the family to overcome the oppression inflicted upon them both by society and by life.

In Barbara Wenk's *One Way Mirror,*[45] Jenny, the heroine, again is a twentieth-century woman, this time a *Star Trek* fan captured to be a slave not in a backwater of the benign Federation, but in the mirror universe of her favorite *Star Trek* episode, "Mirror, Mirror." In the mirror universe, a cruel empire counterparts the Federation, and women are valued for their expense more than for their contribution to society. Slair, the Vulcan third officer of the starship *Victory,* has been pressured to take a mistress from among the captives as an appropriate display of property, and he chooses Jenny out of spite because she seems the least likely to cause him trouble:

> "Beautiful women can provide an officer with problems. I merely require a passably attractive female." He eyed her speculatively, then continued, "You also appear to be of a calm temperament. I do not wish this arrangement to inconvenience me unduly."[46]

The heroine is not happy with her situation but realizes that a worse master or death are her alternatives if the Vulcan discards her. She consciously draws on the example of *The Thousand and One Nights* and holds her Vulcan master's attention by telling him stories from *Star Trek* the television show, and about fandom and fan stories. Here Wenk mixes in a rich stew of insider humor: Gene Roddenberry is a renegade from the Imperial Empire, and the series episodes a "vicious distortion" of Empire politics. The idic, favored in jeans patches and costume jewelry as a symbol of universal tolerance, is "really" the family crest of Vulcan's ruling dynasty overthrown by the Empire; wearing the idic is considered treason. Over the course of their relationship, the Vulcan is amused and outraged by the stories, and impressed with the spunk and determination of the human cast adrift in an alien universe. He begins to see her as companion rather than property, and she falls in love with him in spite of his continuing though less frequent abuse, which Wenk presents as mild compared to the treatment other women of Jenny's station receive in similar circumstances.

Wenk's *One Way Mirror* is a complex work. She begins with an epigram from Jean Cocteau: "Mirrors should reflect a little before throwing back images," and on the first page, Jenny reflects on her situation: "Be careful what you wish for, Dad always says. You may get it." Clearly the story that follows will be a warning to its readers to consider the implications of their fantasies. And yet, the story that plays out is similar to *The Displaced*. While the empire does not enslave the Vulcan people, that society does force the Vulcan Slair into a relationship with Jenny just as slavery forced Spock into a relationship with Susan in the foregoing story. The couples both have sex long before they establish the interpersonal trust that marks the shift in their relationship from temporary and outside-motivated to permanent and inner-motivated. Unlike Susan, however, Jenny has no rescue, and her Slair is the harsh and sometimes brutal man his society has made him. She can never completely let go of the example of Scheherazade but must learn when to stand up for herself, and when doing so will cost her more than she can pay. At the very end of the story, Jenny, who has perceived herself as plain and unsophisticated, wishes she were like a woman she sees fleetingly, then realizes immediately that the other is herself, seen in a mirror.

The message in this story seems to be that a woman can learn to curb the more hostile impulses of a man and win a modicum of respect by standing up for herself and also by knowing when to back down. The mirror Vulcan does learn to love the heroine, or so one is given to assume, and his behavior gradually becomes more respectful, while Jenny grows in sophistication and understanding of the new culture of which she becomes a part. But the lesson here seems to be "make the most of even the worst situation in which one finds oneself."[47]

Differences of opinion are a part of fan life, and I have often met readers who disagreed vehemently with my interpretations of stories, while a sufficient number agreed to make me feel reasonably confident that I had, if not *the* interpretation, at least a reasonable one. My objection to *One Way Mirror,* that it encourages readers to stay in abusive relationships, however, is the one reading that has received no support in the fan community whatsoever. Fans often accuse me gently of taking the story too seriously. It is only play, they say, and the author does use the reflexive humor of the group, mixing fannish behavior with classic literature and the canon of *Star Trek* in a text that is broadly marked as "play" in spite of its romance novel form.[48]

The play aspects of the text, however, are motivated by the reader's insider knowledge of the series, of the formulaic nature of romance novels, and of the fan community itself. Fans see the character Jenny as a reflection of their own culture, and they enjoy her playful use of the series and the materials of their own community while they share with the author the sly literary allusions, and the fun of wildly mixing their genres. If the reader doesn't know *Star Trek,* the community, the *Arabian Nights,* science fiction, romance novels, *and* the theory that they don't mix, she may enjoy the story, but she won't get the joke.

In correspondence the author herself emphasized the play aspect of the novel:

> *One Way Mirror* is a sex/romance fantasy: it has the same relationship to actual male/female relationships that *Three Weeks* did to the Balkan Question and *The Sheik* did to the Mid-East Conflict. The whole point of a fantasy is its amusement value; the more jewels and gold lame, the better. (And surely every reader has noticed that

not once does Slair ask Jenny to clean the cabin or pick up his socks; housework on the ISS Victory is apparently done by Helpful Elves.) There is no message in this story; in the immortal words of a Great Movie Mogul, "If you want to send a message, call Western Union."[49]

As we will see later in this work, the challenge of mastering a form and playing with it may often motivate a fanwriter. Fans who have discussed *One Way Mirror* with me do give the work serious critical consideration, however, both for its subject matter and for its length—well over a hundred thousand words. Most consistently, readers object to my interpretation of the story because I imply that the heroine had a choice in her actions—escaping while planetside, for example. The fan women often explained to me that Jenny could not manipulate the situation for her benefit because she found herself in a culture whose rules she did not know and in which she had neither status of her own nor kin or friendship networks for her support. Her actions, I am told, must be seen as the best available in a bad situation. Above all, they remind me of the words with which the story begins: "Be careful what you wish for . . . You may get it." To fans, *One Way Mirror* acts not as a model for living but as a cautionary tale of wishful thinking gone wrong, in which signals of playfulness deflect the risk of the serious message behind them.

Women in the Eighties

If members reserved their criticism of female characters for those who fit the Mary Sue stereotype, I would have expected to see many female characters develop in the fan fiction with the support of the community. In fact, Johanna Cantor's challenge posed in 1980,[50] "Why is it that in a group that is probably 90% female, we have so few stories about believable, competent, and identifiable-with women?" remains substantially unmet. The term Mary Sue seems to expand to encompass the characters women write to overcome that onus.

All the stories discussed above were in print when Cantor asked her question, and more had come into print by 1984, the time of the debate in *Interstat* described earlier in this chapter. And yet, participants at a panel discussion in January of 1990 noted with growing dismay that *any* female character created within the community is damned with the term Mary Sue.[51]

At Clippercon in 1987, a panel of women who do not write female characters in their stories described similar experiences as the reason they write only about the male characters that appear in the source products themselves:

— . . . [e]very time I've tried to put a woman in any story I've ever written, everyone immediately says, this is a Mary Sue.
—The automatic reaction you are going to get is "that's a Mary Sue."[52]

In her analysis, Johanna Cantor suggests an explanation for the lack of convincing women characters, and for the expanding usage of the term Mary Sue:

. . . Could it also be that we are afraid, as women, to put into our creations that touch of humanity for which read touch of self, that might make them a little too real? I think so . . . "So what if it hurts, if it makes a good book," Lord Peter Wimsey decreed. (Granted, he wasn't the one who was going to write the book, read the reviews, and do the hurting.) We're not going to get rid of the term Mary Sue. . . . But we can be prepared to turn a resolutely deaf ear, as we work on what we want to work on.[53]

I suspect that the matriarch stories we have discussed in the previous section suffer from too much of the self for the comfort of many fans. Whether expressing love in an idealized marriage as do Amanda and Sarek, overcoming adversity as do Susan and Spock, or finding space for mutual respect in a harsh and oppressive culture like Jenny and Slair, all of these female characters are realized in terms of their relationships to men. Their relationships are not incidental in the women's identity, but integral to them; whereas the achievements of the women in the stories may be their own, their status depends on their husbands. Even Cantor, who decries the lack of strong women, makes the status of her female hero T'Pan contingent upon that of Spock. In her story "Rendezvous," T'Pan has agreed to mate with Spock because he is in pon farr and has no bondmate. In exchange, both her family and Spock's have agreed that the child, if any, will belong to her house. Spock and T'Pan are drawn to each other, but T'Pan will not marry because that would cloud the legal status of the child, and because she would have to travel with her husband in case he went into pon farr again. She agrees instead to a pledge that leaves Spock legally free and T'Pan his chattel:

As a chattel T'Pan could not vote, could not own property: she was a non-person. T'Pan brushed that aside. So long as she did not try to vote and avoided using other channels that might activate an inquiry, no one outside their immediate families need know.[54]

As a corpus, these stories seem to say that a man's status depends on appearances and the hierarchy of his culture, but that a woman has no need of these trappings of success to recognize her self-worth. Competence and a relationship built on mutual respect are their own rewards.

Writing the Self

When women in fandom write about women they are talking to each other about themselves in the symbolic language of their literature. With their efforts they pass through stages of their own development as individuals, from the superteen Mary Sue who lingers in the consciousness even of middle-aged matrons who have steadfastly refused to let go of the active agent of their prepubescent years (or fantasies), to the matriarch struggling for dignity against a society that pressures the family into systems of oppression. Few of the stories about women seem to postulate institutional dignity or equal status for women, but in the fan fiction the fan women talk about their struggle for dignity in their relationships. And in amongst the stories of struggle, the reader finds the stray sentence, given little weight in any single story, but that repeated in story after story speaks of the small frustrations that build up into deep-seated resentments over time: "Sarek had never, ever, been one to turn away from her and fall asleep after making love . . ."[55] or the many references to bathing and cleanliness that appear particularly in erotic stories from England and Australia.

While the stories about women do represent the struggle of some women in the community, that number seems to be very small. In a survey I conducted at More Eastly Con (see Appendix C), which attracted a high concentration of fanzine readers, only 9 percent of respondents reported reading Mary Sue stories, and only 14 percent reported that they read lay-Spock stories. By contrast, 20 percent reported reading homoerotic fiction, and 24 percent enjoyed hurt-comfort.

Part of the reason so few stories about women are written or read by fan readers may take us back to the question of distance mentioned earlier in this chapter. Most of the stories that do feature women characters take place in the science fiction universes of *Star Trek* and *Blake's 7*. The different times and different cultures in which they play out stories of women's captivity and redemption offer writers a degree of distance from the situations they write. By contrast, contemporary dramas tie the writer to the here and now. The writer has little fictional distance from which she may imagine alternative ways of relating, and she is always drawn back to the recognition of the way things really are in the world in which she actually lives.

Notes

1. Judy Segal and Shirley Maiewski, taped interview, New York, August 1985.
2. Based on regular review of publications such as *Isaac Asimov's Science Fiction Magazine, Analog: Science Fiction, Science Fact,* and *Science Fiction Chronicles.* The last of these does list an occasional *Star Trek* convention, but their listing is by no means representative for media conventions.
3. The *Star Trek* fans I have met prefer to be called "Trekkers," and consider the term "Trekkies" to be an insult.
4. Beverly Lorenstein and Judith Gran, taped interview, Philadelphia, June 1983.
5. Ibid.
6. Ibid.
7. Judy Segal, taped interview, Cockeysville, Md., July 1983.
8. Ibid.
9. A gathering of friends of a fanzine publisher to put the actual fanzines together.
10. Segal, taped interview, Cockeysville, Md., July 1983.
11. Lois Welling, taped interview, Cockeysville, Md., July 1983.
12. Ibid.
13. Ibid.
14. Ibid.
15. Camille Bacon-Smith, "The Mary Sue Genre in Star Trek Fan Fiction," *Folklore Women's Communication* (1984).
16. Personal correspondence with Paula Smith, September 27, 1990.
17. Paula Smith, "A Trekkie's Tale," reprinted in "Mary Sue: A Short Compendium," *Archives V* (Winter 1980), ed. Johanna Cantor, p. 34 (fanzine).
18. Ibid.
19. Ibid., p. 35
20. Ibid.
21. Cantor, "Mary Sue: A Short Compendium."
22. Ann Pinzow, taped interview, Cockeysville, Md., July 1984.
23. Judith Gran, taped discussion, Cockeysville, Md., July 1984.
24. Roberta Rogow, taped interview, New York, September 1985.
25. The author was referring to my article "The Mary Sue Genre in Star Trek Fan Fiction," which circulated among writers in both the fan and commercial Trekwriting circles.
26. Taped interview, 1986; citation information withheld at request of informant.
27. Diane Duane, *The Wounded Sky* (New York, Pocket Books, 1983).
28. Ann Crispin, letter, *Interstat* (June 1984), ed. Teri Meyer (fanzine).
29. Diane Carey, *Dreadnought* (New York: Pocket Books, 1986).
30. Ibid, p. 167.
31. Ibid., p. 246.
32. J. M. Dillard, *Demons* (New York: Pocket Books, 1986).
33. J. M. Dillard, taped interview, Atlanta, Ga., September 1986.

34. Carey, *Dreadnought*, p. 139.
35. Dillard, *Demons*, p. 156. The ellipses are Dillard's.
36. Ibid., p. 63.
37. Ibid., pp. 138–39.
38. Jean Lorrah, series published by the author from 1975 through the present and including the novel, *Night of the Twin Moons*, and three volumes of collected stories by Lorrah and others.
39. Gran, taped discussion, Cockeysville, Md., July 1984.
40. Lois Welling, *The Displaced* (Champaign, Ill.: self-published, 1978).
41. Welling, taped discussion (with Gran and others), Cockeysville, Md., July 1983.
42. Welling, *The Displaced*, p. 92. Ellipses are Wellings'.
43. Ibid., p. 118.
44. Ibid. First ellipses are Wellings'.
45. Barbara Wenk, *One Way Mirror*, in *Masiform D, special supplement #2* (Brooklyn, N.Y.: Poison Pen Press, 1980).
46. Ibid., p. 8.
47. In personal correspondence with me dated September 26, 1990, Wenk adds her wry objection to this interpretation: "As for the matter of encouraging women to stay in abusive relationships I can only state, categorically and firmly, that I am utterly opposed to their so doing, and strongly urge any woman trapped in an abusive relationship on a starship with an alien nobleman to leave immediately and seek professional help."
48. Note in particular the "dark hero" aspect of the romantic male, as described in Jan Radway's *Reading the Romance* (Chapel Hill: University of North Carolina Press, 1984).
49. Personal correspondence from Barbara Wenk, September 1990.
50. Cantor, "Mary Sue: A Short Compendium," p. 35.
51. Reported by Judy Chien, who attended the panel discussion at Most Eastly Con, Newark, N.J., January 1990.
52. Taped panel discussion, Cockeysville, Md., March 1987.
53. Cantor, "Mary Sue: A Short Compendium," pp. 34–35.
54. Johanna Cantor, "Rendezvous," *R & R XXII* (Bronx, N.Y.: Yeoman Press, 1985), p. 77 (fanzine).
55. Jean Lorrah, *Full Moon Rising* (Bronx, N.Y.: Yeoman Press, 1976), p. 64.

Chapter Five
Second Stage Initiation: Learning about Videotape

The early stages of my initiation into fandom were marked by discussion and literature that revolved around the *Star Trek* series, first broadcast on network television, and then in its many syndicated reruns. In 1985, however, I became aware of the changes videotape was making, both artistically and in the nature of the source products themselves, in the fan community. At More Eastly Con that year I met Jean Curley, who would become my mentor in the British and fringe fandoms.[1]

Fandoms for British Series

When I met Jean, British television programs such as *Blake's 7* and *The Professionals* were still unknown to American television audiences. *The Professionals,* a contemporary action-adventure show, apparently had a very short run on a few independent TV stations in the United States during the 1981 season, but few fans here can remember seeing it. *Blake's 7* was not shown in the United States until late 1986, when it began a popular run on public television stations.

My opportunity to begin a close study of fans of British media arose when I attended More Eastly Con, a five-day convention for three hundred participants organized by the original New York Convention Committee for Labor Day weekend, 1985, and held in a small hotel at LaGuardia Airport. I traveled to the convention with ethnographic photographer Stephanie Hall; Judy Segal, my early mentor in fandom, met us there. As is common at conventions, the three of us shared a room with two other women I had not met before. The room was small for five women and their assorted luggage and recording equipment. Its location, under the flight paths of incoming airliners and above the dance club, made sleep all but impossible. The hotel did offer one interesting perq: several teams playing in the U.S. Open tennis tournament, held at nearby Forest Hills, were also staying there. The young men in their tennis shorts were the subjects of casual approval voiced by many of the women in attendance.

By 1985 I had become fairly adept at finding my way around conventions, but I had not yet attended a room showing of videotapes. Friday night, I followed the directions posted on the convention bulletin board to a room where about twenty fans, mostly women, were watching British television. One woman had brought a PAL system monitor and video recorder to the hotel, and she played tapes she had received in trade from Australia.

I didn't understand the interest in *The Professionals,* an action-adventure program about a civilian antiterrorist squad. In a fifty-minute episode (which I later learned was not indicative of the series as a whole) there could not have been more than ten minutes of dialogue, and there was only sporadic action. The knowing audience laughed at what seemed to an outsider to be inappropriate moments, and clearly the audience in the room was finding significance in looks and glances, small comments, that made little or no sense to me.

However, *Blake's 7,* a show about a band of escaped prisoners and rebels battling the evil Federation in space, had witty repartee and unusual characters, including a Spock-like computer specialist who was clearly the favorite of the group. Group members spoke little and kept to whispers while tapes were playing, although there seemed to be two factions present: those who wanted to watch in silence and those who wanted to play, making comments, joking, or laughing at provocative glances or dialogue. It became clear that several mentors were introducing neophytes to the source material at this convention, while more embedded members of the subcommunity wanted to share their insider humor with other viewers. Some audience members seemed pleased to be seeing clear copy of favorite programs—some even seemed surprised at what a favorite character actually looked like.

Between episodes of *Blake's 7* I had an opportunity to ask some questions of nearby fans who were mentoring new members of the community. The episode just shown, "Star One," falls at the end of the second season of the series, but it is often used as an introduction for neophytes. "Star One," which ends in an intergalactic war, offers developed character relationships, action, and some delightfully "BBC" dialogue—soliloquy in the grand style—wit, and a key revelation or two that fans devour.

From across the room I heard a phrase passed between a mentor and student, "Travis, you can see Travis's road to degradation." In the episode we had just seen, Travis had fallen to his death in some sort of nuclear power station. The fans in the room seemed pleased. I could not see the original speaker, so I asked a nearby fan about Travis, and about Blake, for whom the series is named. My unknown advisor gave me a précis of character relationships:

> . . . So he (Travis) is a homicidal maniac searching for Blake—he has an obsession with Blake . . . and of course, Blake has become a focus for everything that has gone wrong in his life.

A second voice interjected: "Oh, the interactions between personnel is the best part of the show, and "Gambit" will show it even more."[2]

While my two informants filled me in on the background of the characters and their relationships to one another, an interested group of new fans and old hands gathered around us, some to nod agreement, some trying to understand what they have just seen. For many fans, this was a first opportunity to see these products. Although directing their answers to my questions, my two unknown mentors addressed their explanations to the small group around us. The women advised us about the key messages delivered by the program that are seen as important in the fan fiction: About Blake and Avon, a key relationship often seen as a bizarre realignment of the relationship between Kirk and Spock of *Star Trek:*

> Stranger 1: . . . He [Avon] is opposed to it [Blake's rebellion against the Federation]. He doesn't believe that the rabble have the ability to keep the rebellion. He doesn't give a damn about that. He only cares about Avon, but he gets sucked into it again.
> Stranger 2: Blake is the consummate manipulator.
> Stranger 1: Oh, he is!
> Stranger 2: It is extraordinary what he can do with the interpersonal relationships on board ship. And Avon gets sucked in even though he knows what is going on. But he has always stood rather apart from the other figures and has opposed Blake on the stupid moves that he perceives Blake does.[3]

The crimes that each of the seven key characters committed were described, and I asked how Avon, embezzler and "the second-best computer expert in the galaxy" (because the first best is the one who caught him) was in fact detected:

> Stranger 2: He was caught because he trusted someone else— You're never supposed to trust people.

As the next episode began, the first stranger summed up the morality of the series: "There's always the ambiguity: Is Blake a terrorist or a freedom fighter?"

On Saturday the convention committee made a room available for meetings of subgroups. Organizers Devra Langsam and Linda Deneroff gave me permission to set up shop there until someone else wanted the room. On the sign-up sheet outside the room I printed in large letters "The Ethnographer Is In," and I settled in to wait for the stray fan to come in and talk. Several fans were eating lunch in the room, and I apologized for disturbing them. They asked what I was doing, and when I told them, they became my first informants of the day.

Others drifted into the room out of curiosity, or because they had worked with me in the past. Soon the room was filled with fans—some men but mostly women, some known to me, others I had not met before that day. The group interview was the sort that an ethnographer both wishes for and has nightmares about. The room held roughly thirty people and was crowded for two and a half hours. The population in the room was not constant, however; people came in and had their say, listened for a while, and left. Others took their place. The tape recorder ran, and photographer Stephanie Hall moved around the room taking pictures with high-speed film, because a flash might disturb the interaction.

I was so busy directing traffic—making sure everyone who had something to say had a chance to say it, drawing out the opinions of the shy, and curbing the enthusiasm of those who would hold the floor too long—that I actually heard very little of what people were *saying* until I went home and listened to my tape. I did, however, note several *Blake's* fans discussing their interest in that program and other British television products. I seized my opportunity to find out more about this esoteric fandom.

Pam Auditore and Jean Curley, both fans of *Blake's 7* and *The Professionals*, talked about their interest in the British products, and I asked them about the friction between the "talkers" and the "shushers" in the video room the night before:

> Jean: I think the ones who were going around shushing people were the ones who had not been able to see it before, and would probably not be able to see it again.[4]

Pam added a personal confirmation of this assumption:

> That would be my reaction too. I was seeing *Blake's 7* up there (in the video room), and I wanted to memorize as much as I could of it.

And we're not used to memorizing just verbally like that, by watching it.

And here again, there were people talking, and I wasn't to a "shushing" part, but I was putting all my concentration on what was going on, both visually and, uh hearing it, so I could get it.[5]

Jean explained why many people are drawn to the British products: "The majority of things you find people deeply hooked on are almost always dealing with people. Partnerships are very big."

Pam continues this explanation about her interest in *The Professionals* and *Blake's 7*. In fact, she switches back and forth, discussing both shows in her explanation:

> . . . but it's relationships. You start out with two guys who are very wary of each other, then they form a working relationship, then they form a partnership that is a support system.
>
> People like that. If you look at today's world, there are not that many people I'm going to be willing to open my door to and say, "hey, come on in."

Jean adds that good writing in the British products is a key to their popularity, a view that Pam supports:

> Jean: They put all their money into getting good scripts and it shows in the development. Most people who have followed one or the other (*Blake's 7* or *The Professionals*) are very interested in where the characters are going and how they got there, and will talk for hours about what might have been somebody's past experience so that they would react in this situation in this manner.
> Pam: The backgrounds [sets in *Blake's 7; The Professionals* was filmed on location] are really bad . . . It's like when you were a small child and you didn't have umpteen thousand *Star Wars* figures, but you had your imagination, and your little log cabin, and you built things.

The interest fans sustain in these source products depends on characters in ambivalent relationships growing to trust each other, a situation that the fan women see in their own lives.

At the same time, because the British television system did not expend its program budgets for *Blake's 7* in special effects and realistic sets, the fans are called upon to interact with the screen from the outset. The fan must essentially make up the special effects as she goes along, so the ficting process begins with the viewing and easily moves into the writing that is second nature to the community. The inac-

cessibility of the products would have been an obstacle to the spread
of British source products five years ago, but VCR technology has
changed that. Pam talks about how one obtains access to the materials:

> Usually it boils down to, you've got to have somebody who has
> been hooked, who has seen the originals or good quality [video-
> tape]—usually somebody who has been into tape media for a while,
> because they already know the connecting ropes. Because, I know a
> lot of it, for a while, seemed to be coming up from the Southwest,
> up to New England.
> And generally these are people who are too kind to keep good
> things away from their fellow fans. So they immediately start, just
> sort of casually saying, "Oh, by the way, I saw something neat the
> other night. And I'm getting a tape of it, and when I get it, do you
> want to come see it?"[6]

Materials that can be obtained only through the community add a
sense of solidarity within it, while limiting the numbers of participants
to the comfort levels described in Chapter 2.

As a researcher, I determined to examine these products more
closely at the first opportunity. That opportunity came later in 1985,
at the November Philadelphia Science Fiction Conference. Jean
Curley, working as a convention volunteer, recognized me from the
More Eastly Con and took me on as a neophyte in the fringe fandoms.
Jean is tall and slim, with straight brown hair and, ubiquitous in fandom, glasses. When we met, Jean was working several jobs. One, as a
part-time security guard, she kept solely to support her postage expenses—maintaining international correspondence with hundreds
of fans is expensive, especially when trading videotapes and fanzines.
In the years we have known each other, Jean has weathered life-
threatening illness, and she has returned to college for a degree in
computer science, which she received in June of 1990.

A fan of *The Man From U.N.C.L.E.*, *Blake's 7*, *The Professionals*, and a
wide range of other source products, but not *Star Trek*, Jean told me
about her unique entry into the fan community.[7] Like many fans, Jean
read science fiction from childhood, but more unusual for a woman,
she had been a role game player in high school. In 1981, when she was
eighteen years old, she attended her first convention, for role-playing
gamers. Fans generally think of role-playing games as men's activities,
so Jean had to prove her superior competence in the games to win
acceptance. At her second convention, the Philadelphia Science Fiction
Conference (Philcon) later that same year, Jean first learned about
media fandom, and she obtained a few contacts in her interest, *Blake's*

7. Not until her first Spycon, in 1983, did Jean consider herself to be a fully committed member of the media fan community.

Videotape Initiation

At this point, Jean became my mentor in the fringe fandoms. We exchanged addresses, and several weeks later, I received a box of xeroxed copies of *Blake's 7* stories and a long letter giving me some background on the series and the fandom. By February we had arranged a weekend to view tapes.

Jean arrived with a box of videotapes and, since I did not own one, a video recorder. We watched taped episodes of *Blake's 7* for sixteen hours that weekend. Several total immersion weekends are common to the process of initiating the new member in the esoteric product material. She left the box of tapes and the machine with me for a month, and brought another fan with her for our next marathon viewing weekend.

Understanding the tapes of some favorite British source products, such as *The Professionals*, requires a great deal of effort. Poor tape copy and British working-class accents and expressions, combined with open microphone recording on location, make some of these episodes incomprehensible to the uninitiated. The mentor must frequently stop the tape to interpret, first giving an exact but clearly spoken rendering of the dialogue in question, then giving an interpretation in American English. Fortunately for me, the main characters in *Blake's 7* speak BBC English, fairly understandable to any regular viewer of *Masterpiece Theater,* and most of the action takes place on the soundstage, so dialogue is generally clear.

The picture, however, is more problematic. The videotapes are copies of copies, and can be almost impossible to interpret. For the most part, however, Jean's tapes were not that degraded: faces were generally distinguishable, if not well focused.

Since Jean had seen each episode a number of times, she napped occasionally as I watched; however, she advised me on which episodes to watch and the order in which to watch them. She would often stop the tape, run it backward, and replay particular scenes, commenting, "This is where they get that description of Avon from," or, "That is why everyone says they really like each other." Each scene so commented upon is an interpersonal interaction, and each leads me back into the fan stories I have already read.

The writers in this source product emphasize plotting that highlights the psychological manipulation underlying much of the series action. The helpful fans at More Eastly Con pointed this out when introducing new viewers, and my mentor, Jean, did the same for each relevant scene throughout the weekend, telling me who was manipulating whom, and why. When possible, she tied the scenes I was seeing for the first time into the background given in episodes I had not yet seen, and reminded me of scenes I had viewed in other episodes that fans took for explanations of actions that may have seemed incomprehensible standing alone. She taught me how to read beyond the spoken language to the body language—"See how he smiles a real smile after he insults Vila. It's their way of being friends"—and—"Watch how he looks at Cally (or Servalan). He must really love her." She stopped the tape often to replay the scenes that support the interpretations that inform the fan literature.

By March of 1986 I had become part of Jean's circle, receiving copies of stories and fanzines, and meeting with other members on a sporadic basis. On a Sunday afternoon at a weekend house party in New Jersey, a number of fans lounged in pajamas and nightshirts on the open sofa bed, munching pizza and discussing the importance of videotape in the community. Other fans sprawled in chairs or on the floor to watch videos on the television or read fanzines, looking up occasionally to add their opinions to the topic under discussion. Lin Place, a reader of the community's products and active trader in the videotape circuit, explained how she came to collect *Starsky and Hutch* tapes:

> . . . I was reading Starsky and Hutch fiction, but I hadn't seen the episodes in years. So some of the things I could vaguely remember . . . but I didn't remember character names, so I wanted to see the episodes to make the stories more interesting—bring them more alive. And since they weren't showing it, a friend in New York had a collection, and she made copies for me. And then, when they showed it where I live, I got first-run generation. And now friends that I know who haven't seen it in years ask me for it.[8]

Fan interest in a given source product often arises after the original is off the air or otherwise out of circulation, when the only access to the source product may be videotape. The video collector, however, accumulates tapes for reasons other than to reinforce the experience of reading fan fiction. Listening to Lin's comments, Australian fan Shayne McCormack added, ". . . [people collect tapes] for the obvious reason—so you can watch them again. I think there's a lot of the old collecting bug in there too."[9]

A number of fans agreed, but the one partial dissent is equally instructive. Lisa, a longtime science fiction reader, was being initiated into media fandom at the house party. Lisa had already become a regular viewer of *Blake's 7*, which had been picked up by local public television stations in 1986, and she read fan fiction surrounding that source product. The night before the group interview, she had watched at least seven hours of videotaped episodes of *The Professionals*. Songtapes, fan-constructed music videos that use popular songs to highlight favorite visual messages in the products themselves (see Chapter 7), played during the interview, and Lisa was torn throughout between watching the songtapes and participating in the interview. Lisa disagreed with Shayne:

> I generally don't save episodes, but I wound up with a copy of "Star One" [a key *Blake's 7* episode] because I wasn't home [and recorded it to watch later] . . . And it was like, there was "Star One," but I don't want to get rid of "Star One" but I don't save episodes, but I don't want to get rid of "Star One," so I found another space to put it, I still have it, and I'm not getting rid of it, at least until my mother needs an hour [of tape] and there's absolutely nowhere else it can go.[10]

We Control the Video . . .

Lisa's confusion about her own attitude toward the *Blake's 7* episode on her tape is typical of the neophyte's battle against what she often perceives as her own irrational behavior: Collecting reruns is pointless, so why am I doing it? Moving into the video circuit, the neophyte must change attitudes and perceptions of the very nature of mass-produced entertainment. The ephemeral, throw-away nature of television changes, as programming becomes frozen in time at the will of the viewer. Control of the medium also changes hands, no longer the sole province of the broadcaster.

When the "what" of watching falls into the hands of the fan-oriented viewer, the "how and why" of watching undergoes radical revision as well. Concerned because she cannot bring herself to erase her one taped episode of *Blake's 7*, Lisa has been bombarded with experiences that reorder her perceptions of the product she watches. Later, if Lisa follows the pattern of other community members, she will collect her own tapes or borrow tapes from others.[11]

Lisa's training experience would not have been possible if many people all over the country had not spent hours recording and then copying tapes, making contacts, and distributing the product in trade or simply to gratify an eager friend. Most of *The Professionals* tapes Lisa has seen during the weekend derive from one set recorded in the

Dallas-Fort Worth area in 1981–82 and distributed via tortuous channels throughout the country.

Lin, whose episodes we viewed, has copies close to the source— faces of the actors were usually visible, if a little indistinct. While the episodes ran, a second VCR caught them on tape again, to pass them further down the line. Shayne offered to send PAL system first-generation tapes from Australia, where *The Professionals* has been in reruns for several years. Lin said that she planned to purchase a PAL system and readily arranged an exchange for tapes of *Simon and Simon* and *Hardcastle and McCormick*, both mutual favorites, the former running several seasons behind in Australia, the latter not seen there at all.

The international connection is as important in video circles as it is in fanzining, and in what have been known as the fringe fandoms, the two are often parts of one whole. Fans who live in Australia, England, Italy, or Japan cannot wait out the several seasons' time lag between the original showing in the United States and the showing in their native countries. *Star Trek: The Next Generation* did not even begin broadcast in England until 1991, but the new characters have become integral to the fanzine community. Without videotape, stories written overseas for fanzines would be hopelessly out of date for the American market. American fans likewise become attracted to series television shown abroad through the stories that appear in overseas fanzines, and want to participate fully in the fandoms, particularly those surrounding the British products.

The drive to participate fully in the international community is so strong that in 1984, American fans of *Blake's 7*, attracted to the source product entirely through videotapes and British and Australian fanzines, held the first annual Scorpio convention in Chicago. They invited a number of *Blake's 7* cast members as well as Terry Nation, creator of the series. The larger *Star Trek* conventions regularly contract for one or two actors from that series to appear, but Scorpio was unique as a small convention inviting a large number of guests who appeared for travel and expenses but no contract fee. Fans wanted to see what the actors really looked like, and the actors were curious themselves. Paul Darrow, who played the popular misanthrope, Avon, attended:

> It was rather surprising, really, to get an invitation to go to Chicago, which indeed I did [go]. Michael [Keating, Vila on *Blake's 7*] also, and Terry [Nation], and Brian Croucher, who was the second Travis.

And candidly, we didn't know what to expect. We were treated with great love and affection . . . I enjoyed it, certainly, although I was a little taken aback at the enthusiasm. I couldn't quite understand it—when a show has not been put on [the air].[12]

Michael Keating, who played Vila, also expressed his surprise at the knowledgeability of American fans he met in 1984:

. . . It was my very first trip to America, so it was an amazing event for me anyway, and also having never experienced American fandom either, the whole thing just blew my mind . . .

. . . [T]his is another thing, so ridiculous, that no one had seen it officially. The people who had seen it had seen some quite bad copies of it because of course it's a different system. So some of the copies they had, it was like a radio play—you couldn't see anything . . .

It just amazed me that there we had a program that wasn't even seen in the United States and yet people were interested in it.[13]

As Keating so accurately described, the present world video technology does not lend itself to the level of international trading that becomes necessary if a fandom is to spread and make a secure place for itself in a country where the source product is not broadcast. Both Britain and Australia use the PAL transmitting system, and fans who can afford them purchase PAL systems for use solely with their UK videotapes. Less committed fans, or fans with less discretionary income, must settle for "camera copy." Jean Curley explained how fans with PAL capacity equipment convert their tapes for viewing on American television systems. Her description resembled a recipe or list of instructions, so I have formatted it that way rather than as a paragraph:

You know there are three television systems in the world.
Okay, what happens is,
you get a multi-standard VCR,
which will play back in all three systems . . .
They will only play back,
They will not record.
So what you do is
you take your multi-standard VCR,
you hook it up to your American television, okay?
You can play back your tape now.

You have a friend who makes copies—
You take your multi-standard VCR,
you hook it up to your television,
you play the tape.
You take your American VCR camera,
you stand it in front of the television
and you aim. [laugh]
And you get remarkable differences in quality.
Most things are first- or second-generation camera copy.
Second-generation camera copy usually is not that good,
but it's viewable.
Anything after that you just really can't watch.[14]

Whether the program is American or British, direct-to-tape or camera copy, the mentor's training in reading television introduces the initiate to the community's viewing aesthetic and the structure of meaning that fans draw from the television they view.

Mapping Television: The Interpretive Process

Over extended viewing weekends like the one described above, women learn or reinforce among themselves the complex interpretation of media products, generally referred to as a selective reading process,[15] which underlies the creation of narratives in their own literature and art.

Some of the messages coded into the group's narratives are specific to the community, developed over time out of the group's particular communication needs. Trust—the need for it and the difficulty finding it—is a key message in the community, and fans develop sexual symbols (that do not necessarily appear in the source product themselves) as codes for discussing trust in their own literature. Through the long process of my instruction in watching the videotaped series episodes in extended "total immersion" doses, I found my mentors emphasized an understanding of the structure of relationships of characters in the source material to each other, to the setting, and to themselves. My mentor trained me to construct a viewing experience counter to traditional episodic patterns, one that connects each episode of a series in causal relation to every other.

Traditional Viewing Pattern: The Flow

Raymond Williams has described "flow" as the combination of programming and commercial breaks offered by a particular network or station on any given night. According to Williams, an evening of television is constructed around a set of mutually compatible programs designed to keep the viewer in his or her chair. Lulled by inertia and the comfortably predictable ebb and flow of programming, the viewer will not bother to change the channel. To do so would disrupt the flow, for example, of an evening of dramatic presentations, inserting a different tempo—for example, a comedic flow—after the mood has already been set.[16]

This model has a number of similarities to the concept of ludic flow[17] described by sociologist Mihalyi Csikszentmihalyi. While the use of the term "flow" by both theorists seems to have been coincidental,[18] that very coincidence points out the phenomenological similarity of the experience of television viewing and experiences which Csikszentmihalyi finds to be present in play.

In Williams' theory, a viewer sits in front of the television for the prime-time viewing hours. During the viewing, the experience is clear and immediate, but ludic—"flow"—time is always "now": the viewer turns off the television after the nightly news with no conscious perception of the passing of three and a half hours. The rhythm of play produces the experience that the flow of time has contracted.

Plot, the most easily recognized characteristic of narrative, constitutes the part of episodic television that properly belongs to the flow. Action-adventure show producers have traditionally structured their products for the cursory viewer; the program must clearly define its primary message on the surface of the action—the plot—and must deliver that message in the one-hour—less commercial breaks—running time of an episode.[19] The plot must also fit into a typology of genre and subgenre that the viewer recognizes, so the decoding process can continue in spite of distractions during the viewing. The narrative must seem to be complete, even when the real-time attention that the viewer gives to the screen may be much less than his memory of the experience tells him.

Action-adventure plots are characterized by a struggle between good and evil, between right and wrong. Heroes try to capture villains. These programs do not emphasize crime prevention, ostensibly because preventive action is perceived as being dramatically limited. A more complex reasoning underlies the direct catch-a-thief model: If the villain does not complete a nefarious act, the viewer receives an ambiguous message—how bad is a villain who does no evil? How evil is intention without action? How good is a hero who acts aggressively against someone who has not acted? How wrongly may a hero act and still be perceived as in the right?

The ambiguous plot generates questions. It calls upon the viewer to concentrate more intently on the inner world of formulating his questions, while simultaneously keeping track of the external world playing out on the screen. If he spends too much time pondering—trying to figure out—how bad the bad guy is and how good the good guy is, he loses the thread of the ongoing plot. He becomes frustrated because he has missed the information he needs to answer his questions. Producers seem more willing to risk this last question. The cursory viewer may find the hero's actions questionable, but regular viewers have the reassurance of past experience to help mediate the ambiguity: ultimately, the hero must be good because he is the hero.

Importantly for producers interested in syndicated marketing of their products after network runs, however, episodes with a degree of ambiguity in their plots seem to present a new experience upon repeated viewing, lengthening the "shelf-life" of the series. Members of the media fan community recognize and appreciate the ambiguous status of good and evil in their favorite source products. At a house gathering in Illinois, a number of people were discussing the best episode with which to introduce a potential fan to *Star Trek*. Patricia, an academic and fan visiting from Pittsburgh, suggested:

How about the Organians ["Errand of Mercy"] . . . Because it's got all the elements of macho idiotic, uh, sort of men playing off against each other and so on. And all the time there's a whole 'nuther something going on that they don't know about.[20]

In this episode, Captain Kirk is shown to be acting heroically according to norms established in the action-adventure genre. He is sent to protect the technologically unsophisticated inhabitants of a planet from the invading forces of evil Klingons, but the leaders of the alien civilization do not want his help. Captain Kirk uses aggressive tactics to impose the conflict on the planet's inhabitants. The hero, and through him the norms that dictate his behavior, become ambiguous in relation to right and wrong.

At the end of the episode the aliens are revealed to be highly superior beings in no need of assistance, and Captain Kirk accepts censure for his behavior, which is shown to parallel that of his Klingon enemy. But the apparent mediation of the ambiguity is only partially successful: Was the captain wrong in trying to "protect" the Organians against their will, or did he fall from grace because he did not recognize the Organians' ability to protect themselves?

Captain Kirk's position as a hero may be called into doubt in the occasional episode plot, but as Caren Parnes pointed out when she contrasted two favorite source products, *Star Trek* never left the

viewer in doubt for long. By contrast, other products build moral ambiguity into the ongoing characters:

> Caren: (about *Star Trek*) This is America, that's Russia; the
> Klingons, and the flag-waving good guys, no question about that.
> Ethnographer: And in *The Professionals?*
> Caren: You're talking about a whole different ball game. No good
> guys in that series, period.[21]

Miami Vice, with a small following in fandom,[22] did try to interject a
sense of ambiguity in its hero, Sonny Crockett, but in typically American fashion, it qualified the hero's actions with a psychological explanation: Sonny was a burnt-out cop, struggling to do the right thing in
difficult circumstances. It wasn't his fault. By contrast, fans of *Blake's 7*
find the element of doubt central to their enjoyment of the product:
"There's always the ambiguity—Is Blake a terrorist or a freedom
fighter?"[23]

Plot sets the ongoing characters a problem to solve, or a situation
that displays their strongest or weakest points. The specific problem
set before the hero is not important to the fan, however: how he responds to the stress, the traits he displays while he resolves the puzzle
are important because they add to the fans' knowledge of the character and his relationships with others over time.

How to end a series episode may be the most problematic aspect of
the plot. Closure should be sufficient to satisfy the cursory viewer, but
not so complete that the viewer feels content to turn off his set. Nor is
the construction of flow through the evening enough to hold and satisfy an audience. Each viewer creates a personal map of the series that
depends on a sense of continuity from week to week. Series producers
respond to the challenge to narrative form by replacing the denoue-
ment with the tag, a short interaction between regular cast characters
that may refer to events in the plot for the week, or may comment on
a running joke or relationship. Tags and coming attractions for the
following week reverse the closure of the individual episode plot, reminding the viewer that the series, like real life, goes on.

For many viewers, life goes on even when the series is over. When
the BBC ended *Blake's 7*'s four-year run with the apparent deaths of
all of the regular characters, fans, especially in the fanzine community, protested. Fanwriters have created alternative explanations for
what the viewer sees in the final minutes of the episode. Sheila Willis'
fanzine *Fifth Season* draws its title from the apocryphal continuation of
the series, and Sheila included a number of "resurrection" stories in
the publication. Many stories and novels, such as Matthews' *Double-*

Edged Sword, postulate that the entire fourth season exists only as a figment of the character Avon's insanity.

Audience reactions like the ones fans had to the death of the major characters in *Blake's 7* point out that, in series television, plot becomes important not only for what it does, but equally for what it does not do. The plot must seem to give the viewer a novel experience, but in fact it must draw from a small repertoire by which viewers recognize the series genre and subgenre. Likewise, plot must attract the viewer away from the flow of a competing station while maintaining the rhythm of the evening's viewing for viewers already tuned in for the series that plays before it. Each episode must hold viewers in their seats and waiting for more—more series the next week, and more television that same night—when it ends.

Macroflow

Women in the fanzine community may be drawn to particular source products through viewing weekly broadcasts of a favorite program, or they may be initiated during short bursts of compressed multiple-episode viewing. Surprisingly, women in both groups report the same experience—time compression in viewing seems to result in the same cognitive organization of the new material that time dilation in weekly broadcasts produces.

In the early stages of attraction either as a loyal weekly viewer or as a weekend initiate, the fan prioritizes the macroflow.[24] Much of the early ordering of the macroflow involves discerning the nature of the characters portrayed. Barbara Tennison had seen parts of the first and third seasons of *Blake's 7* on tape when she attended More Eastly Con. While at the convention, Barbara saw "Gambit" and "Star One," both popular second-season episodes. In a letter to Jean Curley she tries to fit the two second-season episodes into the shifting structure she is creating out of the macroflow:

> The one [second-season] episode I've seen, aside from "Star One," is "Gambit," which a lot of people seem to like inordinately—why? Is it just the fancy trappings of Freedom City; or the strain of humor which does not seem to me all that strongly in character; or the convoluted intrigue between Servalan and Travis [villains of the series]?
>
> I do recall that Avon there was neither the standoffish automaton of the early first season, nor the unreachable, infallible leader-by-default of the third season. He may not have had much time for Blake at that point, but he was getting on pretty well with Vila.[25]

Barbara suggests several reasons why the episode may be one of the most popular of the series; all but one have to do with the interactions of the characters. She comments on character development and relationships, and dismisses the humor as inappropriate, dropping that contradictory information (that these characters can interact with humor at no one's expense) from the map she is building of the series. As more material becomes available, the viewer makes a conscious effort to fit new episodes into the map she is building; she complains if a current episode contradicts others that preceded it. A picture builds over time to make a unified, coherent, and seemingly complete map of the series universe in the mind of the viewer. That map, however, is constructed out of the macroflow, in which the meaningful combination of the action and the dialogue becomes fragmented and lost. Words become generalized concepts, and action, relationship.[26] Details that reinforce the coherence of the ongoing whole may remain, while contradictory or conflicting information drops out of the meaningful structuring of the series universe.

Caren Parnes' recounting of a *Professionals* episode demonstrates how macroflow works. Caren and I had seen most of the episodes of the series, but several others who were listening had not, and at least one participant in the extended conversation specifically stated that she had not seen the series at all. We discussed how fanwriting based on the anti-terrorist characters and premise seemed much grittier than the fiction centered on the *Star Trek* universe, and Caren demonstrates her point with this summary of an episode of *The Professionals:*

Caren: . . . The end of "Fall Girl" has to be the ultimate ending to an episode, where you're turning and going, "How can you end an episode this way!"[27]

. . . this whole organization that Bodie [an agent] has worked for has set—well, Cowley [his boss] didn't, but even Cowley used him to his own purposes—has set him up. He ran into a woman he loved at one time, and she has been used—um, she is why the episode name is "Fall Girl"—for a political coup MI5, which is a rival agency, and Cowley didn't realize that his man, Bodie, was going to be used as the scapegoat for this episode—where he was going to look like the murderer of, um, this woman's husband that they wanted to get rid of.

And they end up—she does get killed—he thinks at the end of the episode, Bodie thinks that Doyle [his partner] has betrayed him, because he's [Doyle's] been following him all over. Cowley has told him [Doyle] to put surveillance on Bodie, and he's been following him [Bodie] and Bodie saw him [Doyle] tailing him

[Bodie]. And you know that he's deeply hurt and disturbed by this.

Ethnographer: [referring back to the beginning of Caren's description] And he thinks Cowley's set him up.

Caren: (ironic) Well that's a kind of minor, just, detail, yes, he comes in—he's supposed to be allowed to escape when he's captured, Cowley's supposed to have set this up with the man. The man turns around right after he gets off the phone with Cowley and says, "shoot him" [Bodie]. And so, when he makes his attempted escape it's almost not an attempt. It's almost as though—of course, what's he to think but that Cowley set him up?

And this man [Bodie] is not a man who trusts easily anyway. The only two people in the world he does trust are Cowley and Doyle, and both of them have just betrayed him, he thinks. He's on a water tower at the end, with an Uzi. And he's standing alone there against most of the force of MI5 and Cowley comes up at just about the point where this woman he's had an affair with is having a conversation, with him on the water tower, saying, "it wasn't me, I didn't do it," because he thinks that she betrayed him a second time also—she betrayed him once before. And she gets shot in the back by the MI5 people, because she has to be dead for this whole scheme to work.

And they were going to shoot Bodie to get him out of the way, and Cowley comes in and stops the whole thing. And Doyle, like a dodo, is supposed to have been guarding the woman, and he's so worried about Bodie that these guys just shoot her, and it's a very weird sort of ending.

And Bodie comes down, shoves the gun into Doyle's chest and does he say anything to Doyle? No, he doesn't—he just turns and walks away, and Cowley goes after him. Doyle wants to, and Cowley won't let him. There's a total lack of trust and understanding between all of them at the end, and Bodie's just been used.

And it's sort of—it's not typical, but a lot of the episodes ended with that kind of a feel . . . But anyway, it's got a very gritty, realistic feel to it, this whole series.[28]

In examining this recount, we notice several characteristic traits of descriptions in the macroflow. We are given no physical descriptions of scenes, settings, or characters. Only the regular, ongoing characters are named, but in Caren's narrative even the names of key characters are seldom used. Caren uses pronouns for most of her narrative, and her listeners are expected to (and do) follow who is doing what to whom in a structural rather than material sense. By contrast, fans will talk about Marrika, the woman, and Willis, the head of MI5, by name when those details are significant to the point under discussion.

Caren describes only two actual scenes from this episode in even the sketchiest terms: Bodie escapes, and Bodie is on a water tower. The escape is an example, and is told with as little detail as the rest of the narrative. However, the scene on the water tower is the moment that symbolically expresses for Caren the meaning of the series. At this point, she switches into microflow analysis: the setting is explicit, a water tower.

In this segment, Caren uses the names of key characters for most transactions, and she adds dialogue in context, as she remembers it. When Caren crosses over into description of the microflow, however, she still tells us only what she considers significant detail. The setting is described simply as "a water tower," and it is not made clear where the characters in the scene are located in respect to one another—is the woman on the tower with Bodie or is she speaking from a distance? We do not know why MI5 wants the woman dead, why that agency wants the blame to fall on her erstwhile lover, or why said lover must likewise die. These are details of plot that fans perceive as irrelevant to the map the series makes in the viewer's head. In contrast, great care and attention are focused on the assumed betrayal by friends of the central character in this episode, Bodie. That in fact his friends did not betray him but were in their turn betrayed by MI5 does not lessen the stress on betrayal and trust.

Caren's narrative ends where it began, at the episode's final scene, where trust has been lost, friendships broken, and understanding seems far away. Then Caren uses the ending to characterize the series as a whole. It is important to note that the episode Caren chooses to characterize the series is one of its most extreme examples of alienation, and many fans dislike "Fall Girl" for the very reasons Caren describes.

The women in the media fanzine community use their art as well as more objective discussion to comment on and analyze the broader narrative of the macroflow of their favorite source products as it takes shape through the selective reading process. Fans create their own video interpretations in songtapes, music videos that combine a popular song, chosen because it expresses the meaning the fan wishes to explore, with clips from the series. The visual images of the songtape not only expose a message implied over time in the source product but may also reinforce that interpretation of the message by using the very text—clips from the episodes—to identify that same message read across the corpus of the series. The analysis by many women in the fanzine community that women in the *Star Trek* universe shared equal professional status with men arises out of just such a selective reading of the macroflow, which Mary Suskind reinforces in her song-tape that highlights the character Uhura.

In the original television series *Star Trek,* female characters frequently appeared as transitory crew members who abandoned their posts for romance. The ongoing character of Lieutenant Uhura performed her duties competently at all times, however, and under the same stressful conditions as her male counterparts. Mary Suskind's songtape shows Uhura performing competently at her own position and in emergencies at other bridge stations as well. By focusing on Uhura, the songtape supports the notion developed over time in the macroflow that women are competent members of Starfleet.[29] The incompetence of the single-episode female character is discarded, often consciously, while fans refer to the professional title she held to support the view that women perform as competent professionals in many areas of Starfleet.[30]

Of course, not all fans arrive at the same reading when they construct their maps of the program universe: the experience they bring to viewing prioritizes different bits of information. A woman sensitized to the negative portrayal of women on television may incorporate into her map of the macroflow the incompetence of the single-episode female character rather than the high valorization of her title. From this point of view, Uhura may be seen as competent but oppressed. Mary Suskind's songtape may not sway the opinion of a woman entering the community with a minority interpretation, but it will teach her the majority map she must address—positively or negatively—if she wants to engage in the community's discourse.

The macroflow of episodic television series like *Starsky and Hutch* or *Star Trek* is a function of circumstance and group consensus rather than design. Most of the episodes may be viewed in any order without seriously modifying the overall sense of the series.[31] The action is encapsulated, and the growing experience of the actors with their characters is the only clue to development in the macroflow.

For fans of *Blake's 7,* however, the macroflow is built into the source product itself. Over the course of the four seasons, the viewer watches the crew members grow to trust each other, she sees Blake, the title character, devolve into megalomania. Intragroup discussion—in letters, like the following exchange between Jean Curley and Barbara Tennison, or in person—formalizes the interpretation of the doomed struggle of those Blake leaves behind against the forces of oppression and madness.

Jean, writing to Barbara in December of 1985, offers her view of Blake's downfall:

. . . [during the second season] [t]he bleeding-heart leader [Blake] is giving in to the pressures of his position and turning callous and manipulative . . . survival is no longer the goal—retaliation is, and retaliation in a *big* way. Perhaps all the meddling with his mind finally is driving Blake crazy . . . he is willing to kill almost everyone in the universe to get even with the Federation.[32]

In her response, which takes Jean's explanation a step further, Barbara disagrees with the actor's interpretation of his own role:

Gareth Thomas has complained in interviews that Blake started out idealistic but ruthless, and the show got more flashy but less violent, aimed more at children by the second season. He doesn't say anything about the on-camera fighting being replaced by abstract, distant killing, but that's the sort of thing that might have bothered Blake intellectually. If he thought it was necessary, it would have been a pressure on him that might have sent him toward insanity . . . When he realized that any revolution of a scale that would touch the Federation as a whole would inevitably entail massive deaths, he was probably faced with an insoluble problem. He may even have thrown in the towel, mentally speaking. . .[33]

Exchanges like this reinforce a fan's confidence that she has achieved a degree of competence in "reading" the series. She will now begin to make minute-by-minute choices to accept or reject the immediate real-time message based on the expectations that arise out of the internalized "rightness" of the macroflow to which the members of her interest group or circle have contributed.

While the most successful series episodes forward continuity of character definition throughout, bits of character business most consistently appear in the tag. In an untaped interview, Lin Place voiced a common complaint among fans trying to agree on a shared interpretation: syndication packagers generally shorten episodes to accommodate more commercials in the viewing hour. Packagers of syndicated action programming consistently cut tags and bits of character definition in lieu of shortening car chases or eroding plot structure. Fans of popular series may align themselves with opposing viewpoints about characters and their actions based on whether the fan has seen uncut episodes or re-edited showings. Still other viewers may wonder at the poor taste of friends who have praised a series for the very traits that are lost in syndicated repeats.

As Lin Place's complaint about series editing for syndication shows, the picture the fan actually sees is not nearly so complete as she may believe. An equally important part of the experience of watching television is the action the viewer does not see but assumes to have occurred. The perceptual consciousness, the cognitive map of the series universe, includes action seen and interpreted, and action inferred as necessary to arrive at a satisfactory interpretation. Viewers assume the quotidian details—that the characters eat, eliminate, and sleep—are played out in some netherworld that continues after they turn off the television. The appearance of these activities in an episode marks them as symbolically significant, and viewers may prioritize their occurrence in the microflow.

Microflow

The viewer builds out of the macroflow a map of her favorite program, but the macroflow itself is created out of the microflow—clusters of relational movements and contrastive actions that appear in individual episodes, often in the tags, and that absorb considerably more conceptual time than real viewing time. When a *Star Trek* fan spoke of IDIC—". . . [h]ow fast did it last on the show? It went gallop, gallop, gallop, and all of the people are out there going 'Ah!'"[34]—she was describing the experience of identifying pivotal moments in the microflow.

But some elements in the microflow only develop significance when they are repeated over time. The line "He's dead, Jim," as delivered by Dr. McCoy in *Star Trek,* is such an example. The line helps to define the character of the doctor, and in a sense the deadpan scientism of the series. It also points up a major contradiction built into the program—violent death occurs with dismaying frequency on a mission self-described as a peaceful one of exploration and first contact. Fan Leslie Fish has written a song using the line as its title, theme, and chorus, and the line appears on slogan buttons made within the community.[35] Importantly, like other examples of microflow interactions, the line does not appear in the series as often as the attention fans give it would lead one to believe.

The above examples demonstrate that microflow may arise out of a word or a phrase, but slightly longer exchanges may likewise define an aspect of a series. The *Blake's 7* episode "Star One" falls at the end of the second season, but most fans find two scenes in the episode so significant to the development of their map of the Blake and Avon relationship that they often use "Star One" to introduce new fans to the series.[36] In the macroflow, Avon is perceived as a voice crying out in the wilderness—". . . he [Avon] has always stood rather apart from the other figures, and has opposed Blake on the stupid moves that he perceives Blake does" [fan at convention, 1985]. Avon rarely demonstrates his attachments with overt emotional display, but he often proves his loyalty through actions in direct contradiction of his words, as Barbara Tennison describes in an open computer-net letter:

> He [Avon] tends to emote with an eyedropper instead of a waterfall, and always has a 'logical' reason why he's a) saved your life, b) saved the ship, c) saved some planet's population from being enslaved by the EVIL VILE NASTY **FEDERATION**, instead of letting anyone possibly think he might be (at least before the fourth season) a decent human being under all the nastiness. He does this REGULARLY.[37]

A short scene early in the "Star One" episode seems to define the relationship between the two main characters—Avon as unwilling follower, Blake as leader grown obsessive with failure. In the scene, Blake has reasserted his intention to destroy the computer complex that controls the environment on a number of populated planets. He realizes that millions of people will die by his actions. Many fans, mentor Jean Curley among them, memorize Avon's response and deliver it like a Shakespearean soliloquy, as Paul Darrow did in the episode:

> Avon: "As far as I'm concerned you can destroy whatever you wish. Stir up a thousand revolutions. Wade through blood up to your armpits and lead the rabble to victory, whatever that is. When Star One's gone it's finished, Blake. I want it over and done with. I want to be free![38]

In the next exchange the viewer is explicitly told what she implicitly knows: Avon wants to be free of his attachment to the leader, Blake. But it is the soliloquy, over in seconds, that fans remember and recite.

In discussion, community members stress the ambiguity of the relationship between Blake and Avon. Blake is described as "the consummate manipulator—it is extraordinary what he can do with the interpersonal relationships on board ship, and Avon gets sucked in even though he knows what is going on."[39] This tendency of Avon's to follow Blake is set in contrast to the more openly stated disillusionment: "He [Avon] was caught [embezzling] because he trusted someone else—you're never supposed to trust people."[40] In the scene described above, Avon not only sums up his relationship with the rebel leader but also sets their values in contrast—Blake has lost his reverence for life in his quest for "winning," while Avon's cynicism is seen as the result of many disappointments, not least of which is Blake himself.

The second oft-quoted scene from "Star One" falls at the very end of the episode and epitomizes in a few short words this ambiguity in the relationship between the two main characters. Avon has promised an injured Blake that he will hold off an invading alien force, but Blake struggles to the ship's bridge anyway. Avon confronts him: "Don't you trust me, Blake?"[41] Blake answers: "I have always trusted you, Avon, from the very beginning," and leaves the bridge before the battle begins.

The questions of who to trust, how far, and with what, are central to the group's own writing and to its organization as a community. The scene in question surfaces in the source product the most pressing questions in the community. It carries within it the knowledge of community members that trust withheld is trust broken, and the concomitant fear that trust may be offered as a form of manipulation.

In the microflow we find the small segments of interaction that sum up in a stroke a complex of relationships within the source product. In the most striking examples, the interaction crosses the boundary between artifice and art, and acts symbolically within the community itself.

Notes

1. Those interest areas each too small to support a group of their own, but which nonetheless generate some fan fiction and when taken as a group constitute a significant fandom.
2. Taped viewing session, More Eastly Con, New York, August 1985.
3. Ibid.
4. Jean Curley, taped group interview, More Eastly Con, August 1985.
5. Pam Auditore, ibid.
6. Ibid.
7. I did not have a tape recorder with me at the time and so must paraphrase from my field notes.
8. Lin Place, taped group interview, Mt. Holly, New Jersey, June 1987.
9. Shayne McCormack, ibid.
10. Taped group interview, Mt. Holly, New Jersey, June 1987.
11. In 1988 I had a follow-up visit with Lisa. She had added a few *Blake's 7* episodes to her videotape collection but had only recently made her first committed acquisition in the tape library—the collected episodes of a short-lived fantasy-satire, *Wizards and Warriors*.
12. Paul Darrow, taped interview, Philadelphia, November 1986.
13. Michael Keating, taped interview, Philadelphia, November, 1986.
14. Jean Curley, taped group interview, New York, August 1985.

15. For a good description of the selective reading process of romance readers see Janice Radway, "Interpretive Communities and Variable Literacies: The Functions of Romance Reading," *Anticipations, Proceedings of the American Academy of Arts and Sciences,* vol. 113, no. 3 (1984): 49–73.

16. Raymond Williams, *Television, Technology, and Cultural Form* (New York: Schocken Books, 1975).

17. Mihalyi Czikszentmihalyi, *Beyond Boredom and Anxiety* (San Francisco: Jossey-Bass, 1975).

18. Csikszentmihalyi, writing a number of years after Williams, does not cite the latter in his work.

19. Stephen Cannell has broken from this model with shows like *Wiseguy,* in which the action takes place over a number of weeks, and over the course of which a history is built up and called upon much as fans do in their own stories.

20. Taped group discussion, Champaign, Ill., June 1986.

21. Parnes, taped interview, Cockeysville, Md., February 1987.

22. While not ready to challenge the big fandoms for series like *Star Trek, Miami Vice's* popularity in fandom seems to have grown since the show went off the air.

23. Unidentified fan, More Eastly Con, August 1985.

24. The construction of macroflow and microflow in the latter half of this chapter does not draw on the construction described as microflow in Czikszentmihalyi's *Beyond Boredom and Anxiety.* Rather, the terms *micro* and *macro* as used here refer to extent of encompassment, not significance of effect.

25. Personal correspondence, Barbara Tennison to Jean Curley, January 1986, passed on to me with the permission of the sender.

26. Tamar Liebes notes a similar process in Israeli viewers of *Dallas* ("Ethnocentrism: Israelis of Moroccan Ethnicity Negotiate the Meaning of 'Dallas.'" *Studies in Visual Communication* 10, no. 3 [1989]: 48–71). *Dallas,* of course, continued an open storyline from week to week. Study with the media fanzine community points out that the same process goes on even when producers do not deliberately build continuity and development from week to week.

27. Beginning with the ending of a story is also typical of women relating personal experience narratives. See Susan Kalčik, "'Like Ann's Gynecologist or the Time I was Almost Raped': Personal Narratives in Women's Rap Groups," in *Women and Folklore,* ed. Claire Farrer (Austin: University of Texas Press, 1975), pp. 3–11.

28. Caren Parnes, taped interview, Cockeysville, Md., February 1987.

29. Songtapes will be discussed more fully in Chapter 7.

30. Janice Radway describes a similar strategy among romance readers, who award female characters the status of their job titles while discarding the behaviors that contradict the high status of their labels ("Interpretive Communities and Variable Literacies: The Functions of Romance Reading").

31. In fact the episodes shot first for a new series, while actors and writers were still searching for the right formula for characters and relationships, were often shown later in the season. Later episodes, with characters and relationships already developed, were often shown first to attract viewers.

32. Personal correspondence, Jean Curley to Barbara Tennison, December 1985; used with permission.

33. Personal correspondence, Barbara Tennison to Jean Curley, January 1986.

34. Group discussion, More Eastly Con, August 1985.

35. See Stephanie Hall, "Reality is a Crutch for People Who Can't Deal with Science Fiction," *Keystone Folklore* (1989): 19–31, for explanation of slogan buttons, and in particular for the lamination of meanings loaded into the short messages.

36. Ironically, the very significance that fans find in these exchanges is so embedded in an understanding of the series to that point that prospective fans meeting "Star One" as their first experience with the product leave it knowing they have had a meaningful encounter with series fandom, but not knowing what that meaning was supposed to be—the experience of encountering the episode is emptied of content, has not yet taken on symbolic meaning, and is experienced only as a potentially meaningful moment. Fans assume, correctly in many cases, that when they have developed the proper understanding of the series, they will fall back on the memory of their first viewing of "Star One" as a meaningful experience.

37. Barbara Tennison, computer correspondence, October 1985; used with permission.

38. Chris Boucher, rehearsal script for "Star One," *Blake's 7* (1979), p. 13.

39. Unidentified fan in convention video room, More Eastly Con, New York, August 1985.

40. Second fan, adding to conversation, ibid.

41. Script, "Star One," pp. 126–27.

Chapter Six
Reading Fan Fiction

During my videotape initiation into the British and fringe fandoms, I continued to accumulate *Star Trek* fan fiction from conventions and other sources, and *Blake's 7* and other fiction through Jean Curley and her contacts. During this period I discovered more fiction that included women as strong characters, and I began to read the fiction that focused exclusively on the male characters of the source products.

The New Strong Woman

I found that, increasingly, women in the fan community were turning away in their fiction from the ideal of marriage and family for complete fulfillment. Female characters like Susan in *The Displaced*, who had once satisfied a need for women characters of strength and purpose next to their male source product counterparts, fell into the expanding category of Mary Sue. In dismissing their own female creations, fan women were left with a dilemma: what is the strong woman?

Members often perceive strength in each other; they know that they are stronger in their community than they are outside of it. But the models offered up for inspection in the media and in their own products fall short of an ideal they have not yet formulated. When a reader or writer dismisses a story like *The Displaced* as a Mary Sue, she seems to be saying, This model doesn't satisfy me anymore. I want to be something else; I don't know what that is yet, I'll know it when I see it, but I haven't seen it yet.[1]

Part of the problem may be intrinsic to the product. *Star Trek* promotes the belief that the system works for everyone, but shows few examples of women acting with strength and independence. Writer and editor Florence Butler describes a strong, competent Uhura in her fiction, and with co-editor Lee Coleman, encourages writers in her fanzine, *Destiny's Children*,[2] to give forceful portrayals of the women in *Star Trek*. Many fanwriters, however, point to power gained through marriage and family connection as the best opportunity to make the *Star Trek* system work for them.

While the debate about female characters goes on in person and in the letterzines, however, a small but growing number of believable, tough women characters have appeared in the fan literature, particularly of source products based on the premise that the system does not work for anyone. *Blake's 7* includes as characters women warriors in a rebellion against an oppressive Federation and a strong woman villain, leader of the armed forces and later president.

In the many *Blake's 7* stories and fanzines my mentor Jean gave me before the series began airing in the United States, writers here and abroad were using these women characters as strong figures in their own work. In Sandy Hall's "Easy to Be Hard,"[3] Auron rebel Cally is on a mission with the thief Vila to steal crystals from the Federation. They are captured, and Avon and Tarrant, two male rebels, come to their rescue. Dayna Mellanby, the young woman weapons expert, guards the spaceship and stands ready to teleport them all to safety when the rescuers have found their comrades. The ship is attacked, and Dayna destroys six enemy vessels to win the fight. While she defends the ship, Federation interrogators torture Cally. (Vila escapes interrogation, first by feigning aftereffects of the drug used in their capture and later by becoming very drunk on the liquor hidden in the infirmary.)

Auronae are transmitting telepaths. Cally can send mind messages, but she can receive only from other transmitting telepaths like herself. Her defenses crumble under interrogation and she inadvertently transmits her pain to Avon, who nevertheless stands off from rescuing her until the ship has returned to orbit and can lift them off the planet. He explains to his younger companion that they would have no way to hide and would surely be recaptured if they completed the rescue before Dayna could retrieve them all. When Dayna does return after successfully defeating enemy forces, Avon and Tarrant carry out the rescue and they all escape safely on the rebel ship.

This story, characteristic of earlier work in the *Blake's 7* source product, shows the reader two strong women. In the initial landing party, Cally is the stronger of the two: ". . . Locks and safes he [Vila] could deal with very well; but roaming around in dark hallways with guards all over the place waiting to pounce on him wasn't his line at all. It was Cally's, though . . ."[4]

When they are captured, Cally is perceived to be strong enough to undergo interrogation, while Vila seems too weak to withstand the process. Cally's suffering is not that of the damsel in distress but of the warrior in battle, and she is treated accordingly by her comrades. At the beginning of the story Dayna would seem to have been given the passive role, but she proves an active and competent warrior in the space battle, defeating many times her number of the enemy. Hall had to work at putting Dayna in the active position here. Tarrant is the ship's pilot and the more appropriate crew member to leave behind—and to conduct the space battle—but his passive role in the story allows him to do little more than rail at Avon for not rescuing their comrades more quickly.

Because the fanwriters had strong women characters in the source product, *Blake's 7* fiction exhibited much less of the spunky ingenue/superwoman syndrome we see in the *Star Trek* fiction. The women worked competently beside the men, doing as much as their male counterparts, but they didn't need to be better than the men to receive as much respect as any crew member gave another in Blake's crew. Cally might be characterized as more understanding than other crew members, but Dayna was more bloodthirsty, Soolin more distant. They did exist as viable characters.

When the program reached a wider audience in the United States through PBS broadcasting, however, two things changed the shape of the fiction. *Star Trek* fans entered the new media fandom, bringing their established writing models with them, and *Blake's 7* stars began appearing widely on the convention circuit. Paul Darrow and Michael Keating appeared with greater frequency than the other actors, and many writers latched onto the pair as a substitute for Kirk and Spock. Incoming fanwriters shifted their attention to the three men in the first two seasons of episodes, Blake, Avon, and Vila, often assigning to Vila the role Dr. McCoy filled in *Star Trek*. Few stories in the fanzines I have seen since 1987 feature women characters other than the villainess Servalan in any but infrequent subordinate or romantic roles.

In part this creative failure by the majority to portray their own sex seems due to the particular group of *Star Trek* writers who entered the *Blake's 7* fandom and found themselves locked into thought and writing patterns of their own earlier devising. In part, too, it signals a continuing dissatisfaction with the options available to women characters and to women in society. In spite of the radically different social organization of their community life, an overwhelming number of fan readers and writers continue to believe at some level that respect, honor, and happiness should come to them with a fulfilling career and an extended matriarchal family including husband, children, and ancillary relatives whose lives are gently directed by the woman. At the same time, experience teaches them that they can have none of these things—that they will pass through lives not of their own making, often with less than interesting jobs and with families in which they are the dependent, not the powerful, member. Not yet ready to take on the role of woman warrior, they have grown bitter and cynical about the only other model they have.

While the majority of fans languish in this morass of uncertainty about the direction women characters should take, a very few fan-writers have created strong women in fan fiction built around the police dramas. As I have described before, fans configure the media universes around the relationships of the characters; action is the medium in which those relationships are expressed. Fans of series like *Starsky and Hutch* and *The Professionals* value the strong male bond they find in the programs and often resent any efforts by a writer to come between the friends with another relationship. Occasionally, however, a character created in the community does capture the imagination of fan readers. Some of these characters even move from one source product to the other. Deborah June Laymon's Jordan Lang, a geologist whose experience in South Africa has given her training in both mercenary tactics and tribal witchcraft, has appeared in stories set in both the *Miami Vice* and the *Professionals* universes. While she does have sexual relationships in both settings, her identity does not depend on those relationships, nor does she depend upon the men in the stories for her power as an active agent in her own destiny. I have never heard Jordan Lang referred to as a Mary Sue, and in fact, response to her comes closer to "that's it" than it does for any other character I have seen in any of the fan communities.[5]

By contrast, in a very short period of time *Beauty and the Beast* inspired a vast body of fiction in the modern romance mold highlighting a woman character. Catherine escaped the rubric Mary Sue, with its connotation of fantasy self-aggrandizement, because writers portrayed her relationship with the beast-like Vincent much as it appeared on the screen. For many women, however, that relationship symbolized the real struggle of the modern woman: financially secure through her own work as a lawyer in the District Attorney's office, Catherine found sexual fulfillment and family just beyond her reach, across a chasm of difference.

Unfortunately, series creators succumbed to the Mary Sue syndrome where fans had carefully avoided it. In the final season, Catherine did have a brief sexual experience with the leonine beast, Vincent. She was then captured by villains who hold her prisoner throughout her pregnancy, murder her, and steal her child. The final season was Vincent's quest to find, not his lost love, but his son. Fan response did persuade the network not to replace Catherine in Vincent's heart with the new love interest they had hired, but the final season killed the enthusiasm many fans had for the series and the characters.

The Relationship Story

When I first began exploring the fan community, mentors warned me about Mary Sue stories and led me to lay-Spock matriarchal erotica and the male-male friendship story, called the relationship story. Whereas the matriarchal erotica has fallen into disfavor in many circles, stories about male friendships have grown in popularity.

Relationship stories about a hero dyad are integral to every aspect of fan literature. Mary Sue enters into the comradely relationship of the hero dyad, and the erotic matriarch of the lay-Spock story must fit her family relationship with the hero into or around his male relationships.[6]

The television episodes themselves are the principal source of relationship, or male-bonding, stories. The women fans of action-adventure television view the weekly plots as proving grounds, meaningful only to the extent they test the relationships and personal integrity of the ongoing characters. April Selley[7] has pointed out that the relationship between Kirk and Spock in the television series fits the pattern of the archetypal hero dyad described by Leslie Fiedler.[8] Patricia Frazer Lamb and Diana Vieth go further, and cite that same pattern in the fan fiction about male relationships.[9] Fan stories explore the relationships of hero dyads or triads before, during, and after the period covered by the televised episodes, imagining those relationships in female terms that often tie the dyad back into family and community.

In Claire Gabriel's "Metamorphosis,"[10] a childhood encounter with his captain of later life makes up one episode in a story about Spock growing up. The young Spock is reprimanded for daydreaming after he encounters a nine-year-old "Jimmy" in a museum. Jimmy is cocky and sure of himself and his wit, and the young Spock is fascinated by the other child's daring and lack of restraint. Jimmy, of course, will grow up to become James T. Kirk, captain of the *Enterprise* and Spock's best friend.

In Jean Lorrah's *Epilogue* series,[11] an aged Kirk returns to Spock's family on Vulcan for telepathic treatments to cure his failing mental faculties, and he relives with the family Spock's and Amanda's experience during the Klingon-Romulan war against the Federation. The Kraith series by Jacqueline Lichtenberg[12] gives us a Kirk adopted by Spock's family because his association with Spock brings out a latent telepathic ability best dealt with in the Vulcan family setting.

Relationship stories are common in the literature around every source product I have examined, and they often depend on the elements of telepathy and empathy as metaphors for the experience of closeness that women value so highly in their relationships. What the masculine analyst would call weak ego boundary development, women see as the ideal of social relatedness. In Carol Gilligan's *In a Different Voice*, informant Claire, a physician, accurately describes the ethic that informs the metaphor of telepathy in fan fiction. Gilligan says:

> Although a person may not like someone else: "You have to love someone else, because you are inseparable from them. In a way, it's like loving your right hand; it is part of you . . . the stranger is still another person belonging to that group, people you are connected to by virtue of being another person."
>
> Claire describes morality as "being part of something larger and a sort of self-contained entity."[13]

While stories based on *Star Trek* and Vulcan telepathy epitomize the ideal of belonging, as the right hand belongs to the body, stories about *Blake's 7*'s Avon most sharply convey the tension Claire describes, between being a part of something and being a self-contained entity. Sandy Hall's "The Scars That Won't Heal"[14] demonstrates this conflict. As developed in Hall's text, an incident occurring during a fourth-season episode creates out of Avon, Dayna, Soolin, and Tarrant an empathic gestalt personality that Avon can neither accept nor escape. In the story, the characters must first become aware of why Avon is becoming so unreachable—he finds their closeness intolerable—and then take measures to correct the problem.

Although predicated upon a four-part gestalt, the relationships in "The Scars That Won't Heal" reduce to two dyads. Avon and Dayna, the latter of whom tries to protect the former from the painful closeness of his companions, constitute the first dyad, and Tarrant and Soolin, who feel threatened by Avon's rejection of the gestalt, constitute the second. Avon's attitude contrasts sharply with that of the other characters who do not find their empathic relationship burdensome, and on the contrary, wish to draw Avon more deeply into the group rather than see him break away.

Gilligan describes the female image of safety as a web of relationships, in which security is found at the center, anchored at all points by mutual responsibility. The masculine image of safety, by contrast, is a hierarchy marked by separation and diminished responsibility to or for others.[15]

Hall captures this dynamic precisely in her characterizations of the alpha male Avon and his companions in the gestalt. Her story also reflects the ideal minimal unit of social organization within the community. For the women in fandom, the center of the web is the dyadic or triadic[16] friendship that shapes or enters into the wider circles of fan interaction. Women's media fandom takes this configuration not out of some fluke but out of values stated in all its fiction, and most plainly in the relationship story.

One final example by Mystery Frank writing as Victoria Sinall, which appeared in a fanzine based on *The Professionals,* draws on a variety of partnership source products to support the story's premise that explicitly states this belief in the dyadic core at the center of the fan community's social system. In Frank's "Listening at the Keyhole," Raymond Doyle has been injured and a staff physician lectures his assisting interns while he conducts his examination. Unconscious at first, Doyle struggles to awareness, continually calling for his partner. The doctor discovers Doyle is a CI5 agent and admonishes his staff: ". . . He has a partner. And you *never* separate partners. They'll do anything to get back to each other . . . this is how you deal with partners—police, agents, best friends, whatever." He sends a nurse to fetch the partner, upon whose arrival the patient relaxes and is whisked off for treatment. When his younger assistants ask how the senior physician came to recognize the nature of the partnership bond, he names other media characters he has treated.[17] Participants in the fan community recognize these characters from their own relationship fiction, and understand the message that the story is to be generalized beyond the scope of its few short pages.

The reference to best friends in the story is not made casually. Many fans rely on their friendships for support in time of grief or when they are ill. Friends share houses and apartments and often become closer than family. The entire community is based upon the friendship bond, and its reification through all the source products in all its permutations underlies the most important communication of the community: How far will my friend go for me in an emergency, and how far will I go for her? What sacrifice is too much—any? How hard is it to be friends, when friends disagree or find themselves attracted to a new friend, a new source product, or a new genre? How can the new fan, isolated in her native community so long she thought it was her natural condition, accept the close friendship ties so valued

Caren Parnes' cover for *Nome 9* recalls the friendship of Kirk and Spock, and the life-threatening events of *Star Trek: The Motion Picture*.

Ann M. Crouch's Captain Kirk and Mr. Spock, with idic.

in the community? These are the questions fans ask each other, and constantly answer, in their relationship fiction.

Stories about the relationships of the on-screen characters give the writers added distance that the Mary Sue or lay-Spock does not afford them. The work that the fan's own created character did in the communication process is here subsumed under the creations of the commercial providers; the reader or writer can mask her message with her protest that she is only writing the character as it appears to her on the screen, or as the conventions of fan fiction dictate. But her message about caring, about the need to care and how difficult it is to care and to allow oneself to accept the caring of others, makes itself felt in no uncertain terms.

Learning How to Read: The Macroflow in Fan Fiction

Fans use their fiction to communicate their messages about their own lives, but those messages become intelligible by a process of learning how to read all over again. When I first began studying the fan community, it seemed that the women fans had chosen an unlikely set of source products around which to build culture. Members ignored traditionally "feminine" soap operas, with their interconnected structures,[18] for episodic action-adventure that offered few female role models and featured plot lines that seem to exist in a temporal limbo, with no readily discernible connection or order.

Over time I realized that the community draws women who engage the masculine cultural model of active agent, and who are looking for a way of understanding that vigor and integrating it into a female lifestyle. Fan culture teaches them how to reinterpret the heroic figure in mass media in terms of a feminine culture model of emotional relatedness through the process of reading and writing the fan fiction.

Neophytes entering the community may have a knowledge of a given television series, but their reading experience is that of an outsider. At this level the new member does not experience the fan fiction as communication; as yet she doesn't even know that the possibility exists. The community has an interest in using its product as language, however, and training new members in the language of fan literature takes a high priority in fan activities. Training begins with reading, a process that can be compared to the fan's experience of interpreting the television series.

Few fans begin their introduction to fan fiction with one story. Many fans report that, when introduced to fan fiction, they "read everything they could get their hands on."[19] Mentors will often present their neophytes with stacks of fanzines, or engage them in weekend initiations of total immersion in the fan fiction culture. Fans commonly report that they reread many of their favorite works, but the first reading, even for insider community members, tends to be demarcated in inches or stacks rather than in titles.

While the new fan is absorbing the fiction in bulk, however, mentors such as Judy Segal and Jean Curley start the neophyte's education with a liberal selection of stories that relate apparently transparent—"naturalized"—events similar to the experience of the macroflow of television. That is, the reader experiences the literature not as "real" in the traditional sense of fictional "realism," but "real" in the sense that it creates no sense of disjuncture with the map of the series universe she has already created in her head. For example, the mentor may initiate a fan with a story that picks up a minor, perhaps even nonrecurring, character and builds a history of relationships between that character and another shown more prominently in the source product. In the *Star Trek* episode "Shore Leave" by Theodore Sturgeon, the viewer learns that Kirk once loved Ruth and still harbors strong feelings for her. Lynda Carraher's fan story, "Prelude,"[20] posits that Ruth is the communications officer of a ship on which Kirk has temporary command. They are in love, but Ruth releases him, refusing to accompany him when he receives his commission as captain of the *Enterprise*. She knows that he must be free to pursue his destiny among the stars, and they part.

It is possible to appreciate the story without having seen the episode from which the author draws Ruth, but fans of the source product know what Ruth looks like. The fan knows that on the shore leave planet that fulfills every fantasy, Kirk chooses to re-create the Ruth he carries in his memory over all the women he has known and experiences he has had. The knowledgeable viewer brings to her reading a preconception of the kind of woman Ruth must have been, based on the short scene on the screen, and the story satisfies the reader with a possible why and how the affair ended that fulfills the expectations raised by the episode.

Stories like C. E. Roush's "Assignment: Enterprise"[21] help the reader to move single *Star Trek* episodes out of temporal ambiguity and into time frames that shape a history out of discontinuous series episodes. In "Assignment: Enterprise," an expert in group dynamics must determine for the Starfleet admiralty the nature of the *Enterprise*'s singular success. This device allows Roush to examine the "logs"[22] of past adventures, tying them together into a history of events that live on as part of the experience of the crew. At the same time, the device gives the author an opportunity to analyze the working relationships of the crew members to their captain.

When fans move into the community they gain access to a wider variety of fan fiction. As readers they reorganize the body of fan literature they have read—literature that converges with or diverges from the source products that inspired it. Over time and with reinforcement from community members, the new fan selectively creates coherent meaning out of the body of fan fiction: the macroflow grows to include the community's literature. Interpretation operates from both community literature and commercial television to influence the map both sources create together in the mind of the reader.

Stories like Susan Matthews' *Blake 7* novel, *The Mind of a Man Is a Double Edged Sword*,[23] take this selection process a step further and demand of the reader that she create more than one map of a single source product. Some fans of *Blake's 7* feel that the program's direction changed dramatically in its last two seasons, replacing a harsh but hopeful worldview with a nihilistic message that diverged sharply from the preferred aesthetic of many members of the group. Several years before *Dallas*'s Bobby Ewing returned from the dead, Susan Matthews' novel explained that the last two seasons of *Blake's 7* represented the delusions created in the character Avon's mind by Federation brainwashing: it was all a dream.

Over the course of Matthews' novel, Avon must come to realize that his memories are false, that the companions he thought dead are alive, and that he did not do the terrible things he remembers, such as threatening to murder one friend, Vila, and murdering another, Blake. In this work the actions depicted in the last two seasons of the series are denied and replaced with a more acceptable scenario. The violence against the characters perceived as friends comes from outside the relationships in the novel, and not from within them, as postulated in the series.

A work like *Double-Edged Sword* integrates the series episodes into a temporal unity and explains them away again as delusions. If the community member in training accepts the novel as part of a single map of the series she is constructing in her head, she cannot make sense of stories that do not make this assumption. She must learn to juggle a variety of maps, called universes, and learn how to distinguish between them while finding companions who share an interest in the maps, or universes, she prefers.

Play, Humor, and Liminality: Writing a Story

At this point the reader may become an active member, organizing her social life around her preferred reading matter, or vice versa. She may begin to feel competent to manipulate the literary system of the community and express that competence, and her willingness to participate, with a story of her own. The avenues of distribution available to her will depend upon the social organization of her fan experience.

Roberta Rogow's fanzine *Grip* emphasizes a close adherence to the forms of the original source products in serious stories and a high percentage of playful and humorous stories. Roberta developed her publication specifically to give new writers an outlet. The newcomers do not have a broad knowledge of what has been done before, what fans appreciate and what they don't in their serious reading. Like many editors who work with new writers, Roberta frequently suggests that newcomers amend well-worn plots with a humorous twist. She recognizes that the beginning writer may not have mastered the codes and conventions she needs to write a story that the group, her readers, will take seriously. In humor, however, the neophyte inhabits a liminal area where she may practice the manipulation of the community's codes. Her readers will allow her errors to pass as the deliberate crossing of boundaries with which more experienced writers play in their own work.

In marked and extended form such as described here, play and humor signal liminality with regard to membership status in the group, and the work of men who write in the women's fanzines overwhelmingly falls into this category. To write a serious story seems to signal that the author takes the women's fanzine community and its writing seriously. Even men who actively participate in the fanwriting find it difficult to overcome the prejudice against the form in the masculine community. Humor bridges the uncomfortable gap between wanting to write in the fanzines and having expectations that real men don't write Treklit.[24]

Humor for these structurally liminoid participants—members who are not passing from one state to another but remain permanently betwixt and between[25]—signals protective coloration at the boundary of belonging: My writing in the fanzines is only a joke, like the joke I tell in the story. Unlike most of the women who write humor in the community, male trekwriters frequently make use of distorted naming in their stories, such as "Star Trek II: The Rash of Kon,"[26] with character names Captain Smirk, Mr. Spa, Mr. Solo for Kirk, Spock, and Sulu respectively. Changing the character names, like using humor itself, gives the writer a distance from the serious business of making community. "I'm just playing," both devices say, and add: "I'm not really using the same characters at all."

For most of the women who enter the community, however, liminal status occurs when they are learning the codes of the community and deciding that they want to become members, and briefly at intervals thereafter while they move from group to group entering more deeply into community life. Many new writers in the community will create a humorous situation in a first or early story by juxtaposing their friends and the heroes of their favorite source product in an incongruous situation. Fans identified by name may run amok on the starship *Enterprise*, driving Mr. Spock crazy, or the *Enterprise* heroes may beam down to a hotel convention where they may be swept up by the gleeful friends of the writer.

These first stories are usually very short, just a few pages, and they often have a very small circulation, confined to the writer's circle or a few interrelated circles. In an exaggerated way, these early stories parallel the experience of the newcomer: she integrates her friends in the narrative, and the creation of that narrative signals a desire for integration into the group.

When the writer moves more deeply into the community, wordplay in the fiction can function as social control much as it does in conversational wordplay. Experienced writers may use humor to comment indirectly upon the less well developed competence of others. The *Star Trek* parody "Stairs in His Eyes"[27] comments on the stories about Vulcan sexuality—pon farr stories—and the almost universal complaint about typographical errors in fanzines to concoct a mélange of puns and typographical hysteria. In the "story," Spock is in pon farr and has gone to Nurse Christine Chapel's quarters:

> Slyly he siddled across the deck, his face tinged aloof-green in his embezzlement. She smelled of lavatory water and he flushed harder . . .
> "I—am—bewhiched by you! he grasped in short pants as he swepted her off her feet and hoovered over her yawningly . . . she nobbled his ears and he could no longer contain his pission. She felt the bilge in his trousers and knew that her action had moved him . . . She discorded her flimsy negligent and slopped out of her brazier and his eyes lit up at the sight of her rosy tipples . . . They lay prune on the bed and began to divulge in erratic horeplay . . . she thought his technique was admiral, especially below the naval . . .
> "Naturally," he said, erupting into a passion of lava again, "I am a volcano."[28]

This story makes broad humor of writerly errors: typography, as in aloof-green for a leaf-green, which in itself might receive a humorous response, and bilge for bulge; inappropriate word choice, as in lavatory for toilette (water) and brazier for brassiere; and ambiguous construction, as in phrases like "he grasped in short pants" where an inappropriate word choice, grasped for gasped, combined with the prepositional phrase easily conjures the strange image of Spock holding up his short pants rather than breathing erratically.

To fully appreciate the intentional humor of this two-page lampoon, the reader must know the source product and the fiction well enough to make the correct substitutions for the referential humor. "I am a Volcano" makes twisted sense of "erupting into a passion of lava," but it is only funny if the reader knows that Spock is a Vulcan. The incongruity, raised here to the level of hysteria, is inherent in the character whose cool and emotionless facade works at odds with the mysterious and steamy history of the species that Roddenberry aptly named for the god of fire. The reader must also recognize in the intentionally funny work the kind of error that has caused unintended laughter in texts that were written with more serious intent than skill. Stories like "Stairs in His Eyes" both remind the community of its own shortcomings and teach newcomers to pay attention to the details of spelling and word choice in their fiction.

The significance of boundaries in the play of fiction is at its most overt in the cross-universe stories.[29] At their most basic, the author introduces the characters of one source product into the setting of another, and humor arises out of the confrontation between the characters that belong in that universe and those that have crossed the boundary. Cross-universe humor may be as obvious as a time-traveling Captain Kirk meeting an officer T. J. Hooker (both played by William Shatner) in twentieth-century Los Angeles, where both characters disavow any resemblance between them.

Barbara Hambly's published but very fannish *Star Trek* novel *Ishmael*,[30] however, embeds its cross-universe premise so deeply that only highly knowledgeable insiders can decipher it. In a fairly typical time travel premise, Barbara crossed *Star Trek* with the series *Here Come the Brides*. Klingons abandoned an injured Spock in nineteenth-century Seattle, where Aaron Stemple helps him to recover. During his recovery, Spock brings together the characters of Stemple and Biddie, who marry at the end of the book. The book is loaded with references to other source products—Doctor Who makes an appearance, as do Frederick Pohl's literary Hoka, but the book turns on the hook of Mark Lenard, the actor who played Aaron Stemple in *Here Come the Brides* and Sarek, Spock's father, in *Star Trek*. In *Ishmael*, Mark Lenard plays characters from whom Spock descends directly on both his mother's side of the family through Aaron Stemple, and on his father's side of the family through Sarek himself.

Fanwriters do not limit the humorous blurring of boundaries to shifting real friends into fictional accounts of their artificial relations, or of setting fictional characters in incongruous relation to one another. Once a writer is comfortable with the conventions of fanwriting, she may emphasize that fact by deliberately crossing her work with incongruous writing styles. In Marian Allen's "Beau Mudd,"[31] her character, the ever-in-trouble-but-it's-never-her-fault-and-she-always-resolves-the-crisis Bel, fresh from diplomat school, receives her first assignment on the planet Relf, where the dominant group is punk and worships money, and the oppressed group, the Nonesuch, dresses and speaks in Regency romance style and gives money away. Harry Mudd, the recurring *Star Trek* character, pops up here as a leader among the Nonesuch. Some of the humor of the story arises in veiled reference—the prince of the Relf is Prince Rutgerhauer, the name of a popular actor in the fan community, and his pseudonym among the Nonesuch is Percy, an oblique reference to Percy Blakeney's vapid cover persona in the *Scarlet Pimpernel*. Most of the humor derives from the incongruous mixing of the discourses of science fiction, modern punk culture, and historical romance, and from the wordplay with which Marian Allen embroiders the conceit. An early description of the liaison officer on Relf:

> He was dressed conservatively in Byzantine fashion [Byzan is the capital of Relf]. His red long-johns were topped by a tunic made from an olive drab garbage bag. His belt was a purple nylon jump-rope. His high-topped black basketball shoes had bits cut out of them and the laces didn't match. Absolutely off-the-rack.
> Civil Service, thought Tetra.[32]

A few pages later, Bel finds herself with Harry Mudd among the Nonesuch:

> A young buck in turquoise velvet laced with silver, his black locks brushed in the Brutus, approached Harry and made a leg. "Some of your own sort?" he asked, eyeing Harry's enameled Sevres snuff box.
> "Just so," said Harry, closing the box and restoring it to a pocket of his flowered waist coat. "A bit strong for young'uns, Percy. Not to your taste, I'll be bound."
> Percy shrugged, disappointed, and moved off.
> Sound lad, young Percy, Harry thought. But not quite up to snuff.[33]

By the end of the story, of course, Bel has reconciled Prince Rutgerhauer with his family and found a loophole in the Relf law so that the

Nonesuch can continue with their philanthropy. And, she has uncovered the liaison officer, Uriah Slope, as a Klingon agent.

Experienced writers play with juxtaposing a variety of folk and high art forms with the source products. Among the results are fractured and often sexually adventurous fairy tales, and reinterpretations of opera in fannish terms, also to licentious effect. Drawn into the known world of the fan fiction, the writer re-creates the commonplace and known artifacts of mainstream culture, remaking them into the alien and strange. In the process she reinforces the social construction of the group through its source products, and presents for questioning the artifacts of the commonplace in the larger culture. By making the fairy tale sexual she laughs at the culture that bowdlerizes its own products in its mad rush to deny the existence of sex. When she lampoons the opera she does not spurn the form but reminds the reader of the low-culture appeal of melodrama and exaggerated emotionality inherent in high culture. By deliberately taking a liminal position between them, the experienced writer embraces both her cultures—her fan culture and the American or British or Australian one that raised her—and laughs as only one who loves both can laugh at them.

Deeper Reading: Microflow in Fan Fiction

Readers who move more deeply into the community begin to recognize certain nexus points in the literature that operate symbolically to compress into the moment, the phrase, glance, or image, the meaningful experience of the entirety of the message she has previously organized at the level of the macroflow (the microflow). At this point the developing member can easily interpret the most internally referential works, she may produce similar works herself, and she finds herself making "intuitive" judgments about community social situations based on her knowledge of both the literature and the group.

As part of the talk and the literature, she may begin to engage the source products on an "as if" basis: as if the fictional universe were real. Every fan realizes that Mr. Spock and Captain Kirk are fictional characters and as such exist only as constructs of the imagination. But, members often detail the deeds and exploits of their heroes, and even the artifacts of their cultures, as if they truly existed. D. Booker's "Preliminary Report on the Inscription on the *Kh'Marr Bowl*"[34] presents an archaeological study of an ancient Vulcan artifact, complete with footnotes, including one from *The Universal Golden Bough*, Beta Centauri VII, Academic Press. The "article" includes illustrations of the bowl drawn carefully to a scale measured out on the drawing, although Booker is well aware that Vulcans, and therefore the Kh'Marr Bowl, do not exist.

Of course, Booker is making playful use of the academic form, but the "article" illustrates an important point. Independent studies by Tamar Liebes on Israeli *Dallas* viewers,[35] John Caughey on imaginary social relationships,[36] and Janice A. Radway on romance readers[37] all point to a mode of interaction with fictional characters very like that described here for media fanwriters. That is, the viewer/reader develops relationships with fictional characters that are no less real than, while being intrinsically different from, relationships with living people. In interaction with others who share in the fictional relationships, the actions and behaviors of the fictional characters generate discussion and gossip as if the characters were in some way real.[38]

In this sense, all the forms of verbal art can be used fictively or discursively. Some fans write epistolary fiction, and others write about their favorite source product "as if" it were true in personal letters and essays, while still others use the fictional forms to critically study both the fan and the commercial products as fictions. Likewise, personal experience narratives may be related orally or in letters or essays, or they may appear fictionalized and integrated into stories written "as if" the characters were not only real but interacting with the community members as characters.

From Story to Text: Talking Story

In her book *Narrative Fiction,* Shlomith Rimmon-Kenan[39] suggests distinctions between story, narrative, and text that are most pertinent here. In its passage through the fan community, from idea to novella, short story, or poem, a story with as yet no set form may be performed in a variety of ways. The author may "talk" the story orally or "work out" the story in letters. Both of these forms indicate an incomplete narrative, with ideas not fully expressed, and usually without the artful language that positions a text in the community. Women in the community make a distinction between a story's intended form and forms through which a story passes in its process of becoming. Thus, a fan may read to friends a letter in which a story is being worked out. The letter is a finished form, although the narrative discussed in it is not.

Members of the community recognize and act on the knowledge that different forms of interaction serve different purposes for the community, from the giving of personal advice and support to the creation of a sense of experience shared by many participants. To say that most fan artistic production can be divided into convention activity, fanzine activity, club activity, or circle activity, however, would mislead the reader into seeing sharp distinctions based on venue.

Fans actively work at opening up opportunities for the practice and creation of stories, and the writer may exercise the process of creation in almost any situation. She may "talk" her story at club or circle gatherings, or with friends at conventions. Fans engage in talking story more than any other activity, in all social situations and for all types of content. They may tell their own stories, relate stories they have read or heard elsewhere, or repeat the stories of particular episodes of the source products. As described in an earlier chapter, when the women recount stories they give only the most general description of plot, while unfolding the tangled course of characters' relationships in great detail. Some fans invent stories verbally for years before they commit one to paper. Not all community members produce stories or art, but in groups that include writers or artists, peer pressure to produce may continue unabated for years until the participant makes an effort to circulate at least one finished work. The pressure to contribute is so strong that both storyteller and audience assume that any oral narrative using the fictional characters is a precursor to a final form in the print media of the group. When a fan at More Eastly Con said, "It's going to blossom sooner or later. Ideas. Most people who write have been talking [their stories] before that,"[40] her comment implied that, for the group, the finished text remains the goal of talking story. For community members, however, the shared experience of a story's passage from form to form in the process of becoming a text subverts the very idea of form. Formal genres don't so much function to identify the fan community with the mainstream as to mask its activities with the appearance of similarity to that literary mainstream.

Reading the Codes in Fan Fiction

As a fan moves deeper into the community, she finds certain phrases, turns of speech, or uses of language that act as codes within the fan community. In this section, I am using the term "codes" in the linguistic sense, not of a language or dialect but of a way of using language in a particular situation, a contextually appropriate discourse.[41] Themes become codes in the fan fiction when conventionalized language or gestures attach to their presentation, and when that presentation acts as a recognition signal that the theme in question is being used in the community with certain meanings and to certain effects in a particular body of the work.

The codes in fan fiction combine descriptions of images as they appear on the screen and distinctive diction developed over time in the fanwriting both to draw the community's art together and to distinguish particular genre categories from each other. As an example, series producers often use food and drink as indicators of moral character and viewers read the use of food and drink as a code according to cultural expectations shared by series creators and middle-class American audiences. *Star Trek* positively reinforces the ethos of modest display when heroes eat simple food from simple dinnerware. Captain and crew grab sandwiches on paper plates at their stations and drink coffee out of paper cups. Mr. Spock, the ultimate super-egoist, is a vegetarian. Villains, however, often announce themselves at dinner tables laden with sumptuous banquets served on ornate platters, as series episodes "Cat's Paw" and "The Squire of Gothos" demonstrate. Heroes continue the marked distinction between good and evil by abstaining from the bounty offered them or by choosing a small portion of the simplest food. Temptation is avoided, and we suspect that, had Captain Kirk been in Adam's position, the human race might never have left the Garden of Eden.

By contrast, *Blake's 7*'s Vila exhibits the lower moral standing of his class status by overindulging in futuristic alcohol. The sinister villainess Servalan often seduces her prey with food and drink as well as promises of sexual favors before she murders them. The fan fiction continues the tradition of heroically modest display, while it adds to its repertoire a convention of food use developed in a number of source products. That is, a preference for junk food becomes a character trait that signals boyish eccentricity or harmless commonality with the viewer—Avon likes ice cream, Starsky likes burritos, Bodie likes swiss rolls, Diana Troi likes chocolate—while falling within the bounds of modest display and therefore morally appropriate behavior.

The fanwriters do not always adopt the codes of the source products with their meanings intact, however. The theme of telepathy appeared in both *Star Trek* and *Blake's 7*. In the former, Mr. Spock's apparently uncommunicative facade harbored a capacity to understand the other at the level of that other's own thoughts and feelings. Telepathy broke down the barriers that Vulcan culture erected between individuals. By contrast, the telepathic alien Cally on *Blake's 7* could send thoughts but could not receive them from any but another sending telepath. Separated from her own people, Cally could communicate with others at the level of the mind, but she could never receive like communication in return. Whereas for Spock telepathy diminished the solitude of the alien, for Cally telepathy only made her alien solitude more acute. In both cases, however, the television series depicted telepathy as alien, not human.

Women fanwriters, however, have developed telepathy as a code for the ideal form of understanding, empathy expanded to include thought as well as emotion. Fanwriters use telepathy both as an integral part of Spock's Vulcan culture and as a metaphor for the understanding that accompanies deeply felt interpersonal relationships. In the Kraith series, Captain Kirk, a highly intuitive military officer, develops telepathic abilities. Spock's family adopts the captain to train him in Vulcan techniques for controlling his talent. To "Kraith" writers this development of one of Spock's more important relationships, his friendship with Captain Kirk, was inevitable. In the *Blake's 7* character Cally, who can never experience the telepathic presence of another because her people are dead and the humans cannot communicate on that level, the loneliness of many women who feel that they give understanding but receive nothing back to nurture their sense of belonging finds representation.

To the women of the media fandom community, telepathy codes the possibility of complete understanding of another person, of incorporating into the self that other being with all its strangeness, and of exposing the self to the stranger. Mr. Spock represents the positive value of an understanding merged with the other, while Cally represents the tragedy when comprehension of the totality of the other is forever denied. And yet, even in its most positive aspect, the telepath must temper comprehension with the right of the other to retain some privacy, some mystery.

At a most basic level, telepathy codes love as an overwhelmingly positive union with the alien other. In Jean Lorrah's NTM universe, the human Amanda and the Vulcan (alien) Sarek are telepathically bonded in Vulcan marriage. Sexual intercourse shared telepathically as well as physically becomes so intense that the mind-melding Vulcan male loses consciousness after orgasm:

> . . . she could stand the suspense no longer and had to let them spiral into satiation. She glimpsed her husband's utter astonishment at that moment, but then, as always, he sank momentarily into unconsciousness. . . .
>
> Already Sarek's consciousness was returning, and she braced herself for his reaction. He put his arms around her and turned onto his side, gathering her protectively against him as if to assure himself that it was still she, Amanda, that he held before he asked, //Have you always been able to do that?//* [42*]

*"//" is an orthographic convention for telepathic communication.

In "Aftershocks," a story written about characters from the *Blake's 7* television show, Deborah Walsh describes a sexual encounter between the human male, Avon, and the alien female, Cally:

> He pulled back from this link, trying to control the level of psychic involvement, but the demands of his body overrode his control, and at the moment of orgasm, he was dimly aware of riding on the head of a shooting star, all of space surrounding and enveloping him, until at last he ceased to exist.
>
> A little while later, the fragments of the personality that was Kerr Avon began to reintegrate, and he stirred slightly. He had collapsed unconscious on top of Cally, her arms holding him close . . .
>
> "I don't understand why you Auronae [alien race] took up cloning if that's any example of your sexual norm," he whispered hoarsely.[43]

In the sexual literature we can see where fanwriters place the concept of other: not on themselves, the female, as feminist literature so often does, but on the male. In the Jean Lorrah excerpt, the telepathic alien is male and in the Deborah Walsh excerpt, a female. In both cases, however, the male lost consciousness, and the woman retained control of the sexual act. When Lorrah and Walsh established their categories of like and unlike "us," consistently the sexual male is perceived as other, while the female is coded as "one of us," even when she belongs to an alien species.

Typically with the use of codes, telepathy does not have specific meaning in and of itself in the fan fiction. Rather, the appearance of the conventional language of the code signals that the writer is entering a particular subdivision of the fan fiction discourse. In the above example, both authors used the language of telepathy to describe strong women who take control of their own sexuality. Whether human or Vulcan, the male remains the alien in both stories by the very nature of his sexual experience. The code, in essence, transforms the content according to the rules of the discourse.

Visual Wordplay: The "Dress Code"

Not surprisingly, most of the play in the community revolves around the use of codes. In her recent article "Reality is a Crutch for People Who Can't Deal with Science Fiction," Stephanie Hall[44] described the many uses science fiction fans make of slogan buttons. As in the SF community, the two-inch buttons caligraphed with densely coded aphorisms and arcane words and phrases constitute the most wide-spread form of wordplay in the media fanzine community. Unlike the science fiction buttons, however, a majority of the slogan buttons re-ferring specifically to media fandom make use of direct or deliber-ately distorted quotations from the source products themselves, or direct or deliberately distorted titles from the same. Examples span a range from the generally well known, like "Beam me up, Scotty, there is no intelligent life here," to the most arcane, such as "Weekend in the Gutter."[45] Most media fans have many buttons, and no fan I have ever met has none.

Slogan buttons signal competence in the manipulation of the codes of the community and act as cues by which participants with equal lev-els of competence may recognize each other in the public sphere of the convention. A participant wearing a button with the motto "He's Dead, Jim" signals an interest in *Star Trek* and a satiric frame of mind, but does not necessarily demonstrate an esoteric knowledge of the source product. A button that says "Maltz Choa Choo" (translation: "Beam me up, Maltz"[46]) signals that the wearer does have esoteric knowledge of the source product. Participants who have as intense an interest in *Star Trek*, or in Klingons, as the button wearer will recog-nize the reference to the movie *The Search for Spock*, while others may question the button, signaling a wish to increase their esoteric knowl-edge. "I'm not Expendable, I'm not Stupid, and I'm not Going" like-wise indicates not only a knowledge of *Blake's 7* but also an interest in the character Avon, who says the line in an episode of that program. I have noted that media fans wear more buttons when they attend general science fiction conventions than they do in special-interest conventions, and they also wear more buttons at larger media con-ventions (500 or more participants) than they do at the very small con-ventions (75–150 participants). Since the button acts as an identifier of the fan to others, it becomes less important when participation it-self already marks at least one, or even two, levels of selection.

The standard fan wardrobe may contain almost as many T-shirts as buttons. T-shirts, because they have a larger surface with which to work, often display screen printed or iron-on graphics as well as slo-gans. While commercial shirts with registered logos are popular, shirts decorated within the community often refer directly to the group's own products. Story illustrations are popular on T-shirts, and often reflect the community's humor (for example, Leah Rosenthal's cartoon-style drawings for the satiric Bizarro 7 stories she creates with Ann Wortham). Importantly, however, T-shirts and buttons may signal not play but the mask of play, while they serve the serious functions of confirming the identity of the wearer[47] and marking out of public space the private "mobile geography" of a dispersed small town.[48]

Conversational Wordplay: Competence and Solidarity

Members of the fan community highly prize humor in conversation, which occurs most often in the form of quips and wordplay that juxtapose the esoteric knowledge of the community's literature with the mundane experience of the outside world. Participants may share anecdotes and humorous personal experience narratives, but conversational repartee is more popular.

Fan conversational genres differ from the more studied forms of riddles and jokes. The joke or riddling event is highly marked, set apart from the flow of everyday conversation, whereas breakthrough into speech play is subtly marked. Skilled participation in speech play often dictates that the witticism must fit easily into the conversation and not affect its flow or divert attention from the point of discussion.[49] Conversation in the play mode will have many such witticisms, often bits of stories and references to episodes of favorite series. Fans may also add humorous personal experience narratives to the conversation, but in conversation marked as play the narratives are generally kept very short. They may still include markers such as "that reminds me of the time" or "do you remember when," but the flow of the conversation still overrides the performance of the narrative. In fact, I have seldom heard anyone introduce a narrative unknown to other members of the conversation at these times. Often members of the group share the narration of the experience. Telling such a narrative seems to establish inclusion in the group rather than separation into those who tell the story and those who listen.

The women do not seem to perceive the speech play as an event hierarched into performers and audience. In fact, many instances of wordplay are framed by an invitation for general participation within the flow of the conversation. In one such popular form of play, a participant suggests a topic and adds the first humorous commentary. Others in the group make their own pithy contributions. The following example took place at a hospitality house gathering in Champaign, Illinois, in 1986, by which time I had passed through many of the initiatory phases in the community, and I felt that I had attained the level of a reasonably knowledgeable insider, though I was not yet privy to certain bodies of core information.

Most house gatherings take place over weekends, and except for the occasional neophyte invited specifically for initiation, most of the

participants know each other. A hospitality gathering like the one described here brings together fans who, while experienced in the fan
community, may be known only by reputation or may be new to each
other altogether. On this occasion several community members, including one member of the Champaign circle, had formed a panel to
talk about the women's fandom at the Women's Studies Conference
located that year at the University of Illinois in Champaign-Urbana.
They had invited me to join them and discuss my ethnographic work
in the community.

As is traditional, the local circle put us up in their homes and
gathered to party after work and on the weekend to make us feel welcome. The event described below took place on Thursday night, the
day before our papers were scheduled, in the wood-paneled television
room–auxiliary kitchen in Lois Welling's converted basement. Videotapes played on her twenty-five-inch television set while she made
copies on several of her VCRs. Lois and a close friend[50] sat on the
Early American sofa with Sean, Lois' dog, on the floor between them;
I was in the farthest chair, Patricia Frazer Lamb stood nearby, and Judith Gran, the most recent arrival, stood at the counter that separated
the auxiliary kitchen from the television room.

Discussion revolved around the stories of an author whose work is
generally liked in spite of (or perhaps because of) the fact that she
writes saccharine, cliché-ridden prose. As the more specific conversation winds down, Patricia broadens the topic to include clichéd descriptors for characters in the fan fiction in general.

Patricia: Give me, give me words you can't stand.
Judith: Let me, let me, first of all, let me tell you this. I started writ-
     ing this, a sonnet, but I can't remember uh, I don't think I ever
     ended it, see. It's something like this—
     My lover's eyes are nothing like a pool
     —you know, the hazel pools—
     If hairs be wires, black wires grow off his chest.
     His wetness welcomes not, he's dry and cool
     I think I much prefer him fully dressed.
     —got to finish it someday.
Patricia: Sounds good. New words—
Ethnographer: Well, sated and satiated both just sort of grate on
     me.
Judith: Soft-furred chest.
Lois: That's Sean.
[General laughter. The original referent was an erotic description
     of any number of hirsute heroic pectorals, but Lois applies it to

her dog, whose belly she rubbed to emphasize the point. Sean began to groom his anus, to more laughter.]

Lois: Oh Sean, was that necessary?

Ethnographer: Obviously it was—it was the first time he got attention all night.

Friend: That was an editorial comment if I ever saw one.

Lois: [laughing] It was disgusting!

Patricia: More silly words.

Friend: [to Sean] You mean mamma doesn't scratch your ass for you? Come on, Lois, be a good mommy.

Lois: [to Sean] You're disgusting and gross.

Patricia: [returning to silly words] What about globes?

Judith: Globes, which ones? [Tone indicates an overabundance of choices, rather than a cliché she does not recognize].

Friend: Oh God, yes.

Patricia: The ones on Kirk's ass. Always golden globes.

Judith: The golden globe award.

Friend: Marshmallows, I mean there are so many.

Patricia: I suppose the deep hazel pools.

Judith: Twin hazel pools.

Friend: Or the precious hazel pools.

Ethnographer: Or the sparkling or mischievous.

Lois: Golden lock [of hair on Kirk's forehead].

Ethnographer: I love the golden lock. That's such a hoot.

Friend: And if I hear one more time "Spock's velvet pine forest" [The referent is clearly to genitals, but the word that follows is obscured by laughter.]

Patricia: Gee, I was thinking that.

Lois: Keep your shower clean. [hysterical laughter]

Friend: Pine Sol.

Lois: That's how he cleans the toilets.

[Voices at this time become so obscured by laughter that the speakers can no longer be identified.]

————: I can see Kirk sneaking into the bathroom and "that's how he does it—He pisses Pine Sol." Mr. Clean.

————: Who is it who smells like lemons?

————: Well that's probably next.

————: Vulcans will smell like lemons. They smell like room fresheners.

[Voices at this point become differentiated again.]

Judith: They will. They've been described as lemon and cinnamon.

Friend: Sandalwood and cinnamon.

Judith: Sandalwood.

Ethnographer: Sandalwood and cinnamon?

Patricia: Myrrh. I just read a story where they smelled like myrrh all over.

Judy: Oh no, really? What does myrrh smell like?

[Obscured by laughter, but I think there is a reference to frankincense and myrrh and movies. Conversation then lulls, and Lois puts on a tape of a British comedy, the early work of a favorite actor among the group members.][51]

Two overlapping contexts shape the wordplay in this example. The first is the fan literature from which these descriptors are drawn. In their usual context, the descriptors are generally not meant as humor or play, nor do they necessarily produce more than a passing wince in readers who have come to recognize the phrases as clichés over the years. Humor places them in a new, reflective, context—don't we do some silly things when we are trying to be serious. The reader would find a few of the clichés widely interspersed in the community's texts, but their presence to such excess marks the context as play, much as it did in the written "Stairs in His Eyes" discussed earlier in the chapter.

The second context is the social setting in which this particular play episode took place. Lois was our hostess. Patricia and Judith were both experienced fanwriters, but they did not know Lois personally. I had known Lois for several years, but I was not a part of her circle and I had never been to her home before. Lois and the friend sharing our visit are members of the same circle. The two live close to each other, visit back and forth frequently, and have similar staff positions at the same university, although in different departments. In some ways the wordplay was a friendly test. As a newcomer to the group, Patricia offered both to demonstrate her sense of humor and to position herself with reference to knowledge of the conventions of the fan fiction. Judith took up the offer of play with a performance of a funny poem she was writing, indicating she recognized part of the signal, to talk about the descriptive conventions of many fan stories, but she did not read the intention that the session open up to include more participants trading reciprocal quips.

Judith received polite laughter, but the resident circle did not pick up the play. Patricia signaled the game again, and I offered an opinion, followed by Judith—still the outsiders engaging—while the insiders decline to participate in the play. At this juncture, Lois turns the point to the mundane, bringing the descriptor, furred chest, around to a mundane referent, her dog, and the insiders switched the conversation to the dog. I add a comment about the dog, joining the insiders' conversation not because I am an ethnographer,[52] but because I have

Illustration for a *Starsky and Hutch* story, "The Tomb," appearing in *Zebra 3*, vol. 5.

Fanzine editors Laura Peck and TACS. TACS is best known for her artwork.
Both are active in British media and *War of the Worlds* fandoms.

known Lois for several years and have met and talked with her friend
on several occasions.

Neither of the newcomers to Lois's circle joins in the dog talk, but
Patricia again solicits silly descriptors, and this time she includes an
example, buttocks as golden globes. The insiders join in, and the
laughter increases to a level at which I can no longer distinguish
voices, or even some words, on the tape. The humor turns on shifting
the sexual referents (descriptions of how sexual partners smell) to
household cleaners, and then attributing the cleansing properties of
the household cleaners to urine. The laughter peaks during this
exchange in part because the incongruous juxtaposing of sex and
cleaning the bathroom is funny. Equally important, however, the
laughter signals a release of social tension, as the newcomers are fitted
into the group for the duration of the weekend.

As Rayna Green has pointed out, women commonly discuss sexual
matters in a humorous manner among themselves,[53] and talk similar
to that described above occurs at all fan gatherings I have attended.
This particular example is more highly structured than occurrences
of wordplay that fall incidentally into a conversation, and represents a
game of competency that results in solidarity extended to strangers.

TACS's portrait of *The Man from U.N.C.L.E.*'s Napoleon Solo.

In some ways the verbal wit described here resembles the verbal dueling Gary Gossen observed among the Chamula: the wit turns on sexual innuendo, and participants try to offer increasingly outrageous contributions to the exchange.[54] Unlike the verbal duel, however, the goal is augmentative rather than competitive, and the purpose is to demonstrate competence in deciphering and manipulating the codes of the community. Unwillingness to participate is signaled by silence

Another Leah Rosenthal cartoon, this time for short-lived American series
Alien Nation.

and indirection rather than by direct confrontation, which is consistent with the norms of group behavior outside of play.

Notes

1. This analysis is generated out of a number of conversations of a sensitive
and deeply personal nature that I was not permitted to tape. For the same
reason, I am protecting the identities of those who spoke to me in these
conversations.
2. Florence Butler and Lee Coleman, taped interview, Cockeysville, Md.,
1985. *Destiny's Children,* ed. Butler and Coleman (fanzine; Washington, D.C.:
Florence Butler, 1985).
3. Sandy Hall, "Easy to be Hard," *Fifth Season 2,* ed. Sheila Willis (fanzine;
Greenbelt, Md.: Spice Press, 1983).
4. Ibid., p. 56.
5. Deb Layman, who created Jordan Lang, reported in a 1989 telephone
conversation that some fans *have* complained that her Lang stories are not
sufficiently "fannish," an indicator that some groups are still uncomfortable
with the new strong women characters. I have not included discussion about
Princess Leia Organa of *Star Wars* here because of the uneasy relationship the
fandom has had with Lucasfilm. However, many of the fans in *Star Wars* do
see Princess Leia as a strong role model.

6. Aside from the physical attributes of the actor playing the part, Sarek stories are popular because the character has many of Spock's most interesting traits of alienness and control, but none of his entanglements with *Enterprise* bridge crew. The writer's alter ego character therefore shares an erotic relationship untrammeled by her mate's obligations to male bonding, while her maternal relationship to Spock gives her a place in the life of a son committed to his male companions.

7. April Selley, "'I Have Been, and Ever Shall Be, Your Friend': *Star Trek, The Deerslayer*, and the American Romance," *Journal of Popular Culture* 20, no. 1 (1986): pp. 89–104.

8. Leslie A. Fiedler, *Love and Death in the American Novel* (New York: Scarborough Books, 1966 [1960]).

9. Patricia Frazer Lamb and Diana Vieth, "Romantic Myth, Transcendence and *Star Trek* Zines," in *Erotic Universe*, ed. Donald Palumbo (New York: Greenwood Press, 1986), pp. 235–89.

10. Claire Gabriel, "Metamorphosis," *Quartet Plus Two* (fanzine, Gross Pointe Park, Mich.: Ceiling Press Publications, 1987 [1975]).

11. Jean Lorrah, *Epilogue* and *Epilogue 2*, originally published in fanzines *Triskelion #4* and *Triskelion #5*, and as *Sol Plus*, special editions in 1977 and 1978. Reprints are self-published by Lorrah (Murray, Ky).

12. Jacqueline Lichtenberg, *Kraith Collected*, 3 vols. (fanzine, Detroit: Ceiling Press Publications, 1982).

13. Carol Gilligan, *In a Different Voice* (Cambridge, Mass.: Harvard University Press, 1982), p. 57.

14. Sandy Hall, "The Scars That Won't Heal," *Fifth Season 2*, ed. Sheila Willis (fanzine, Greenbelt, Md.: Spice Press, 1983), pp. 204–87.

15. Gilligan, *Different Voice*, p. 62.

16. In spite of the commonly held notion that close friendships in threes are unstable and ultimately leave one member feeling an outsider, I have seen that form of relationship work very well in fandom.

17. Victoria Sinall (Mystery Frank), "Listening at the Keyhole," *Chalk and Cheese*, ed. Mysti Frank (Lexington, Ky.: Whatever You Do, Don't Press!, April 1988), pp. 34–37.

18. For the structure of the flow of soap operas, see, for example, Tania Modleski, "The Rhythms of Reception: Daytime Television and Women's Work," in *Regarding Television*, ed. E. Ann Kaplan (Los Angeles: The American Film Institute, 1975).

19. Lois Welling, taped interview, Cockeysville, Md., July 1984.

20. Lynda Carraher, "Prelude," *Masiform-D #13*, ed. Devra Michele Langsam (fanzine, Brooklyn, N.Y.: Poison Pen Press, 1983).

21. C. E. Roush, "Assignment: Enterprise," in *Maine(ly) Trek*, ed. Mary Ann Drach (Temple, Maine: Walking Carpet Press, 1985), pp. 14–42.

22. The series uses the same device, beginning each episode as an entry in the captain's log.

23. Susan R. Matthews, *The Mind of a Man is a Double Edged Sword* (New York: Strelsau Press, 1983).

24. A very small number of men do in fact write serious stories in the fan fiction, and Winston Howlett, for example, is a well-known editor in the fan community. The number of men who do write fan fiction not only remains small, however, but continues to grow smaller.

25. Victor Turner, "Liminal to Liminoid, in Play, Flow, and Ritual: An

Essay in Comparative Symbology," in *The Anthropological Study of Human Play* (Houston: Rice University Studies, 1974), vol. 60, no. 3, pp. 53–92.

26. "Star Track II: The Rash of Kon," *Grip*, no. 18, ed. Roberta Rogow (Fair Lawn, N.J.: Other Worlds Books, 1984). The author's name has been withheld because he could not be located for permission to release his identity.

27. Bawdry Aker and Calory Vollage, "Stairs in His Eyes: A Phonographic Tail of the Spice Age," unknown date and origin.

28. Ibid., p. 1.

29. In recent years, as the biases against the fringe fandoms have broken down, an increasing number of writers have been working to create serious cross-universe stories that bring together characters and situations from series that may cross genre boundaries, but that nevertheless share a mood or attitude consistent with the tone the writer sets in her story. However, many writers still combine series' universes incongruously, for humor.

39. Barbara Hambly, *Ishmael* (New York: Pocket Books, 1985).

31. Marian Allen, "Beau Mudd," *Masiform D, #16*, ed. Devra Langsam (fanzine, Brooklyn, N.Y.: Poison Pen Press, 1988), pp. 37–64.

32. Ibid., p. 38. The character Tetra was created by a friend of the story's author, Claudia Jane Peyton, who also does the illustrations for Allen's "Mudd" stories.

33. Ibid., pp. 42–43.

34. D. Booker, "Preliminary Report on the Inscription on the *Kh'Marr Bowl*," *Masiform D, #13*, ed. Devra Langsam (Brooklyn, N.Y.: Poison Pen Press, 1983), pp. 16–20.

35. Tamar Liebes, "Ethnocriticism: Israelis of Moroccan Ethnicity Negotiate the Meaning of 'Dallas,'" *Studies in Visual Communication* 10, no. 3 (1984): 46–73.

36. John Caughey, "Imaginary Social Relationships in Modern America," *American Quarterly* 30, no. 1 (Spring 1978): 70–89.

37. Janice A. Radway, *Reading the Romance* (Chapel Hill: University of North Carolina Press, 1984); and idem, "Interpretive Communities and Variable Literacies: The Function of Romance Reading," *Anticipations*, Proceedings of the American Academy of Arts and Sciences, vol. 113, no. 3 (1984), pp. 49–71.

38. Fieldwork I have been conducting among professional science fiction writers likewise points to a common practice of thinking about characters as if they were real people, to the extent that professionals, like the fanwriters, may claim that a book made an unexpected turn when a "character took over."

39. Shlomith Rimmon-Kenan, *Narrative Fiction: Contemporary Poetics* (London: Methuen, 1983).

40. Taped group interview, New York, September 1985.

41. Dell Hymes, "Social Anthropology, Sociolinguistics, and the Ethnography of Speaking," in *Foundations in Sociolinguistics* (Philadelphia: University of Pennsylvania Press, 1974), pp. 83–117.

42. Jean Lorrah's "Amanda of Vulcan," *NTM Collected* (fanzine, Murray, Ky., self-published, 1978), p. 70.

43. Deborah Walsh's "Aftershocks" appeared in the fanzine *B7 Complex*, ed. Deb Walsh (Malden, Mass.: Moonrise Press, 1981), p. 46.

44. Stephanie Hall, "Reality is a Crutch for People Who Can't Deal with

Science Fiction: Slogan-Buttons among Science Fiction Fans," *Keystone Folklore* (1989): 19–31.

45. The latter distorts the episode title "Weekend in the Country" from a British series, and only a small group of fans understand that the button refers to an imaginary convention where favorite actors from all the source products would be the guests of the "con committee."

46. Maltz was the second in command of the Klingon bird-of-prey starship in the movie *The Search for Spock.*

47. Erving Goffman, *The Presentation of Self in Everyday Life* (Garden City, N.Y.: Doubleday Anchor Books, 1959).

48. My paper "Breaking the Frame: Intrusion on a Costume Event" (presented at the annual meeting of the American Folklore Society, Cincinnati, Ohio, 1985), which draws heavily on frame analysis of Bateson and Goffman, demonstrated how buttons, T-shirts, and costumes marked space in the science fiction community. The same can be said for the media fan community.

49. Similarly, Kanako Shiokawa found, in her study of ghostlore among Japanese speakers living in America ("Between Here and There: Reinforcement of Expectations in Supernatural Experience Narratives of Japanese Speakers," presented at the annual meeting of the American Folkore Society, Cambridge, Mass., October 1988, and expanded in nonpublished form January 31, 1989), that the narratives were likewise interjected as part of the conversational exchange. In fact, breaking the flow of conversation for either an inappropriate offering of ghostlore or an overly affective rendition of the narrative is perceived as a breach of etiquette.

50. Name withheld at the request of the informant.

51. Taped discussion, Champaign, Ill., June 1986.

52. In a humorous encounter like the example, the ethnographer can only react as a participant and hope she doesn't put her foot in her mouth.

53. Rayna Green, "Magnolias Grow in Dirt: The Bawdy Lore of Women," *Southern Exposure* 4, no. 4 (1977); 29–33.

54. Gary Gossen, "Verbal Dueling in Chamula," in *Speech Play*, ed. B. Kirshenblatt-Gimblett (Philadelphia: University of Pennsylvania Press, 1976), pp. 121–46.

Chapter Seven
Visual Meaning

Video as Art

Videotape is important for introducing fans to the more esoteric source products, but it serves another purpose as well. Fans use the video to create their own art form, the songtape. In 1985, while I was learning about alternative fandoms and the video connection with Jean Curley, I met Mary Suskind Lansing, who became my mentor to songtape fandom. In this community that depends on technology for the creation and dissemination of its art, Mary was one of the first of a growing number of artists who are taking advantage of the possibilities of video as an art form. Taking their inspiration from MTV and the amateur film tradition in science fiction, some visual artists began to construct their own videos, which they called songtapes.

In an article that appeared in *Consort 2*, a fan publication, Mary Suskind Lansing described the equipment a songtape artist needs: "We are looking at three machines: the video source, the audio source, and the video/audio sync."[1] The audio source can be an audio- or videotape machine, compact disc, or phonograph. The audio/video sync is the video machine that records both the images from the video source and the soundtrack from the audio source onto what will become the songtape master. The tape artist also needs as much source material as possible, in as clear copy as possible. In a letter describing her *Star Trek* songtapes, video artist Ellen Morris explained some of the technological limitations of the songtape:

> The artist is really limited by how many episodes he/she has on tape, the generation quality and the sound quality . . . Generation quality is a big problem. By the time a music video is finished, the viewer is seeing a second generation of an image. You can tell just

by looking that the picture is breaking up because it's been copied twice already. It's like making a xerox copy from a xerox copy from a xerox copy. Every time you make a copy of a copy, the print breaks up a little more, and makes viewing a bit more difficult because the picture quality is worse. Then there are the [sound] dropouts.[2]

Artists become extremely sensitive to the technology of videotape; they will often discuss at length the advantages of laser disc for source material and the higher quality of the Beta system as compared to VHS. Lansing is an exception in her access to advanced technology, however; few community members are able or willing to devote the financial resources necessary for the use of multiple technologies. Another fan, who has created several *Blake's 7* songtapes, describes her plight as an artist:

The equipment I work with is so difficult to work with that really, once you finish and it doesn't work, you've really got to rework it [from the beginning—few machines have the capacity for correction]. Frame advance, huh [not available on her machine]—me and the pause button are real close friends, you know.[3]

The variable quality of the equipment used by the artist makes a difference not only in the technical clarity of the picture, but in the amount of time it takes to construct a three-minute songtape. Mary can complete a three-minute song in three hours, while the video artist referenced above, with much less sophisticated video capacity, takes up to twelve hours to compile the video images and match them to a song.

In a songtape the artist deconstructs the texts of both source products—video and audio—and reconstructs not only their forms but in many cases their messages as well to create a new narrative. Not surprisingly, the community's writers, rather than its graphic artists, have taken up the new narrative form of the songtape most enthusiastically.

To create a successful songtape, the video artist must have a thorough knowledge of the visual and musical material at her command, as well as of her technology, so that she can fit appropriate visuals to the music she selects. Mary Suskind Lansing has made extensive use of songs created inside the community—*filksongs*—particularly those written about the source product the songtape illustrates. Songs such as Leslie Fish's "He's Dead, Jim,"[4] satirizing the frequent use of that line in the *Star Trek* television series, and her "Engineer's Song,"[5] told from the point of view of Engineer Scott, again a character from *Star Trek,* are particularly suited to visual interpretation.

Artists can and do use folk, rock, classical, or easy listening music, but soft pop is used more frequently than all other forms of music combined. At a gathering of local fans who had come to an academic conference in Houston to meet a group of scholars giving papers about *Star Trek* fans, Patricia Frazer Lamb, a *Star Trek* writer, college professor, and lifelong classical music fan, told a local video artist how she used to feel about popular music and how her experience with the songtapes has changed that:

> Patricia: . . . I mean, I know from nothing [in contemporary music]. I do not like it. I never listen to radio. And my, my kids would say, "Mom, you've just got to listen to this," and I'd say, "No, I hate it. Put on some Mozart and shut up" . . . Every [popular] song I know I've learned in the last eight or nine months, since I saw those first *Trek* [song]tapes at Lois Welling's place.
> Video artist: What, from watching songtapes?
> Patricia: Yeah. This is my introduction to contemporary music. Mary's [Suskind Lansing] Shore Leave [convention] songtape was the first one I had. Flora did it [copied the tape] and sent it to me.
> And I sat and I watched that thing until, like, my eyes were falling out of my head. And I went into my classes in September . . . I went into my class and I said, "Okay, we're going to do Keats and so forth. Does anybody have any Air Supply tapes?"
> Fan: Did you get anyone to loan you one?
> Patricia: Yeah. Yup. Uh huh. Got a bunch of stuff. [laughs] They think I'm crazy.

In the songtape, the text of the chosen song sets the theme of the piece. Songs of love or adventure, paeans to comradeship, or anthems of social consciousness are popular. Choosing from the available videotaped canon, the artist will cut together scenes from the source product and replace the original soundtrack with the song. When assembled into a new whole, the clips set up a narrative or lyric message in the video portion of the songtape that reinforces the text in the song or runs counter to it for an ironic or humorous effect.

A Mary Suskind Lansing songtape, constructed around the sweetly romantic song "Follow Me,"[6] pulls together clips from *Blake's 7* in which the hero's nemesis, Travis, repeatedly attempts to kill the hero. Rather than building on the theme of affection and devotion expressed in the song, the videotape runs counter to it, expressing in black humor the hate relationship between the hero Blake and his archenemy. The overly sweet music, together with the soulful text, run exactly counter to the hard, bitter relationship expressed in the video source product. And yet, the combination of visual image and song text does catch in humorous reversal the truly obsessive quality of the relationship portrayed.

A songtape producer like Mary or Ellen, or the video artist who talked with Patricia and me in Houston, must have a strong sense of the art of collage translated into movement. She exploits for effect the knowledge shared with other members of the community about the context of some clips, while in other scenes she must see the multiple possibilities in kinesics and shot composition, and then separate the action from its context to make a statement only subliminally present, if at all, in the source product. At all times, however, she must be aware of the symbolic content that the community has vested in certain actions or characters. Cuing from the lines of the song, the experienced viewer selectively accepts or discards the context where applicable, making a series of rapid judgments about the clips of tape that may last only seconds each.

Viewed as a body, the songtapes can also be used to train newcomers in what to look for in the source products. Some songtapes are made particularly for newcomers—the song "Holding Out for a Hero"[7] has been used for most of the source products and is a valuable introductory lesson for newcomers. Mary Suskind Lansing has done a number of tapes specifically designed to interest newcomers in the *Blake's 7* product. While she keeps most of the symbolism simple in these videos and tries to minimize reliance on context, she still slips in some of the more sophisticated messages for her own pleasure. She finds that newcomers do not recognize the hidden messages, but that more experienced community members pick them up and often comment appreciatively on those very aspects of the songtapes that newcomers do not see at all.

Testing Competence: Video Play

Because songtapes derive from the source products directly, fans must bring to the interpretation process a well-developed memory of the visual context in which their heroes move and act, and must make a second-by-second judgment whether the artist is cuing to the context or using a scene out of context to illustrate a line of the song. A prizewinning songtape at a fan convention used the song "Living Years"[8] to set Thomas Magnum's relationships with his father, who died when he was a child, and his living but feckless grandfather against his relationship with his daughter. Fans automatically recognize how well the song illustrates the emotional context of the well-chosen scenes, pulling together out of the macroflow of the series a single theme: the deep and abiding love that enmeshes the characters in painful and problematic family relationships. The result, for even cursory fans of the show, is one of the more deeply moving songtapes created in the community. To a nonparticipant untrained in deciphering the tapes, or for a participant who has not seen the series, however, the songtape has no meaning at all.

In spite of the complexity of the songtapes, fans trade them actively through the mail and at conventions. Some fans collect only those tapes that draw on source products they know and like well, but others collect all the songtapes they can, when the opportunity arises, assuming that one day they may have a meaningful context in which to fit the songs they do not readily understand at the moment. Songtapes have become the standard background for many house gatherings. Fans generally give full attention to new songtapes presented by the artist at a gathering, but at other times the tapes play relatively unnoticed: a wash of sound and image over the hubbub of a party. When conversation lags, participants will spend a few minutes looking at the screen, perhaps pick up a thread of conversation from the image, and turn their attention back to each other, away from the screen.

As songtapes have become an established art form, however, they have added a new dimension to a traditional game. In fandom, trivia contests calling upon specific knowledge of the source products are popular. Played formally at conventions and informally wherever fans gather, the contests serve a number of important social functions. Among established fans who do not know each other well, trivia contests, like the wordplay described in Chapter 6, provide a gauge of the knowledgeability of each participant, so that members can carry on conversation and negotiate status at an appropriate level. They provide topics of conversation when discussion lags, and they educate the neophyte in the codes of the community.

In a relatively recent twist on the game, fans watching songtapes created in the community will identify the context in the episode and source product from which the video artist drew individual scenes that make up the songtape. The player must then determine whether the video artist has used the scene for its visual or contextual value. Of course, the fan must go through this same process very rapidly and usually unconsciously to make sense of the songtape at all. As a game, however, identifying each scene, or particularly crucial scenes, serves a number of purposes. First, like much of women's play, the game is augmentative rather than competitive. That is, the point is not to win but to participate.[9] Enjoyment results when the fan demonstrates her competence in deciphering the community's codes and can claim for herself a place in that community. Second, calling out the scenes gives important information to new community members who may be present but who do not have enough information about the source products to identify the scenes or to make sense of the video. Third, the commentary offers a critical assessment of how well the songtape fits into the corpus of the community's product. If the artist is not present, word will reach her indirectly to tell her which of her choices of scenes seemed most apt and which seemed less well chosen, so that she can take the community's taste into consideration in her next effort.

The Process of Interpretation

Learning how to make, interpret, and play with songtapes gave me new insights into the process of interpreting images in the community. Generally, interpretation is a function of what actually appears on the screen—a combination of craft, employed with the intention of communicating a message, and unintentional messages based on tacit assumptions the creators of the source products make about the real world and unconsciously incorporate into their art—and the cultural assumptions or worldview of the viewer—what he or she expects to find in an image.[10]

At the same time, the technical limitations inherent in compressing a live-action scene onto an average diagonal screen size of nineteen inches, and the variable quality of in-home reception of that scene, may create wholly unintentional messages. The viewer makes choices to accept or reject both the intentional and the unintentional messages based on their fit into the range of possibilities her culture recognizes.[11]

To some extent, the viewer and the producer of the source product have a tacit agreement. The creator of the series will try to target a pleasurable experience for a wide variety of viewers, and in turn, the individual viewer will accept the interpretation the producer wishes her to make. That experience may be the concrete presentation of an abstract concept: Gene Roddenberry wanted to embody an idea in *Star Trek*—"He [mankind] will learn that differences in ideas and attitudes are a delight, part of life's exciting variety, not something to fear"[12]—and he did this in part with plots and dialogue, but more consistently and concretely with the ethnic mix of the bridge crew. Another producer may target a particular set of readings for the characters, as director Gerry O'Hara analyzed *The Professionals'* Bodie and Doyle in a discussion published in *Primetime* television magazine:

> . . . [T]he secret of these two characters is that the audience sees them differently, sees them as they want to see them . . . Little girls see them one way, as the fellers they long to have for themselves; young boys in another way, as the heroes they want to be; I've got a strong suspicion that mothers and fathers see them as the sons that they would like to have. Now that sounds absurd, because they whip out guns and shoot people to pieces—but I think they're turn-ons, they're adrenaline-releasers for all the different kinds of people in the audience.[13]

Series creators expect female viewers to find the heroic characters sexually attractive in a nonthreatening way because these characters are also charming, naughty boys appealing to the caretaker in the adult woman.

When Caren Parnes narrates "Fall Girl" (see Chapter 5), her story is vague about the political machinations acted out in the plot, but her description of the hero's loss and his need for someone to trust, someone to comfort him, focuses acutely on the very facets of the character series creators expected her to see: naughty boys occasionally scrape their knees and need someone to set them on their feet again. Brian Clemens produced his series in England, but American viewers can recognize such favorites as Dave Starsky and Thomas Magnum in Gerry O'Hara's description. Women fans of these series see in their heroes similar traits of lack and need in the juxtapositioning of the sexual and the childlike. Songtape artists use popular songs like "Stand By Me" and "By Your Side" together with rescue scenes from the source products to emphasize the hero's need for supportive companionship.

Pattern Recognition and Meaning-Pleasure

In general, the viewer may read the visual images of television or movies as:

1. Intrinsically meaningful (interpretation at the level of the flow)—codes in general use in the cultural representation of similar images;
2. Patterned and then meaningful (interpretation at the level of the macroflow)—codes specifically constructed for reading the particular series; or

3. Simultaneously patterned and meaningful (interpretation at the level of the microflow)—codes the meanings of which resonate beyond the context of the scene in which they appear.

Intrinsic Meaning

When a viewer watches a new series, she may perceive the images either as intrinsically meaningful or as chaotic. The viewer of the narrative at this level brings to the experience expectations that certain patterns of action and behavior—the conventions of the genre—will be present in the narrative. She finds the narrative meaningful when expectations are met, and ambiguous when expectations are overturned. Chaotic images are untenable and, for the most part, are discarded uninterpreted. Pleasure occurs when meaning is recognized, but the pattern of the conventionalized code remains largely unconscious at this level of viewing. Here is where the viewer's response to the image on the screen is most like that of viewing a painting or photograph, or a single, rather than series, film.[14]

Importantly, of course, the meaning of these images is not intrinsic, a fact that a Texas fan pointed out at a gathering in Houston.[15] She described a fan story based on the television show *Hardcastle and McCormick:*

> It [the fan story] rings so true. The only things wrong with it are the things wrong with any television show. You know, we are asked to believe that through plastic surgery these people are made to look exactly like Hardcastle and McCormick. [general laughter] And we all know that in real life that can't happen, but it happens on television all the time.

Conventionalized images such as the "evil twin" described above strain credulity, but the naturalistic film style of most action-adventure series invites the viewer to interpret the image as if it were a natural event. In the willing suspension of disbelief, the conventionalized images specific to the genre come to be read transparently as intrinsically meaningful in the context of any action-adventure movie or series.

Patterned Meaning

If an image formerly discarded as chaotic recurs, either as a meaningful development of a concept or characterization, or as the unintentional product of technical limitations, it may approach the recognition level of a pattern in the macroflow of the source product. When a pattern of occurrence emerges out of the macroflow, the viewer can neither discard the image nor maintain it as both patterned and meaningless. She must either store the fragment for future incorporation or construct a meaning for it: in the macroflow recognition of the pattern and understanding of the meaning are separate experiences. Gombrich describes the work of ascribing meaning in the process of visual discovery this way: "When paintings have aroused our interest in certain configurations, we may look for anchorage and confirmation and use every hint in a visual experience to find there what we sought." [16]

For each bit of information added to the map created in the macroflow, then, the viewer has two distinct experiences. The first is the surfacing of awareness that an image is not random but patterned—constructed in a certain configuration. The second is the understanding of the meaning of the pattern. As an example, in the *Primetime* discussion above, *The Professionals* producer Ray Menmuir explains how series creators invited an open reading of their programs by inserting deliberately meaningless patterns:

> I believe that the audience is really clued in. They pick up on *behavior and actions* [italics in original]. . . . People in general are constantly surprising, so I always resisted 'motivation.' It has never been questioned by the audience, but it was questioned by just about everyone working on the series. 'Is he moving his flat *again?*' for instance. Audiences don't care about things like that. It's a floating crap game. So he's in a different flat, so he's got 28 different apartments, they accept that and we never once explained why. You can make up your own reasons, you can participate. [17]

In practice, women in the fanzine community recognize the constantly changing apartment set and establish not only a reason for it—security—but a patterned regularity to its occurrence—usually quarterly, with emergency moves as required by breaches in security.

Likewise, viewers read actions and behaviors as patterns, systematically according to an organizing principle based in movement and proximity. That means the women in the group generally pay less attention to visuals with intrinsic but not necessarily meaningful content, such as a beautiful or handsome face, or the classic build of a body. Rather, they attend with fierce concentration to visual actions that are intrinsically empty of content but carry relational, processual meaning, as in the fan response to Martin Shaw's portrayal of Raymond Doyle in *The Professionals*. A Houston fan explained:

He [Shaw] takes different people in different ways. Because, when I tried to get a friend into this [fandom], she said, "that has got to be the ugliest man I ever saw." But it's the way he moves—with him, that's it.[18]

Fans interpret and debate kinesics and proxemics, and describe characters as handsome based not on static attributes but on how they move and relate in physical space to the people and things around them. Likewise, fans interpret the image as erotic based not on the state of undress or the apparent passive receptiveness of the figure, but on the interpretation of glances, gestures, and postures that signal a focus on an equally engaged second figure. While the women in this study attend most keenly to images in actual motion—video and movies—the response remains strong for still graphics that symbolically represent movement in relation to some other. Introspective scenes seem to count as relational engagement, even though the "other" in the picture is the portrayed "self." Out of the patterns of relations discovered in the macroflow, viewers develop a gestural code that may be read as tacit knowledge or may surface in the artistic conventions of the songtape.

Meaningful Patterns

Of the three levels at which viewers read television, microflow gives the greatest sense of completion, while imparting the least amount of information. It is not the place of the microflow to give information, but to act as a nexus point, where the product seems at its most whole and true. That effect is produced when the viewer experiences simultaneously the pleasure of recognizing a pattern and the pleasure of understanding a meaning contained in a gesture or word that stands for all the complex experience she has of the product.

At its simplest, creators of television products may import symbols immanent in the culture in the hope that the audience will impute to their products that same symbolic meaning. The fallen hero of "shot in the heart" episodes fits this description. The heart has deep symbolic meaning in Western culture as the location of courage (as opposed to the "faint-hearted") and love. While medicine may have changed the definitive organ of life and death to the brain, the heart still holds that position in the symbol structure of the culture. And thanks to heroic medicine, prominently displayed about the hero, the form can act out the resurrection myth, with mankind represented by the "code" team standing in for God.

TACS's illustration for a story, "The Need," based on *The Professionals* and appearing in *Discovered in a Graveyard*.

At its most complex level, the symbol may arise in the macroflow and reach a critical mass at the level of code, until it resonates with a new depth of relational importance. At that point the newly empowered symbol may move out into the wider culture. Very few visual images make this leap into the mainstream culture, and they seldom carry the same meaning they did in the more narrow context of the television series. *Star Trek* has contributed two visual symbols to the culture. One is the *Enterprise,* the ship in which the crew explored the galaxy. More than any fictional design since Tom Swift's rocket ship, the *Enterprise* seems to symbolize the future to air and space professionals and aficionados. The original model of the ship has flown in the National Air and Space Museum of the Smithsonian Institution, and NASA named the shuttlecraft's prototype *Enterprise* after the fictional ship. Roddenberry's ship has become a symbol of the message of technological positivism he deliberately communicated in *Star Trek.*

The second image, or action, to take up a life of its own is the Vulcan greeting: arm held with the elbow close to the side of the body and the hand upright, the second and third fingers spread to form a V. While Nimoy borrowed a Judaic religious gesture to create the salute, that symbolic use is meaningful to a relatively small number of the people who recognize it as "alien" or "Star Trek." The gesture seems to have become the symbol of the popular aspects of the television show, which has itself become a symbol structure in the culture, even among people who do not watch the series or attend the movies.

Pattern Recognition and Anxiety

Each step in interpreting the source products generates its own pleasures and anxieties. For the viewer strongly engendered in the mainstream masculine culture, the interpretive process gives pleasure when it reinforces his sense of control over his situation. Patterns to which no meaning has been ascribed are not yet set within the hierarchy of the controlled image, and they produce anxiety accordingly. Until meaning attaches to the image, it remains a threat to whatever position he has taken in relation to the product.

Aesthetically, however, many women find pleasure in recognizing patterns—not just narrative patterns but all manner of regularities. This same aesthetic pleasure in recognizing patterns underlies quilt and other needlework designs as well as early child rearing. Here, perhaps, we can see the problem Laura Mulvey[19] addresses in "Visual Pleasure and Narrative Cinema." In the Hitchcock films she describes, and more explicitly in films like *Looking for Mr. Goodbar,* analyzed by E. Ann Kaplan,[20] the meaning of the patterns is threatening to women who nevertheless may find recognition pleasure in the narrative pattern of the film. The woman viewer finds herself in the paradoxical position of experiencing pleasure and displeasure from the same images, and in direct opposition to the masculine response to pattern recognition and meaning. For the masculine viewer the anxiety ceases when he recognizes the meaning of the image, but for the woman the conflict between aesthetics and communication remains. For the woman, the two responses do not cancel each other out but create anxiety the viewer must defuse either by denying that she experiences pleasure in pattern recognition or by denying the meaning of the images.

With television, however, the situation is made more complex by the message coded into the gestural language at the level of the macroflow. In the flow, television, like film, offers up a message of threat to women, but the macroflow is made up of positive relational devices that tie ongoing characters together from week to week. The meanings of patterns in the macroflow are not threatening, but they often do not include women in the structure of relational ties they create. The viewer, then, experiences pleasure when she recognizes the generic and particular patterns of her favorite series while she diffuses the anxiety of her own nonthreatening absence from the product by incorporating herself into the meaning through creative interaction with the characters and situations as they exist in her head.

Gestural Code

When informants recapitulated series episodes as oral narratives, I could identify the narrators' understanding of the message and the verbal cues they drew from. Visual codes, however, remained difficult to crack. Some articulate informants, particularly fan artists, did offer insightful arguments for their interpretations of visual images as cues and their recapitulation of them in their own art. But their numbers were limited, as was the nature of the cues they could discuss.

Both fans and creators of television images stressed the importance of the expressive use of the eyes. Descriptions for the eyes of characters abound in the fan fiction—"hazel pools," "flashing sapphires," "eyes stormy as the North sea"—and video artists often fill their songtapes with close-ups of eyes. Graphic artist Fanny Adams stressed the importance of the eyes to catch the essence of the character she draws:

> I would say that when I draw, I draw the eyes first, if I don't get them right I dump the picture. There's no point in going on. You can fudge on anything else, but the eyes.[21]

Blake's 7 creator Terry Nation described an encounter during the production of that series. According to Nation, Paul Darrow approached him triumphantly because he had devised a way to make the eyes of his character, Avon, "go cold."[22] Nation interpreted the gesture as adding a special menace to the character, but fan Patricia Frazer Lamb asserts that "Paul Darrow can convey agony with the flick of one eyebrow."[23] The gesture is correctly interpreted as lack of emotion, but Nation (and Darrow) conceived that lack to be absolute, while fans generally register Avon's emotionless exterior as being a protective camouflage hiding deep emotion.

Eyes may speak a kind of language, but for communication to occur, that expressiveness must be directed at some other in the picture. Fans of *The Professionals* often point to the episode "Backtrack" as a favorite. In a scene frequently singled out by mentors for repeat viewing, a middle-aged woman informant treats one of the young protagonists preferentially. She flirts with him verbally and with occasional pats to the knee and face, while dismissing his partner as a "lout." Unable to make verbal comment, the two partners carry on whole conversations using their eyes and small facial gestures to carry the primary messages of solidarity and outraged humor.

To a regular viewer or initiate, these scenes are very funny and signify a close and playful relationship between the two partners. The first time I saw the episode I had no experience with the program, and the scenes I can now read as enjoyable in the context of the macroflow made no sense to me at all.

Trying to move beyond eye contact in the construction of gestural codes, however, I resorted to the community's own songtapes. One important clue appears in the choice of songs and the scenes used to illustrate them. "Wind Beneath My Wings"[24] is a popular favorite to comment on Spock's relationship to Captain Kirk. I have seen four separate videos done by four different people or groups to several versions of the song. Along with scenes of deep and meaningful eye contact, each one includes many scenes of Spock walking a pace behind the captain.

"Holding Out for a Hero" likewise draws on the larger-than-life moments of derring-do of all the source products. Swinging from ropes, galloping on horseback, diving over automobiles or furniture, fighting with fists or swords are popular images in the songtapes, and a surprising number of series, both contemporary action-adventure and science fiction, have all of these conventional images, including sword fighting.

For more subtle clues to gestural codes, I passed control of the pause button on the videotape machine to the fans and mentors with whom I came in contact. I discovered that most informants who could not *say* what they saw could point to it when they saw it on the screen.[25] Some of the gestures fans pointed out can be interpreted based on the kinesic code of day-to-day interaction. For other gestures, repeated appearance in similar contexts provoke similar reactions in the responding characters, giving the action symbolic meaning specific to the relationships in the series.

A raised eyebrow may have a generalizable meaning in daily life of skepticism for most viewers. When *Star Trek*'s Mr. Spock raises his eyebrow, however, the regular viewer responds as she has been trained to by many such occurrences, to the symbolic intent to communicate surprise or to acknowledge humor. The viewer recognizes which symbolic meaning is intended from the context in which the gesture is made, and she makes judgments about the relationships she sees based on the appropriateness of the responses by other characters on the screen. When Captain Kirk reacts to the raised eyebrow in a contextually appropriate manner that suggests he understands and accepts the code of Vulcan gestures, we make the connection that Kirk and Spock are friends. When other characters misinterpret or do not register the raised eyebrow, the viewer perceives the gesture as part of a code shared by the captain and his first officer but not by outsiders. The friendship becomes more significant when the two men share a secret gestural code.

Likewise, the way characters move around each other and touch each other may be transparent when those motions are uniformly distributed. The actions become symbolic when they are directed at only one or a few characters, designating relational discrimination. If Hutch normally holds himself aloof but touches Starsky, the relationship with Starsky becomes marked as more significant than other relationships, even if the touch is only to the arm or shoulder. The significance is not necessarily in the generalized social meaning of the particular gesture, but in the degree of divergence from normal behavior the gesture represents in the character.

Most surprising, I found that fans make preferential readings of the visual messages separately from the verbal ones. At one gathering, where fans had come to my home to introduce me to a new source product, we were watching an episode while discussing the homoerotic fiction produced in the community. I complained that I could not see that kind of relationship with this particular source product, because the characters didn't seem to like each other very much. My mentor responded by turning off the sound on the episode we were watching. Without the discussion, in which one character disdains the use of snub-nosed bullets suggested by his partner, the image tells a very different story. One character lies on a cot stroking his face with a handgun while the other sits beside him drinking from a coffee mug. The first man sits up, they speak for several seconds with their heads very close together, and then the second man takes a sip of his coffee, licks his lips, stands up, and walks away.

Stripped of the verbal argument, the erotic message was visually striking, but I wanted to be certain that my response had not been influenced by my knowledge of the fan stories. To test my reaction, I showed the clip to a fellow ethnographer with no experience of the literature of the group. Her response to the scene was stronger than mine; she commented, somewhat sarcastically, "Why doesn't he put the gun barrel in the cup and be done with it!"

Reading visual messages separately from the verbal ones, fans likewise become sensitive to interactions gone awry. In Houston, fans discussed their disappointment with *Miami Vice*, a program that interested only a limited number of fanwriters:

> Speaker 1: When it first came on I thought, "Oh boy, this is going to be great. These guys [Crockett and Tubbs, the police-partner heroes] are gorgeous." I watched it a couple times, but—
> Speaker 2: You could *tell* they can't stand each other.
> Speaker 1: No chemistry, no chemistry at all.
> Speaker 3: Now Castillo is very interesting.
> Speaker 4: I heard somebody [in the fan community] was writing a Castillo/Crockett novel.[26]

The partners, who in the conventions of action-adventure must depend on each other to survive, do not seem to care about each other. When asked why they think this is so, fans often answer that the two partners never meet each other's eyes and seldom even look at each other.

However, there have been a number of longer works that feature Martin Castillo, the Hispanic superior officer. Castillo, the lieutenant to whom the partners report, holds an almost magical sway over the imagination of many fans, and he does so with minimal dialogue even in episodes that feature his character. Caren Parnes, a Castillo fan, says of the character, "Well, he doesn't do well with language at all. I mean, he's actually fairly inarticulate."

Edward James Olmos, who plays Castillo, uses the gestural codes with such precision, however, that fans easily read intense relational feeling in his actions. One scene in particular strikes Parnes. In the episode "Duty and Honor," Miami experiences a series of particularly brutal murders reminiscent of serial murders Castillo tried to solve during the Viet Nam War. As the investigation begins, a stranger arrives whom Castillo knows as Trang, the Vietnamese policeman who worked with him on the case in Saigon. Parnes says of the meeting in a Miami police interrogation room:

> He [Castillo] sits down and they [several of the series regulars] are all around him watching the two of them [Castillo and Trang] and then with this little kind of half-smile he says "hello." And there is this—again—this very Oriental feel to the exchange. It's very short, not a lot of words, but it's this complete understanding between the two of them. A real, very strong bond there. And then a face is shown that he [Castillo] very rarely shows the people in his department. Very, sort of approachable.[27]

Lin Place invited me to her home to view this episode on videotape. I found that Olmos created with contrasts the mood in the scene Caren Parnes described. As Castillo he delivers most of his lines with his head lowered, markedly avoiding eye contact when he speaks. By contrast, when he enters the room where Trang, played by Haing S. Ngor, awaits him, Castillo makes and holds eye contact with the Vietnamese officer while he speaks to his men. At no point in the short scene does he look at anyone but Trang, nor does he ever look away. When he rises to leave, the two men say good-bye and clasp all four hands in farewell. The effect of the scene arises not only through the intense focus of the eye contact, but also because the viewer has been trained to see eye contact in this character as a rare gift he bestows sparingly and when words fail him.

Like Caren Parnes, Lin Place reads the visual codes of the episode, calling to my attention the particular images that make up the visual content of the message. Taking notes while I viewed the scene, I missed the handclasp the first time. Lin called it to my attention, then ran the tape back and played it over again so that I could see the important image of the four hands clasped in close-up.

Caren identifies the moment of significance in "Duty and Honor" as having an "Oriental feel," and the description is not accidental. Through contrasts in settings and behavior the character achieves a strange ethnic reorganization, almost as if a Hispanic Clark Kent were suddenly transformed into a Samurai Superman. As the viewer regularly sees him, Castillo seems almost to cave in upon himself, his shoulders hunched, his head bowed. Always taciturn, his movements slow and cautious, he wears a conservative black suit belted unfashionably high at the waist, white short-sleeved shirt, and narrow black tie.

Castillo's alter ego appears surrounded with signs of Eastern culture. In the episode "Bushido," he meets a former friend in a Buddhist shrine, and later, armed only with a samurai sword, he takes on Russian spies armed with submachine guns. In "The Golden Triangle," he demonstrates superior skills in Eastern martial arts, during which his posture and bearing shift, his movements become swift and precise. In each instance, verbal referents recall to the viewer Castillo's past in Viet Nam during the war and later as a drug enforcement officer in Burma; however, the program makes the real distinction between the thoughtful, serious, but tongue-tied Hispanic leader and the orientalized larger-than-life action hero through gestures, actions, and backgrounds that carry the message "quotidian" or "exotic."

In this example, the episodes in question can only be understood in the flow by an audience versed in the conventions both of police action series and martial arts movies. The contrasting states in the character can only be read in the macroflow, where the viewer has learned to anticipate and interpret certain forms of behavior.

Occasionally, fleeting gestures that resonate with more intimate symbolic meaning may create a sense that all the viewer's knowledge of a person, relationship, or situation is immediately present in the moment. At that point, the gesture becomes not only code but also symbol. In the *Miami Vice* episode "Honor and Duty" described above, the symbolic resonance of the microflow occurs at two points. The first has already been analyzed as it adds to the macroflow: Castillo uses eye and hand contact to signal a relationship with the mysterious stranger. The second occurs when the mysterious stranger, who has been introduced as Trang, a South Vietnamese police officer, but who the viewer later discovers is really from the North, must escape capture from the Miami officers he has aided in capturing the villain. Trang hits Castillo on the head, rendering him unconscious. Before making his escape, however, Trang tells the unconscious Castillo that they are still friends. He strokes Castillo's face once and disappears (not in a puff of smoke, but out the back door).

Fans perceive hands as sensual and faces as vulnerable. Hands touching a face may be perceived either as threatening, or, when the gesture is used in an environment of trust, as protective. In this context, the verbal affirmation of friendship is insufficient to counter the visual experience of the physical blow, but the gesture of hand stroking face reestablishes Trang's relationship with Castillo as mutually protective. The blow, read transparently as necessary for Trang's escape in the flow, could be read as a sign of betrayal in the macroflow, but its sign value is overturned by the contrasting symbol of the gentle touch to the face.

Intimacy, Identification, and the Narrative

The viewers in this study make judgments about the characters in the source products based on women's cultural definitions of intimacy. Those same cultural definitions govern the way the fan women relate to characters and action within the frame of the television screen. Accordingly, how they situate the fantasy relationship within the source product is a function of their conceptualization of a frame as a psychical as well as physical boundary.

The positioned interaction with the images inside of the frame has been called "the gaze." In Laura Mulvey's formulation,[28] movies are created by men for men. The woman in the frame becomes an objectified presence for both the satisfaction of the male scopophilia, or voyeurism, and the male narcissistic identification with the controlling male in the frame. According to Mulvey, even as object the female poses a danger because her lack of a penis connotes the threat of castration—thus the male as voyeur or as identified with the hero sees the sadistic images of destruction of women not as attack but as defense. The female viewer, however, is given no position from which to gain entry into the film experience. As a viewer she has been constructed out of the gaze.

Feminist critics such as E. Ann Kaplan[29] and Annette Kuhn[30] have taken up the challenge posed in Mulvey's article to analyze classic film psychoanalytically in terms of the gaze, using Lacanian and Freudian models. Unfortunately, the very model used to construct an understanding of male and female viewer positioning constitutes the female as immature. According to Nancy Chodorow, the woman's Oedipal phase remains incomplete because she cannot fully separate from the mother,[31] a view countered in the work of Carol Gilligan:

Since development has been premised on separation and told as a narrative of failed relationships—of pre-Oedipal attachments, Oedipal fantasies, preadolescent chumships and adolescent loves— only successively to erupt and give way to an increasingly emphatic individualism, the development of girls appears problematic because of the continuity of relationships in their lives . . . girls, seen not to fit the categories or relationships derived from male experience, call attention to the assumptions about relationships that have informed the account of human development by replacing the imagery of explosive connection with images of dangerous separation.[32]

Gilligan, like Chodorow, recognizes the connection of the woman to her primary relationships. She sets female growth in a context not of a failed male development but of a successful realization of a different cultural model. The viewer is not a half-created male but a fully realized woman. The style of that engendering does not of necessity lead the woman to a masochistic pleasure, but does regulate, to some extent, the relationship she maintains with the screen. Unlike the male voyeur, the media fan women in this group make little direct relationship with the product *across the frame*. Rather, the viewer looks inside the frame for characters giving and receiving visual attention; she makes an identification with one, with two, or alternating between two or more.

The women in my study do take the voyeuristic position across the frame in certain highly defined instances, such as when a character deliberately breaks the frame by leaving the set to talk to the viewer, or when the viewer catches a fragmentary view, in passing, of an image gazing out of the screen. While that point of view can attract the attention of the women viewers, it fails to meet the aesthetic preference of most of the people in my study. Part of this difference in the way the fan women preferentially correspond to the images within the frame of the screen may relate directly to the very different experiences of viewing a single movie and an action-adventure series on television. Unlike film, the macroflow level at which most fans view series television poses no sadistic threat to the woman but does give her an opportunity to indulge in many empathic identifications with men inside the frame. A common technique in both the songtapes and the fan stories will demonstrate this latter point. Fan artists often construct a songtape or story about a character from the standpoint of a member of the screen relationship and then pick up and reiterate the same sequence of events from first one and then another viewpoint until the reader has "seen" the events from the points of view of all the major characters present in the narrative. The writer will explore each character's feelings about the events, and many fan plots hinge on the true motives of the character—already known to the reader—being revealed to each other. The aesthetic here is not just to know the alien on the screen, be he Vulcan or human male, but to become him, and then to enmesh him in the social matrices that the female viewer finds "sane."

A Female Gaze and an Erotic Sensibility

When we contrast the female gaze developed here with the male gaze postulated by Mulvey and others, we can see a systematic divergence in the mode of attending to visual images. According to the materialist-psychoanalytic model, the Western male responds across the frame to the subject of the visual image as an object of both fear and possession. The object represents the threat of castration and must be diminished, transformed fetishistically into the thing it threatens: the penis. At the same time, the male's ownership of the fetishized object asserts his dominance not only over the objectified female but also in the hierarchy of males of his acquaintance.

From this we may derive that the fantasy of the male so constructed resides both in his ownership of the valued object and in the status ownership gives him: he is more desirable, more sexually powerful, than those who consider themselves his peers. The emphasis on fetishism in mainstream film, and on genital nudity in male-oriented erotica, seems to indicate that for men power is located in genital sex. The fantasy does not broaden to include a relationship of diapering babies and taking out the garbage, but remains forever idealized in the perfection of woman as sexual work of art and phallic man as art collector.

As we have seen in this chapter, the media fan women make a fantasy relationship inside the frame, not across it; the fantasy depends on no illusory possession of the object-image to give the viewer power among her peers. In fact, there is no real "object" at all. She sees as "handsome" characters who relate kinesically to other characters in the frame. Desirability can only be judged within the relationship between two or more subjects. Objects are not desirable, passivity is not desirable; therefore, the objectification of the relational other in the frame makes no sense as a fantasy.

The fan women's erotic engagement with visual media likewise seems to be less dependent on graphic detailing of genitalia than on the presence of an object of sexual focus in the frame. Paradoxically, many fan women reported that graphically explicit images actually dampened their erotic interest in the fantasy. No women reported erotic interest in the depictions of passively "seductive" unaroused nude males.

Many women in the fan community prefer images that reclaim the sensuality of the whole body. As shown earlier in the chapter, hands are perceived as sensual, and faces as vulnerable. Hands touching a face in an environment of trust symbolize sensuality as protective, and fans will often express romantic arousal—sighing, giggling, falling back in their chairs—during scenes in which hands caress faces, run through hair, or brush away a tear while both characters maintain eye contact. Conversely, fans read similar gestures made in an adversarial context as extremely threatening.

Kissing seems to be arousing only when tempered with restraint. A short pause for eye contact heightens the effect, while scenes of extended non-stop kissing turn fans off. Part of the problem may be that characters cannot maintain eye contact while they kiss. Kisses to the neck, the wrists, the inner arm elicit at least as strong a reaction as mouth-to-mouth osculation; women viewers seem to value the rediscovery of some of these more neglected erogenous zones. More graphic sexual scenes on television or in film generally elicit stronger demonstrations of arousal—laughing, shrieking, blushing, bouncing, nudging each other—but many fans define this kind of viewing experience as "fun," enjoyable in small doses but palling quickly as compared to the serious interpretations of more subtle gestures. This response is in sharp contrast to the appreciation of sexual material in their own work, and seems to demonstrate a difference in the aesthetics of the depictions of sexuality, and not in the fact of that depiction.

Because the women in the study respond to a wide range of subtly expressive touches and near-touches, dramatic gestures not intended as erotic may be read as such. As we have seen earlier, some women write erotic stories about the love relationship between Captain Kirk and Mr. Spock. It can be no coincidence that the gesture enacting the "mind meld" between the Vulcan and the character he most often melds with—the captain—is structurally very similar to that viewed as most erotic in sexual situations. That is, the Vulcan's fingertips are positioned on the cheek and temple close to the face-framing hair of the captain. Most of the songtapes representing a sexual relationship between Kirk and Spock include at least one mind-meld scene.

Women who write in the media worlds of *Star Trek* or *Blake's 7*, of *Starsky and Hutch* or *The Professionals* stress that it is the relationships of love and trust they see between the characters that draw them to these products. While a majority of the writers limit this relationship to an intense friendship, many fans do extend these relationships into the overtly, genitally sexual. When women characters are present in ongoing relationship to the hero, the fan writer will seize upon them as quickly as other fans explore male homoerotic relationships in their fiction. *Blake's 7*, for example, includes a number of strong men and women characters whose relational gestures can be read as a subtext of erotic interest in each other against an overt text of professional respect and mutual dependency. Writers often surface this subtext, and less homoerotic literature is written about this television product than any other.

In source products that focus on a pair of male heroes, however, there are no long-term women involved in equal relationships with the key characters. The conclusion drawn by some women fans becomes obvious. Either the hero is a cad incapable of intimacy or his relationship with his partner is so significant that it eclipses all others in his life.

Since few viewers like to think they would freely choose to admire a cad, many fans come to the alternative conclusion. The partners, or heroes in close working relationship, love each other. Again, the operative word here is "love," a passionate but nonsexual friendship. Much of what is written in the *Star Trek* universe falls into this model, while a growing body of the literature posits a sexual relationship between the captain and his first officer.

Female Symbols of Intimacy in *Beauty and the Beast*

For many years fan women dismissed male-female partnership series as unsatisfying. These series often surfaced the sexual tension between the characters into the text, adding verbal reinforcement to the visual interpretation that the characters are attracted to each other. In the process, however, they seem to lose the cues that signal solidarity. There seems to be less eye contact between characters in these programs, less sense of trust.

The most striking exception to this observation is *Beauty and the Beast,* a combination of action-adventure and romantic fantasy featuring the "other" as mythic beast loving and loved by a spunky assistant D.A. "beauty." Vincent, the leonine male lead, appears in full facial appliance makeup. Fur covers his clawed hands. In the absence of the many small gestures that fans usually read as sexual cues, fans remark on the way the character runs and walks, on the way he carries himself, and the way he tosses his head so that his flowing mane streams out behind him.

The women remark on the sensual nature of the actor's voice, but in group-viewing situations the viewers respond most vocally to the lingering glances between Vincent and Catherine, the female lead. Without exception, every woman who has discussed the program with me finds Vincent, the Beast, beautiful (although not all find him sexually attractive). Nowhere is the evidence stronger that eye contact is the most attractive visual cue to women: as can be expected, the media fans have incorporated this product into their repertoire more rapidly and widely than any series since *Star Trek.*

Fans of *Beauty and the Beast*, like fans of other source products, value the visual cues of the process of establishing and maintaining a sensual relationship between characters. They are adept at shifting their attention to the appropriate cues in the absence of more traditional gestures. However, the reaction of fans to the visual context with which the series creators surround the action in *Beauty and the Beast* is unique for source products adopted by the fan community. Viewers treat *Star Trek*'s *Enterprise* as a character to which other characters relate, but only in *Beauty and the Beast* is the background itself a deeply felt source of attraction. The particular contextualizing images that attract the greatest amount of attention in the group can only be described as uterine symbols. Vincent passes through long tunnels underground, he and his people live in vast underground caverns; both the tunnels and the caverns are lit with a diffused red glow. Spirals are intensely felt feminine symbols, and at the end of each episode the credits roll over a view down the center of a lacy iron spiral staircase, again lit with a hazy red glow.

Beauty and the Beast is an extreme case of visual images compensating for a perceived lack in the verbal narrative of the series. Fans often complain about the writing and the plots, and they object when the story takes the action above ground, in the phallic world of New York skyscrapers (where the heroine lives, of course). For significant verbal interaction, fans point to the reading aloud of Romantic poetry, which together with the visual setting and kinesic expressions of the relationship, creates the meaning the series has for these women viewers.

Notes

1. Mary Suskind Lansing, "Making Your Own Songtapes," *Consort 2* (Reprehensible Press, December 1986 [fanzine]), pp. 48–53.
2. Personal correspondence, Ellen Morris to author, February 22, 1987.
3. Name withheld, taped group interview, Houston, Texas, March 1987.
4. "He's Dead, Jim," and "Engineer's Song" are written and performed by fan Leslie Fish.
5. Ibid.
6. John Denver, "Follow Me," performed by John Denver on *Take Me to Tomorrow*, LP #LSP4278, RCA, 1970.
7. John Steinman and Dean Pitchford, "Holding Out for a Hero," performed by Bonnie Tyler on *Footloose*, Columbia Records #JS39242, 1984.
8. Mike Rutherford and Brian Robertson, "Living Years," performed by Mike and the Mechanics on *Living Years*, Atlantic #CS81923-4, 1988. *Magnum P.I.* relates the adventures of a formal naval intelligence officer who makes a marginal living as a competent but unambitious private investigator. His family relationships, and those formed during the Viet Nam War, figure importantly in the character's motivation.

9. In his article, "Learning Non-Aggression" (in *Learning Non-Aggression,* Ashley Montague, ed. [New York: Oxford University Press, 1978], pp. 161–221), Colin Turnbull describes physical games played by the Mbuti pygmies of Central Africa that strive toward a similar goal: the game is played well when everyone cooperates, and played poorly when noncooperation spoils the configuration of the game. A preference for noncompetitive games seems consonant with a social system based on nonaggression, as the women's community is.

10. See Sol Worth, *Studying Visual Communication* (Philadelphia: University of Pennsylvania Press, 1981 [1974]), and Worth and John Adair, *Through Navajo Eyes: An Exploration in Film Communication and Anthropology* (Bloomington: Indiana University Press, 1972). See also John Fiske, "Television, Polysemy and Popularity," *Critical Studies in Mass Communication* (1986): 391–408, for a culture-criticism analysis of the phenomenon.

11. Using a psychoanalytic model, feminist film critic E. Ann Kaplan has posited useful alternative readings for classic films (*Women and Film* [New York: Methuen, 1983]). Her analysis assumes there is a "correct" masculine reading which must be countered by the strategic repositioning of the female viewer. Kaplan's demonstration of reading "against the grain" (citing Judith Mayne's "The Woman at the Keyhole: Women's Cinema and Feminist Criticism," *New German Critique,* no. 23 [1981]) seems increasingly important as cinema focuses more narrowly on the target market of teenaged boys and men under twenty-five than it did in the years before television.

12. Stephen E. Whitfield and Gene Roddenberry, *The Making of Star Trek* (New York: Ballantine Books, 1968), p. 40.

13. Christopher Wicking, in *Primetime* 1, no. 2 (1981), pp. 5–8. John Fiske discusses polysemy and ethnic interpretations of television in his article "Television, Polysemy and Popularity." He is less successful in extending his argument (*Television and Culture* [London: Methuen, 1987]) because he identifies action-adventure with a specifically masculine reading, whereas successful action-adventure series creators target and reach an audience of men and women in a broad range of ages.

14. See, for example, E. H. Gombrich, "Visual Discovery through Art," in *Psychology and the Visual Arts,* ed. James Hoss (Baltimore: Penguin Books, 1969), pp. 215–38; or the section "Art and the Perceptual Process" in Bill Nichols' *Ideology and the Image* (Bloomington: Indiana University Press, 1981). Gombrich, in particular, also presents clues for the discovery of patterns in the macroflow.

15. Taped group discussion, Houston, March 1987.

16. Gombrich, "Visual Discovery," p. 237.

17. Ray Menmuir, quoted by Wicking, in *Primetime* 1, no. 2 (1981): 6.

18. Taped group discussion, Houston, March 1987.

19. Laura Mulvey, "Visual Pleasure and Narrative Cinema," *Screen* 16, no. 3 (1975): 6–18.

20. Kaplan, *Women and Film.*

21. Fanny Adams, taped interview, Chicago, 1987.

22. Terry Nation, untaped conversation in Philadelphia, March 1986.

23. Patricia Frazer Lamb, taped discussion, Houston, Texas, March 1987.

24. Larry Henley and Jeff Silbar, "Wind Beneath My Wings," performed by Gary Morris on *Why Lady Why,* Warner Brothers, #CS4-23738, 1983.

25. Judith Mayne ("The Woman at the Keyhole," pp. 27–43, as cited in

Kaplan, *Women and Film*) has challenged the female viewer to position herself at the projector, to take control of its speed, its motion. The projector has never become an integral part of the well-equipped home, but fortunately the video recorder has.

26. Taped group interview, Houston, Texas, 1987.

27. Caren Parnes, taped discussion, Cockeysville, Md., February 1987.

28. Mulvey, "Visual Pleasure."

29. Kaplan, *Women and Film.*

30. Annette Kuhn, *Women's Pictures: Feminism and Cinema* (London: Routledge and Kegan Paul, 1982).

31. Nancy Chodorow, *The Reproduction of Mothering: Psychoanalysis and the Sociology of Gender* (Berkeley: University of California Press, 1978).

32. Carol Gilligan, *In a Different Voice* (Cambridge, Mass.: Harvard University Press, 1982), p. 39.

Part III
Transgression and
Identity

Chapter Eight
Identity and Risk

In my study of the fan in the East, Mid- and Southwest, I found that most community members treated the rare radical feminist among them with benign tolerance. For most, fandom is where they go when the garden club or the people at the office don't understand their preoccupation with the ideas of *Star Trek* or their need to write, draw, talk, and fantasize about stakes higher than the spots on the stemware. Smart women, dreamers, artists of all political persuasions can come here in peace and acceptance—as can the lonely, the shy, the battered, the frightened, and the just plain weary. In fiction, the women of the fan community construct a safe discourse with which to explore the dangerous subject of their own lives.

Community, Genre, and Danger: The Conservation of Risk

In the fan community, thematic narrative content organized according to the specific conventions of each genre is the most consciously meaningful aspect of the women's creative expression. As we have seen, thematic genres have specific names in the community, and group members often identify themselves by their particular involvement with one or more of the thematic genres.

Genres symbolically structure topics deemed appropriate for discussion in the community, and they shape the metaphor with which real-life messages will be constructed for social interaction. They establish limits on whom the writer will meaningfully address with her message, and how the message will be read. Further, each genre functions at a different level of abstraction, moving the writer more deeply into metaphoric distance from the personal story she tells as she passes from genre to genre.

The genres that operate at the most abstract levels create the greatest psychological distance between the writer and the issue with which she may identify, so they carry the least risk of personal exposure. These genres are the most difficult to read symbolically, and are found more deeply embedded in the community than genres operating at less esoteric levels. In some cases, the community may trade similar messages both in a genre with a low level of abstraction and in one that functions at a high level of abstraction. The individual writer can then match her message to the genre that offers the degree of distance she needs to feel safe, based on the level of risk she perceives in speaking about the issue in her story. The danger of the issue in discussion is not eliminated, but only displaced, in a process I call the conservation of risk.[1]

In the fan community, risk is often displaced onto the theme of the genre. An example is a fan who may want to talk about sexual relationships. She must choose the potential for personal revelation present at the low level of abstraction in the genres about women in relationships with men or other women, or opt instead for the high-level abstraction of male homoerotic fiction, which carries a high-risk theme—male homosexuality—while providing a correspondingly greater literary distance from the author's own life.

Of course, the experience of selecting and writing in the genres is not homogeneous. The perception of risk and the options open to a writer depend most particularly on the position of the participant with regard to the community: creating a story in any genre is qualitatively different for fans working at the periphery of the community, to whom fanwriting constitutes a part-time hobby, than for fans who live in the group as their primary community. The former may write in relative solitude, may integrate the forms, structures, and themes of the literature, but may never use those forms, structures, or themes to ask or receive personal support from the group.

The core member may engage in a complex cycle of interactions with readers and other writers during which she may receive and give communal support both face-to-face and in the written work. Her choice of source product and thematic genre will determine to a large extent whom among the community's readers and writers she will touch with her work. Conversely, the group in which she participates may determine through its preferred choices in reading and writing material the genre a fan will use to communicate her message. A high-risk genre like K/S, with a high level of abstraction, may represent the individual writer's need for metaphoric distance from her topic, or it may reflect that general need in the group to which she belongs by accident of geography or friendship, and who are the readers she wishes to address.

Community as Risk

The two chapters that follow deal with the genres considered most dangerous in the community—homoerotic fiction, called K/S or slash, and hurt-comfort—but all participants feel that they risk something by participating in fandom. Some fear the ridicule of friends and family, as participants at More Eastly Con described:

Speaker 1: Have you ever met somebody who never reads S.F.—
Speaker 2: I have a mother who worries about me a lot, and she keeps on saying, "But darling, you're old enough now—you can live without those things now." Mother, get out of my house and leave my bookshelves alone . . . what does she mean I had too many books on the floor?
Speaker 3: That's what my mother said too.
Speaker 4: When I was a teenager, my father thought that this was just one of those passing fancies . . . [Everyone in the room laughs in recognition of the experience.] Now that I'm thirty-one, he's more or less resigned that this will probably go on forever.[2]

Others see their participation as a struggle to communicate the thoughts and feelings that make them different from outsiders. At another group interview, at Shore Leave in 1984, a fan confided,

Many of us don't have much confidence in our ability to use words. As one of my friends said this morning, that we ought to go learn Vulcan—I don't think any of us has said what we want to say.

A sense of failure in the outside world brings many women like Ann, the informant quoted below, to the community where they take risks to try again:

Until this period in my life, I had no ambitions in my life except to be a good wife and mother, at which I was failing miserably. If I had been succeeding at it, possibly—I am not a mother—I would not have turned to fandom, or discovered that I was a writer or a fan . . . these things irritated my husband because he married one type of woman and I was turning into another type of woman.

Ann's marriage ended in divorce—the papers stated her involvement with science fiction as a contributing factor, but now, she says,

> I look at my friends and I say, Gee, I am the friend of these people, and they are my friends because I'm me. A lot of people have friends to look good. It's more like they are my friends because I'm worth it. And I am their friend because they are worth it . . .[3]

Lois Welling took a similar risk when she decided she wanted more out of life:

> I was the great tradition, you know: get married, have kids, which I did. And along about ten years into that, I told my husband, "forget this shit."
> And he said, "No, we made a deal and I'm supposed to be the mind."
> And I said, "I don't care. I'm changing all the rules." And I started going [to conventions] anyway.

Lois's husband accepted her decision, and she feels that her participation in fandom has strengthened their relationship, but her life has not been easy. She says of fandom, "It's what keeps me going through the bad times and the boring times. I can't imagine what life would be like without this."[4]

Women who aspire to or who do write commercially, or who have any jobs in the publishing industry risk loss of income. One professional writer[5] explained that editors warned her to stay out of fandom if she wanted publishers to take her seriously. Publishers turned down a science fiction book she wrote, saying that it too closely resembled *Star Trek*. When she asked how, they responded that it had a spaceship and an alien, both staples in the form long before Gene Roddenberry borrowed them for *Star Trek*. This writer followed the warnings of her editors, but found her books sold no better and she was bereft of the companionship she had found in fandom for many years. With regret for the time she lost, and regardless of the risk, this writer has returned to her community.

Employers of another woman who works in publishing threatened her job if she participated in the community. She takes the risk, but under a pseudonym, as do a number of established commercial writers who enjoy the shared creation of fan fiction.

Most fans bring with them their bourgeois dream of white picket fences, husbands, two kids, and the dog, and their bewilderment that the dream doesn't work. Some have it all, but have discovered that it never has been enough. Some never came close to having it at all and still don't understand why. Even more never wanted it in the first place and don't understand why, as they grow older, they feel like they've had something important stolen from them. One lesbian informant has commented upon the heterosexist bias of the fan community but another gay participant expresses a deeper confusion. He still wants the bourgeois dream, and he feels cheated because his sexual attraction to men puts the dream out of touch. Many fear growing old alone.

Fanziners don't gather in each other's homes and in hotels around the country to march on the male heterosexual bastions and demand their rightful place. They come together for mutual healing, for protection from the outside, and to ponder the most pressing questions in their lives—Who am I? What do I really want? Why can't I have it? Why does life hurt so much?

As I studied the primary source material, I realized that, yes, there is danger in revealing these secrets, in telling too much. The risks are high. And yet. And yet. While the ethnographer pieces together the puzzle put before her, a niggling doubt pierces the euphoria. Conservation of risk is at work here. In their discourse, community members select a level of signification that protects them from risk of personal exposure, but the risk is real, it doesn't go away. Rather, the communication system they choose conserves and rechannels the risk into a form with which the participant feels more competent to cope. Often the answer is to contain the risk.

Containing the Risk

The community contains the risk inherent in asking oneself probing questions about life and one's place in it in a number of ways. Some fanwriters use pseudonyms to mask their identities from community members they don't know, or from outsiders who may stumble upon the material accidentally or in a work of scholarship.

Anonymous Authorship and the Pseudonym

As I grew more knowledgeable about the K/S fan community in particular, I realized that many of the writers and artists used pseudonyms when they published their work in fanzines. Writers and artists sometimes fear reprisals if the nature of their work becomes known outside the community. Australian schoolteacher Meg Lewtan, for example, values her pseudonym both for the protection and the privacy it affords her: ". . . [It's] my protection, and sort of the wall between me and the world and everything I put out."[6]

One informant underscored the feelings of many writers about their anonymity:

Because of the moral climate in this country lately, people, people who have been unafraid to attach their names to things are now not going to publish without pseudonyms. We'll continue to publish that material, but not under our real names.[7]

In a separate interview, Lois Welling commented about this fear: "People have jobs that they want to keep."[8]

The risks inherent in publishing erotic material about other people's characters are real, even inside the community. *Blake's 7* actors first learned about the homoerotic fiction during personal appearances, when participants asked facetious questions from the audience. The questioners tended to be marginal members who had little real experience with the community's literature, and the actors passed off the genre with indifference and humor. When one actor discovered the real identities of the slash writers in his source product, he found they were not strangers but included members of his own inner circle of fan acquaintances.

Reasonably, since the genre made him uncomfortable, he withdrew his friendship from these fans. Less reasonably, he took strong steps, including open letters to letterzines, to blackball the circle of homoerotic writers from the fan community. His efforts were largely unsuccessful, because the fans were well known and established not only in *Blake's 7* fandom but in many fandoms and for many years. The actor based his actions on false assumptions about his own importance in the community (see Chapter 2) and on the community's reaction to the erotica.

But the controversy, coming as it did at a time of stress in the growth of the interest group, did turn many fans away from that source product completely. A few fans left the community, many moved into other interest groups, while others participated in circles that gave little attention to the actors. The actor retained a smaller cadre of followers among the fanziners, but the controversy created many bitter feelings of personal betrayal for participants who were part of the fandom at that time. Over more than a year, the community as a whole adjusted to bear the strain, but interest in *Blake's 7* declined sharply within the fanzine community, as did the popularity of that actor among many fans.

Anonymity is important in a writer's relationship with the outside world and with some insiders. But as Lois Welling notes, anonymity is not the only value traded with the use of pseudonyms. They can become a status game: "It, it becomes sort of an 'in' thing. People know. If you're in, you know who this person is."[9]

Fans turn pseudonyms into a game as well. Meg, who participates not only in *Star Trek* fan fiction but also in other esoteric fan interests, was quick to assure me that she enjoyed the playful aspects of pseudonyms:

> I like to track down stories. I was thrilled to be able to find out that someone who had written my very very very very favorite K/S story, um, was also a writer in this fandom.
>
> She wrote—she writes in K/S under at least two pseudonyms that I know of, and I know her real name, and we had a correspondence.
>
> And she wrote back to me and said—this was really quite funny—um, that she was now in this fandom, that she had a couple stories, named them—one of my favorites—and said, "Do you know a letterzine from Australia?"
>
> And I had to write back to her and say, very blushingly, "Yes, I know of it. Not only do I know of it . . ." [Meg published it.][10]

In spite of status considerations and the playlike attitude of many pseudonym hunters, the anonymity of some writers does remain intact, as Meg describes: "I like to track down stories . . . So it can be very frustrating. I mean, I'd like to know who wrote 'Endgame.'"

Most community members consider "Endgame," a story written in 1982, to be the best example of a death story written in its fandom to date. To mention this story even today will elicit the reaction of the reader to her first reading of it, no matter how long ago that reading may have been. This is a particularly affecting story, and unlike many other works on the circuit (see below), the merits of its literary style or plot devices are not debated. A typical answer to questions about it is, "Any reaction you have to that story must of necessity be valid." Members of the fandom feel that the story forces truth not only *on* the reader but *out of* the reader as well. A number of works have been written in response to it, and yet, after eight years, the author's identity remains a secret closely guarded by the very few privy to the information.

Limited Access and the Circuit

While some fans use anonymity to contain the risk they take in the community, we have seen that it is not always successful. A more effective approach is to limit formal access to the materials. Community members find out about fanzines by attending conventions held by community members, where fanzines are sold at tables in the huckster rooms and fliers for planned publications are displayed on tables near registration and information. They may read directories produced in the community, or see advertisements for new publications in other fanzines, or hear about them by word of mouth.

As we have read throughout this study, access to the community is difficult and requires both acceptance on the part of the local group and commitment on the part of the newcomer. Sometimes, however, even the limited access of the fanzine community at large seems too open. The circuit limits access to a circle or set of trading circles, or to fans who have already demonstrated an interest in a less widely accepted kind of fiction.[11]

A story will usually begin its run on the circuit in the home circle. The writer will give copies to several members of the home circle, who will make copies for other members of the circle. Those members will send copies to friends in other circles, who will copy and pass the story on again. Access to the circuit requires contact with a circle that has at least one member who regularly receives and distributes stories from other circles. (See Chapter 2.)

Star Trek fandom, the oldest and largest of the fan groups, continues to produce large numbers of fanzines, but some *Star Trek* stories travel a limited circuit to gather commentary before a final draft for a fanzine is written. Sometimes an author will write a story for which she does not see a fanzine market, or does not want to put in the extra work that writing for an editor would require, and she will circulate that story privately among friends as well.

Some of the new fan interests, such as *Blake's 7*, continue in the fanzine tradition with only a limited circuit, whereas other fandoms are trying new methods of distribution. One fandom, while it continues to publish a few fanzines, passes most of its literature through the complex photocopying network of a subfandom-wide circuit. In exchange for limited access to the circuit, I had to promise not to identify the source products around which it has formed or those who write in it anonymously.

At the 1986 Clippercon convention, during a group discussion about the circuit, Lois Welling, a *Star Trek* fanziner who also participates in the more hidden fandom, contrasted how the perspective on copying for private circulation differs in the two groups, in spite of the fact that a high percentage of the memberships overlaps:

> You know, in *Star Trek* fandom you wrote a story that was probably going to go in a zine. You know, you'd show it to people. If some-

body sent it to you for proofing and comments, you kept it. In this fandom, it's like—Shit, xerox fifty copies and push them out.[12]

An unidentified speaker added to this thought:

> I'm sure that if xerox capability had been there when *Trek* started, that it would be in the same place this fandom is now. When *Trek* started it was mimeo, because that's what people could get their hands on.[13]

Photocopy remains prohibitively expensive for extensive distribution in less urbanized regions of the United States and abroad. However, in major American metropolitan areas a growing number of copy centers provide the service for relatively low fees. Fans of this one source product have adopted the technology wholeheartedly, while fans of other products use photocopying to expand their reach as well. Lin Place explained how and why she copies for representatives of a number of fan circles:

> . . . Down in the college area there's two [copy centers]. It's just cheaper for me to copy . . . and I'm not going to send my originals out anyway. I used to do it by hand, to save the penny [per copy difference in the price] for five and a half cents each [page] and I said, "If they want the extra story they're paying the extra penny" because I just can't stand here anymore. I just divide single-sided and double-sided, and I tell him I want two sets of those and three of that and four of that and they're really good.[14]

While the cost per copy in urban college centers may be low, the scale of copying is extensive, and Lin estimates that she spends roughly one hundred dollars on each foray to the copy center, most of which is reimbursed by the fans for whom she copies. Fans like Lin, who copy for others, develop a working relationship with the proprietors or clerks of the copy centers they patronize:

> Lin: I wasn't in for a while, because nothing new had come in on the circuit, and these guys said, "where were you, we missed you, we're going to go bankrupt if you don't start coming back."[15]

The content of some material, particularly explicit art, can be a problem at copy centers as it is with some printers, but Lin's experience having a fanzine re-bound seems fairly typical:

I went up to this guy, because I go in there quite often and I said, "Now you, um, don't mind doing, you know, adult graphic art, do you?" and he said, "Nah, let's see what it is." He says, "Oh, no, I don't mind." He said, "That's pretty interesting, too, isn't it?" And I could see him perusing it [the fanzine]. I can't really stop them. They have a nice attitude about it where I go.

In this and other accounts of her experiences with the photocopy centers, Lin's voice recaptures the experience of asking a male clerk to handle women's erotic fiction and art. She mimics her hesitation to ask him to bind the fanzine and the clerk's effort to make her more comfortable by demonstrating acceptance of the material. In spite of his averred interest, however, the clerk is still an outsider. Lin clearly would prefer some alternative to exposing the material outside the community, but recognizes the effort both parties must make to keep the system operating.

Unlike fanzines, which depend on fairly large runs to be economically viable, the circuit functions on a diffused dispersion system based directly on the networks between community circles. The system has drawbacks—unequal distribution, poor availability, and high prices of photocopies in some parts of the country and outside the United States. The cost, even at prices such as Lin pays, exceeds the comparable cost per story of a fanzine, but the circuit offers the advantage that a participant need not buy a whole fanzine. Meg Lewtan, an Australian fanwriter visiting America for a series of conventions, gave her perspective on the pressures that have turned many fans away from fanzines and toward the development of the circuit:

The circuit started off as friends passing stories to friends, who introduced them to friends and by the cheapest possible method, which was xeroxing. Then the circuit grew. People started swapping from England to America, and Australia got in the act as well . . .

And the thing [about fanzines] that's worrying, I think particularly the Australian fans, is that we've got three strikes against us. One is distance, two is the exchange rate, and three is the cost of mailing.

And there are times—not often, I'm pleased to say,—that people have been taken for money. We're laying out this much money, and if it doesn't turn up, what recourse do we have? . . . But mainly, it was that people were worried about the escalating cost.

And I know people who have said they would much prefer to just read stories. It's very nice to have illos, very nice to have poetry, but there's a lot of white space in a zine. Plus stories are tied up for a long time.[16]

In her comments, Meg underscores the main reasons why fans in Australia and England have been drawn to the concept of the xerox circuit. As has been described, fanzines have become increasingly expensive, and the cost to fans overseas is increased by unfavorable exchange rates and very high mailing costs. When the cost for postage exceeds the cost for the product, the purchaser is more than ever conscious of the "white space" or blank paper in a zine, paper for which the purchaser has paid postage but received no product.

The risks for fans participating at large distances are correspondingly greater as well. Fanzine fandom runs by payment in advance for products shipped in the mail, and purchasers eight thousand miles away have two concerns over and above the initial cash outlay. They may have ordered from the less than 1 percent of overambitious zine editors who cannot deliver the product they have promised, or the product may be lost or stolen in the mail. Fans in the mainstream of the community are more likely to have information about the reputations of editors, and have greater recourse to tracing lost packages in the domestic mails.

Meg's last comment, that fanzines tie up stories for a long time, is a common complaint, particularly among members of the fandom accustomed to the rapid distribution of the circuit. Karen Brandl, a well-known and highly respected editor in the fandom, explained that she generally takes two years to produce each issue of her fanzine. For many fanzines a year to two years' preparation time is the norm. As Meg implied, stories travel much more quickly on the circuit. My own experience is common.

After five years of research, I decided to try my hand at writing a story. I chose the fandom that distributed stories through the circuit because at the time I believed it to be too small to be significant to my study, but I wanted to see if I had absorbed enough of the group aesthetics to produce a story that the members would find satisfying. I gave the story to my contact with permission to distribute it, provided that my name was not attached to the story. She volunteered to act as go-between for comments that might be returned to the source. During this portion of my study I sent several stories through the circuit, and submitted several more to a fanzine editor using a pseudonym.

When I released my stories on the circuit, I did so anonymously for a number of reasons. I did not want fans to apply more or less stringent criteria to their criticism because of my researcher/outsider status. At the same time, I wanted to preserve my outsider status as a protection for my informants, who might be inclined to tell me as a participant things they would later be dismayed to find in print. The decision fit comfortably into the system of the circuit, however; almost all of the circuit stories circulate with either no name or a pseudonym. As described above, some writers in all of the fandoms have used pseudonyms for many years, but it is here, where the highest risks are taken in themes and levels of eroticism, that anonymity is most strongly preserved. But fear for personal reputation in the outside world is only one part of the drive toward anonymity in the circuit, as an informant pointed out:

> People can write stories, "first draft, get it off my chest, I want to write this situation" stories, and put it out on the circuit without their names on it [and] without being critiqued.[17]

In fact, fans do critique stories on the circuit, but the most vulnerable group of writers—first-time and relatively new writers—tend to be immune. A reader/critic may be incensed to find awkward first efforts in a fanzine for which she has paid twenty dollars. That same fan will let the same story fall by the wayside on the circuit, where the expense for the single effort is small and the volume is high. On the circuit, only stories that offend the group ethic seem to attract serious censure.

Stories that do receive criticism, or discussion, generally fall within the accepted aesthetic, and critics compare the quality of the story to others by the same author, recognizable by pseudonym or style, or point out high or low points in characterization or action. This was the kind of critique I sought for my first story, and within six weeks fans from as far away from my home in Pennsylvania as California and Nevada had responded to my contact with their comments. One of the respondents included an illustration inspired by the story. Within four months I had a request from an Australian editor (through my contact) to have the story withdrawn from the circuit and placed in her fanzine, which my contact did for me. I have since filtered three more stories anonymously into the circuit, and the immediate response to them has pinpointed for me where the aesthetic eluded me.

Until I actually sent stories through the circuit I had access to the identity of very few writers in it, and I thought I knew few fans of this product. The similarity of the circuit stories to works in other fandoms surprised me. After I made it known in a limited way that I had written a story on the circuit, some of the fans were concerned that my study would endanger the anonymity of their group. Others accepted me as they had not done before, and many more circuit writers spoke to me about their work in the source product. I discovered that I already knew most of them for their writing in other source products. A number of them, like Lois Welling, had been enthusiastic informants since the beginning of my study: I thought they had "told all," but in fact they had been participating in the circuit fandom without telling me about it since we began working together in 1983. In all that time I had not suspected their interest in this fandom—for much of that time, my informants kept secret the very existence of the circuit.

When I first became aware of the circuit, I wondered what the effect on the aesthetics would be when unmediated art passed into the open distribution system. Editors of fanzines act as arbiters of taste, suggesting changes to stories that may not meet the aesthetic criteria of the group. Without editors, could the circuit maintain the integrity of the community's forms? In what directions would changes develop with no one to impede the introduction of innovation? Would the circuit remain accessible to fans of other source products, or to new fans of this source product introduced through the fanzines? To what extent would the fanzines reflect the changes in the literature on the circuit?

The answers—and the reasons for them—came as a surprise. In fact, the circuit showed evidence both of conservatism and of change. The source product had a contemporary setting, and at least part of the production of most circuit writers and artists conformed to the canon-established characters and settings, based on a system of interpretation recognizable by fans of any source product used in the community. Stories that present themselves as conforming to canon are analyzed for their success by the community in face-to-face discussions, personal correspondence, and letters of commentary. While the source product was not science fiction, the writers continue to express the messages they traded in the *Star Trek* fan fiction, and in other source products.

As fans accepted that I had become knowledgeable in the circuit and revealed their identities, I began to understand why the aesthetic remained relatively unchanged. Because the circuit is so well hidden, only the most experienced writers and readers have access to it. These experienced fans work consciously to preserve the standards of fan fiction developed over time in *Star Trek* and other fan literature; at the same time, the very depth of their experience gives them the freedom to explore new ways of expressing the messages most important to them.

The alternate universe story—one which claims no connection to the series canon—is a staple in all the source products, but diverging as it does so markedly from the canon, it carries with it greater risks for the author. What happens when you break the aesthetic rules of the community? How far can you go? Will fans accept the alternate world as a likely or believable one? What communication will the move into a new and different context open up in the community? Will it, on the contrary, close doors to the writer open in the more canonically recognizable forms?

In the protected environment of the circuit, writers of alternate universe stories have the freedom to transcend the limits set in most mediated forms. While they retain in their work a greater or lesser resemblance to the two or three main characters, circuit writers and artists may recast these characters into historical stories, fantasy stories, and even cast them as new characters in the stories they write for other media products.

The movement away from the canon has not been entirely easy, however, even for writers in the circuit. Meg Lewtan, who has written both canon-oriented and alternate universe stories, feels ambivalent about the historicals and fantasies even while she writes them:

> I have a real problem with it [alternate universe] in that I like to hang my stories on the series. I very rarely write alternative universe stories . . . in fact, I've written three . . . [she describes two stories that stayed close to source.]
>
> . . . one that I've done which is just absolutely for fun is a Victorian—there's no other word for it—it's a Victorian melodrama. But all I have done is just pick up two people, two characters, and put them in a story. Now that is a transference.
>
> Whether you agree with doing it or not, it's up to the individual. I personally think it's fun. I do it for fun.[18]

For other writers, the new settings offer meaningful metaphors with which they can present their messages. Fanny Adams, who writes both canonical universe and alternate universe stories, explained in a letter why she writes fantasy:

> Magic is, for me, another metaphor. I think of it as a word that refers to all human potential . . . All words are symbolic, of course, but words having to do with spirituality are more so.[19]

While alternate universe stories expand the range of possibilities for fanwriters, the circuit has not descended into a disordered array of idiosyncratic forms. Rather, the stories fall into just a few new categories—historical and fantasy fiction—that coincide with the readership preferences in commercial fiction. Science fiction stories do appear occasionally, but most of the writers reserve their science fiction work for *Star Trek* and other source products where such stories conform to canon.

Fanzines published in this fandom have come to reflect the aesthetic changes that first appeared on the circuit. Fantasy stories in which one or all of the main characters are elves or vampires, or in which the human heroes interact with same, have appeared in fanzines for some time, and a number of fanzines now being prepared will offer historical as well as fantasy and canon-oriented stories.

Over the years the circuit has changed to include new source products and a new community involvement in a number of original products created entirely within the community. Some creators of these original products invite groups of fanwriters to participate just as they do with media products, while others are preparing their original creations for potential commercial sale.

The Library

In 1983 the volume and unpredictable distribution system of the circuit surpassed Karen Brandl's tolerance threshold for disorganization. Karen, a longtime participant known for the fanzines she edits and the conventions she organizes, decided that the circuit needed a central clearinghouse to give some sense of order to the growing number of stories, sequels, and series. In a letter, she explained:

> . . . By the end of 1983 things were really getting out of hand. The women I was getting stories from were also feeding many others, and the costs were becoming prohibitive. I, too, was passing stories on to many other fans, and I could not afford to continue the amount of xeroxing I was doing. So gradually, the idea of a Library took shape, and in early 1984 I started it.[20]

Presently, most writers send Karen at least one copy of their stories for inclusion in the Library. Through her circuit sources Karen obtains most of the other stories available for general distribution. The circuit's product comes from all over the world, and from writers or photocopyists with varying qualities of equipment. According to Karen, hundreds of stories reach the Library in barely legible condition. Some fans therefore contribute to the Library by retyping the more illegible works.

Community members from the United States, Canada, England, Scotland, and Australia subscribe to the Library service for a small fee, almost all of which pays for copying at the local copy center. Subscribers receive a bimonthly update on the available stories, organized alphabetically by title. Stories in series are also subheaded under the title of the first story in the sequence, so that fans can keep track of continuing storylines.

A subscriber may borrow up to ten stories on the list for a period of two weeks, reimbursing the Library for the postage cost. The subscriber, who may request packages at any time after she returns her last borrowing, usually photocopies the stories for her own collection before returning them.

According to Karen, the Library had 114 members in 1987, but that number varies as new members subscribe, and others drop their subscriptions.[21] Karen, who fits her Library, fanzine, and convention activities around her work running a cleaning service, remarked that she used to worry that she might not be able to provide adequate service to the expanding list of subscribers, and adds:

> . . . but not anymore. I have got used to always being 2 or 3 weeks behind with Library work, and the members have got used to a bit of a slow-down from the early days. The membership list isn't expanding all that quickly—I seem to pick up 2 or 3 new members every two-month period, usually more after a con[vention] . . . several fans use the Library mostly for the lists, as a way to keep their own records in order.

One reason the subscriber list now remains fairly constant returns us to the circuit. While some subscribers to the Library participate alone, many are part of smaller photocopy circles, who pool their resources. A photocopy circle usually depends on at least one participant's access to reasonably priced copying facilities. Some photocopyists own machines. In a circle, perhaps two or three members will have subscriptions in the Library, and they will pool their borrowing so that everyone in the circle receives a copy of all of the stories as they become available. Photocopy circles often make contact with each other, and a new circle can greatly accelerate its acquisition of the material by tapping into the older circle's collections. And so the Library's stories, coming from the circuit, are filtered back into the circuit once again.

Conservation of Risk: Metaphoric Distance

As we have seen, some fans contain the risk of participation in fandom by using pseudonyms or by trading their stories on the circuit.

Other fans need distance not from their readers, but from the very questions they seek to ask. One we have talked about already is the metaphoric distance the various genres afford the writer as she works out in fictional models the possibilities she imagines. Science fiction gives temporal distance: mores and customs can change over time. The hero is an alien, not a human—his feelings have nothing to do with my feelings. Many community members need more distance than science fiction alone affords them. Male-male friendship and homoerotic fiction, by eliminating the female character with whom the writer or reader may identify too closely, offers a greater metaphoric distance from which the writer can work out her questions. If challenged, she can respond, "It's what I see, those are the characters on the screen I have to work with."

Friendship stories, called relationship stories in the community, are the most common genre, and address the most widely asked questions the community asks of itself—the meaning of friendship, of depending on others, and of supporting others in turn. Many fan women find in fandom their first experience of community and close friendships with women. The community must work out its questions— What does my friendship mean to you? What does it mean to me? What are the limits to friendship?—without offending members, or preaching to them, or frightening them away. Sometimes, however, a situation will confront the community with which it cannot deal by indirection. When that happens, members fall back on the tenets of community life for which the relationship stories serve as blueprints.

Testing the Boundaries: A Case History

In the fan community, the very process of creation generates the social situation. Fans gather to trade and sell their fanzines, to tell stories, to watch the source products and the music videos, and to construct lives based on the tenets they build into their fiction. Among the most important beliefs are the trustworthiness of fans and the willingness of fans to contribute to the good of the community in the spirit of IDIC—the joy of Infinite Diversity in Infinite Combinations. Community members use their serious fiction to explicate their belief system, and their humor and play to enforce it. In some cases, however, even the most well intentioned may fail in their obligation to the community so markedly that the usual forms of social control—indirection and playful humor—do not succeed in stabilizing the situation. At such times, the community faces the danger of breaking its own rules of caring and acceptance. To survive as a group, members have to find a way to repair the damage caused by the broken trust. The following is the story of one such rupture of the social fabric of the group and how the community coped with honor.

The case of Syn Ferguson's *Courts of Honor* demonstrates the paradox that the fan community is often at its best when it is at its worst. Syn Ferguson[22] wrote to me of her struggle to write *Courts of Honor,* a homoerotic novel with many scenes of hurt and fewer, perhaps, of comfort. The novel is about love and honor and putting oneself on the line, personally, for what one believes. It sets the hero a test: to win as a "hero" Kirk must sacrifice his personal honor; to retain personal honor he must relinquish his position as a hero in the eyes of the Federation. Spock, imprisoned and brutalized in the novel, comes through his experience with a new understanding of himself and his relationships.

During the roughly four-year course of writing the novel, Syn struggled with that creative effort, often at the expense of basic life necessities. She lost jobs, found jobs, and lost them again. She received support, including food and shelter, from a succession of fans and non-fan friends and lost that support. Advances paid for copies of the novel went to buy food and pay rent, and for one or two weeks when everything else failed, Syn lived in her car. Not everything she did was sensible or appropriate in the community. Fans are not allowed, by law, to make a profit on their ventures, and Syn had priced her novel accordingly. She lived on the advances, although she had no profit margin in her price to pay for production of the actual book.

A number of fans who had sent her up to twenty dollars for a copy of *Courts of Honor* sent her hate mail, and one even left a mutilated toy dog on her front lawn. In her letter to me, Syn sums up:

> Poor Syn. Poor Spock. How terrible it is to be imperfect and need other people. Easy to see why Spock needs Kirk. Harder to see why Kirk needs Spock. I think it is to let the weakness in. You cannot love weakness or failure. You might love an individual who was weak and failed. (Spock as the Trojan horse, taking destruction to the city, taking in wildness, taking in weakness and failure and yielding and guile. Offering what the hero lacks and needs to be whole.)[23]

Syn's letter is one long account of risk and suffering, of courage and the limitations of that courage in herself and in her community. *Courts of Honor* is a good read but no *Finnegans Wake*. The obsessive drive to create an association with the genius resides also in the mid-level talent as defined by literary norms of masculine culture,[24] but Syn is a genius in her own right. Writing about honor and obligation and love in the discourse of the community, Syn creates the archetypal fan work, while the history of that creation carries the discourse out into the community itself. Syn is the weakness the community takes in to be whole. She cannot meet the standard of ideal behavior in the community, nor can the community treat her lack with the ideal of tolerance its philosophy dictates. Real people are cranky and difficult to live with, they expect return in pages written for their food and shelter, and opportunism lurks on both sides of the equation. Would the fan community have extended as much support for Syn the person as it did for Syn the producer of highly valued fiction? Should Syn have taken so much from the community—assistance freely given, and funds sent to her for a different purpose entirely—to complete a work that would create more controversy than printed copies?

Syn offers no answers, but the story continues past her letters, back out into the community, and shows us that once again the apparent questions are not the most important ones. About to abandon fandom and the completed manuscript, Syn confided her intention to one friend. While respecting Syn's wishes that her whereabouts remain hidden, the friend assembled a committee of editors and writers to save the manuscript. My account of the action to save *Courts of Honor* has been put together from interviews with a number of the committee members, including Flora Post, well-known fan poet, and Victoria Clark and Barbara Storey, editors of the fanzine *Nome*.

The committee gave notice to the community at large: they could not take responsibility for the funds already spent, but they would print *Courts of Honor,* priced no higher than the original offering. Committee members accepted no prepayments but instead put in shares of their own money to pay for the initial printing. If a fan wanted a copy she could order it for payment on receipt. She would have to pay all over again, but she would be assured both of receiving a copy of the novel and of losing no further money. The committee auctioned Syn's small fan art collection and promised that any profits which might accrue from the sale of art or the sale of the novel would be distributed on a pro-rata basis among the creditors who lost their money on pre-paid orders with Syn.

As I examined the remarkable history of this work, I was constantly reminded of the Kohlberg ethical development tests discussed by Carol Gilligan.[25] Rather than judge human weakness and failure in black and white terms, community members asked themselves, "What is best for the community?" No one in the community condoned Syn Ferguson's behavior: she had betrayed trust, the single most important aspect of fan life. After the initial uproar, however, the community accepted the limitations of the human being and reified the importance of her message. The committee published *Courts of Honor,* the fans bought it, and many believe it to be the best work of its kind produced in the community to date.

Homoerotic Fiction: Voices Against K/S and Slash

The level of metaphor at which Syn wrote did not cause her problem, but it limited both the distribution of the final work and the amount of support some community members would offer. Homoerotic fiction addresses some of the most risk-laden questions in the community. At this level of abstraction, the author achieves the greatest distance from direct exposure of some of her deepest anxieties, but conserves the risk with a metaphor that poses the greatest danger of censure from within and without the community.

When *Newsweek* mentioned fan interest in ideas about "S & M" and homosexuality among the *Star Trek* characters,[26] it was exposing the fan fiction genres of hurt-comfort and K/S to public shock and amusement. Even within the community, however, fans disagree on the value of K/S. Some members are vehemently opposed to the homoerotic material on religious or moral grounds, and it offends them that they are called upon to accept this particular difference in the spirit of IDIC. With no exception, fans who offered this opinion refused to discuss their objections with me on tape. The community ideal to accept difference seems to exert pressure on members to make clear distinctions between opinions that reflect the community and opinions that affect the self, and while members would openly discuss their personal feelings, they would generally allow me to tape only those opinions that concerned the community.

Over the eight years that I followed the community, the amount of open opposition to the genre has fallen off sharply. Increasingly, fans direct their opposition less at the genre itself than at the logical consistency of its premise in particular circumstances. Lois Welling writes slash relationship fiction for another source product but hesitates to use the genre for *Star Trek:*

> The picture of them together won't run in my head. As for . . . that (other relationship) I can see. The difference for me is that these two do not have 430 crew people looking to them for their safety.[27]

Roberta Rogow, in an editorial from her fanzine *Grip,* agreed with Lois:

. . . I've made some judgments in the past, and I have revised my opinion about a number of things . . . [T]here is the K/S premise, which is that Captain Kirk and Mr. Spock are "more than just good friends." I've been pretty vocal about this for a number of years, and I've gathered a remarkable batch of feudists en route. I refuse to believe for one minute that "our" Captain Kirk will do anything to put his career in jeopardy, and "our" Mr. Spock isn't going to have a sexual relationship for any reason but propagation of the species. However . . I've read a few 'alternative' K/S stories that make a little more sense, and are not as involved with the mechanics of the relationship as they are with the emotions. So . . . another qualified revision of opinion.[28]

It is the "mechanics of the relationship" that disturbs some fans. Ann Pinzow objects less to the genre itself than to the explicit nature of some of the stories.

There have been some very explicit K/S stories . . . Personally, I'm not against the homosexual aspects of them, although they are very unreal . . . they don't tell it like it is. I object to the pornography in them. Some of them are very good. Some of them are not pornographic. Some of them . . . explain a type of relationship that otherwise may—could not be explained.[29]

Pinzow also expresses a concern that the stories may cause embarrassment for the actors who originally created the characters that fans appropriate for sexual reinterpretation: ". . . [T]he important thing is, and I agree, to keep the actors separate from this type of thing."[30]
Fans of *Starsky and Hutch* agree so strongly with this last concern that the mere threat of exposure to the actors in that series drove the fan product underground in the community.

Speaker 1: . . . You were there at the panel yesterday, when Karen said that the first issue [of a homoerotic fanzine], you know, she only sold to people she knew. She was very protective of it, because some people didn't like the idea.
Speaker 2: Well it was mainly because some people were threatening to send copies to the actors.
Speaker 1: Yeah, and we don't do that kind of stuff to our actors.
Speaker 2: At this point, it's ten years later. Who cares.
Speaker 1: Yeah, it's not going to affect them.[31]

While acceptance of the form has grown in the community, there still remains a core of resistance to the material. Vicki Clark and her co-editor, Barbara Storey, named their fanzine *Nome*, a word that Clark says was created in the *Star Trek* series to mean an infinite diversity of things that combine to make existence worthwhile. The meaning was apt, because Clark and Storey wanted to accept any well-written material that handled its subject in an adult fashion. Things did not work out quite as they expected, and Vicki reflected on the experience:

> And it made me kind of sad. Once we decided that we would reflect as much fandom as we could, including K/S—once we began accepting K/S, doors were closed to us, because there were certain other areas of fandom which will not, who will not send material to a zine that has K/S, even if it [the fanzine] is only partial K/S . . . so what has happened is, *Nome* has become primarily K/S relationship.[32]

Ironically, neither Vicki nor Barbara writes K/S herself, preferring to stop short of a sexual relationship between the characters.

To this point we have listened to fans who objected to the homoerotic fiction on its own terms, for what it is. Among the opposition, however, some participants are more concerned about the loss to the community of the female presence in the fiction. As described at length in Chapter 4, fans including Johanna Cantor and Linda Deneroff complain that the literature needs more strong women characters. In their work and in their editorships they encourage other community members to imagine strong women in equal sexual relationships with the television heroes.

Conservation of Risk: Hiding in Plain Sight

Conservation of risk is most active between the insider and the outsider, where exposure is both the risk and the prize. As an ethnographer, I found myself searching for the heart of this community: what made it tick? What single unifying factor tied a neophyte Mary Sue writer together with the reader and creator of the domestic dynasty of the lay-Spock, with the writer of the slave story or the five-page homosexual vignette? The deeper I penetrated the community, the more elusive my goal became.

Of course, a community gives certain signals when an outsider approaches the heart of its culture. In the beginning the heart is hidden—often in plain sight—passed over, casually dismissed by those in the know. Later, as the importance of the practice, object, or belief starts to emerge from the dense fog of apparent communal indif-

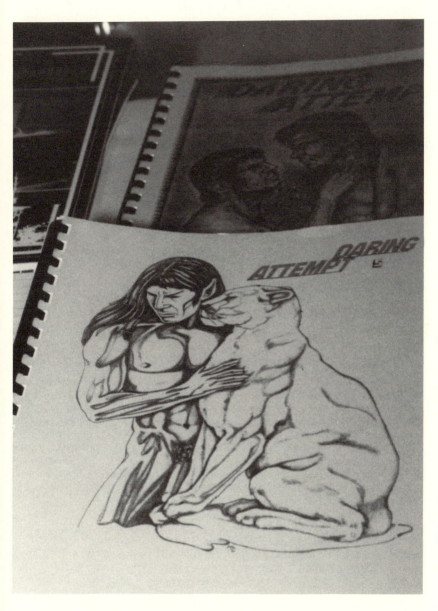

Exploring risk in the community.

ference, the intrepid ethnographer finds herself swamped with data—explanations that agree too closely with one another, that offer tidy answers to her questions with no loose ends left to unravel.

When the investigator gets too close, the community sidetracks with something of value, something that conserves the risk the ethnographer knows is present but that does not expose *too* much, that does not reveal the heart of the community. Homoerotic literature *is not* the heart of the community, but my introduction to the genre came late in my study and with all of the symptoms of being headed off at the pass I described above. That does not mean that K/S—generically, slash—is insignificant. In fact, for me understanding the genre was a necessary precursor to my understanding the community. Graphic homoerotic literature is the one thing that is almost as dangerous to know about as the heart, but that no one can read or write without knowing she is doing so. The action, if not the meaning, remains at the level of consciousness, which is not necessarily true of the symbolizing heart of the community. However, when we understand slash, we begin to understand danger.

Notes

1. I first became aware of the conservation of risk when working with a group of women in state-of-the-art technical fields who relied heavily on intuitive knowledge that on occasion took on the aspects of psychic experience. The women began to discuss their experiences and agreed to let me tape the discussion. As soon as the tape began to roll, however, the women shifted the conversation to the topic of rape. The new discussion conserved the risk of the earlier one. Discussion *on tape* of what one would do if raped seemed equivalent in risk value to off-tape discussion of leading-edge technical function by intuition. I have since noticed a similar correspondence in other interactive situations.

2. Group discussion, More Eastly Con, La Guardia Airport, Long Island, N.Y., August 1986.

3. Ann Pinzow, taped interview, Shore Leave, Cockeysville, Md., 1983.

4. Lois Welling, taped interview, Shore Leave, Cockeysville, Md., 1983.

5. For obvious reasons, she has asked to remain anonymous.

6. Meg Lewtan, taped interview, Cockeysville, Md., July 1986.

7. Taped interview, Cockeysville, Md., February 1987.

8. Lois Welling, taped group discussion, Cockeysville, Md. July 1986.

9. Ibid.

10. Meg Lewtan, taped interview, Cockeysville, Md., July 1986.

11. I have personal experience of several circuits, which function, for the most part, in the most hidden fandoms. Of the circuits I know, only the largest, described in this section, relies heavily on anonymity. The others are so small that anonymity becomes irrelevant—if you find the circuit, that can only mean you already know who is writing in it, and what kind of work they write.

12. Taped group interview, Cockeysville, Md., February, 1986.
13. Ibid.
14. Lin Place, taped group interview, Mt. Holly, N.J., June 1987.
15. Ibid.
16. Lewtan, taped group discussion, Cockeysville, Md., February 1986.
17. Taped group discussion, Cockeysville, Md. February 1986.
18. Lewtan, taped group discussion, Cockeysville, Md., July 1986.
19. Personal communication, Fanny Adams to author, August 1987.
20. Personal correspondence, Karen Brandl to author, July 1987.
21. Ibid.
22. Personal correspondence, Syn Ferguson to author, October 1987.
23. Personal correspondence, Syn Ferguson to author, October 1987.
24. Here I use the term *masculine* rather than *male* advisedly, for I mean to imply neither that the specific complement of genitalia and composition of hormones constitutes a culture, nor that the culture constructed as American and masculine operates independently of family and ethnic influences. Some women espouse the masculine culture while some men reject it, and others grow to adulthood enculturated with different expectations altogether. The most visible culture in the popular media, however, and certainly the culture with the largest share of the wealth in the West today, does identify itself through traits that are culturally gendered masculine. (See Carol Gilligan, *In A Different Voice* (Cambridge, Mass.: Harvard University Press, [1982].)
25. Gilligan, *In a Different Voice.*
26. Charles Leerhsen, "Star Trek's Nine Lives," *Newsweek*, December 22, 1986.
27. Personal correspondence, Lois Welling to author, undated [1986].
28. Roberta Rogow, writing in the Editorial in *Grip 23*, ed. Rogow (fanzine; Fairlawn, N.J.: Other World Press, 1986). All ellipses except the first are in the original.
29. Ann Pinzow, taped group interview, Cockeysville, Md., July 1984.
30. Ibid.
31. Taped interview, Cockeysville, Md., March 1987.
32. Victoria Clark and Barbara Storey, taped interview, Tyson Corners, Virginia, August 1985.

Chapter Nine
Homoerotic Romance

The turning point in my initiation into fan culture came in 1985. Jean Curley introduced me to British and fringe fandoms, and Mary Suskind Lansing taught me how to interpret songtapes. Judith Gran, whom I had met early in my study, gave me entrée to the male homoerotic fiction about *Star Trek,* called K/S, produced in the community. Judith, who edited the mixed-genre zine *Organia* with Beverly Lorenstein, introduced me to Vicki Clark and Barbara Storey, who edit *Nome.*

Although they do not write homoerotic fiction themselves, Vicki and Barbara publish the genre in their fanzine, and the two women act as a focal point for fans of *Nome.* Both Vicki and Barbara granted me interviews, at which we discussed both homoerotic fiction and other genres. Over the next year I became provisionally accepted as part of their group, and I was regularly invited to their closed gatherings at conventions.

Homoerotic Fiction

With some surprise, I discovered that the traditional romance formula missing in the fiction about women in relationships with men and each other shows up here, in the fiction about men in love with men. Some of the stories are graphically sexual. While the explicit stories do form a category recognized in the community, often called "with plumbing," the style per se does not differ from the romantic fiction described in this chapter. In fact, some of the stories quoted here do have graphic depictions of sexual acts. I have not included excerpts depicting the female writers' version of male-male sex because many community members have asked me to exercise discretion in quoting their material. Also, I must consider that the characters depicted do not belong to those writers but to commercial providers who practice an uneasy tolerance for the clandestine form at best, and then only as long as it remains hidden.

Of course, while depictions of graphic sexuality are common (and often copied verbatim from story to story), many other stories that community members classify as K/S, or slash, describe the relationship and foreplay but stop at depiction of sexual acts. Still others have no sexual content at all, but set the adventure or threat in the context of a sexual partnership.

Subgenres of Homoerotic Fiction

Like mass market romances written for women, the vast majority of stories written in this genre are *first time* stories, in which the hero and his ultimate sexual companion discover their physical attraction for each other for the first time. The form, with or without graphic depictions of genital sex, is so popular that one recurring *Star Trek* fanzine is devoted entirely to first time stories about Spock and Kirk.

In a typical first time scenario, each character secretly harbors a desire for the other. By accident, or at great personal risk, they must confront their feelings and in doing so find that the feelings are reciprocated. In "A Wish Come True," for example, Spock, on the shore leave planet where fantasies are brought to life by alien amusement park attendants working deep underground, imagines a loving embrace from his captain:

> Kirk smiled in assurance and reached out without words to draw Spock into a loving embrace. Spock stiffened automatically before realizing that it was, after all, his fantasy that he was fulfilling. He let himself go in the warmth of the strong, somehow familiar arms then, finally returning an almost bone-crushing response as he realized that this was a reality he would never know.[1]

Of course, the fantasy turns out to be real, and captain and first officer return to the ship with a mutual promise to discuss their new relationship when they are "thinking more clearly." Typical of many K/S stories, consummation of the relationship does not take place in the pages of the story. The key emotional pivot is the realization that the love one has for the other is returned:

> "Don't you see, you foolish Vulcan? We dreamed each other up! I still can't quite believe it, but what could be more perfectly beautiful than finding out it's a reality?"[2]

Here romantic love is fraught with risk—of trust broken, of exposure or even loss of the self, of society's disapproval, or of misinterpretation of the intent of the partner—and the prize for risking all is perfect physical and psychic fulfillment. In a twist on the typical first time story, the initial meeting may be a "chance encounter" between strangers. Alternate universe "slave" stories often follow this form, with one hero a captive whose sexual favors are sold to the other, who comes to the encounter as a stranger. True to the community ideal, however, the stories reach their happy conclusion when the two heroes recognize their love for one another, and when the "slave" is rescued and freed by his lover.

Another popular form, the *Pon Farr* story, brings the two men together out of necessity—the Vulcan must have sex or die, and the only available partner is his captain, who may have harbored secret sexual thoughts or may offer his services selflessly and later discover a true love for his partner. In the most famous of this form, *Courts of Honor,* the end of pon farr leaves the two partners bereft. The biological drive of pon farr gone, Spock is no longer responsive, but his captain still yearns for the sexual relationship they had so briefly. Flora Poste's sonnet "Lessons," inspired by the novel, captures the torment of the moment:

Now teach me not to love you. Tell me how
To turn away from that intensity
We shared together, for I want you now.
I need you still, as once you needed me.

You needed me, and from that need I learned
How necessary was the hungry touch
That taught desire, with all the love you spurned
In aftermath. You think I want too much.

I know how much I want. Unfailingly,
I reach for what you will no longer give.
Now turn to me again, look back and see
How I have learned from you, how I will live
To give you back that knowledge which love brought:

Now let me teach in turn, as I was taught.[3]

For over one thousand pages in *Courts of Honor* the captain and his first officer suffer trials, tribulations, and adventures, until at last and at great personal sacrifice they find love again.

"Old married couple" stories, which set the plot in the context of an established sexual relationship, are also popular. Like the heterosexual stories of Vulcan marriage, K/S emphasizes the importance of bonding in the mind meld. Source products that do not offer a telepathic hero likewise receive the mind meld treatment, with references to "almost telepathic" rapport. Fans often scorn the more sentimentally domestic of the form, with exaggerated references to Spock in a housedress and Kirk in bobby socks, but the long-term sexual relationship of two male heroes, particularly relying on some representation of the mind meld to represent psychic intimacy as well as sexual attraction, as in the example below, seems to be the ideal.

In Mary Suskind Lansing's story "Divorce, Vulcan Style,"[4] Captain Kirk and his first officer still love each other, but they have separated because their devotion to each other had proved hazardous to the ship. Kirk must, and eagerly does, return to Vulcan for pon farr, however, and in this scene we see the importance to the fanwriter of the mind meld:

> . . . The needs of his body retreated before the needs of his mind. Raising Kirk back up, he brought them face to face, hand stretched out to bond back his love.
> "Spock, I love you. I've missed you so badly. I need your mind. Now!"
> "Now, Jim."
> Like a paper wall before a flood, the shields dropped between them. Kirk's thoughts flowed into his.[5]

The story continues with a fairly graphic depiction of a week of sexual bliss, darkened only by the impending separation when Kirk must return to his duty without his lover. In a surprise ending that surprises no devout fan of that genre, Kirk decides at the last moment to take a safer posting at headquarters, one that will allow the bonded couple to remain together.

While the subgenres described above do not exhaust the range of homoerotic stories, they do account for the largest number of them, and the categories are recognized by most fans of the genre.

Because It's There: Gestural Codes and the Frame

As I read and discussed the stories with fans of K/S and other slash fiction, I had to develop an understanding of the dense links between visual images perceived as carrying erotic content on the screen and the community's own literary codes of romantic homoeroticism. All the forms of the homoerotic romance share a rich attention to the images from the source products translated as erotic in the community, and key phrases make up a fantasy code of sensual attention to the body.

But where does this idea come from? Why are the homosexual stories romanticized? The answer arises, surprisingly, in the images the viewer sees on the screen, and the way women read those framed images.

On television, characters move and interact in a space defined by the twelve- or nineteen- or twenty-five-inch diagonal of the television screen. Directors and editors focus the viewer's attention on the expressive code written on the body with the manipulation of close-up and long shot, and point of view of the camera. In the article, "Television, Polysemy and Popularity," John Fiske limits the intentional meaning of the extreme close-up in an action-adventure drama to aggression or intimacy.[6]

In my review of roughly thirty hours of fan-produced songtapes, I did find examples of extreme close-ups used many times to represent an intimate relationship between series characters. When I returned to the context of the episode from which the clip had been drawn, however, I found no evidence that the director intended the scene to be read as intimate, and no evidence that the scene was intended to express aggression or that viewers ever read the scene as doing so.

Tania Modleski offers a clue to the extreme close-up when she points out that soap operas use close-up shots so that the viewer can clearly see the actor's expression of any emotion in the face, particularly in the eyes.[7] Like the close-up, the extreme close-up allows the viewer to read emotion, but in uncomfortable proximity—the shot is not a sign for particular emotions, but acts as a syntactic modifier. That is, the extreme close-up shot does not tell the viewer that the actor is expressing a particular emotion but that whatever emotion he portrays is both strongly felt and under tight control.

The paradox of grand feelings displayed in small actions—a twitch of the jaw, tightening around the eyes—and held in uncomfortable symbolic proximity to the viewer adds a level of tension to the scene. If the control slips, the emotion may be displayed in terms that the screen cannot contain, focused as it is in the tight shot. The viewer is held, drawn into the tight focus, but emotionally prepared to spring away should the almost expected explosion of fear, anger, passion, or pain threaten to exceed its boundaries. The fact still remains, however, that my informants did interpret the extreme close-up against the narrative grain of the plot, and in terms of intimacy when the characters in the scene had an established friendly relationship.

The television director makes a conscious choice to use the extreme close-up, but setting a scene as simple as two or more characters in conversation so that viewers can correctly interpret it presents a problem in logistics. If the figures are set far enough back in the scene to allow for representation of appropriate proxemics for friends who are not sexual intimates or engaged in aggressive power relationships, the viewer cannot see the emotions projected through the actors' facial gestures. When the actors are shot in sufficient close-up for the viewer to read facial expressions clearly, they cannot maneuver appropriate social distances and still look at each other while they are speaking. Of the two social gaffes, inattention is deemed the least acceptable because it might suggest lack of interest to the viewer, who may respond by changing the channel. So, actors portraying friends consistently break into each other's spheres of intimate space.

While watching songtapes, a group of fans in Houston talked about how their favorite characters moved in relation to one another, and in particular about what one fan called "the Starsky and Hutch syndrome":[8]

Speaker 2: Starsky and Hutch always look like they can't stay away from each other.

Speaker 1: That's true.

Speaker 2: And with the others [probably Bodie and Doyle from *The Professionals*] it's slightly uncomfortable and creates great conflict and tension. I really like it.

Speaker 3: They did that [invade personal space] in *Blake's 7*, but they used the pulled-back camera and stuff, so there's absolutely no reason, you know, for them to have to do that [invade personal space]. But Avon, he's always trespassing on people like that. It's his favorite intimidation tactic.

A scene from *The Professionals*[9] appears on the songtape and I point out the obvious: "They are hanging all over each other."

Speaker 4: It's like he's [Doyle is] looking for Bodie to protect him in that episode, more than in any other.

Speaker 3: We like them to be vulnerable, right.[10]

In this conversation, viewers perceive and agree on at least three different interpretations of intrusion into personal space: interpersonal intimacy, aggression, and dependency. At least one, Avon's intimidation through infringement on personal space, is an intentional message. The scenes in question are not shot in close-up, so the actors had space to represent appropriate distances and did not do so. But the suggestion that fans misinterpret technological expediency as meaningful action does not explain the viewers' perceptions of proxemic intimacy and vulnerability. A viewer who can reinterpret a raised eyebrow as meaningful code for a variety of emotions in one series can certainly adjust for the physical limitations of a nineteen-inch screen and move the characters into conceptually "safe" relational distances in another.

There are, however, a number of reasons why the fan women do not "correct for" appropriate social distance on the screen, and the first is perhaps the simplest. Many women perceive a deep and loving relationship between characters on the screen because series creators put it there. The homosocial partnership has been a staple of Western romance tradition for at least two thousand years, as compared to heterosexual romance, which did not arise in Western culture until the Age of Chivalry. Leslie Fiedler has demonstrated the pervasiveness of the homosocial adventure tale throughout the history of American literature.[11] The concept of two males forsaking all others in the name of whatever goal they mutually seek is central to the Western literary consciousness, and April Selley has ably shown how this tradition continues in the television series *Star Trek*.[12]

In his review of the movie *Star Trek IV*, David Denby takes the homosocial relationship a step further when he characterizes Spock and Dr. McCoy this way:

> Leonard Nimoy [Spock] and DeForest Kelley [Dr. McCoy], in their scenes with each other, are at their most amusingly snippy. Are these two working out some private joke? When *Star Trek II* came out, I noted that "America's beloved players Nimoy and Kelley exchange huffy looks like rival hatcheck girls vying to serve a big tipper." In the case of this film, I would amend that to read, "America's beloved actors Nimoy and Kelley appear to be playing two aging gays dishing each other at a party while vying for the attention of William Shatner."[13]

Nor is *Star Trek* an exception on American television. An example from the shooting script of "Sweet Revenge," the final *Starsky and Hutch* episode, serves as a graphic example of this tendency in "buddy" action-adventure television. The episode offers the traditional "shot in the heart" plot, and in this scene, Hutch is at the bedside of his wounded partner:

> Dir: Hutch stares down at Starsky and feels an overwhelming sense of helplessness. Hutch ventures another step closer, and then bends

down, getting as close as he can, as if, somehow, in that crowded little room, he can still share a private moment with his friend.
Hutch: You've gotta make it. And you know why? 'Cause without you, Starsk, there's no me.[14]

Starsky does recover, and Hutch climbs into bed with him to share the hearty meal Hutch has smuggled into the hospital, a sure sign of his partner's recovery. As striking as the visual realization becomes on screen, the stage directions are more so, couched as they are in the intense, one might even say florid, language of the gothic romance. While Paul Michael Glazer's Sergeant Dave Starsky may seem an unlikely damsel in distress, he holds that position in this and in a number of episodes in the series.

The British, not to be outdone, offered a homegrown buddy pair in *The Professionals*. England's independent Channel 4 produced a parody of the series, "The Bullshitters," in which the two leads dash about London in leather jackets and bikini briefs. A surveillance job toward the end of the half-hour results in a kiss and a clinch during which the "heroes" roll out of their hiding place and down a hill.[15]

Fans, who watch their source products with as much avid attention as critics or other producers, pick up the same clues and read them in predictable ways. Some examples will illustrate this point. As we have seen, the extreme close-up, which focuses on eyes and eye contact, can be interpreted as a display of intimacy regardless of the actual gloss the context put on the shot. Not surprisingly, fanwriters lavish descriptive attention on the romance of eye contact. Caren Parnes writes about Captain Kirk's eyes, as perceived by Mr. Spock, in "A Wish Come True":

> Spock recalled now the *warm, excited glow in the hazel eyes*, and his own subdued reaction to his Captain's enthusiasm. Jim had merely smiled at the *mockingly lifted eyebrow* Spock had bestowed on him after his comment . . . He said the last words with soft assurance, but the *intensity in the hazel eyes conveyed the words left unspoken:* with you. Spock felt himself getting *lost in those eyes* and pulled himself back with an effort.[16]

And *Blake's 7* fans likewise attend to the eyes of their heroes:

> Give me that wonderful smile and light me with your gold-lit eyes and that soft laugh.[17]

And add to eyes the action of seeing, with erotic attention to the object of the gaze:

. . . As those glowing eyes burned a trail from the shiny ebony hair, over the sharp planes of his face, his nose, mouth, lingering on the upswept ears, then back to his eyes, Spock longed to know what thoughts and feelings the wistful gold reflected.[18]

Fans code for more than eyes in the homoerotic genres, and in conscious reflexivity, recognize the conventionalization of the codes with humorous compilation stories like *Alien Beuty* [*sic*], which collected a page of descriptors for a particular hero and shaped them into one effusive scene, a sample of which is:

. . . [S]maller than he was, lighter, and eye-catchingly vulnerable, slender-wristed, with over-long curls, eyes wide with almost-fear . . .[19]

Like the above descriptions, the mind meld codes romantically for a deep sexual commitment, including as it does eye contact and the touch of fingers on the face to visually represent the deep psychic link. In contrast to the heterosexual and friendship stories, a first telepathic union in a context of homosexual love may be fraught with both attraction and danger:

The meld as a medium of love . . . !
He thrilled at the thought of it, trembling in anticipation.
Each time he'd seen Spock initiate a meld, it had always seemed so sensitive, so intimate a thing . . . To him it had always looked like love. And on the few occasions he had experienced it himself it had felt like it, too . . . though he believed he had succeeded in shielding that response from Spock. Secretly, he now acknowledged, he had always been fascinated by the possibilities of a meld *for* love and not as a means to some other end.
"Jim . . . no . . ." Spock moaned as though reading his thoughts and rejecting them. With infinite regret he let his fingers trail away from Kirk's face, breaking the tentative link.[20]

The codes develop an expectation of content so strongly that the reader interprets the content as implied, even when the author has not included or intended such content. The case of Della Van Hise's commercial *Star Trek* book, *Killing Time*, demonstrates how significant codes become in the group's literature. Community members who read K/S know Van Hise for her amateur fiction in that genre. Her commercially published novel had no explicit homosexual liaison between the male characters and, indeed, had a heterosexual one between Spock and the Romulan Commander from the original *Star Trek* episode "The Enterprise Incident."

In the novel, the *Enterprise* experiences strange distortions of reality that cast it into an alternate universe in which Spock is captain and Kirk an ensign whose career was destroyed when he was wrongly accused of murder. The Kirk in the alternate universe is tormented by strange memories of being captain, alternately believing himself trapped in the universe of his disgrace and insane for believing things should be different. Spock gradually realizes not only that the ensign is not mad but that the stability of the universe depends upon the deaths of himself and Kirk in the alternative reality created by the Romulans. Early in the novel, before reality has been altered, Van Hise describes the interaction of the two characters with this language:

> "Indeed," Spock murmured. Kirk was normally a very private individual; but now the hazel eyes seemed alight with a combination of embarrassment and mischief . . .
>
> Kirk glanced up from where he'd been studying his boots, and felt the familiar telepathic door swing open between himself and the Vulcan. It was something which had formed between them over the years, something which had saved their lives countless times and made them brothers. He *did* want to discuss it, but only with Spock.[21]

Coming, as these passages do, in the first few pages of the book during the first interaction between captain and first officer, we see two markers which readers of the fan genre interpret as setting up a homoerotic context for the story: a reference to the captain's hazel eyes and a reference to a telepathic bond of long standing.[22]

Throughout *Killing Time* the linguistic markers of a passionate romantic relationship alerted readers of that genre to place the action of the story in a sexual context:

> He tasted a moment of fire—illogical, un-vulcan anger at the sudden rejection. Kirk had led him on, had practically asked for the meld, and now the human was hurling jagged knives into vulnerable tissue. With an effort, he wrestled himself back under control, choosing a less personal approach . . .
>
> But before he [ensign Kirk] could complete the sentence, he found himself sprawling to the ground, the Vulcan's arms wrapped tightly and unexpectedly around his legs. Lethal anger flared in the human's eyes and he fell painfully into the dirt; he kicked, but to no

avail. Without completely knowing what he was doing, Spock rolled over, covering the ensign's writhing body with his own . . .[23]

The implications to fans of the genre seemed clear. A sexual relationship accepted by both partners in the "real" universe has been lost in the alternate one, as has Kirk's command. The struggle both to comprehend the sense that they have shared a deep and intense friendship, and to deal with emotions no longer appropriate in the new context of the altered reality lead to the contrasting images of the meld, which begins as a positive value to both partners and becomes a symbol of invasion—rape—completed explicitly as "Without another thought to the matter, he injected himself into the human's unshielded mind."[24]

In bodice-ripper style, Kirk surrenders to the psychic possession, and regrets his struggle against it: "He took a deep breath, tired of fighting, and surrendered to the pleasant vertigo that accompanied the meld . . . for an instant Kirk tasted regret . . . regret over what his actions had obviously cost the captain."[25]

The appearance of *Killing Time* disturbed many fans. Community members who do not generally object to K/S were concerned about the allusions to sexuality in this book—allusions that occur not specifically in the content but in the language Van Hise used to express content, and which language is read as sexual in the group. Fanwriters worried that the book would call undue attention to their own works. Both the fans of the genre and those who object to homoerotic fiction in the community protested within the community and to the publisher. Pocket Books pulled the book and issued a revised edition in which all the quotations but the first given here were deleted or extensively revised. A number of other smaller-scaled excisions—references to pliant flesh and psychic nakedness—stripped the book of its more obvious markers, although enough remain to cue the regular K/S reader that the book situates linguistically in that genre.

Why Homoerotic Fiction?

When a mentor points out the cues fans interpret as indicative of a homoerotic relationship, the "why" of the genre seems obvious. For most fans, however, the idea did not occur spontaneously. Leslie Fish's interest in homoerotic fan fiction began at the very birth of the genre. According to Leslie, a long-standing fan well known for her work in fan fiction and particularly in filksong,[26] the idea did occur to a number of fan fiction readers and writers independently:

I was in the beginning of the K/S argument. In 1975 . . . [*Star Trek Lives*[27]] was the first printed material anywhere to say that "all right, what there is between Spock and Kirk is love."[28]

Of course, us females said, "OK, we know all too well that when you say love you can also mean sex" . . . and so, a lot of people were whispering underground, "why not, why not?"

Nobody would dare, except this one suggestive thing by Diane M.—she lived in Australia, so she didn't care[29] . . . And I figured, what the hell, I'll be an icebreaker here too. And I started to write a K/S story.[30] And . . . while I was looking around for a taker, Jerri D. printed *Alternatives* [a collection of K/S poems] and the fat hit the fire . . . [I] found a taker, *Warped Space Double X*, issue twenty, and the rest is history.[31]

In personal correspondence, Leslie explained that American fans who may have considered writing K/S stories earlier held back because they feared lawsuits from Paramount, a fear that the Australian fan did not have to consider.[32] From my own observation, I would add that American fans also faced the censure of fellow fans, a situation that continues, to a much lesser extent, more than fifteen years later.

When I asked Leslie what attraction K/S material held for women, she responded:

Well, on the one hand [there is] the general attraction of gay men for women. It's the only way we can even—[in] fantasy—we can be the one and have the other.

A number of fans have echoed this explanation. Women who read and write the material do so because it is sexually exciting, among other reasons. They can share in the fantasy of sexual relationships with both of the male screen characters with whom they already maintain an imaginary relationship. The fan can imagine giving and receiving both physical and emotional love from the point of view of one or both of the characters. The tendency to identify with more than one position is so strong that some of the less experienced writers lose control of their point of view in sex scenes, as they simultaneously identify with all of the characters in the scene. Their readers may find it impossible to sort out who is doing what to whom, or to whom a passage of descriptive ecstasy refers.

The sexual response to the genre, while its most obvious characteristic to an outsider, represents but a single one of the many complexly interwoven reasons why women write homoerotic fiction. As Leslie Fish continued:

> Our culture so thoroughly denigrates the personalities of women that women can't imagine themselves as heroic characters unless they imagine themselves as male.

Women writers traditionally have had great difficulty creating active, powerful women heroes to take center stage in their own works.[33] Contrary to Carolyn G. Heilbrun's criticism of women's literature, however, women science fiction and fantasy writers have created strong female heroes since the thirties.[34] Clearly, some women in the extended community that includes both science fiction and media fandom do write strong women, and the fanwriters have that work as model. The question that I pose, therefore, is not quite the same as Heilbrun's. That is, rather than ask how women are to derive models for strong female heroes, I ask why, when such models are available, and when their own community expresses an interest in them, do women writers choose not to use those models in their own literature? What work does homoerotic romance do in the communication of personal needs and experiences that cannot be done more effectively in other genres?

The fans themselves have a variety of answers, some of which take on the very question of female characters. At a panel discussion on homoerotic fiction someone from the audience asked why the participants did not write more women characters. These are some of the answers:

> Speaker 1: I wouldn't write it, because I don't care.
> Speaker 2: I don't want to see them involved with other women. I don't want to see them with me either, I wouldn't put me in the story.
> Speaker 3: I wouldn't either.
> Speaker 4: There's no woman you could put in the story that would suit the ideal.[35]

While the group concluded that they simply did not want to write about women, one remark was very telling. In discussing the typical female character on action-adventure programming, including *Star Trek*, the fan objected, "I say this is a bimbo and not me." Science fiction offers the woman writer models of active, engaged women in print, but little in the visual media gives women that kind of model for their work. Leia Organa of *Star Wars* gave some women a role model, but her strong position faltered in the later movies. Ripley from the two *Alien* movies commanded the center of her adventure with an un-compromising strength, but events in the movie left her alone with cats and children at the end, insufficient for the emotional engagement fans look for in their characters.

The visual media, still overwhelmingly controlled by men, send out a clear message to women: female heroes don't have satisfying sexual relationships unless they learn to take second place in their own adventures. Late twentieth-century filmmakers echo the message mid-nineteenth-century clergy sent out to women: " . . . [S]tep outside [your proper confines] and you will cease to exist."[36] For the male filmmaker, Ripley the hero can only exist outside of sexual relationships. In television, she cannot exist at all.

Having given this argument its due, however, I must point out that neither in the movies nor, certainly, on television does the writer find any model for the sexually involved homosexual couple as active co-heroes in their own story. Contrary to the assertion of more avid fans, the idea springs to mind spontaneously and independently in few women with whom I have spoken. Mentors introduce most fans to the concept of homosexually involved hero dyads slowly and carefully. I am not alone in having found the concept disconcerting when first introduced to it. Joanna Russ, in her article, "Another Addict Raves about K/S" describes her own first experiences with the genre. When K/S fan and scholar Patricia Frazer Lamb asked Russ if she had heard of the material, Russ reports:

What I said was, "No!" and then . . .
"WherecanIgetsome!" [*sic*] . . . Once I had got a package of zines from Patricia, I showed them to all my friends, and (if the friend was female and had liked *Star Trek*) her reaction was just like mine—embarrassment conflicting with sheer delight.[37]

I should make it clear here that the astonishing part is the sexual relationship, not the intensity of the friendship, which, as Selley points out, follows the traditional homosocial (but not homosexual) model described by Leslie Fiedler as the basis for much of American literature. Patricia Frazer Lamb and Diane Vieth, independently of Selley, draw on Fiedler as well, and then extend his argument into the overt sexuality of the homoerotic fiction,[38] and fans themselves have a variety of explanations for their interest in stories that revolve around a sexual relationship between the two male hero figures.

With the full weight of so many traditional forces working against the realization of strong and erotic female characters, many fans echo

Leslie Fish's argument about the difficulty women writers encounter creating believable female heroes. At a discussion among thirty or more community members at More Eastly Con in 1985, a fan again brought up the question that preys on the minds of many fans: "But why aren't we writing love between equals between men and women?" Many women in the room responded with the reasons they prefer the homoerotic fiction:

> Speaker 1: Because you don't have to worry about who's going to be on top.
> Speaker 2: Because we were raised in this culture and we don't believe women are equal.
> Speaker 3: That's why you're not seeing women gay, or women's slash.
> Speaker 4: I have seen a number of Nurse Chapel stories [general laughter in the group[39]].
> Speaker 5: There's a long tradition of romantic emotional entanglement between men going back 1500 years . . . It's sort of an archetype—the fated friendship between men, and anyway, who wants to be role playing between two underdogs in the slave pit. I mean, let's be equal and the top of the heap.
> Speaker 6: But it's so nice to be able to, ah, what you're doing is obviously reading an idealized romance. One, they are not just into it for the body—knowing somebody from the toenails out.

All of this is true, politically. But as an ethnographer, I had to admit to myself it sounded too intellectual, too politically correct, and for a reason that became situationally evident. The fanzine *Nome* had just printed Joanna Russ' article, "Another Addict Raves about K/S," an early draft of the article she subsequently published in her book, *Magic Mammas, Trembling Sisters, Puritans and Perverts.*[40] The article as it appeared in fan publication enthused about the specifically female nature of K/S writing—Russ goes so far as to say, "K/S is the only literature I know that celebrates female sexuality, and its relation to love and vulnerability . . . the woman's vision of erotic excitement exists nowhere else but in K/S." After the group interview, a number of the interviewees came to me and recommended the article, including the editors of *Nome*, who had published it. They freely admitted that, while they had come to the same conclusions independently, they had been favorably influenced by her article.

In her fan article, however, Russ dressed the homoerotic genre in its Sunday best, all shiny and scrubbed for the insider audience, and then presented the material in a different guise for the readership of

Magic Mammas. She worked from another academic's basic concepts, with a very small corpus, and in "study meetings" with a very small group that included only three or four established writers in the field. Several of those cited by Russ have complained that she interpreted their remarks somewhat freely, including Syn Ferguson: " . . . I admit to being naive, an idealist, I was hurt by Joanna's comments in *Magic Mammas* as much by being classified with pornography as by her misquote."[41]

Russ did not refer to the K/S material as pornography in the *Nome* version of her paper, and fans of both reading and writing the genre are frequently amazed that even the most sexually explicit material should be considered pornographic:

> To me, it seems the difference is so clear that no reader could mistake it, that once explicit sex is portrayed as love, it should leap to the reader's awareness that the problem with pornography isn't how graphically sex is portrayed, but that sex has been confused with domination.[42]

While those involved with the article itself had ambivalent feelings about it, the article as it appeared in *Nome* had already worked its way into the public face of K/S fandom when I interviewed fans in the summer of 1985. Clearly Russ' arguments resonated with meaning for some of these women, while for others the article validated their involvement with homoerotic material without revealing the meaning involvement had for them. Still others, however, resented both the claims the article made and the public form in which *Magic Mammas* later made them:

> I mean she's [Joanna Russ] coming into this with her own perspective only . . . And I said to myself, "Well, I'm a woman, and I don't think that way, and not only that, but I'm in this group![43]

Others who objected to the article pointed out that Russ gave a biased and incorrect impression about the community. As I have shown, homoerotic fiction is one of the last of the many forms of fan fiction to which community members introduce neophytes. One fan, talking to me about my study, reminded me:

> This stuff is private stuff, and taking it out [to the public] is not going to get you very well liked. That's blunt, but it's absolutely true . . . This is one of the problems about being under the microscope,

which is what you're doing to us. Because, as I was telling you before, there's a lot of people out there with some hesitation.[44]

Fans like this informant are unwilling to expose their activities to a
wider public audience. Some children's librarians and schoolteachers
have expressed concern that they could lose their jobs under morals
clauses in their contracts if it became known that they participated in
writing or other creative aspects of K/S. Others cite loss of professional credibility as a possible outcome of the exposure of their
material.

At the least, many participants in the genre fear that they will be
made to look foolish or aberrant for activities that make sense in the
context of the community. They worry that even scholars who participate as active members of the community will misrepresent them. An
unexpected effect of Russ' article, however, was the change some fans
saw in a new wave of writers entering fandom. Russ had implied by
omission that all of the women in the community wrote homosexual
erotica. My informant voiced a common complaint that Russ' book attracted new writers who entered the homoerotic fiction subgroup of
Star Trek fandom without going through the usual initiation. Members of the closed, protected community share a philosophy they express in their literature. The community does not want to attract
people who are drawn to it merely for the exotic sexual literature.

New members introduced to the concept of fan fiction through the
scholarship on K/S have not been educated in what the stories symbolize to the group or in how to write in the group's aesthetic. Some of
the long-standing members of the *Star Trek* fan group continue to
work in the *Star Trek* medium and persevere in maintaining the fiction
as a discourse for discussing issues important to community members.
Others have fled into *Blake's 7* or other less well known source products where fans continue in the fanzine tradition or participate in a
circuit of privately circulated material.

Are They Really Women?

When a writer makes use primarily of male characters she adds a further level of signification between her own personal message as a
woman and her reader, also a woman. But does that necessarily mean
that the male characters are surrogate women? Many fans, Joanna
Russ among them, would have it so. Russ asserts:

What the authors are describing [in sex scenes] is female, from the
overriding importance of touch to the slow thoroughness and sen-

sitization of the whole body . . . the plethora of male penises . . . are so insistent that they become something like the name cards you see at conventions: "Hello, my name is ———." The K/S card reads: "Hello, I have a penis and am therefore male." (often the behavior at that point is what would be seen—in social stereotype that is—as "feminine.")[45]

In Russ' analysis, the penis is a sign, literally, behind which the woman can express femaleness free of male domination. As we have seen before, however, thematic genres are deeply complex systems of discourse capable of communicating layers of meaning from the most mundane to the most arcane, from the most consciously wrought to the most ineffably symbolic, in a way to which Syn Ferguson alludes when she says:

> I didn't pick my metaphor [K/S], it picked me. Art, like science, is a series of problems. K/S is a problem for me. I'm working through it. I can't tell my unconscious, "No, bring me something else," after all it's been through. I'm committed. I have to write until this problem is solved—whatever the problem is—and the way I solve problems is telling stories.[46]

The example that Russ uses metaphorically, penis as name card, is in a most mundane sense literally true. Fans group socially by a shared interest in a particular genre. If a community member wishes to socialize with a group involved particularly with homoerotic fiction, she will signal her interest by reading, writing, and discussing that genre. Some women, like informant Judy Chien, would not have considered reading or writing homoerotic fiction, but when introduced to the genre as the predominant discourse in their social groups, they grew to accept it and even find support for the concept in other source products.

The genre has the capability of carrying most messages that can be carried in other genres; the writer need learn only the particular conventions of the genre for expressing her message. An author interested in kinship ties, for example, may involve the homosexual couple with parents, siblings, and even children conceived outside of the relationship but absorbed into the family bond. Alternatively, the fan may engage the group socially because she shares with it an interest in themes specific to the genre itself, such as sexual equality.

At the level of conservation of risk, however, the homoerotic fiction writer can deal with personal needs that carry a high-risk lading for her in a genre that removes the woman from the direct experience

about which she writes. For some, homoerotic fiction as sexual material provides an outlet for sexual feelings, while not personally threatening or frustrating the reader. As one lesbian informant explained,

> . . . [O]n the most personal level, I've realized that slash writing,
> and indeed all the male-centered fannish writing by women, is a
> way of expressing the sexual feelings I do have for male images and
> types. I know from experience that the interest doesn't extend to
> actually enjoying sex with men for its own sake, but . . . I do have
> some notions that men might be attractive. As objects, and purely at
> a distance, but the notion is there.[47]

Distanced from the material by the absence of her gender, this lesbian
reader/writer can experiment with a sexual attraction she may not
wish to experience in the physical sense even in her imagination.

Sexual experiences with men as they are presently encultured can
seem intimidating even to heterosexual women. Many heterosexual
community members writing in all the genres openly express a need
for more satisfying sexual relationships. They describe their regret
that they do not have the kinds of relationships with men they would
like. Homoerotic fiction interest groups, however, seem to include a
much higher percentage of women who seem to find relationships
with men simultaneously attractive and threatening. For some heterosexual fans, and equally for some lesbian participants, the homoerotic
stories stimulate sexually through the fantasy while at the same time
they distance the woman from the risk sexual relationships with men
represent.

Heterosexuality is only part of the risk that sex represents. Attitudes deemed politically incorrect inside the community or morally
deviant outside the community may be ascribed to the character and
the fiction rather than to the writer. The woman can imagine an equal
relationship, or she may even envision an unequal one without revealing her personal need to feel dominant or submissive in a relationship. This is a particularly interesting thought because, in spite of the
community's own rhetoric to the contrary, many of the homoerotic
stories describe unequal relationships.

The risk is not just to the individual writer, however. A lesbian
writer answered my question, "Why are you interested in writing
about male-male sexual relationships?" much as heterosexual women
did, but with two important additions:

> There may be an element of gay solidarity in it, too . . . some of the
> sociology of being closeted and oppressed (little though that is used
> in most slash fiction) transfers whole for either sex as gay . . .[48]

Writing about the gay male means writing about the risk inherent in pursuing an oppressed sexuality. Heterosexual women, like lesbians and gay men, are constrained to silence by Western masculine culture. Interacting with that masculine culture, they find it difficult to publish when they write, difficult to gain an audience when they speak. Any interest women express in an erotic life outside of the monogamous heterosexual relationship classes them immediately as degenerates. Women are allowed a certain level of success only when they conform to the image of the "feminine" that masculine culture holds for them: femininity which includes the giving of sexual pleasure, but not the active seeking out of sexual pleasure, particularly in print or picture that excludes the heterosexual male from the experience altogether.

More than any other genre I have studied, the interest group around women's homoerotic fiction excludes males. Outside of the genre, male participation is roughly 10 percent; within it, I have heard of only three gay men who write, and perhaps one or two more who participate regularly as readers. The idea that their most beloved heroes might share a homosexual love relationship seems to both enrage and terrify most men who are deeply enculturated in heterosexual masculine culture. At the same time, the sexuality actualized in the fiction represents a woman's vision that many gay men find passingly curious but not engaging over the long term.

Solidarity or a sense of identification notwithstanding, women don't write erotic fiction for political reasons. Which leads me back to hiding things in plain sight. Many women who write homoerotic fiction are writing consciously and deliberately about men, not women. I would hazard the broad statement that most fan fiction, regardless of its genre, is about men, and homoerotic fiction most decidedly so. Men are the alien, the other. Surveys conducted within the community,[49] as well as my own observations, indicate that a high percentage of the women in fandom were not involved in relationships with men at the times the surveys were taken, and many considered themselves celibate. Some of these were divorced, or post-relationship but others had never had a long-term, loving, sexual relationship with a man. A small but still significant number of the women in media fandom suffer from extreme, health-threatening obesity, and that group tends to cluster in the homoerotic genres.

Writing about men, sometimes solely and obsessively about men, does not add to a woman's knowledge about women, nor, in fandom, need it do so. Women talk, work, live together, share their stories and their lives in a unique language of connection. Women in fandom don't want to change real women—themselves—but they have no patience with the images of women created by men: "I say this is a bimbo and not me." Taking the point of view of a fictional man, originally created by a man, in a story she writes herself, however, a fanwriter can explore her feelings about men. When they write about men in sexual relationships with other men, fans tap intuitively (and some, consciously) into knowledge expressed theoretically by Eva Kosofsky Sedgwick about English literature written by men:

> The importance—an importance—of the category "homosexual," I am suggesting, comes not necessarily from its regulatory relation to a nascent or already-constituted minority of homosexual people or desires, but from its potential for giving whoever wields it a structuring definitional leverage over the whole range of male bonds that shape the social constitution.[50]

A bit later, Sedgwick explains:

> The fact that what goes on at football games, in fraternities, at the Bohemian Grove and at climactic[51] moments in war novels can look, with only a slight shift of optic, quite startlingly "homosexual," is . . . the coming to visibility of the double bind . . . for a man to be a man's man is separated only by an invisible, carefully blurred, always-already-crossed line from being "interested in men."[52]

A very small number of the women who write homoerotic fiction inside the community had a prior interest in gay male literature, and few have extended their interest beyond the community once exposed to it. The writing in fandom *is* female, as Joanna Russ claims, but the subject, the purpose, is at one level to understand men as they are. The homosexual gives the writer distance from her theme: she need not subject herself, even in her imagination, to the stresses of a relationship with man-as-he-is.

Equally important, as one slash writer reminded me, no one expects her to have firsthand knowledge of male-male sex. A few fans, including some married women, have privately admitted that they don't write heterosexual erotica because they are afraid everyone will know that they have been "doing it wrong all this time." No such pressure to demonstrate expertise is placed upon the female writer of homoerotic fiction.

At a deeper level, the writer uses male homosexuality to reconstruct men, to "wield the structuring definitional leverage over the whole range of male bonds," and change them into people with whom women can coexist more comfortably:

I think what my unconscious may be doing is starting with the hero, who is easy to write about, he is nowhere in the world, everywhere in literature. I change him a little bit by saying, "No, but if he had all that integrity, how would he really have to act?" And then I try to write about what decent, whole, individuals would be like, how they relate to each other . . ."[53]

Many slash fans declare they write about men together because men, holding power, can relate to each other as powerful equals. By the very representation of male-male love, however, they strip their characters of their power in the masculine culture. Many "first time" stories, in which the characters first enter into a sexual relationship, debate the very issue of risk in pursuing a forbidden union, the potential loss if the relationship were to become known. Stories in which no such problems exist for the characters are still *written* in a culture where even writing about such a union means taking a risk.

It's not that a woman writer thinks a man stripped of power would make a better mate. Rather, at some level, many women who write homoerotic fiction in the community want to tear down the very institution of hierarchical power that constructs men as individuals, not as parts of a whole. Power, as reconstructed in the stories, comes from the union of complementary parts, even when that union must exist as an anomaly in an otherwise hierarchical order that may be seen as oppressive in itself or as benign in its neglect or admiration for the value of the union.

But what are the men that thrive stripped of the power of the individual in a hierarchy? What do they look like, sound like? How do they treat friends and each other? The answers are as varied as the characters in the source products with which the women choose to write. Patricia Frazer Lamb and Diane Vieth tell us: "Androgynous . . . Unlike a female Henry Higgins, the K/S writer does not cry 'why can't a man be more like a woman?' She instead asks, 'Why can't we all just be human?'"[54]

Earlier, Lamb and Vieth set out the complementary matching of Kirk's feminine traits to Spock's masculine ones, and conversely, the matching of Kirk's masculine traits to Spock's feminine. Many of the traits reflect differences between masculine and feminine in masculine culture: taller and stronger masculine and shorter, weaker feminine, reticent, rational masculine, verbal, intuitive feminine, masculine leader fulfilled in himself, feminine follower fulfilled only within the union. In *Star Trek* fan fiction the traditional traits that masculine culture defines for male and female gender roles are more apparent than in later entries among the source products, but even here the traits do not define one character or another as masculine or feminine. Rather, each character takes up some of the masculine role and some of the feminine role.

While the writing starts with a certain shared ideal, the actualization of that ideal in each writer's mind varies greatly, as does her concept of the ideal relationship. Some writers in all genres strongly feminize one character over another: they may emphasize a difference in height and bulk between the pair, such as Hutch's height or the broadness of Kirk's shoulders. When no such distinctions are apparent in the source product, in *Blake's 7* or *The Professionals*, for example, the writer may create the stereotypical shift in relative sizes in her descriptions.[55] Some writers place one of the participants in the role of "wife," even if he is a working wife. Other writers leave both characters firmly in the masculine sphere and write of the struggle two dominant personalities have in establishing an equable relationship. I have never seen a story in which two submissive personalities try to decide what to do.

In all the permutations of relationships from all the source products in all the stories I have read, however, two traits stand out as the androgynous mean, regardless of other factors of personality and culture: (1) Both participants in the relationship recognize, or come to recognize in the course of the story, that the entity constituted of the integrated union represented in the relationship is more powerful and enduring than any individual, including the individuals they once were, and (2) Communication is vital to the integrity of the relationship as an entity. The less communicative partner must learn to express himself verbally and not withdraw or act out rage, pain, or hostility. The more communicative partner must learn both patience and persistence in eliciting verbal communication from his partner while at the same time insisting that his own verbal communication be heard and understood.

Androgyny for women does not mean men in dresses or even, necessarily, women in pants. Rather, we return again to Carol Gilligan: androgyny, as it can be extracted from the fan stories, means trading in the hierarchical pyramid of individuality for the safety net of relationships. The relationship between two particular equals becomes a paradigm for trust in the fan community.

Nowhere does this become more evident than in the romantic coding for the mind meld in homoerotic relationships. In the stories of homoerotic love, the writers underscore the romance of the forbidden with telepathy as penetration of the mind, as taboo. Telepathy

Mr. Spock looking at Captain Kirk in a mirror. Caren Parnes' illustration for "Intermezzo," from *Nome 9*.

still means closeness and understanding, but the hero must pay the price of knowing the other. That price is equal knowledge of himself.

Notes

1. Caren Parnes, "A Wish Come True," *T'Hy'La #5* (fanzine; Santa Clara, 1985), p. 48.
2. Ibid., p. 49.
3. Flora Poste, "Lessons," *Nome 9*, ed. Victoria Clark and Barbara Storey (fanzine; New York: Jumping Dik-Bat Press, 1986), p. 69.
4. Mary Suskind Lansing, "Divorce, Vulcan Style," in *Consort 2* (fanzine; Reprehensible Press, 1986), pp. CII-217–CII-269.
5. Ibid., p. CII-244.
6. John Fiske, "Television, Polysemy, and Popularity," *Critical Studies in Mass Communications* 3 (1986): 397.
7. Tania Modleski, "The Rhythms of Reception: Daytime Television and Women's Work," in *Regarding Television*, ed. E. Ann Kaplan (Los Angeles: The American Film Institute, 1975), pp. 67–75.
8. Taped discussion, Houston, Texas, March 1987. This excerpt is a continuation of the interview previously cited in Chapter 7 under "Gestural Codes." I continue with the identification convention established earlier: the reader can add the comments in this section to the comments by the same fan in Chapter 7 for a more complete picture of each fan's views.
9. The episode, "Mixed Doubles," juxtaposes the training of two secret agents against the training of two hired assassins. The episode seems to say that there is little to distinguish the two sides of the law. The most important visual distinctive between the two pairs is that the heroes touch each other a great deal, and the villains do not.
10. Taped discussion, Houston, Tex., March 1987
11. Leslie A. Fiedler, *Love and Death in the American Novel* (New York: Scarborough Books, 1966 [1960]).
12. April Selley, "'I Have Been, and Ever Shall Be, Your Friend': *Star Trek, The Deerslayer*, and the American Romance" *Journal of Popular Culture* (1987): 89–104.
13. David Denby, "Back from the Future," *New York*, December 8, 1986, p. 108.
14. "Sweet Revenge," *Starsky and Hutch*, draft date February 1, 1979, p. 12, scene 16.
15. London Weekend Television, shown on Channel 4.
16. Parnes, "A Wish Come True," p. 46; emphasis added.
17. Excerpt from "Reluctant Rebel," published pseudonymously in *Southern Lights Special Issue 2.5* (Altemont Springs, Fla., 1986), p. 39.
18. Parnes, "A Wish Come True," p. 48.
19. "Alien Beuty" in *Discovered on a Rooftop* (fanzine; Sunshine Press, 1985), pp. 128–29.
20. Elwyn Conway, "And Never Parted," *Nome 8*, ed. Victoria Clark and Barbara Storey (fanzine; New York: Jumping Dik-Bat Press, 1985), p. 316. The elisions are Conway's.
21. Della Van Hise, *Killing Time* (New York: Pocket Books, 1985), pp. 2–3. Italics are as they appear in the original.

22. Fanwriters who limit the relationship to an intense friendship often use the telepathic bond to demonstrate the strength of that friendship, but stories that include the particular markers of personal description and telepathy are often accused of teasing about a sexual relationship when one does not appear in the text.

23. Van Hise, *Killing Time*, pp. 172–73.

24. Ibid., p. 175.

25. Ibid. The last set of ellipses appear in the original.

26. Leslie has recently sold stories in C. J. Cherryh's commercially published shared universe Merovingen Nights.

27. Jacqueline Lichtenberg, Sondra Marshak, and Joan Winston, *Star Trek Lives!* (New York: Bantam Books, 1975).

28. Ibid. I should point out that while the book inspired Leslie Fish to consider the idea of a sexual relationship between Kirk and Spock, nowhere is that intimated or indicated in the book itself. Lichtenberg specifically referred to a fraternal order of love, a concept she develops in her fan fiction. For many years Lichtenberg herself opposed the K/S genre as contrary to the meaning of *Star Trek* as it was conceived by Gene Roddenberry.

29. In subsequent correspondence, Fish identified the story for me as "A Fragment out of Time," published in Lori Chapek's *Warped Space* #6, Lansing, Michigan.

30. Again in correspondence, Leslie gave the title of her story as "Shelter," published in *Warped Space XX* (issue 20).

31. Leslie Fish, taped interview, Atlanta, Ga., August 1987.

32. Personal correspondence from Leslie Fish to the author, October 12, 1991.

33. Carolyn G. Heilbrun, *Reinventing Womanhood* (New York: W. W. Norton, 1979).

34. C. L. Moore's *Jirel of Jory* is an early science fiction example, and writers including but not limited to Ursula LeGuin, Joanna Russ, Marian Zimmer Bradley, Andre Norton, Tanith Lee, Nancy Kress, Pat Cadigan, and Suzette Elgin Hayden, just to name a few, have not only envisioned strong women in central roles but also have worked to redefine the male hero, an agenda equally vital for envisioning a better future.

35. Taped panel discussion, Cockeysville, Md., April 1987.

36. I first came upon this quote of Patricia Albjerg Graham ("Women in Academe," *Science*, September 1970) in Carolyn G. Heilbrun's *Reinventing Women*, p. 89.

37. Joanna Russ' "Another Addict Raves about K/S," published in the fanzine *Nome 8* (1985), pp. 28–37, later appeared in a considerably revised and more formal version in Russ' *Magic Mammas, Trembling Sisters, Puritans and Perverts* (New York: Crossing Press, 1985), pp. 79–99.

38. Patricia Frazer Lamb and Diane Vieth, "Romantic Myth, Transcendence and *Star Trek* Zines," in *Erotic Universe*, ed. Donald Palumbo (New York: Greenwood Press, 1986), pp. 235–89.

39. Chapel, whose sole function in the show seems to have been to suffer unrequited love for Spock, is not widely respected as a character.

40. Except where specifically stated, I refer to the *Nome 8* version of the article, because that is the text to which members of the fan community generally responded in their interviews (see note 37 above). This version is marked by a less radical position; the word *pornography*, for example, never

appears in the *Nome 8* text, nor is there any implication that the readers or writers have any particular sexual orientation.

41. Personal correspondence, Syn Ferguson to author, October 1987.

42. Ibid.

43. Taped interview, Cockeysville, Md., February 1987.

44. Ibid.

45. Russ, "Another Addict," p. 34.

46. Personal correspondence, to author, October 1987.

47. Personal letter to the author, February 17, 1987.

48. Ibid.

49. Judith Gran and Dorothy Laoang: "Kirk/Spock Survey Results—Part 1," in *NTS*, undated. Judith and I have spoken at length about this and other surveys she has conducted within the community specifically involved in homoerotic fiction about Kirk and Spock.

50. Eva Kosofsky Sedgwick, *Between Men: English Literature and Male Homosocial Desire* (New York: Columbia University Press, 1985), p. 86.

51. I've always considered this an interesting double meaning of the term climax. How strange that, in commercial romance books for and about women, the climax in both its literary and sexual sense are conjoined and occur only in the mind of the reader and after the book has ended. If I were politically minded, I might carry the metaphor into the boudoir *propre*.

52. Sedgwick, *Between Men*, p. 89.

53. Personal correspondence, Ferguson to author, October 1987.

54. Lamb and Vieth, "Romantic Myth," pp. 243–44.

55. *Blake's 7* is an anomalous product in that class, status, and character seem to contribute at least as much as sexual relationship to the depiction of the relative sizes of the characters. The effect seems as much a result of film technique as of unconscious attribution of traits. Long before I ever saw a piece of homoerotic fiction in this source product I had read many action, relationship, and nonsexual hurt-comfort stories that depicted the delta-class Vila as smaller, slighter than the two alpha-class males. My own viewing of the series, perhaps preconditioned by the stories, substantiated this common description. It was therefore a complete shock when I met Paul Darrow and Michael Keating in the green room at the Batscon convention in Philadelphia in 1986. With the two actors standing side by side in real space, they seemed to me to be identical in height. Although their different styles of dress made it impossible to be certain, their builds did not look very different either.

Chapter Ten
Suffering and Solace:
The Genre of Pain

Hurt-Comfort and the Ethnographer

In hurt-comfort fiction, one of the heroes suffers while the other, or a character created for the purpose, comforts him. (In *Blake's 7* fan fiction the comfortee may be one of the female characters, but is more often one of the men.) The source of the suffering may in some instances be illness, but more often inflicted injury causes the pain. Unlike sadomasochistic fantasy material,[1] hurt-comfort places the source of the injury outside of the dyad of sufferer and comforter. Alternatively, the story may originate the hurt within the relationship and move toward eradicating the hurtful behavior through better mutual understanding by the ending. At no point in any of the literature I have read does the sufferer enjoy or deliberately seek out pain.

As a researcher, I found hurt-comfort the most difficult form to study. My own strong aversion to violence inhibited my early efforts at an unbiased analysis, and the community seemed to support my negative judgments about the genre. Judy Segal, who introduced me to fandom, dismissed hurt-comfort as the special interest of a small group while she guided me toward more acceptable material for a neophyte.

As I progressed in my study of the community and its products, I asked a number of writers and editors who occasionally act as mentors to new fans why people in the community chose to write or read hurt-comfort stories. Mentors know how to talk to outsiders. They could not give me core information because I was not yet sufficiently enculturated to make sense of it, but they did mediate for me in language I could understand. Barbara Storey, co-editor of *Nome*, a fanzine that publishes homoerotic fiction, explained:

Some people have problems with sexuality, but they do like closeness, those emotional ties. I think that's the reason why a lot of
people like hurt-comfort, which happens to turn me off completely
. . . they cannot allow, for whatever reason, a sexual relationship between those two characters . . . but it is all right if they are just extremely close, they hug each other, if one of them gets hurt, that
allows them an outlet for that deep emotional feeling, without
having to delve into sex.[2]

Co-editor Vicki Clark seconded this opinion, including her dislike of
the genre, but added, "I can see it if it's part of a whole story. What I
can't see is when that is the whole point of the story."[3]

Barbara and Vicki's explanation highlights an example of conservation of risk. The writer balances the very basic needs to be touched,
caressed, against the strictures placed upon physical contact in society.
Sex and pain are the two situations in which masculine culture allows
physical and emotional intimacy between adults of the opposite sex. If
sex is prohibited by the social constraints under which the writer
works, either because the participants are not of opposite sexes or because the writer feels constrained to limit sexual material of any kind
in her work, she may substitute the only symbolic alternative to sexual
intimacy available to her.

Lois Welling, a frequent mentor whose stories often contain strong
hurt-comfort elements, said much the same thing in more simple
terms: "I think they just like the comfort, and the hurt is an excuse to
get there."[4] When pressed for a more detailed explanation, Lois
backed away from the emotionally fraught question of hurt-comfort
to a mundane level I have observed among many community members who move from genre to genre and from source product to
source product (Lois writes in several "universes" and in a number of
genres): "I sometimes think that as a writer progresses in her writing,
the situations get more complex and daring, and really have no sub-
conscious meaning for the writer."[5]

Each option available in the community affords the writer or artist a
challenge to her skill as an artist and as a communicator. Can she deliver her message in this genre? In this source product? In some ways,
the self-conscious writer may consider taking on a socially ambiguous
genre like a mountain climber takes on the Matterhorn: she pits her
skill in presenting her material against the risk she takes in the subject
matter.

While some authors may engage the genre at the level of challenge,
or because of sexual prohibitions, others find that their particular

message places them in hurt-comfort without their volition. Shirley Maiewski wrote the story "Mindsifter," in which Klingon interrogation has rendered Captain Kirk bereft of both his memory and his sanity. The Klingons dispose of their victim by time-transport to the 1950s, where Kirk is hospitalized in a mental institution. In the story, a nurse helps Kirk to recover both his memory and his confidence in time for his rescue by the *Enterprise*.

According to Shirley, a mental institution near where she lives motivated her to write the story:

> . . . And you go to these state hospitals, and they're beautiful out front, and then you go 'round the back [a pregnant pause follows, giving me time to imagine the terrible conditions that lurk out of sight of casual passersby, some of which are dramatized in Shirley's story]. And there's a large one right near where we live, and a lot of my neighbors work there, and they've told me stories. Well, I got to thinking what would happen if one of our [*Star Trek*] characters, you know, was trapped in one of those places. And it wrote itself.[6]

Shirley Maiewski had an immediate and pressing social need to expose an injustice in her fiction, but she did not associate "Mindsifter" with the genre until a reader wrote her a letter and asked her about the hurt-comfort in the story. The idea that she might be writing hurt-comfort so distressed Shirley that she stopped writing fiction altogether.

The basic plot for "Mindsifter" grew out of the televised *Star Trek* episode "Errand of Mercy," in which the Klingon, Kor, interrogates Spock using a device called the mindsifter. In the episode, Spock, with his Vulcan mind controls, withstands the machine but he tells the captain that a human would not survive the ordeal with his sanity intact. Shirley was surprised to find her story considered hurt-comfort because her plot originated with the series universe itself, but many writers in the genre use series episodes as starting points for their stories. Both fans of hurt-comfort and community members who do not like the genre often dismissed my questions about its origin with the assertion that the idea wasn't theirs but came from the screen.

To test this response, I did turn to text analysis and found it to be true, up to a point. In the *Star Trek* episode "The Empath," Kirk, and then McCoy, are methodically tortured to test the compassion of one representative of an empathic race. Other episodes made a similar point less directly. *Starsky and Hutch* fans produce the highest percentage of hurt-comfort fiction, as writer Fanny Adams pointed out to me:

In *Starsky and Hutch,* especially at the beginning of the fandom, there was a lot of hurt-comfort, and there may be a lot of different reasons for that, you know, I won't want to go into it, but there will always be hurt, physically hurt . . . beat 'em up, let's hurt 'em, bleed 'em.[7]

In fact, a whole *Starsky and Hutch* fanzine was dedicated to "slow poison" stories, in honor of that common theme in action-adventure television, *Starsky and Hutch* in particular. A review of the *Starsky and Hutch* corpus was still surprising, however.

I was less interested in my interpretation of the action on the screen than in the intention to communicate hurt-comfort concepts on the part of series producers, so I examined the press release for each episode in the press pack sent to *TV Guide* magazine by the Spelling-Goldman organization. In at least 33 percent of the episodes, the press releases mentioned as central to the plot injury or directed threat of death to one of the two heroes, while the other worried or saved him. In almost as many episodes, the threat was to a friend or family member outside the dyadic hero relationship.

Clearly, fans drew basic concepts from the screen, but why these products inspired an artistic response, or why hurt-comfort fans grew decidedly misty when they admitted to their fan interest, still eluded me. To my persistent questions, most fans responded that they didn't know why they liked hurt-comfort. They just did.

While participants at the core of an esoteric practice have the most knowledge about it, those participants also have a knack for knowing when the questioner isn't ready to understand any answer they can give. My informants did not lie; the thing they did not know about their interest was how to tell me what they knew. We did not share a language, and my informants politely refrained from informing me that my question made no sense.

At this point I still had trouble reading hurt-comfort fiction, and I finally realized that I would never understand it until I had read more deeply in the genre. Armed with this grudging insight and the general explanations equally uneasily given by informants over my years studying the community, I proceeded to ask hurt-comfort fans at an action-adventure convention for the title of their favorite story. They named most frequently "Strange Days Indeed,"[8] a story 105 single-spaced, eight-and-a-half by eleven pages long. To desensitize myself to the difficult genre so that I could work with it, I read "Strange Days Indeed" four times in one weekend. Over that weekend I learned to look past my own response to the graphic depiction of violence and to seek out the patterns of interaction embedded within them.

In "Strange Days Indeed," the abuse begins when the villain beats the first hero, breaking several of the hero's ribs and damaging his appendix. An extended scene of homosexual rape of the second hero follows, from the point of view of the partner held in a room adjacent to where the rape is taking place. The partner can only hear what is happening to his friend, but at the same time he cannot stop listening. The two hurt friends are abandoned in a comfortable cottage with everything one might need but a doctor. The first hero develops a drug dependency under the pressure of caring for his raped companion. They quarrel, and finally the rape victim realizes that his companion is in equal need of attention. In spite of their respective fragile conditions, they crawl into bed together for a supportive embrace. By the end of the story, they realize they love each other.

As I have since found to be most usually the case, the violence and abuse in the story arises outside of the friendship relationship. At no point is either character attracted to the perpetrator of the violence. At no point is the abuse written as sexually exciting to the hurt characters, nor does either hero take pleasure in the abuse of the other. The presence of the friend as witness to the sexual degradation of his companion increases the suffering of the witness and the pain of humiliation of the sexually abused partner. At all times the first hero's concern is for the well-being of his companion. The second hero reciprocates this attitude and returns the care and attention as soon as he becomes aware that comforting is needed. The distinction between good and evil is clearly drawn and unambiguous. Importantly, at no point does the story seem intended to appeal sexually to its audience. Criticized by scholars for not considering the erotic possibilities of the story as I described it here, however, I returned to the community and asked those who recommended the story what they found erotic in it. The question puzzled the fans, who did not understand how anyone could find the torture portions of that particular story sexually exciting, and I had to expend some effort to rehabilitate my position among community members who took my question as an expression of my own feelings about the story. They did agree that the discovery of true love at the end was pleasurable.

I then began reading the many stories in the genre that I had put aside, and I discovered that "Strange Days Indeed" was an unauthorized rewrite of an earlier story, also anonymous, in which the first hero is not severely beaten, and a third party with no relationship to the hero dyad attends to the care of the sexually abused man. Many fans of the genre found the first version less satisfying because the third party replaces what readers construed as the proper source of the comfort; a loving friend is present and concerned, but not the ac-

Merle Decker's illustration for "Notes of a Madwoman," a mild hurt-comfort story in which a woman character created by the fanwriter provides comfort to the injured Kirk and his companion.

tive giver of care. Other fans, however, preferred the first version because the amount of suffering depicted in the story is less extreme,
and the attention of the knowledgeable third party seems more appropriate than the ministrations of his less adequately prepared
friend. Both versions of the story maintain the same pattern of pain
coming from outside the dyad, but the more popular version adds
two interesting factors along with the additional violence that seemed
gratuitous to some: (1) it reestablishes the main source of comfort
within the relationship; and (2) it balances the equation—both partners experience pain and both receive comfort. In fact, the story
seems to say that one way of dealing with personal pain is to recognize
the suffering of those we care about and return their attention and
comfort.

The Types of Hurt-Comfort

Once I developed a working knowledge of the hurt-comfort literature, many things I had heard over the years began to make sense to
me. Each genre has its particular categories that distinguish one type
of story from another in the body of work. In "slash" fiction, "first
time" stories, in which the hero dyad first become lovers in the physical sense, make up a distinctive subgenre. Heterosexual stories are generically identified by the name of the hero with whom the female
character has a relationship, such as "lay-Spock." Amanda and Sarek
stories make up a sub-genre, and there is some unnamed distinction
made between twentieth-century characters imported into the future
worlds and characters who are contemporary with the settings in
which they are placed. Only in hurt-comfort, however, did I find a
wealth of types categorized by name.

Hurt-comfort represents both a generic term for all the stories in this
category and a subset within the genre. In the subset of stories, one
member of the hero dyad is wounded, or occasionally, ill, and his
companion comforts the wounded party. If both heroes are hurt or
ill, they comfort each other. Hurt-comfort stories may substitute an
invented character to provide the comfort, or an invented character
may provide support and observe the comfort given by the dyad. A
hurt-comfort story may precipitate a sexual relationship or occur
within the context of an ongoing sexual relationship. Alternatively, no
sexual tie need be present at all.

Get-'em stories generally include a great deal of pain and very little
comfort. The story may occur temporally before the dyadic relationship has formed, or the hurt member of the dyad may be separated
spatially from the source of comfort. Many fans rate pain inflicted in

the presence of a partner or lover willing but unable to give comfort as more intense than pain inflicted outside the knowledge of the partner, since the sufferer must experience not only the basic pain, but also a sense of humiliation at being helpless in front of a respected other and regret that the situation is upsetting the partner. Occasionally both members of the dyad have separate but parallel hurt experiences, either as background that explains the affinity they have for each other, or to show the danger of separation.

Slave stories range from the traditional capture and rescue of the television source products to covert or institutional slavery, often with the slave as an unwilling sexual partner of the captor. In many stories an outsider enslaves one partner and the other undergoes great danger and hardship first to release his partner and then to help him overcome his experience. Other stories postulate a captor and slave relationship between the hero or heroine and the partner that transforms into a more equal relationship over the course of the story. These stories postulate no preexisting relationship; they attribute the growing equality to the love the pair discovers for each other and to the indomitability of the captive. Most slave stories are also rape stories, but the reverse is not true.

Rape stories likewise include a number of types. Rape may be inflicted as part of torture or as part of establishing the pecking order in an aggressive all-male social setting. The rapist in these stories is usually outside the hero dyad. Occasionally the rapist may be a partner in the dyad who acts to protect the other from a worse fate, such as gang rape or rape by a stranger. The latter stories often lead to a sexual relationship between the partners—not because either participant enjoyed the rape, but because a strong but heretofore hidden emotional and physical attraction is revealed in the ensuing arguments. In rarer instances, sexual tension between the pair, which erupts in forced rape as an act of aggressive sexual dominance of one partner over the other, leads to a sexual relationship. In these stories the victim leads his aggressive partner to accept a more equal and loving, less emotionally explosive, relationship.

Death stories, called *wallows* in England and Australia, often begin with the death of one member of the dyad, and the rest of the story focuses on the grief of his companion, which sometimes results in the companion's death soon after. Alternatively, one member of the dyad may be lingering in death while his anguished partner first tries to save him, and then sacrifices his own life rather than be parted at death. I have never seen a fan story consider the death of a hero as a transcendent or uplifting experience, as Spock's death was depicted in Paramount's *Star Trek: The Wrath of Khan,* nor is death ever given the

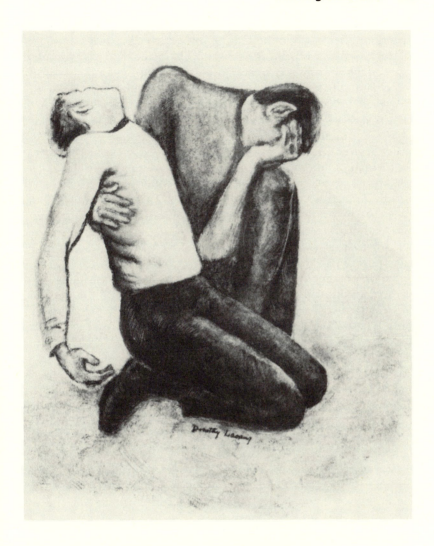

Dorothy Laoang's illustration for "He Stopped for Me," a hurt-comfort story in *Consort 2*, shows the influence of Edvard Munch.

passing insignificance a television series may give it when a series character suffers death by contract negotiation. Rather, death of the hero in his prime is *always* seen as horrific, anguishing, and marking those around it for life. Only death by old age seems to hold transcendent significance for writers of fan stories.

Resurrection stories, like death stories, are seldom created for a transcendent affect. While the method of resurrection may vary, an underlying subtext of outrage that this character might be considered expendable in any way pervades all of the stories in this type. The very name of the category is misleading in many ways. While some stories that deal with Spock's resurrection do take place in the context that real death occurred and intervention by Vulcan culture and the Genesis project overturned it, most stories in this genre based on other source products propose that death never occurred. Dream, hallucination, brainwashing of a point-of-view character all appear in the stories as reasons why the television or movie viewer incorrectly believed that a favorite character had died. Fans of *Blake's 7* had to be particularly inventive in this type of story, because the BBC killed all the lead characters at the end of the fourth season. To evolve their writing universe, *Blake's 7* fans had to show how the events of at least the episode "Blake" never happened.

I have only seen one instance where fans overturned a death story created in the community. In the story "Endgame,"[9] the hero dyad has established turn-taking routines for entering dangerous buildings. The point-of-view character should enter a suspected bomber's hideout first, because it is his turn to take the greater risk, but he allows his partner and lover to do so instead. The bomber had planted a vibration sensitive bomb under the floorboards, and it explodes, killing the partner. Overcome by guilt and grief, the point-of-view character sets out on a course of self-destruction in the Middle East. Captured, and by now quite mad, he murders fellow prisoners and guards, until he is tried for espionage and murder and is himself beheaded.

The story depicted the bombing death with such shattering reality, and the partner's grief with such gothic melodrama, that a number of community members felt it necessary to soften the impact the story had on readers. One response story relegated the entire event to a dream. Another rescued the guilt- and grief-driven surviving partner from the sword while magically permitting him some final days with his partner. Over the course of the new story, the survivor came to terms with his guilt and accepted his own continued existence as necessary. Still a third contribution to the story dealt with a third character's response to the deaths of the two heroes.

I have not mentioned a named category of stories based on the exploration of psychological pain or manipulation here. A story type particularly focused on the effects of psychological manipulation as torture, and particularly the fear of madness, had been developing in *Blake's 7* fandom. As I pointed out earlier, the existence of this type

Suzan Lovett's death-and-resurrection illustration for the poem "All Stories New," which appeared in *Nome 8*. Note the religious referents: cross, flames, touching hands from Michelangelo's *Creation of Man*, and the three principals from *Star Trek*, all set against a background of stars and planets.

Fanzine editors Barbara Storey, Karen Swanson, and Victoria Clark publish
material in the *Star Trek* and *Beauty and the Beast* fandoms.

seems threatened by the influx of fans more accustomed to using sexual and romantic relationships as metaphors in their work. However,
it would be misleading to take the lack of a named subcategory to
mean an absence of psychological pain in the fan stories. Fanny
Adams, after asserting that there will always be the physical violence
she described in the *Starsky and Hutch* fiction, pondered why there was
not as much violence in stories about another police-type action-
adventure show, *The Professionals:* "I realized it's because in *Pros*
fiction, it's psychological hurt-comfort. They're always getting emotionally battered."

I pointed out that the *Professionals* heroes were emotionally battered in the series, and she agreed, adding, "Starsky and Hutch did
too, though, but in a classic American television way." [10]

Until *Miami Vice,* American television had sanitized the emotional
lives of its heroes, inflicting no more than an hour's worth of angst
from which the hero completely recovered in time for the next episode. By contrast, British television seemed overlaid by an existential
weltschmerz that leant itself perfectly to the depiction of hurt-comfort
fiction.

In spite of the confident positivism that pervaded the worldview of American heroes like Kirk and Spock, however, I have found more depictions of psychological pain than any other kind of pain, and in combination with every form of physical hurt. In fact, psychological pain pervades all the genres, if not all stories.

Hurt-Comfort and Community

I saw hurt-comfort in action in the community long before I understood the genre, but the experience has stayed with me in spite of the fact that I could neither tape nor take notes. It was my first realization that something important was going on in the genre, and it is the single reason why I never gave up trying to understand the implications for community life of stories I personally found upsetting to read.

The New York Convention Committee's More Eastly Con took place on Labor Day weekend in 1985, just weeks after the death of fanwriter Toni Cardinal-Price in a hit-and-run auto accident. Toni's work was highly respected in the fan community, and her death shocked everyone who knew her and many who had only read her poetry. I had met Vicki Clark and Barbara Storey, editors of the fanzine *Nome* and close friends of Toni, earlier that year. When they saw me in the dealers room at More Eastly Con they invited me to their room for a small get-together they were holding to remember Toni.

When I arrived the room was full of women clustered on the beds, on the floor, leaning against the walls. Around the mirror friends had taped snapshots of Toni Cardinal-Price at home and with her friends, a number of whom were present in the room. Someone had brought in a VCR, and *Star Trek* songtapes were playing. Most of the videos recounted the strong friendship between Captain Kirk and his first officer, and many dealt with Spock's death, which shocked fans when they first saw *The Wrath of Khan*.

Throughout the evening the fan women watched the videos, commented softly about them, and cried. From time to time the experience would become too much for someone in the room and she would head for the bathroom for quiet talk with one friend until she was calm enough to rejoin the group. People drifted in and out of the room, some stopping only to pay their respects, others lingering to stare at the videos and share in the warmth of each other's company and the freedom to let down the bright face and mourn. Vicki and Barbara told me how they had been on vacation in California when they received the news on the same day Toni had died in New Jersey, and how they had traveled four hundred miles off their scheduled route to be with mutual friends, who took time off from work to be with them and share their grief. It became strikingly clear to me during that weekend that fans did not write hurt-comfort for fun, but that the genre fulfilled some of the deepest needs of community life.

I kept the experience of More Eastly Con in mind while I accumulated explanations of fans and a working knowledge of the literature by title and author. Finally, I figured out where my original question had gone wrong, and once again I ventured into the field. This time, I asked a number of the writers what was happening in their lives when they wrote particular stories I mentioned by title. One woman, who wrote about a man losing his young son to leukemia, explained that she was working out her feelings about an adult daughter's drug addiction. Another woman wrote a "get-'em" story about a hero captured and tortured while his partner, believing him dead, goes mad. At the end of the story the captured hero is rescued by third parties and brought to the place where his partner awaits his return to take him into death. Both men are debilitated almost beyond recognition, but the story offers only the glimmer of hope that they are still alive, together again. Writing the story helped that author struggle with suicidal depression. She told me that she had originally planned to write the comfort part as a sequel but found that when her depression lifted she could not go back to the story again.

In all cases when I asked about specific fictional stories I received descriptions of real psychic pain. Some fans who read but did not create in the genre dealt with physical disability in their lives. In general, however, I found that women experiencing physical turmoil in their lives were more likely to write the most idealized relationships in their fiction.

I might have been tempted to stop here, with a phenomenon and a symbolic function of the text, but my knowledge of the genre and the duration of my study put me in an ambiguous position. While some fans feared that my study might reveal too much about them, others had grown used to my presence. When I showed an interest in hurt-comfort, they included me in fan activities that focused on the genre. I had not seen these interactions earlier because it would have been inappropriate, according to fan standards of behavior, to subject me to discussion about a topic I found distasteful. Over the years fans had occasionally asked if I liked the material, but when I said that I found it uncomfortable reading they quickly dropped the subject. I now realize that I had put some of my informants in a double bind, asking about a genre while admitting I didn't like it, but at the time I thought I could learn about the fan relationship to the genre without actually reading the stories. As I later discovered, I was wrong.

When a fan has an idea, she calls friends and tells them that idea—
it's called talking story, and, as discussed in earlier chapters, it is the
most common activity at any fan gathering in any media product or
community genre. It is far more acceptable to talk story widely in the
community than to express feelings of hopelessness and despair in
the outside world. Through the process of talking story, the fanwriter
or reader has direct and immediate contact with warm and caring
friends. She can ask for advice about her story from any fan of the
genre and, while they talk story, the participants move back and forth
from the personal to the grammatical, hiding in sentence structure
when the feelings become too intense or when a stranger passes by.
With their literature for symbolic discourse, fans band together this
way in a conspiracy of support for their members.

But this support does not occur in woeful sob sessions. Pain is
present, recognized, shared, but art is also present, and art is joyful.
Fans learn to laugh with their friends, to stave off the fearful darkness
with potato chips and chocolate ice cream and preposterous exag-
gerations of their own genre. "Shot in the shoulder, point-blank
range with a high-power rifle and he's up and running the next day,"
one writer characterized her own story; "What I like best is the
realism."

Further along in the process, the writer may see her story incorporated into the community with illustrations in a fanzine. Its worth is
reified because fans outside the immediate circle buy it. Isolation continues to break down as new readers discuss her work. The writer
even finds satisfaction in helping others when fans tell her that her
story has affected them and offer stories of their own in turn.

Hurt-Comfort and Risk

In this section I have talked a lot about meaning and risk. I knew that
homoerotic stories carried a high-risk value in the community. I also
realized that at the heart of the community something both more
meaningful and more dangerous lay hidden, probably out in plain
sight where I had been ignoring it for years. In fact, Jacqueline Lichtenberg almost told me the answer directly when I first began my
study. Her advice on doing the ethnography was simple: when I
found the place where the tears fell, I'd know I'd gotten to the heart
of the community. Lois Welling had given me another clue when she
called hurt-comfort stories more daring than other genres, but at the
time I didn't understand her comment in the context of the conservation of risk.

I didn't want hurt-comfort to be the heart of the community, I didn't want to accept the fact that pain was so pervasive in the lives of women that it lay like a wash beneath all of the creative efforts of a community they had made for themselves. But there it was, nonetheless, laid out so clearly I could no longer deny it. Shirley Maiewski wrote it without realizing it. Other fans wrote to work through their own problems of personal suffering.

Hurt-comfort fiction, as constructed in the fan community, is a complex symbol system for the expression of strong feelings that masculine culture defines as unacceptable. In it, fictional theme and personal experience come together. Stories about suffering mask real suffering, sometimes immediate and overwhelming, sometimes remembered, and sometimes only observed. That suffering may objectively appear to be intense, as in the cases described above, but in many cases it may seem inconsequential to outsiders. No story serves only one purpose here; at least one level of meaning, and often many levels, lie close to the raw-nerved living surface of the writer and the reader. Outside of the group one may not speak of the real anguish of death and pain but must put on a "brave front," a "stiff upper lip," and go on. Most decidedly, one does not refer to the relationship between suffering and power. In hurt-comfort, however, the writer does explore this relationship, often with her own impulses fully engaged.

At its least emphasized in the fiction, hurt-comfort represents such an obvious fact of life that readers, and writers like Shirley, do not even realize it is there. At its most extreme, the genre becomes almost impossible for many people to read, either because the story taps too deeply into the hidden feelings of the reader for comfort, or because the particular pain expressed by the writer is so different and so horrifying that the reader finds it difficult to comprehend or share. The community refers to only the more extreme forms that focus particularly on pain as hurt-comfort, but the discourse of self-sacrifice pervades most of the fiction.

Sadism and Self-Sacrifice

Many hurt-comfort stories make use of a relational triad: an outside villain who causes pain and relates to the hero only as the giver of suffering; a hero in a dyad experiencing the pain; and second hero in the dyad who offers comfort to the suffering partner. In the triadic relationship, the author can play out an unconscious sadistic rage against the loved male from the distance of "outsider," defined as "bad," while she plays out the part of protector and comforter from inside the relationship. I have read few stories in which the author used the point-of-view of the character inflicting pain.[11] In the *Blake's 7* story "The Haunting of Haderon,"[12] we see how much symbolic distance the writer can place between herself and the source of the inflicted pain: her villains, disembodied spirits, flay victims Avon and Vila with sandstorms.

There is no question that the depiction of excesses of inflicted pain arouses strong emotions, including both titillation and revulsion, in many readers. But hurt-comfort does not reflect the murderous rage of man-hating women against their oppressors. Rather, even the most extreme forms of the genre reflect a profound ambivalence as expressed in the triad love-hate-object (of emotional focus). Hatred is present, as is love, and above all the profound confusion of experiencing toward a single focus opposite extremes of an emotional continuum. To some extent, the genre may reflect what Karen Horney refers to as the "overvaluation of love,"[13] particularly in the stories that combine romance and hurt-comfort. Social forces that Horney described in the thirties have in many instances become even more widespread as more women move into nontraditional roles. The women must cope with the backlash of sexual rejection and must come to terms with men they both desire and fear in the workplace and in social relations.

The hurt-comfort story allows the woman writer and reader the opportunity to explore all the roles in the triad of ambivalence—she can experience her rage through the character inflicting pain, her empathy and love in the person of the comforter, and her confusion and dread as the victim. Some *Blake's 7* fans interpret the continuing character of Servalan as embodying the very ambivalence they struggle to express. In the fiction of these fans, Servalan may fill the place of both enemy and lover, both inflicting injury and trying to rehabilitate the very situation she has caused with her rage. These stories remain very rare, however—possibly because with Servalan as point-of-view character, the writer must accept both the rage and the love in herself. In the more traditional splitting of the triad into three characters, the writer and her reader may experience each one separately, disavowing those emotional roles they wish to disown in themselves.[14]

Of these roles, masculine culture allows women social expression only of the comforter. Women are not supposed to feel rage against an oppressive society, and they are looked upon with contempt if they claim that they have been made victims. And yet, story after story expresses the real fears of women—of rape in particular, but of other forms of physical and psychological abuse as well—and the equally strong urge to strike back at those who control them with that fear. In fan fiction the woman's position in relation to the comforter is equally subversive. While masculine culture allows her the role of comforter, it has no place for women as the recipients of comfort. But in her fan fiction, the woman hurt-comfort writer can both give and receive comfort.

It would be remiss to recognize in the emotional content of the genre only the writer. As in homoerotic and relationship genres, the purpose of many hurt-comfort stories is to explore and reconstruct the male with regard to his own suffering, rage, and need for comfort. Her story is both an unconscious expression of her own emotions and a conscious reproduction of her observations about the behavior of men. Men inflict pain and men also suffer. Men need comfort, and men need to learn how to give comfort. In hurt-comfort stories, women try to understand the violence at the core of so many men, and the inability of more men to understand women's needs for comfort.

In the course of a typical hurt-comfort story, one hero will be injured, or more commonly, he will be captured and injured, while his companion worries about him, empathizes with his pain, and finally offers comfort, signaling the end of the abuse. Throughout, the victim remains powerless, but through the story domination undergoes a transformation: beginning as the product of force—bad, masculine power—it becomes the reflection of his need for caring—good, feminine power. While the victim remains powerless, the move from masculine power to feminine power transforms the victim as well. When the woman begins the story, she may identify the victim as female in spite of the male character that represents her, but as the story progresses, the woman as comforter holds power, even when represented by a man, and the victim or situationally submissive partner has become Man tumbled from his position of power by female compassion and love. In this fictional transformation we see the transmutation of the sadistic urge into the maternal role of self-sacrifice, while the masochistic position of victim remains ever problematic, both attractive and repellent.

Heroic Sacrifice and Western Masculine Culture

If fictional narratives about suffering heroes occurred only in the women's fiction, I might have been tempted again to stop, with a psychological evaluation that placed the heart of the community in ambivalent relationships with men. When I reexamined the source products, however, I found pain depicted throughout, though very differently than in the fan fiction. Through the selective recombining of elements from the source products, fanwriters engaged the mythic structure of action-adventure television in a dialogue about suffering, redefining the very acts of on-screen bravery and self-sacrifice as women see them.

To understand hurt-comfort, therefore, one must first understand perceptions of pain and heroism in masculine culture. René Girard speaks with smug certainty about the superiority of the secular state over religion, the latter of which requires in ritual at least the metaphoric image of human sacrifice, and the former of which does away with such need.[15] And yet, in its wars and in its internal law enforcement, modern Western culture often requires the deaths of its young men in numbers that would give an Aztec priest pause. The young and the fit among its males, who represent at one and the same time the potential power of the male and the structural powerlessness of youth, must die so that the society, as directed by its old men and as idealized in the images of women and children, can continue.

The situation presents the society with a number of problems: the more unstable the position of the state, in respect to internal or external pressures, the greater the need to reestablish equilibrium at the cost of willing victims. Soldiers must go to war because they believe in their cause, or they must believe simultaneously in their powerlessness to fight their own state and their power to overcome the external danger through sacrifice of life or limb if all else fails. Forced armies can seldom internalize two such paradoxical beliefs—that they hold power with regard to the outsider but not with regard to those who direct them. The Viet Nam War amply demonstrated that an unwilling force will have neither the will to succeed nor the self-discipline to regulate itself. Given the high frequency of post-traumatic stress disorder after that war, we can see that the soldier who does not believe in the purpose of the state has no support structure for coming to terms with his own actions and experiences carried out in its cause.

Stories of heroic suffering and sacrifice serve the same purpose for the state as they do for religion. The death of Christ on the Cross and the many tales of the martyrdom of saints serve as models of religious devotion for Catholics. Catholic schools regularly regaled students both with the lives of ancient martyrs and with parallel horror tales about religious persecution in the countries of our political cold war enemies. When I speak with women who attended Catholic schools in the sixties and before, they agree that their goal in fifth grade was to die a martyr's death and go straight to heaven. The less secure among them decided to first become nuns and then become martyrs, in case they weren't quite good enough to get into heaven simply by dying for the faith.[16]

Likewise, the state must prepare its young to die for its causes as surrogates for the decision makers. Freud emphasizes the Oedipal conflict of the young boy who unconsciously wishes to murder the father and replace him in relation to the mother, but he denies the Judeo-Christian myth structure that consistently puts the son at risk at the hands of his father. Abraham sets out to sacrifice his son at God's command, and in the New Testament, God himself sacrifices his own son. In the mythology of the state it is the young foot soldier who sacrifices his life for his country, not his general.[17]

The state, like religion, must supply models of valiant pain and death to imbue its youth with the desire to sacrifice itself in like fashion for personal glory and patriotic zeal. During the cold war and Viet Nam, series about World War II were popular on television, as were police action-adventure series. The latter remain popular today, whereas the grim reality of Viet Nam on the news seemed to have killed the popular taste for war fiction on television for a time.[18] But how do these popular culture constructs prepare the appropriate group to sacrifice itself for the good of the society?

As Fanny Adams pointed out, the psychological effects of pain and conflict are downplayed in a typical American action series—when a policeman has murdered a villain, he shows little affect. When an innocent bystander suffers the same fate, the policeman may demonstrate remorse for a single episode, but he is back the next week as if the event never happened. Police drama television makes the nightmares and the memory of the horror of taking life disappear. The death of a comrade is likewise dispensed with in a single episode, often with as little psychic suffering on the part of the hero as he demonstrated for the dead villain.

Killing and watching others die is only a part of what society expects of its chosen. The warrior of the streets at home, like the warrior in battle with external enemies, must willingly accept death or injury as part of his job. Television makes sacrifice attractive by separating pain from suffering and showing only the former. A television policeman takes a bullet in the arm or leg and grits his teeth. The next week he returns completely healed. As we have already seen, "shot in the heart" episodes are popular in any police series. The type, like "slow poison" and other near-death plot lines, tells the viewer that if he sacrifices his life for the state his friends will love him and the state will resurrect him with its advanced medical technology. Moreover, he will be returned to normal health by the next episode.

Only in the dramas of returning warriors, from the Greek-period "Heracles"[19] to the contemporary *Coming Home*, does the society begin to reveal its ambivalence toward the surviving warrior. If we accept that at some unconscious level the soldier is a sacrifice made to ward off the dissolution of the state, then his return poses the society a problem. While it pays to reassure the young man about to rush into the breach that his continued existence has meaning, sacrifices are supposed to stay dead. Medics try to patch them up and noncommissioned officers try to keep them alive because at the level of consciousness the victim becomes a person, and the lives of persons are valued even if troops are not. But the returning soldier represents a serious danger to society for practical reasons of his skills and for the primitive fear that lingers in the civilized mind that the sacrifice has been rejected, and that the society will therefore suffer the consequences of that rejection.

Re-creating the Hero

In hurt-comfort fiction, the women fanwriters reunite the hero's pain with suffering. Death as they create it becomes final, while they reject the casual death laid before them by the television. Fans of *Blake's 7* regularly dismiss the offhanded deaths of the characters as dream or delusion, or they shift the story line away from the source product somewhere before the final season. In the fan story "Endgame,"[20] however, the death of the first hero is disconcertingly real. The reader experiences the pain and fear of the dying man, and the overwhelming grief of his partner.

One scene particularly demonstrates the anguish that violent death leaves behind: immediately after the explosion described earlier in this chapter, the surviving partner slips a hand beneath his comrade's neck to ease the man's discomfort. The dying man's silver chain, broken in the explosion, slips into the survivor's palm. When he returns home from seeing his dead partner in the hospital the chain is still clasped in his hand:

Death comes as the end. The phrase seemed familiar, and he wondered where he'd heard it. Finis. R.I.P. Friends Romans countrymen I come to honour Caesar not to bury him not yet because his killers still live vengeance is mine cry havoc and let slip the dogs of war and fill the gap with English dead and bright life-blood spreads liquid ruby—he became aware that his right hand was closed tight in a fist, nails digging into his palm, fingers caked and glued together with dried blood. No longer red but black-brown. And in his palm was a silver chain. Warm. He did not open his fist, that would let in the cold. Life is warmth. So why did he feel so cold? . . .

He closed the bathroom door, ran the hot tap in the hand basin, and put his fist under the water. Blood flowed again . . . And as the water grew warm he turned his hand and opened it. Washed clean, the bright metal glowed under the steady stream, and he stared at it, hypnotized, until the pain of near-boiling water forced him back to awareness.[21]

In this scene the author juxtaposes quotations about heroic death in literature against the personal and intimate experience of a lover's blood on the survivor's hand. Unlike Lady Macbeth, the survivor does not cry, "Out, damned spot," but cherishes the blood until, at last, he must let it go. Relinquishing that last part of his companion, the hero in some way experiences the finality of death as a recurrence of death—"blood flowed again."

There is nothing transcendent in the women's depictions of untimely death, no Kirk declaring that he feels young again as a new sun rises over Spock's casket. Death hurts deeply, even when it comes at the end of a long and full life. Death of youth and vitality is overwhelmingly painful. It even hurts heroes. Women know this as a fact, and neither Shakespeare nor television can convince them otherwise. When they rewrite the hero, it is with the realization that pain and death cause suffering, not only of the victim sacrificed to the need of the state, but also of those who knew him, cared about him.

Fanwriter Syn Ferguson explained in a letter how the hero stands between the writer and the meaningful women characters she would like to create:

> Our culture makes it difficult to like and respect women, even if you are one. Particularly if you are one and you've been indoctrinated with the hero as a pattern of virtue, because then you have to accept as virtue those very things which are just the opposite of what you must do to survive.[22]

Syn, like other fanwriters, reconstructs the hero in a feminine sensibility of the human being in society. Referring to her book, *Courts of Honor*, she says this about her reconstruction of Kirk:

> Kirk spoke very directly about heroes and images all through the book, he resisted Farrid's efforts to make him larger than life, he was resisting to the end, insisting on the individual. He was prepared to fail, and he would have failed if he hadn't had a lot of other people on his side . . . To me, Kirk was saved by his luck and his friends, by his community, if you will, rather than because of his virtue . . . the hero may have saved the day, but everyone else saved

the hero—a little fact about privilege that is left out of most stories.[23]

Like Syn and the anonymous author of "Endgame," women who write hurt-comfort reconstruct the hero in two specific and important ways: they reintegrate suffering with pain and death, and they draw the hero into the web of relationships discussed earlier as fundamental to women's lives and sense of security. In the process they move closer to an image of a hero that feeds their own need for autonomy but does not succumb to the masculine myth that constructs a hero unsuited to living beyond the end of his story.

Torture and Power

When the fanwriter reconstructs the hero, she is making use of an understanding of the relationship between torture and power in the absence of empathy. Elaine Scarry points out that physical pain, by its very nature, cannot be shared.[24] The imagination fails to grasp what language cannot express, and pain has been particularly resistant to verbal expression. The inexpressibility of pain in the presence of a will to dominate often produces a political relationship which Scarry refers to as the conversion of real pain into the fiction of power. That is,

> . . . it [torture] bestows visibility on the structure and enormity of what is usually private and incommunicable, contained within the boundaries of the sufferer's body. It then goes on to deny, to falsify, the reality of the very thing it has itself objectified by a perceptual shift which converts the vision of suffering into the wholly illusory but, to the torturers and the regime they represent, wholly convincing spectacle of power. The physical pain is so incontestably real that it seems to confer its quality of "incontestable reality" on that power that has brought it into being.[25]

The torturer surrounds himself with the verbal and material manifestations of inflicting pain. Because of the very interiority of suffering, he does not share the experience of pain with his victim, but creates out of it the illusion that his power to cause pain confers power over the wider political sphere. Scarry does not consider psychic pain in her work. She says that, unlike physical pain, psychological pain has an object, a way of projecting itself onto the external world. My study would indicate, however, that the reality of terror arises when the terrorist first creates the psychic pain and then denies not only its object but its very existence. Alternatively, the terrorist may admit the pain exists but turn the object back on the sufferer. The most successful terrorist does both simultaneously: your pain, which I have created, does not exist, but if it did it would be the result of your own inner weakness; it's your own fault. Any one of these strategies effectively shuts off the sufferer's avenues of externalization and leaves her in a closed loop with only herself as the object of her suffering.

The use of both techniques to control the actions of women has become so embedded in Western culture that those who participate in it are not always aware that they are doing so. Discussing the prevalence of rape stories in the fan fiction, I mentioned to a male psychiatrist a widely publicized statistic, that one in four women over the age of twelve in the United States would experience rape, and referred to the United States as a rape culture. He scoffed at me, asked if I thought all men were rapists, and implied that my "overreaction" to the statistic indicated a personal psychological problem with men. He did not seem to recognize the fact that everyone in a culture need not be a rapist to constitute a society built on rape, just as everyone in a regime need not be a torturer to constitute a state built on torture. Nor did he recognize that the publication of the statistic, "objectively," with no concomitant improvement in the protection of women and no harsher penalties for rape, constitutes psychological terrorism. He was, however, ready to close the loop on my anger, attributing it to a flaw in my psyche.[26] In much the same way, the advice given to women in most reports on the statistic—to stay indoors at night and not to travel alone, to beware even when dating—closes the loop on the potential victim, making the woman responsible for her own rape by virtue of going out of doors alone. And this occurs in a culture where the male urge to rape is so widely accepted that heterosexual men fall prey to their own propaganda in their dealings with homosexual men.[27]

I have used the example of rape in this section for two reasons: it presents a clear example of both physical and psychological terrorism intrinsic to the culture in which the fan community writes, and it appears as an act of torture in an overwhelming majority of stories that fall within the recognized hurt-comfort genre. The rape story overlaps almost every other subtype in the genre, although it seldom appears in death stories. But why do women write about the very things they fear? What benefit can be gained from stories that graphically describe pain and suffering, that offer comfort after the fact but do not postulate, do not reconstruct, a society free of deliberate torture?

The women who write hurt-comfort stories are working at some level with the understanding that the reverse of Elaine Scarry's formulation is also true: if real pain can be converted into the fiction of power, then the fiction of pain can be converted into real power. Pain destroys language, but language can re-create pain. All hurt-comfort fiction tries to express pain and suffering so that the reader can share the experience directly, both of the sufferer and of the comforter. If the torturer can be made to share the pain of his victim, he can no longer deny that pain, that suffering, into invisibility. He must deal with the pain he inflicts as his own pain, and not alone of some other. Experiencing the pain, focused on the suffering, he must transform it. Scarry uses the example of the story of Christ as a fundamental transformation:

> The change from God's disembodied relation to man's body in the older writings [the Old Testament] to God's embodied relation to man's body in the younger is itself a transformation that conforms to the description given earlier of the transformation of the weapon into the tool. The weapon acts directly on sentience, while the tool only acts on sentience by providing it with an object.[28]

In the hurt-comfort fiction, pain finds its object, and in the act of creating it, ". . . deprive[s] the external world of the privilege of being inanimate—of, in other words, its privilege of being irresponsible to its sentient inhabitants on the basis that it is itself nonsentient."[29] Suffering, made unreal by its perpetrators, is remade in the fiction. Remade, it denies the power of the oppressor to unmake the experience of the sufferer. It offers him a way out of his own acts of infliction and the suffering he must share in the fiction: he may become the comforter, giving comfort instead of pain, trading the artificial power of pain for the real power of healing.

Notes

1. In the sadomasochistic fantasy material I reviewed, the violence was much less extreme than in hurt-comfort fiction (I found only one threat of permanent injury, and no representations of serious physical damage such as broken bones and abusive beatings). In most cases the point of view was that of the submissive partner, and the attitude of the submissive partner was gratitude for the humiliation and ritual abuse meted out to him by his dominant partner. Examples drawn from *Drummer* magazine, 1980–81.
2. Barbara Storey and Victoria Clark, taped interview, August 1985.
3. Ibid.
4. Personal correspondence, Lois Welling to author, 1986.

5. Ibid.
6. Shirley Maiewski, taped interview, New York, September 1985.
7. Fanny Adams, taped interview, Chicago, March 1987.
8. "Strange Days Indeed," anonymous and undated circuit story.
9. "Endgame," anonymous and undated circuit story.
10. Adams, taped interview, New York, September 1985.
11. Those exceptions have all been in *Blake's 7* fiction, and the point-of-view character was always series regular Servalan, for reasons that will be discussed later in this section.
12. "The Haunting of Haderon," *Liberation #5* (fanzine; London, undated). The author's name is withheld because she could not be reached for permission to release her identity.
13. Karen Horney, *Feminine Psychology*, ed. Harold Kelman, M.D. (New York: W. W. Norton, 1967).
14. In "Romance, Eroticism, and/or Hurt-Comfort: What's Really Going On Here?" (paper delivered at the National Women's Studies Conference, Urbana, Ill., 1986), Patricia Frazer Lamb points out that British and Australian K/S exhibits more strictly sadomasochistic characteristics than the American forms. That is, the injury is inflicted within the relationship by the dominant partner who may be either Kirk or Spock, and the submissive partner learns to accept the domination and love his captor. I have not seen this in the fiction from America or using source products other than *Star Trek*. However, I have noticed a number of stories about domestic violence from abroad that seem to move toward reconstructing the violent partner rather than depicting the acceptance of the victim. Since a number of fans complained that they felt compelled to leave K/S fandom because of the nature of the violence in the stories, I suspect that this manifestation is for the most part limited to a small group specifically interested in using *Star Trek* to explore sadomasochistic fantasies.
15. René Girard, *Violence and the Sacred*, trans. Patrick Gregory (Baltimore: Johns Hopkins University Press, 1977).
16. Victor Turner's brilliant article "Religious Paradigms and Political Action: Thomas Becket at the Council of Northhampton," in his *Dramas, Fields, and Metaphors: Symbolic Action in Human Society* (Ithaca, N.Y.: Cornell University Press, 1974), demonstrates how the Church's teaching both romanticized martyrdom and set it as the model for Becket's ultimate and self-willed destruction.
17. Given a Judeo-Christian interpretation of Western masculine culture, the Oedipus complex can be read quite differently, and in a way that places the diminished value of women in society in high relief. The boy must fight his father not for the love of the mother, but for self-preservation, the mother becoming a secondary prize in the contest of mutual murderous intent.
18. It is interesting to note that the recent spate of movies and television series about the war in Viet Nam began at a time when a generation born too late to be affected by the televised war is coming of soldiering age. That this trend has arisen in a time of conservative government and a breakdown of internal social systems should not surprise us, nor should the fact that the reconstruction of the earlier war was necessary before that new generation could be motivated for the recent Persian Gulf War. By controlling the images of the Persian Gulf campaign released to the American people through the news cameras, and even the code-naming of the action, the government like-

wise controlled the image of the war and separated it causally from the images of devastation in Kuwait and in Iraq released after the close of the official campaign.

19. Girard, *Violence and the Sacred*, pp. 40–44. I agree with Girard that the returning hero sets his society in an ambiguous state because of his ritual impurity, but prefer a different interpretation of the source of that impurity.

20. "Endgame," anonymous and undated circuit story.

21. Ibid.

22. Personal correspondence, Syn Ferguson to author, October 1987.

23. Ibid.

24. Elaine Scarry, *The Body in Pain* (New York: Oxford University Press, 1985).

25. Ibid., p. 27.

26. This one psychiatrist's response is hardly unique. Karen Horney's work, which offers cultural factors dealing with the oppression of women as the underlying cause of many psychological ills of women, was rejected by the psychoanalytic community (Carolyn Heilbrun, *Reinventing Womanhood* [New York: W. W. Norton, 1979]).

27. While teaching Joe Haldeman's book *The Forever War* (New York: Berkeley Books, 1974) in my science fiction class, I asked my students why the protagonist in the book accepted women's homosexuality more easily than the same practice among men. While the women in the class suggested that men are more accustomed to seeing women being demonstrative to each other, the men in the class agreed that they felt personally threatened by the possibility of homosexual attack from men and presumed the protagonist would likewise feel threatened. They assumed the women would feel the same way and were quite surprised when none of the women in the class expressed any fear of lesbian assault, and in fact found the very idea bizarre.

28. Scarry, *The Body in Pain*, p. 214.

29. Ibid., p. 285.

Chapter Eleven
Looking Backward: Play, Creativity, and Narrative

In the past, scholars have approached the media fanzine community much as the three blind men tried to describe the elephant. By focusing on one particular facet of the literature, and not on the context of its production or the wide variety of options open to writers and artists in the community, scholars such as Joanna Russ[1] have inadvertently projected a distorted picture of the group as a whole. Russ describes the community from a radical political perspective held by only a small minority of the participants. Her implication of lesbian dominance in the community does an injustice to both the majority of heterosexual women and the lesbian minority who make up the group, both of whom enjoy and depend on their female friends for companionship and support regardless of their sexual orientation. Russ' emphasis on the explicitly pornographic nature of the homoerotic fiction belies the fact that only 25 percent of the material written is predicated upon any kind of homoerotic relationship. While much of the total corpus does revolve around intensely romanticized friendships, a much smaller percentage includes explicitly graphic depictions of either heterosexual or homosexual activity brought to orgasm.

More recently, communication scholars such as Henry Jenkins III have used the group to further their political agenda as well.[2] In Jenkins' portrayal of oppressed women struggling to create their own entertainment, the graphically sexual is passed over for the description of strong female characters created by the women. The corpus of homoerotic fiction is dismissed as being large in volume but disliked and ignored in the community, again a minority opinion in a group that has produced surprisingly few strong female characters in its twenty-five years of existence. Neither Russ nor Jenkins is wrong, exactly. They have simply described the trunk and tail at opposite ends of a very large elephant.

I began my study with an agenda no more praiseworthy than that of my colleagues: curiosity. During a survey study of the science fiction community, I heard many of my male informants speak with scorn about the "trekkies," and I discovered that many of my female informants had entered the fan community through their involvement with *Star Trek*. I wanted to know why a group of women so obviously intelligent and so involved in commercially published science fiction would spend so much of their time pursuing an art form that earned them venomous disdain on the one hand and no hope of financial reward on the other. But neither Russ nor Jenkins had written their articles yet, and my own political position—a firmly held "undecided"—gave me no direction but to follow the group in search of the answers they found for themselves. In my zeal, I went looking for Truth as the community I studied lived it.

Conservation of Risk and the Ethnographer

When I began my study, I had not yet become aware of the risk participants experience when they engage in community activities, nor did I understand how my own efforts to understand compounded that risk. Exposure is the ethnographer's prize and the community's fear: when my investigations took me too close to sensitive topics, the community sidetracked me with something of value, something that conserved the risk I as ethnographer sensed was present but that did not expose *too* much, that did not reveal the heart of the community.

The symbolizing heart of the community, by its very nature, remains both dangerous and out of sight even to most of the participants, who incorporate its forms and structures integrally throughout their work. Community members do recognize the nature of the perceived risks attendant upon their work, however. They surround the fiction with appropriate layers of defensive language and protective secrecy from the outsider.

The search for meaning in fandom took eight years and moved me deeper into other people's fears and pain and conflict than I ever wanted to go. I remember sitting in an Omni Hotel room with a fellow ethnographer after a particularly wrenching interview, my hands over my ears and my eyes closed, repeating over and over again: "I don't want to know this, I don't want to know this." The deeper I went into my study, the more often I found myself experiencing this response. The most difficult part of ethnography is not necessarily finding the information that the ethnographer needs, but keeping her eyes and ears open when that information challenges her sense of how the world works.

This Truth[3] as I found it, then, and if such a term can be applied to any human being's perceptions of the actions and motives of others, lay not at any mean between the two extremes of Russ and Jenkins, but in the limitless variety of positions available to any participant in the community. While issues of support and comfort and creative expression draw the women together, each brings to the community her own individual preferences, tastes, and politics. Precious few generalizations apply in a community founded on Gene Roddenberry's concept of IDIC: infinite diversity in infinite combinations. In spite of which, however, I will try to isolate a few mechanisms that seem to underlie fanzine culture as a whole.

The Marketplace of Culture

Everywhere I looked in the women's community created around fan fiction I found apparent simplicity on the surface that upon closer examination unfolded level after level of complex interaction. At first, media conventions seemed like a supermarket of goods and experiences purchased by an entry fee. That observation gave way to an understanding of the convention as a place where various groups of men and women from all over the United States and abroad take part in gender- and/or interest-segregated communal activities. Moreover, conventions are only the surface of a social order that for some revolves around club activities but for many women and a few men is built around the creation of art and literature based on media characters and settings.

Like middle-class women in the nineteenth century,[4] the fan women travel extensively to visit with one another in small groups. They maintain long-term, intense friendships. They create together in a community of women, a concept that, far from being new, has been debated for centuries. The reader of this book should find the following a familiar description:

> Let us imagine a little community of young women, among whom, to do an act of disinterested kindness should be an object of the highest ambition . . . and where those who were known to exercise the greatest charity and forbearance should be looked upon as the most exalted individuals in the community . . . women do know what their sex is formed to suffer, and for this very reason, there is sometimes a bond existing between sisters . . . chiefly out of their mutual knowledge of each other's capacity of receiving pain.[5]

In *Communities of Women,* from which this Sarah Stickney Ellis quote is drawn, Nina Auerbach describes the nature of women's communities as debated in literature—a debate that continues in the fan community. Some women, like Trek novelist Diane Duane, who define themselves as part of the commercial establishment only peripherally connected to the wider community, believe that each must determine her own destiny as an individual.[6] Others, like Lois Welling, find that the tightly knit community of women enriches their lives and strengthens their work in conjunction with marriage and family. Yet others find in the community of enterprising women their only source of social relationship and communal support.

The women of fandom share more than their own interior debate with the literary communities of women. Auerbach points out that such communities have been an object of curiosity and revulsion to men since Herodotus described the Amazons as self-mutilated warriors, physically incomplete as their society was sexually incomplete. The reaction of Western masculine culture to the serious enterprise of creating women's culture is no more accepting today than it was in antiquity or the nineteenth century. Lois Welling has won the support of her husband, but her writing teacher at the local university refused to consider seriously her media-based work in class.[7]

Almost without exception the women fans have complained that their interests are trivialized at the least, and are often criticized by family and workmates.[8] In spite of ridicule and paternalistic disregard, however, the women in media fanzining continue, in this, the twenty-fifth year since *Spockanalia* first appeared, to create a vital community behind a mask of play which is not always of their own choosing. Fanwriting is, after all, not a money-making enterprise. It's just a hobby.

But science fiction fandom has a set of terms known to the media fans as well: for each fan who declares fijagdh—fandom is just a God-damned hobby—another replies that fiawol—fandom is a way of life. The co-existence of the two terms is, of course, one of the esoteric paradoxes in which fans delight. If one knows the term fijagdh, fiawol is more likely the case. A fan won't know the words unless she is a part of the community, by which time fandom indeed has become a way of life.

Play

The existence of the two terms in the context of a recreational community highlight a thorny issue: Is it play? By the definitions of Western masculine culture,[9] which alternately seeks to elevate the category of play to include the sacred and the significant and at the same time to trivialize those same processes under the rubric of play, the answer would seem to be yes. Calvin and the other good puritans who guide not only our work ethic but our scholarly hand in the construction of theories of play would have it that a hobby is play. Central to this issue seems to be the functional value of the activity in the material sphere. Does the participant act for material gain? For profit?[10] In Western culture this translates to money, and the members of this community create and disseminate their arts under specific prohibitions against making a profit.

A covariant in the work-versus-play binary axis is the pleasure principle. That which is pleasurable, in particular that which creates what Czikszentmihalyi[11] calls a state of flow, is play. Work is by definition not pleasurable, and those who find pleasure in activities that others define as work are met with ambivalence and suspicion by their more properly striving fellows. In Czikszentmihalyi's early analyses, he looks at surgeons who attain the state of flow, but he cannot comfortably decide whether the surgeons may be said to be playing at those times, or whether the state he defines is no more relevant to play than to any other activity. In some cases enthusiastic researchers have suggested that religious ritual is likewise play, being both intrinsic—creating no discernible profit—and producing in participants the pleasurable state Czikszentmihalyi identifies as flow.[12]

More traditional modern Western art worlds, steeped in the ideal of flow, have teetered on the brink of respectable work, rescued from triviality by the network of profit-making support industries that surround them and by financial valuation on the artistic product.[13] Like religious ritual, fan activities produce no intentional profit and frequently generate a pleasurable state identifiable as flow in participants. However, neither of the latter activities can be viewed as intrinsic on any but the most material terms, nor, given the poverty of most struggling artists, can the creation of art within the institutions of the avant-garde or other schools be seen as existing for the profit-making peripheral structures of gallery and patron.

If we move away from the materialist and physiological, however, more pertinent and perhaps more generalizable distinctions begin to emerge. Games, Brian Sutton-Smith[14] and others have told us, refract the cultures in which they arise. Pleasure results from learning and functioning competently within the overt rules of the game and the covert rules of social relationship taking place in the game, and in developing the physical or mental skills necessary to demonstrate that competence. At the same time, the player exercises, and often learns through manipulation of the symbolic structures of the game, the rules of his culture. He develops competence not only in the game but in his relationship to the social institutions the game symbolically represents. Games can teach players the existing institutions, they can reify those institutions, they can even give the player practice in resisting those institutions. Play cannot, however, change those institutions.

Nowhere is this more graphically demonstrated than in Clifford Geertz' model of deep play, as he describes it in his article "Deep Play: Notes on the Balinese Cockfight."[15] According to Geertz, deep play raises the level of risk in the game, but not to the extent that it has a concrete effect on the actual social status of the players. In deep play participants flirt with the possibility of status change; players must perceive the risk as real on the symbolic level of value prescribed in the society—in the case of the Balinese of Geertz' example, wagers and betting alliances. Deep play often represents those stresses and tensions inherent in the social institutions that cannot be expressed more directly without risking real damage to the social structure. It may vent the frustrations of members of the group, thus allowing the structures to continue without change. The most important point here is that deep play may lessen rather than increase the potential for change in a culture, but cannot stop change from occurring outside the game. Change came violently to Bali in 1965 in spite of, not because of, the cockfight.

Imaginative play, carried on with companions or as solitary play, represents greater freedom and less structure than that which defines either less fraught game activity or the high-risk deep play. However, even imaginative play reflects the rules and structures of the fantasist's culture. The content of imaginative play draws on a repertoire of images available in the culture which also restricts and defines how the player will manifest the imaginative play in the real world. As a common example, many children fantasize in church or school but find their actions severely curtailed if they act out the fantasy. These children are likely to imagine scenes that mix everyday behavior with the airplane or monster they've created out of existing culture models in their heads.

Nor, as John Caughey has pointed out,[16] is imaginative play truly solitary. Rather, the mind of the fantasist is populated by a host of characters from real life, television, and other media, with which characters the imaginative player interacts according to the rules of her culture or in deliberate inversion of those rules. Some practitioners of imaginary play even share their fantasies in structured role-playing games such as Dungeons and Dragons.[17]

During play, the cultural symbols continue to manifest their affective presence, and may create a short-term change in the ambient affect generated among the participants. Through the affecting presence of the culture symbols in play participants may carry away a stronger sense of their culture, a lessening of tensions about social structures that constrict or limit action in the world, or even a sense that the players have defied those limits. The end result, however, is what many critics see in the fan community: a turning away from active resistance, tacitly accepting the oppression they fight only in imagination.

Play, Imaginative Play, and "Real Life"

But what about imaginative play, "make believe"? What about playfulness? In fact, the boundaries that define imaginative play are the most permeable, in that the fantasist, operating essentially out of sight of the guardians of social institutions, can most freely cross the line out of play without being noticed and ushered back into the realm of symbol without power to create change. Imaginative play represents the highest risk to any society, because the society's power to control only extends to what it knows. Imaginative play, combined with a talent for recombining cultural possibilities in unlikely constructions and a high tolerance for risk, can move the "solitary" player from play into the effectively playful, which we label creativity. Out of the secret lives of the playfully imaginative, the creative members of Western culture, have come such diverse culture-changing developments as the Salk vaccine, relativity physics, and the personal computer.

Truly creative people are the most courageous members of society because they must recognize, first, that their actions may have profound effect on some cultural institutions and, second, that, on the contrary, those ideas may make no impact at all. Then the creative person must set aside knowledge of that double-edged risk and "play" with the culture symbols as if they had affective presence only. By moving into a play mode, creative people can test a variety of possibilities. When they move out of play they take with them only the most viable of their test models with which to transform the reality of their culture. Playfulness, which may be defined as action based upon the perception of fluid boundaries between imaginative play, the nonreal, and "real life," may in fact be the most serious, and certainly the most dangerous, activity arising within a culture. Its joyfulness can exist only in people who recognize that "la grande bouffe"[18] really means laughing in the face of painful truth, in full knowledge that laughter can change the very nature of truth itself.

The Mask of Play and the History of Women's Media Fandom

But what does this have to do with the women of media fandom? As we have seen in Chapter 2, women at the core of their fan community have created their own social institutions, they share in some of the institutions created by other "hobby" groups such as science fiction fandoms, and they actively shape their lives around the structures they create. Women regularly travel thousands of miles to participate in the conventions where they strengthen community ties through face-to-face interaction with their counterparts from all over the world. Members re-create the institutions in their homes and move long distances to participate more actively within a particular circle. They share in the creation of their work through the process of "talking story." When I asked fanwriters for permission to quote their work in this book, they often responded that I should also recognize a friend who created a character or developed the idea from which a final work was drawn. Communal culture exists in every aspect of fan activity, in units as small as the sentence or as large as the corpus that defines the group.

Many fans in the fanzine community report feelings akin to those of ethnic immigrants when they interact with the mainstream culture of job or town. They feel like outsiders whose true identities reside elsewhere. While some community members participate on a more peripheral basis, staying in the play mode when they do so, core members practice creative playfulness in the construction of alternative social institutions and ways of relating to each other in what they term "real life."

This does not mean that the fan women never play. In parodies and sketches, and in the highly prized witty conversation,[19] women's play carries out the program of play we have already examined: the women's play teaches the rules of the art and the culture of the media fan community. In play the women joyously demonstrate their competence to manipulate those forms while they reify and critically comment on both the institutions they create and the material with which they create them.

Creating a Culture

If we accept the possibility that a group of women who write, illustrate, edit, and publish a fanzine, consuming all of their discretionary income and a great deal that others would not consider discretionary in the process, are not participating in a game but are inventing a culture, we must next ask the question "Why?" Why create a culture using a method that outsiders perceive as play, by definition "not serious"?[20] The answer is twofold:

1. The history of oppression experienced by the generation of women who constitute the fan community would direct them to mask their culture-building activities in the guise of trivial pastimes, and
2. The narrative properties of imaginative play and creative playfulness lend themselves to the work of constructing new culture models, or reconstructing models that have been lost.

The first of these responses addresses why, if the women in this group are masking their serious activity, do they feel the need to hide? As an oppressed group women often have been perceived as mysterious and dangerous. The masculine culture minimizes this discomfort it creates for its members by devaluing the women it oppresses: "If women are incomplete men, unfinished, not fully grown, they are like children. Developmentally they *are* children." Children—so white, masculine middle-class culture tells its members—are weak, helpless, and under the control of men, therefore safe. Historically, women who refused to be so categorized found themselves alone, abandoned by a culture that refused to see them as mature, capable, or equal.

Organized feminism, which presented itself as "to be taken seriously," set itself the program of storming the male bastions and demanding admittance. The feminists met with opposition both from men and from many women who disagreed with the stated program of the organized groups. Many women inside the feminist groups found this program unsatisfying and open resistance to a dominant masculine culture exhausting. These women were looking for community ties in a fragmented world, and they needed a safe harbor against the day-to-day battle to survive. Women's activities that the masculine culture could view as trivial and women could see as nonthreatening might flourish unnoticed, or meet with smug tolerance should they come to wider public attention. If they were beneath notice, they were safe.

Adult play meets this criterion, since it is implicitly nonserious behavior, a "trivial" exercise for passing the useless time between working and sleeping. Fans use this cultural bias to mask their culture-building activities behind the appearance of play. The imaginative play they do engage passes unseen into the creatively playful, masked by the symbols recognized as play in masculine culture but bearing a different set of meanings in the hidden fan culture. To put it more simply, the women media fans use television characters as the basis of the activity for two purposes:

1. the familiar characters connect their activities to the entertainment sphere, the not-serious, in the masculine culture, and
2. the television products provide members with a ready-made symbolic discourse shared by initiates and outsiders alike—a pidgin, metaphorically speaking—with which they can begin to narrate their lives.

Imaginative Play and the Playful Construction of Narratives

Earlier in this chapter I enumerated two reasons why fan women have created their culture in the sphere of the playful. As we have seen, the mask of play protects the group from detection as a serious alternative to masculine culture. Perhaps more important to the positive action of the group, however, is the fundamental connection between imaginative play and narrative.

In his article "In Search of the Imagination," Brian Sutton-Smith points out that

> . . . The discovery that children remember their scripts better than their categories in recent developmental psychology research (Bretherton, 1984) has turned more attention to the fact that the mind works better as a narrator than as a categorizer. As a result, we are suddenly at liberty to realize that the imagination as narrative is contributing to the linguistic mode of intelligence such as much as the imagination as logic is contributing to the logical mode of intelligence.[21]

To this description of the narrating imagination I would suggest the possibility that all imaginative play, spatial-graphic or verbal, requires at least an underlying assumption of narrative, a "what if" carried out to its structural completion. The child who roars like a jet engine and dashes across the room with his arms extended at both sides does not merely imagine himself to be a jet airplane. He is an airplane going somewhere for some purpose, all of which may be actualized as visual images, as verbal story, or remain implicit. For the fantasy to have meaning, however, it must be grounded in a context which can be defined as narrative.

When the fantasist moves out of play and into creative playfulness, she still operates in a realm of narrative, but with the clear awareness that in this state the construction of narrative may redefine the perception of reality for herself and for those who hear her words or see her pictures. The mathematician like the novelist must create in the context of narrative: what if energy and matter were not different things but different states, and the speed of light were the factor that distinguishes them? Theoretical physicists have been plotting the mathematical "what happens next" for almost a century.

Through narrative,[22] language gives us the fundamental power to create reality:

1. Narrative affords structure for communicating and sharing experience with others in the culture.
2. The levels of structure in narrative organize experience in an aesthetically satisfying way.
3. Over time, the organization of experience in structures that can be communicated and shared develops into a worldview.

Narrative and the Containment of Culture

The inverse of the above, however, is also true: to create the worldview, a community needs narrative structures that can communicate the experience that community members actually have. This book demonstrates that the alternative structure for organizing experience does exist, and is recognized and shared by many women, but it has no place in the worldview created out of the narrative experience of masculine culture. Its falsehood lies in its incomprehensibility to members of that culture. Authorities[23] and cultural gatekeepers regularly dismiss narratives created by and for a women's sensibility as unstructured and therefore false not only in a personal sense but in a cultural sense.

Joanna Russ has ably summarized women's struggle to gain access to narrative in any form in the public sphere.[24] As I have described before,[25] however, women who try to broaden the infringement upon accepted narrative forms into the public sphere meet with even greater opposition. Their narrative reality is dismissed as unformed, unstructured, and unworthy of a public audience. Only when a woman has sufficiently mastered the narrative structures of masculine culture may she win the right to compete for a place in the public arena. Since a woman cannot reach a wide audience unless her message conforms to the expectations of masculine culture, she has no opportunity to offer women alternative narrative realities that might be more satisfying to them. Deprived of alternatives for expressing her experience, she is left in the position of the insane: her reality can find no common ground in the culture of power.

Narrative and Imagination

The description of narrative given above would seem to militate against change in the culture. In this context, we must ask how the process of imagination works on the narrative givens to create alternative narrative possibilities in which change may occur. The very complexity of narrative seems to provide a clue. In the rational world-view, the content of the narrative is closely linked to the structure. Airplanes are made of steel, and girls are sugar and spice. How they are defined as content organizes their behavior in the structure of cultural expectation. In the nonrational worldview, content is not so tightly linked to the structure of cultural expectation, or more precisely, content may move among several mediating structures. A man has the same fortune in life as his father, or he suffers the harassment of demons or the wrath of God, or he may even experience a miracle.

In imaginative play, content and structure come unstuck. Content held to content in the structure of the narrative has the potential to become separated and recombined in "unreal" combinations. Little boys can be airplanes, and little girls can be captains of spaceships. Content, which operates on the surface of narrative, is more available for renegotiation in imaginative play than the more deeply hidden structure of the narratives of cultural expectation. Like content, however, the pieces of structural reality can be fragmented and recombined, alternative structures may be recaptured and put to new uses. Most importantly, the implications of suppressed models can be explored and their application broadened in the imaginative realm. The media fan community engages in this process when it first fragments and then recombines the pieces of its favorite action series (as described in Chapter 7) and later, when it creates its own stories out of the fragments.

Narrative, the Mask of Play, and the Construction of Culture

In the foregoing sections of this chapter I have described a way of thinking about play and a way of thinking about narrative. On the one hand, masculine culture sets play in the leisure world and values it as trivial. On the other hand, narrative is seen as powerful, dangerous, and accordingly, is closely guarded by masculine culture. Women have access to play, and in fact many of women's serious creative endeavors are classed as play by masculine culture. Commercial and academic institutions alike deny women the right to an alternative cultural experience of narrative. Gatekeepers in commercial publishing filter out narratives structurally organized to be aesthetically satisfying to women, and gatekeepers in academia collude to deny in women's narratives the very existence of structure or of truth.

Women in the media fanzine community use this outsider perception of their activities as a mask of play. They explore narrative, but with the characters and scenarios of television, valued as more trivial even than play. Hidden from sight by their own secrecy and masked by the trivial appearance their activities wear to outsiders, community members move in and out of play freely, testing models of narrative and models of social interaction and incorporating them into the structure of a worldview. The group can be playful because of the way it sees itself, where it places the lack in masculine culture, and thereby where it places the risk in its own exploration. The risk is real; many fanwriters and artists share a sense of danger from exposure even when the specific content of their own work seems less than threatening. More importantly, however, the perceived lack is so great that any risk is worth taking to fill it, the need so obvious that it hardly seems innovative to try to meet it.

The women in fandom need to find ways of organizing the information about their experience structurally, according to a grammar that is aesthetically satisfying. They want narratives that express cultural experience in forms that resonate with structures of cultural institutions within which that experience may comfortably be shared. As they experiment with narrative forms, they likewise experiment with ways of relating to one another. The search for expression feeds the struggle for social organization and vice versa, but always both are founded *not* upon an ideal of how things might be if they were different, but upon how women feel right now, and how they can sanely hold on to what they are. They resist all dictates to change themselves to fit either a masculine or feminist ideal, insisting that structures should build upon the way people are, and not the reverse. They create narratives to meet current needs of communication and sharing, of community, and not to anticipate a politically correct feeling one might wish to have.

When a fan writes a story that touches the way women feel or relate in the group, she knows it because she feels it. Her readers feel it, and both readers and writer joyfully affirm for each other the knowledge that a way of thinking, of feeling, is shared. When fans engage in the play-forms of parody and puns and witty conversation about their own material, they strengthen the sense of shared community, shared

Farewell. A self-portrait of artist-fiction-and-song-writer-singer-editor Sheila
Willis. Many active members of fandom participate in more than one form of
expression, though few are as multi-faceted as Sheila.

structures. The incomprehensibility to outsiders of many of the serious forms created in the community points to more than the simple divergence in content one might expect about, for example, a book one has not read. Rather, the structures and language that fans use arise out of a distinct cultural model, a worldview separate from that of masculine culture.

The significance of this model for theorists of women and film cannot be overestimated. Laura Mulvey condemned the pleasurable experience of film narrative with the statement, "Sadism demands a story."[26] The importance of the statement, however, is not in its connection of narrative pleasure to sadism, since all patterns of behavior likewise demand a story. Rather, Mulvey goes on to describe the narrative sadism demands: "Sadism demands a story, depends on making something happen, forcing a change in another person, a battle of will and strength, victory/defeat, all occurring in a linear time with a beginning and an end."[27]

In this quotation, Mulvey describes binary oppositions such as victory/defeat, and implies the binary opposition of winner and loser in a battle of will and strength. The narrative structure she describes—linear time, with a beginning and an end—is consistent with the structure of the masculine worldview in Western culture. Her solution, to create alternative films that deny narrative pleasure to the viewer, is ultimately counterproductive. Women need more narrative forms, not less of them. They need choice in the narrative of life with which they will identify. By denying narrative pleasure, theorists would impoverish women of the narrative choices they need to reconstruct their own reality.

Notes

1. Joanna Russ, *Magic Mammas, Trembling Sisters, Puritans and Perverts* (New York: Crossing Press, 1985).

2. Henry Jenkins III, "*Star Trek* Rerun, Reread, Rewritten: Fan Writing as Textual Poaching," *Critical Studies in Mass Communication* 5, no. 2 (1988): 85–107.

3. For a discussion of "Truth" in ethnographic and documentary studies, see Bruce Jackson, "What People Like Us Are Saying When We Say We're Saying the Truth," *Journal of American Folklore* 101, no. 399 (1988): 276–92.

4. Carroll Smith-Rosenberg, "The Female World of Love and Ritual: Relations between Women in Nineteenth Century America," *Signs* 1 (Autumn 1975): 1–29.

5. Sarah Stickney Ellis, 1843, as quoted in Nina Auerbach's *Communities of Women: An Idea in Fiction* (Cambridge: Harvard University Press, 1978), p. 17.

6. Diane Duane, taped interview, Philadelphia, 1984.

7. Lois Welling, untaped conversation, 1987.

8. Taped group interview, New York, September 1985.

9. See Brian Sutton-Smith, "The Metaphor of Games in Social Science Research, in *Play, Play Therapy, Play Research,* papers presented at an international symposium, Amsterdam, 1985 (Berwyn: Swets North American, 1986).

10. John Huizinga, *Homo Ludens* (New York: Beacon Press, 1959). This is one aspect of Huizinga's definition of play that seems to linger implicitly in more modern debates about intrinsic (play) and extrinsic (work) activities. (See Barbara Kirshenblatt-Gimblett, "Speech Play and Verbal Art," in *Play and Learning,* ed. Brian Sutton-Smith (New York: Gardner Press, 1979), pp. 219–37.

11. Mihalyi Czikszentmihalyi, *Beyond Boredom and Anxiety* (San Francisco, Jossey-Bass, 1975). Czikszentmihalyi's work follows that of Raymond Williams' use of the term *flow* by eighteen years. Although he seems to be unaware of Williams' work on the flow of television through an evening of viewing, the state he describes is in some ways similar to that which Williams asserts is created in the viewer. Specifically, time seems to pass unheeded by the viewer experiencing the flow of television and, to use one of Czikszentmihalyi's examples, the chess player in flow during a game of chess. Likewise, the perception of the experience seems heightened at the time of the experience, but the memory is no more detailed than for experience not in the flow. It is not surprising that both models should compare quite closely, because they both use the metaphor of the flow of fluids in a channel. The properties of the metaphor lead the use of the term in certain directions, rather than the direct knowledge of the other's use of the term.

12. Steven Fox, "Theoretical Implications for the Study of Interrelationships Between Ritual and Play," in *Play and Culture,* ed. H. Schwartzman (New York: Leisure Press, 1980).

13. Howard S. Becker, *Art Worlds* (Berkeley: University of California Press, 1982).

14. See Brian Sutton-Smith, ed., *Play and Learning* (New York: Gardner Press, 1979); Sutton-Smith, "Games of Order and Disorder" (paper presented to symposium on "Forms of Symbolic Inversion," at the American Anthropological Association, Toronto, 1972); and idem, "Cross Cultural and Psychological Study of Games," in *The Folkgames of Children* (Austin, Tex.: American Folklore Society Special Series no. 24, 1972), among other sources.

15. Clifford Geertz, "Deep Play: Notes on the Balinese Cockfight," in *The Interpretation of Cultures* (New York: Basic Books, 1973).

16. John Caughey, *Imaginary Social Worlds: A Cultural Approach* (Lincoln: University of Nebraska Press, 1984).

17. Gary Alan Fine, *Shared Fantasy: Role Playing Games as Social Worlds* (Chicago: University of Chicago Press, 1984).

18. Mikhail Bakhtin, in *Rabelais and His World* (Bloomington: Indiana University Press, 1968), describes the marketplace in pre-Renaissance France as inversion, where the cultural institutions are laughed at. Implicit in the festival definition of the great, primordial laughter of medieval man is that the status quo remains after the festival is over. In the ongoing festival atmosphere of the marketplace, however, cultural transformation can in fact occur. Modern scholars have given a materialist reading to the meaning of the marketplace, but such a reading is only viable in the materialist context. In fact, equally transformative employment of the playful occurs in ritual contexts and, as we see here, in contexts where profit is not perceived in material

terms at all. As applied to imaginative play, however, *la grande bouffe*, laughing at the devil, so to speak, can exist as a concept in the mind of the creator, or it can be shared subversively outside the traditional avenues of public communication.

19. See Chapter 6 for a detailed description of play in the group.

20. Brian Sutton-Smith and Diana Kelly-Byrne address this very issue in the book they edit, *The Masks of Play* (New York: Leisure Press, 1984). In particular Sutton-Smith describes how activities I here define as not-play take place behind the mask of play, and likewise, how play is often carried on disguised as not-play.

21. Brian Sutton-Smith, "In Search of the Imagination," in *Education and Imagination*, ed. D. Nadarer and K. Eagen (New York: T. C. Press, 1987). The full citation for the Bretherton work cited in the excerpt is I. Bretherton, *Symbolic Play* (New York: Academic Press, 1984).

22. See Appendix A for a more detailed discussion of language, worldview, and narrative.

23. An example will demonstrate the point. Several years ago a well-known male sociolinguist (for obvious reasons I feel it politic to protect the identity of this prestigious scholar; I will note, however, that the sociolinguist in question was *not* Dell Hymes) was discussing ghost-sighting reports. He was not concerned with the reality of the ghosts, but wanted a gauge for the belief of the narrator—did an experience occur, and did the narrator believe that it was a ghost? He used two examples. The first, told by a man, was a short, linear narrative. The second, told by a woman, was a long circumlocution filled with extraneous detail, digressions, and with references to other people and events during the period surrounding the experience. The sociolinguist declared that the man had in fact experienced some event which he believed to be a ghost encounter; his story was clear, concise, and neither anticipated disbelief nor courted the researcher's belief. The sociolinguist determined that the woman was lying, however, because her story kept to no structure. He said it was diffused, overly complicated, temporally scrambled, and assumed disbelief in its constant references to peripheral people and events as evidence. Of course, a number of women scholars in the audience recognized the woman's narrative for what it was—a personal experience narrative as they are told by women.

24. Joanna Russ, *How to Suppress Women's Writing* (Austin: University of Texas Press, 1983).

25. Camille Bacon-Smith, "Spock among the Women," *New York Times Book Review*, November 16, 1986.

26. Laura Mulvey, "Visual Pleasure and Narrative Cinema," *Screen* 16, no. 3 (1975): 14.

27. Ibid.

Appendix A. Methodology

Ethnography

Ethnography is a data-intensive method in which the researcher studies the culture of informants where they gather in their own native habitats—in this case the homes and convention hotels where fans establish face-to-face contact, and in the letters, phone calls, and fanzines in which those contacts are maintained over long distances for extended periods of time. The particular ethnographic method used in this paper relies heavily upon the work of Dell and Virginia Hymes, and on the work of Clifford Geertz. From ethnolinguist Dell Hymes[1] comes the deceptively simple dictate: If you want to know what something means in a culture, ask. But to understand the answer, you have to speak the language—the special symbolic dialect—of the community, the audience you wish to study. Critical theorists have their own dialect, as do folklorists. So, too, do *Star Trek* fans, Ralph[2] members, and the fans of Japanese animation.

The ethnographer develops a knowledge of the structure and meaning of the fan language with a number of techniques. First, she must listen carefully to the speech of members with each other and, in the beginning, the very different way people talk to her as a newcomer in need of instruction. The ethnographer can chart her progress into the community by the diminishing distance between these two forms of speech. When community members "forget" that the observer's purpose is to observe, and begin to treat her as a knowledgeable insider, she has learned enough of the basic interactive system to begin the next step. At this point, however, scholarly ethics require that the ethnographer find some way of reminding the community that information passed in front of her will appear before a wider, outside audience. In my case, I wore a tape recorder microphone by a strap over my shoulder, with the tape recorder itself in view at all times. Whenever feasible, I wore a slogan button with the motto "Intergalactic Ethnographer" on it to further identify myself to the science fiction oriented group.

When the ethnographer has established a working knowledge of the language, the next step is a close analysis not only of the informational content, but of the relationship of the spoken words to community actions, and how the one influences the other. As an example, Chapter 6 details how a word game is used to test participants at a fan gathering for membership in a particular social group. The ethnographer examines language—in games and stories, puns and poems—not purely as artistic expression but as social process and a medium of exchange with which community members pay their way in the culture.

To the language of the community the ethnographer must add a growing knowledge of the relationship between visual images coded for cultural information and their transformation into literary language. I am using the term "codes" in the linguistic sense, not of a language or dialect, but as a way of using language in a particular situation, a contextually appropriate discourse.[3] The ethnographer must learn how the codes in fan fiction combine descriptions of images taken from the screen and distinctive diction both to draw the community's art together and to distinguish particular genre categories from each other. Themes become codes in the fan fiction when conventionalized language or gestures attach to their presentation, and when that presentation acts as a recognition signal that the theme in question is being used in the community with certain meanings and to certain effects in a particular body of the work. As an example, telepathy is an important theme drawn from the source products that the community codes in a variety of ways as deep, often passionate empathy in a relationship. Telepathy does not have specific meaning in and of itself in the fan fiction, but the choice of the particular conventional language for describing the telepathy signals that the writer is entering a particular subdivision of the fan fiction discourse. The code, in essence, transforms the content according to the rules of the discourse, and the ethnographer cannot grasp the meaning of the literature until she has developed an understanding of the codes implicit in it.

The use of codes in the fan community reminds the researcher that language serves *two* purposes: to facilitate social interaction between community members and to obscure social secrets from outsiders. Sometimes obscurity is intrinsic to the inside-outsider nature of any communication system, but sometimes language and actions may deliberately lead the researcher away from the goal of understanding.

The only way to distinguish between the two uses of language is to gather as many examples as possible, from the widest variety of sources in both formal and informal settings, and compare them.

If half a dozen people who do not know each other give a similar answer to the same question, then that answer represents at the least a view the community holds of itself. Group discussion is usually more useful than individual interviews, until the researcher has established some relationships with knowledgeable insiders. It is much easier for an informant to direct the ethnographer away from sensitive information in the one-on-one question-and-answer format of the formal interview than it is in a large group discussion in which the ethnographer interferes with only the occasional question or comment.

Oblique questions and comments in a group setting, touching upon but not directing the line of inquiry on which the researcher wishes more information, produce results least biased by the observer's predisposed opinions. Community members often drop their guards in nondirected group settings, and may offer key information in the heat of the discussion. At the same time, less knowledgeable members may be corrected by more established participants in the group setting, giving the researcher both a check on information provided in good faith and a test of how misconceptions are dealt with inside the community.

Spoken language is the easiest form of communication for the novice in a community to decipher, but as ethnographers progress in their study the physical world speaks to them as well. How people relate physically in time and space to their environments and each other, how they read those relationships in others and represent them in art and literature all offer up their corroborative or contradictory evidence to the ethnographer.

The final step in the researcher's pursuit of knowledge is participation. Through mistakes they make, and community members' corrections and opinions of them, ethnographers test the extent to which they have actually understood what they have seen and heard. In the case of this study, after five years of research I offered a series of stories anonymously, two to a fanzine editor, three others to local circles and the circuit. One story was written with the advice of various circle members at each step and with participants giving their suggestions as to what should happen next.

From editorial comments and from the suggestions of community members on my contributions, I learned how poorly I had internalized the aesthetics of the group, but those comments gave me the specific information about my errors that I had lacked before. Meaning became transformed for me when I explored it in the language of the community as that language unfolded in the interplay between observed use and expressed gloss. At every turn, however, I had to concede the limitations a researcher's outsider position places on access to specialized knowledge.[4] The ethnographer is always dependent on the kindness of strangers.

The Theory: Language and Narrative

Ethnography is a method of looking, listening, and writing down as much of what the researcher experiences in the search for knowledge as possible. To make sense of the observations, however, the ethnographer must work within a theoretical framework, in this case, a linguistic-narrative theory of cultural development.

The Sapir-Whorf hypothesis tells us that the structure of its language underlies each culture's worldview; that the words and grammatical and metaphorical structures available to a native speaker define the postulable universe and the speaker's behavior in it.[5] That is not to say that culture becomes a "natural" imperative driven by its language. In fact, no one has adequately described how language as a system of abstract signs[6] that represent both concrete and abstract concepts arises. Language as defined here, conjoined with culture—the traits, symbols, and structures that express a group's social relationships with its members, its environment, and the ineffable—seems to be integral to the concept of humanity. The problem of consigning function to either language or culture arises with the realization that no group of humans exists without both factors. It seems most likely that language and culture exert a constant pressure on each other to contain reality.

Narrative takes us deeper into the matrix of culture and language and possibility. Narrative uses verbal language and visual images to bind memory of the experience of culture to expectations based on experience. The act of speaking the narrative orally, in print, or in visual images, in prose, poetry, or drama, shapes and extends the reality of the experience and enmeshes it in the social matrix. Fragments of narrative—stories alluded to but not retold, turns of phrase that depend upon shared knowledge of a history of thought, pencil sketches, and snapshots that depend for their interpretation upon a context that is story—define the limits of the social matrix and bind its members in a web of experience weathered together. In narrative, experience is contained and filtered through the prism of culture and language.

Dell Hymes calls narrative the Grammar of Experience.[7] According to Hymes, narrative organizes the information about experience structurally according to a grammar that is aesthetically satisfying. The narrative satisfies because it expresses cultural experience in a form that resonates with other structures throughout the cultural system. Over time, the organization of experience in structures that community members can communicate and share develops into a worldview. The cognitive hunger for order drives the narrator to take hold of the contextual world with language to produce both the world-view and the narratives that fit personal experience into communal knowledge as expressed in that worldview.

Like the question of language and culture, however, the exact relationship of narrative to worldview remains a mystery. As with language, there exists no culture without a way of explaining what happens to its members. Members of the culture fit their experience to the content and structure of similar experiences described in the stories of others. They are satisfied when their experience, which they understand in light of culturally possible experiences as defined in the worldview, reaffirms their place in the culture. They are like others, for their story is like others.

But what happens if the experience is not like that of others, or does not fit into the structures the culture allows for expressing experience? What if the words to describe the experience do not exist? Change becomes possible when narrative and worldview fail to integrate experience.[8] The fan community is a product of just such a moment in the lives of its members, who bring with them disillusionment about love and marriage, about careers and independence (and how it was supposed to be possible to have it all and do it all, but somehow it never worked out for them), or hope that they can create a better future.

Accordingly the group produces narratives vigorously and activates them in a wide variety of uses. I have observed community members use fictional narratives to discuss personal, real-life situations. At the same time, fans don't just fit their experience to their narratives; they also explore narrative alternatives to organize experience not available to them in the larger culture. My task, therefore, was twofold: (1) to explore how fan fiction acts as a language, and (2) to explore how fan fiction acts as narrative to organize experience.

Narrative Truth and Levels of Abstraction

In this study I have considered the narrative process as if all its products were perceived truths of the narrators and audience, or "true" reflections of cultural experience. According to this model, a narrative that is untrue is not fiction, it is incomprehensible, a "bad" story because it somehow fails to satisfy the sense of rightness of its social group. Narratives found acceptable in the group differ from each other not in the degree of truth they tell but in the level of abstraction from which they tell it and the symbolic forms they use in the telling. The level of abstraction and set of conventions from which a given narrative is told will depend on the perceived social appropriateness of any given form. The lamination of many levels of symbolic abstraction acts to distance the narrative from the social danger its more direct recounting represents in the perception of the community or the individual writer or reader.

Fiction differs from other forms of narrative in its level of abstraction, which is at a greater remove from experience than, for example, the personal experience narrative. That is, in fiction an author consciously creates narratives that are not literally true accountings of experience, but that represent some belief, understanding, or "truth" from which the author feels a need to build distance through additional layers of signification. Sometimes those layers of signification represent an attempt to hide the message from those for whom it was not intended, or dilute it for those to whom direct confrontation would prove too painful. Often, however, the author uses a high level of abstraction to represent something—a feeling, a situation, an opinion—for which no language exists in everyday discourse.

In a narrative system like the one the women's fanzine culture has produced—which includes concrete aspects of literary narrative in the material products of the community, such as graphic art and costume, as well as the fictional narratives themselves—the very process of creating and disseminating the literature functions with the richness of symbol making that we find in ritual. Victor Turner and others have demonstrated the symbolic nature of ritual processes both in tribal and in industrial societies,[9] and Turner looked at the ritual-like aspects of certain secular processes in postindustrial societies as well.[10] Ritual-like processes, among which narrative holds a place, both generate symbolic forms and act symbolically themselves. I use the term *symbol* advisedly to designate those signs and systems that generate the dynamic potential out of which culture can be shaped.

Notes

1. The two best known works of Dell Hymes are *"In Vain I Tried to Tell You"* (Philadelphia: University of Pennsylvania Press, 1981), and *Foundations in Sociolinguistics* (Philadelphia: University of Pennsylvania Press, 1974). Unfortunately, Hymes has not published much of his most seminal work. My own

understanding of his methods and theories comes from working with the Hymeses and their students over many years.

2. Fans of *The Honeymooners*.

3. Dell Hymes, "Social Anthropology, Sociolingusitics, and the Ethnography of Speaking," *Foundations in Sociolinguistics*, pp. 83–117.

4. This is the problem Clifford Geertz addressed in his seminal theoretical article, "Thick Description," in *The Interpretation of Cultures* (New York: Basic Books, 1973).

5. Edward Sapir, *Language: An Introduction to the Study of Speech* (New York: Harcourt, Brace and Jovanovich, 1921), B. L. Whorf, *Language, Thought, and Reality: Selected Writings of Benjamin Lee Whorf* (Cambridge, Mass.: MIT Press, 1954).

6. By *signs* I here diverge from early language theorists by including not only verbal utterances but also visual linguistic gestures as well.

7. Dell Hymes, "Narrative Form as a 'Grammar of Experience,'" *Journal of Education* 164, no. 2 (1982): 121–42, and idem, *Foundations in Sociolinguistics*.

8. This argument parallels that of Thomas Kuhn in *The Structure of Scientific Revolutions* (Chicago: University of Chicago Press, 1970 [1962]). Kuhn says that, when the weight of evidence against a scientific theory exceeds the capacity of the system to withstand a change that would discredit the given knowledge within it, a revolution occurs that is most often fought by those whose positions are threatened by the new knowledge. Kuhn predicts that no scientific revolution is complete until the last proponent of the old knowledge has died. The primary difference between the institution of science as a paradigm and the consideration of culture as a whole, of course, is that science is by the nature of its inquiry searching for change at the same time it resists change. Culture, on the other hand, is by the nature of its inquiry searching for stability, and so resists change more tenaciously than science does.

9. Almost anything by Victor Turner is relevant, but good examples are: *Revelation and Divination in Ndembu Ritual* and *The Ritual Process: Structure and Anti-Structure* (both from Cornell University Press), and *Image and Pilgrimage in Christian Culture* (Columbia University Press).

10. Victor Turner, "Liminal to Liminoid, in Play, Flow, and Ritual: An Essay in Comparative Symbology," *The Anthropological Study of Human Play*, Rice University Studies, vol. 60, no. 3 (1974), pp. 53–92. Interestingly, Turner's definitional characterizing of the differences between liminal and liminoid states would lead us to examine the women's media fiction community as a tribal culture rather than as an aspect of the larger postindustrial culture, and this in spite of the high dependence on technology by its members.

Appendix B. An Introduction to the Language of the Fan Community: Glossary

We have described here the building blocks of a literary culture: literature, which has a (social) structural relationship to the culture it is creating, which has content categorized in thematic genres by the group and a process of creating literature and art that acts symbolically in and upon the community. These are, however, processes and actions found at the core of the community. That's why ethnography takes so much time. This study has taken eight years both to establish my bona fides as a person worthy of trust[1] and to develop an understanding of the underlying drive mechanisms of the social structure of the group as it is internalized by its members, spread through the processes of narrative production, and recorded in the artistic production of the members.

But first, I had to learn the language, a combination of references to television series and movies past and present, words created in the community, and words borrowed from mainstream culture but given meanings so different inside the fanzine community that they cannot be understood without a glossary. To help the reader with this linguistic stumbling block, I offer the following glossary. It does not, of course, contain all the words created in the fan community, but it does give the reader enough to understand as much of the culture and literary life of the community as I could record on the following pages:

Glossary

Alien Nation: Short-lived Fox Network series set in 1995. A ship of half a million alien slaves has crash-landed in the Mojave Desert. As at Ellis Island, the officials have replaced the hard-to-pronounce alien names with American ones—Hero "George" San Francisco, Edgar

Allanpoe, Betsey Ross, and Dallas Fortworth. The team of heroes include Matt Sikes, an unmarried working-class policeman struggling with his own prejudices and sense of alienation, and his partner George Francisco, an uptight, suburban alien. Plots revolve around social issues like gender stereotyping and racial prejudice, and combine single-episode adventures with developing character situations.

Amanda: The human mother of the half-Vulcan Mr. Spock (see Spock; also Vulcan).

Andorian(s): Aliens indigenous to the *Star Trek* series and characterized by blue skin, straight, silver-white hair, and short, fleshy antennae.

Apa: Amateur press association. The acronym also stands for the publications collected from subscriber-contributors and distributed to the closed membership in the apa.

Auron: The name of a planet in the *Blake's 7* series, and home world to the Auronae, a race of telepathic senders who can receive messages only from other senders. Regular series character Cally is Auronae.

Avon, Kerr: Antihero of *Blake's 7,* the character is a semi-sinister white-collar criminal who begins as a hero against his will, and later becomes one against his better judgment. Best known for killing Blake, the leader for whom the series is named.

Beauty and the Beast: CBS series in which a beautiful young assistant district attorney, Catherine Chandler, is rescued, befriended, and loved romantically by the leonine beast, Vincent, who lives in an exotically costumed culture in the tunnels below New York City.

Blake, Roj: The leader and namesake of the series *Blake's 7,* he is a middle-aged, spacefaring rebel discredited on the basis of false accusations of child molestation. Escaping from his prison-bound spaceship to a derelict supership, he leads a small band of miscreants against the evil Federation.

Blake's 7: The BBC series in which Blake and his merry men travel through the galaxy striving ineffectively to overthrow the evil Federation.

Bodie, William: In the London Weekend Television series *The Professionals,* an agent in the apocryphal CI5, a police super-agency involved in matters of national security. Known for his checkered past, his love of junk food, and his refusal to use his first name.

C3PO: Protocol droid—robot—in the *Star Wars* movies. R2D2's best friend, and Luke Skywalker's companion.

Cally: Auronae rebel against the evil Federation who joins Blake's band in the fourth episode and dies at the start of the fourth season.

Castillo, Lieutenant Martin: The mysterious and mystical ex-D.E.A.

man who served as Crockett and Tubbs' superior officer in *Miami Vice*.

Chandler, Catherine: The Beauty half of *Beauty and the Beast*, an investigator for the New York District Attorney's office who develops a passionate relationship with her leonine rescuer after a devastating knife attack.

Chekov, Pavel: In *Star Trek*, the male ingenu and weapons officer. The Russian member of the multinational *Enterprise* crew.

Chewbacca: In *Star Wars*, a seven-foot-tall fur-covered alien who travels with hero Han Solo in the ship *Millennium Falcon*.

Conventions: Organized gatherings of fans held at regular intervals throughout the year. Media fans have a calendar of conventions, and also meet at the established science fiction conventions.

Crockett, Sonny: The down-and-out, cynical, but still idealistic vice cop who eschewed socks, rode around in a Ferrari Testarossa, and made the Armani jacket a household word.

Cross-universe: Fan stories in which the characters from one source product meet and interact with the characters from another. (See Universe.)

Crusher, Beverly: In *S.T.:T.N.G.* (*Star Trek: The Next Generation*), the chief medical officer of the *Enterprise* and mother of the precocious Wesley Crusher.

Crusher, Wesley: In *S.T.:T.N.G.*, the precocious teenaged ingenu. Wesley is an engineering genius and serves as helmsman with the rank of acting ensign.

Darkover: The planet created by Marion Zimmer Bradley on which the characters of her many books have adventures in a complex culture over many hundreds of years. Also the name of a convention specifically for fans of Ms. Bradley's books, and the generic referent for all the books in the series. Darkover is particularly popular among feminist fans for its Renunciates, a guild of women guides, midwives, and warriors who swear allegiance to the guild, take no permanent husbands, and return any male children of temporary liaisons to their father's families when the boys are five years old.

Data: In *S.T.:T.N.G.*, the android science officer and Sherlock Holmes buff who wishes he were human. The most popular character in the new *Star Trek* series, he seems to have developed some of the cachet of Mr. Spock from the original.

Datazine: A regularly issued catalogue of fanzines available for purchase or seeking contributions of art or writing.

Doctor, the: Title character of the BBC children's science fiction series *Doctor Who*. The Doctor is a Time Lord, a species with two hearts and the capability to travel both in space and time. Best known for his unpredictable disposition and the fact that he can regenerate a new and completely different body whenever the BBC needs to replace the lead actor.

Doctor Who: The longest-running science fiction series in the history of television, a BBC children's show with strong popularity among adults in the United States. The title character, a Time Lord from the planet Gallifrey, travels in time and space with trusty companions he picks up along the way, to defend the universe from such nasty villains as the robot Cybermen, the bioengineered Daleks, and "The Master." At this writing, the BBC has suspended production and is considering bids for private funding of the series.

Doyle, Raymond: In *The Professionals,* the agent partnered with William Bodie. His background is established as a local working-class policeman transferred to the "elite" CI5, and he is best known for his scruffy dress and his occasional disapproval of his partner's past.

DWFCA: Doctor Who Fan Club of America. At one time the BBC-licensed group controlled organized fan clubs all over the United States. Now valued primarily for its merchandise and newsletter, DWFCA no longer exerts any control over local clubs, which have expanded to include other source products like *Blake's 7.*

Enterprise: Starship class space cruiser, the home on their space exploratory mission of *Star Trek's* regular cast of characters and 410 other crewmen, of whom the viewer sees only the occasional representative. Most series fans espouse a loyalty to the ship equal to their loyalty to its crew.

Fandom(s): Term used by members of the related groups self-identified by their interest in written science fiction, in science fiction and action-adventure television and film, in comic books, Japanese animation, and costuming.

Fan language (Fannish): The special argot fans use among themselves. Many fan words are acronyms, distortions of standard English, or standard English words used with specific meanings in the fan community.

Fanwriter: A writer of amateur fiction, poetry, or commentary in the fan community.

Fanzine: An amateur, nonprofit publication focused on the dissemination of written information, fiction, poetry, or commentary about favorite book, television, movie, role-playing, or computer gaming products.

Fanziner: A publisher, editor, writer, or illustrator of fanzines. Only occasionally used for the purchasers and readers of fanzines as well.

Federation: In the *Star Trek* universe, the positivistic United Federation of Planets, a voluntary association of independently governed planets who unite for the purpose of trade and a shared police and military arm, Starfleet. In *Blake's 7*, the term represents the corrupt and repressively bureaucratic government of Earth and her far-flung colony planets against which Blake and his band rebel.

Fiawol: Fannish term for the phrase "fandom is a way of life."

Fijagdh: Fannish term for the phrase "fandom is just a God-damned hobby."

Filker: Someone who creates or performs filksongs.

Filksong: Fannish term for a science fiction folksong.

Force (the): Religious concept from the *Star Wars* movie series. Means the spiritual force of the universe. A believer who goes "with the force" may use that spiritual power to develop quasi-magical superhuman strength and skill, but the term also means a way of living, becoming one with the force of the universe, and flowing with it. A good luck wish is "May the force be with you."

Gen-zine: A fanzine that includes a variety of genres, all suitable for a general audience. Based on the movie rating system and the term fanzine. In particular, gen-zines do not include slash relationships even in nonsexual stories.

Hardcastle, Judge Milton: Independently wealthy retired judge who takes on the rehabilitation of a paroled convict sentenced in his court in the series *Hardcastle and McCormick*.

Hardcastle and McCormick: The ABC television series in which the above-referenced retired judge and his parolee try to solve the cases that got away from the courts when the judge served on the bench—while having many personal adventures involving friends, relatives, and vacations gone wrong along the way.

Holt, Laura: Female detective who named her agency after a typewriter manufacturer, then had to adapt when a British con man stepped in as the nonexistent Remington Steele.

Hurt-comfort: Stories in which one of the protagonists is injured—accidentally, or intentionally by villains—falls ill, or in its extreme form, is tortured, and a fellow protagonist from the source products or developed by the fanwriter tends and comforts the hurt party.

Hutchinson, Kenneth: The tall, blond, college-educated detective on the series *Starsky and Hutch*, a violent police action show of the seventies most notable for its male bonding.

IDIC: A Vulcan philosophical concept from Gene Roddenberry's *Star Trek*. The word itself is an acronym for "infinite diversity in infinite combinations." It means the delight in difference coming together in peaceful diversity, and is symbolized by the idic, a circle penetrated on the oblique by the apex of an elongated triangle. The idic can be found as jewelry, or as a painted or stitched design on many items of fan memorabilia.

Jedi: In the *Star Wars* movie series, a mystical knighthood of warriors who call upon the Force (see above) for their extraordinary powers.

K/S: Fiction, poetry, and art created by fans depicting Captain Kirk and Mr. Spock of *Star Trek* engaged in a sexual relationship. (See Slash.)

Kenobi, Obi Wan: In the first *Star Wars* movie, thought to be the last living Jedi. Luke Skywalker's mentor.

Kirk, Captain James T.: In *Star Trek*, the charismatic captain of the *Enterprise* known for his intuitive command style and his susceptibility to women.

Klingon(s): Aliens with swarthy faces and upturned eyebrows in the original *Star Trek* series, where they appeared as the dastardly villains, uncouth and violent. In the new *Star Trek* series, the Klingons have strange ridges on their foreheads, called turtles or crabs by fans. They are no longer the villains, although they are still violent and uncouth.

Kobayashi Maru: A command test from the *Star Trek* movie *The Wrath of Khan.* In a simulated exercise, the Kobayashi Maru was a freighter spaceship besieged by enemy warships in neutral territory. The test is designed as a "no-win situation": the command cadet cannot save the freighter and his/her ship, but is graded on response to an inevitable loss.

Kraith: The unofficial *Star Trek* universe created in amateur stories by Jacqueline Lichtenberg and later shared by other fanwriters. Also, and only in Lichtenberg's Kraith universe, a ritual cup used in Vulcan ceremonies stolen at the beginning of the series and recovered several stories later.

Kuryakin, Illya: A character from the 1960s spy spoof *The Man from U.N.C.L.E.* Kuryakin was a Russian cryptographer and spy working with an American partner, Napoleon Solo, for the apocryphal United Nations Corps for Law Enforcement.

La Forge, Geordi: In *S.T.:T.N.G.*, black chief engineering officer. Best known for the wide-spectrum visor he wears to compensate for his blindness, and for his love of model sailing ships.

Lay-Spock: A fan story in which an adult heroine meets and has a sexual relationship with a character from the source products. The name after the hyphen may vary, such as lay-Kirk, but the type of story is generically called lay-Spock because they were the most common stories of this type when the designation was coined. May be called simply "lay" story.

Leia Organa (Princess Leia): A character from the *Star Wars* movie series, she was the leader of the rebel forces working against the evil Empire.

Letterzine: A fanzine devoted almost exclusively to letters between fans, the letterzine may have some news about upcoming productions or events, or an occasional review as well as the letters.

McCormick, Mark: In the series *Hardcastle and McCormick,* he is the ex-con paroled into the retired judge's custody to do yardwork around the estate and legwork for the judge trying to solve old cases. From a relatively expedient beginning, show developed a strong and sensitive relationship between the two title characters.

McCoy, Doctor Leonard: In *Star Trek,* the irascible chief medical officer on the *Enterprise.* After Spock, Captain Kirk's most trusted advisor, particularly on emotional matters.

Mary Sue: A fan story in which a very young heroine, often in her teens and possessing genius-level intelligence, great beauty, and a charmingly impish personality, joins the heroes either on the bridge of the starship or on the streets with the spies or police. She generally resolves the conflict of the story, saves the lives of the protagonists who have grown to love her, but dies heroically in the process. The term is also used to describe the heroine featured in the story. Mary Sue has become a derogatory term in the community.

Mellanby, Dayna: A teenaged high-tech huntress from *Blake 7*'s third and fourth season. Notable for waking Avon with a kiss at their first meeting.

Mixed media: In the community the term does not mean a combination of channels for production, such as books and television. Rather, it describes a fanzine in which stories from a wide variety of universes are featured (such as a story about *Star Trek* characters followed by one about *Blake's 7*). The term does not necessarily mean that more than one universe is represented in any given story, nor does it preclude cross-universe stories. May also refer to a songtape in which many characters from a wide variety of universes come together, most often for humorous effect.

Nasfic: Acronym for North American Science Fiction Convention. When Worldcon (see below) is held outside the boundaries of the continental United States, Nasfic is held the weekend before or after at a location as voted by fans who attended the Worldcon two years before. Fans who cannot afford to make the trip abroad attend Nasfic; some fans attend both conventions.

Picard, Jean-Luc: In *S.T.:T.N.G.,* the captain of the new and improved *Enterprise.* Middle-aged and very formal, Picard is French but speaks in RSC (Royal Shakespeare Company) English. He pays more attention to the Prime Directive than his predecessor, Captain Kirk, ever did.

Pon farr: A concept of Vulcan sexuality developed in the *Star Trek* episode "Amok Time" and used as the basis for a vast number of amateur stories. Pon farr is a breeding imperative that occurs every seven years in an adult male Vulcan's life. During that time he loses rationality and must have sex with the wife to whom he is bonded in childhood. If he cannot have sex with the wife at that time, he grows increasingly irrational and violent, his metabolism destabilizes, and he dies. Pon farr is supposed to be a big secret from the rest of the universe.

Prime Directive: In *Star Trek,* the most important law in the Federation, and one most often observed in the breach. It meant that a starship could observe cultures but could take no steps to influence their development. In dealing with less technologically developed societies, the Prime Directive extended to hiding the crew's identities as members of a spacefaring culture. In *S.T.:T.N.G.,* Picard tries harder to follow the dictates of the Prime Directive than his earlier, more impulsive counterpart, Captain Kirk.

Professionals, The: A violent British police action series in which a buddy-style partnership modeled after *Starsky and Hutch*—in this case agents of an elite intelligence and enforcement service—save Britain from spies, criminals, and psychotic agents.

Prydonians of Prynceton: Located in central New Jersey, one of the largest amateur regional Doctor Who fan clubs in the United States. The Prydonians have also expanded into *Blake's 7* fandom. They publish a newsletter and maintain an extensive fanzine library.

Quantum Leap: Recently discovered fan favorite on NBC. Sam, a well-meaning physicist, travels around in a time period bounded by his own lifetime, leaping into the bodies and lives of the people who live there. At first, Sam believed that the computer used in the experiment—Ziggy—was guiding him, but he has since concluded that God is sending him to right wrongs and save lives with the help of a holographic sidekick, Al. The show is most popular for its flexibility—it "crosses" well into the universes of many other shows. Many fans use Sam's time travels to correct errors or poorly conceived ideas in other favorite shows.

R2D2: A droid, or robot, featured in the *Star Wars* movies. Shaped like a garbage can on wheels, R2D2 is most noted for carrying the Princess Leia's SOS message, meant for Obi Wan Kenobi, to Luke Skywalker.

Remington Steele: Television series in which a woman private investigator invents a male alter ego to impress her clients and finds herself saddled with a suave con-man who fast-talks his way into the role of the never-seen Mr. Steele.

Restal, Vila: In the series *Blake's 7*, a pickpocket sneak thief and safe-cracker thrown in with Blake's band when Blake leads a breakout from a prison planet in the beginning of the series.

Riker, William: In *S.T.:T.N.G.*, first officer of the new and improved *Enterprise*. Riker is the dashing, square-jawed hero-type in the new series. After the first season he grew a beard and a sense of humor.

Robin of Sherwood: A 1980s British remake of the Robin Hood legend with strong paganistic overtones.

Romulan(s): A race of aliens in the *Star Trek* universe, Romulans are members of the Romulan Empire, portrayed as more honorable and courteous than the Klingons, but still enemies of the Federation.

Saavik: In the second and third *Star Trek* movies, the command-tracked half-Vulcan, half-Romulan cadet whose mentor was Captain Spock.

Sarek: A character from the *Star Trek* series. Spock's father, and the Vulcan ambassador to Earth.

Scott, Montgomery: *Star Trek's* chief engineer of the *Enterprise*. Most notable for his love of his engines.

Servalan: The villainess of *Blake's 7*, first as supreme commander of the armed forces trying to capture the rebel band and later as the president of the Federation. Best known for her severely short dark hair and the stiletto heels and white evening gowns she wore throughout the first two seasons (in the third season, she switched to black but kept the stiletto heels).

Sime-Gen: The universe created in Jacqueline Lichtenberg's *Zeor* and other books, with the advice and writing of Jean Lorrah, which has a fandom of its own, including newsletters and fan fiction. In the Sime-Gen universe, humanity has divided into two branches, the Gens, with slower metabolisms who process food for energy, and the Simes, who survive by vampirically sucking the energy out of the Gens with tentacles protruding from their forearms. The books and stories chronicle the efforts of both branches to survive.

Skywalker, Luke: In *Star Wars*, the real last of the Jedi (see Obi Wan Kenobi). He begins as a naive young farmboy who runs away to save the beautiful princess who turns out to be his sister, learns the arts of Jedi Knighthood from Kenobi, and then discovers that the evil Darth Vader is his father.

Slash: Homoerotic fiction using the characters from the source products. The term is derived from the virgule, (/), used to separate the names or initials of the two or more characters involved in a sexual-romantic relationship, and distinct from names or initials separated by a dash or an ampersand indicating only a friendship or familial relationship. Many of the stories are highly romantic, some are explicitly erotic, but the presence of a sexual act in the text is not necessary for the categorization; only the implication that the action takes place in a fictional universe where such a relationship exists is needed.

Solo, Han: In *Star Wars,* a smuggler traveling with a seven-foot-tall alien partner, the Wookie Chewbacca. He is drawn into the rebellion against the evil Empire against his will, falls in love with the beautiful rebel leader-princess, is flash-frozen at the end of the second movie and recovered at the beginning of the third.

Solo, Napoleon: Dapper, suave, and womanizing super-agent in the 1960s series *The Man from U.N.C.L.E.*

Songtape: A fan art form. Clips from favorite source products (see below) are recombined on videotape to popular songs to tell a new story or make a critical/editorial point.

Soolin: In *Blake's 7,* a young blonde woman mercenary who joins Avon and his band in the final season of the series.

Source product: Television series, movies, books, and other commercially produced fictional narratives from which fans draw characters, settings, and some plots that serve as the sources of their own art and literature.

Spock: Most popular character on the *Star Trek* television and movie series. Son of Amanda, a schoolteacher from Earth, and Sarek, the ambassador from Vulcan, Spock was the science officer and first officer on the *Enterprise,* later made Captain when Kirk was promoted to Admiral. Most noted for his hyperrationality and his superhuman strength, and for his devotion to his commanding officer, Captain James T. Kirk.

Starfleet: In *Star Trek,* the military-police arm of the Federation government.

Starsky, David: The shorter, darker, working-class policeman with the ethnic New York accent in the television police action series *Starsky and Hutch.* Best known for eating junk food and driving a bright red Torino with a white racing stripe.

Starsky and Hutch: The quintessential buddy series. Partners Dave Starsky and Ken Hutchinson rescue each other and their friends and relatives from the clutches of Los Angeles criminals while angsting over each other's injuries and cavorting in a pranksterly boyish way.

Star Trek: NBC science fiction television series of the late sixties that refused to die. For three seasons the crew of the starship *Enterprise,* led by the intrepidly square-jawed Captain James T. Kirk, boldly went where "no man had gone before," to seek out new life and kill their computers. When overcome in battle with the ratings, fans rallied to save crew and ship, first in cartoon form, later in comic books, paperbacks, movies, and a second series of episodes with a new *Enterprise* and crew. Possibly the most culturally tenacious flop in television history.

Star Trek: The Next Generation (S.T.:T.N.G.): The new syndicated series of episodes based on the adventures of a new and improved *Enterprise* sent out on exploratory and diplomatic missions by the same Federation that directed Captain Kirk and his crew. Their mission continues to be to seek out new life, but now they "go where no one has gone."

Star Wars: A three-movie series which recounts the efforts of a band of rebels to free the universe from the clutches of the evil Empire, and the more personal story of a young man's struggle to grow into his power as a Jedi knight, to defeat the evil side of his own nature as represented by his father, and finally, to return his father to the forces of good from which he had turned during the war.

Steele, Remington: Suave con-man whose "real" name the audience never really discovers. He tangles with the Remington Steele Detective Agency and stays on as the mysterious and romantic title character.

Story tree: A group of stories written by one or more fanwriters and built around a central plot line.

Sulu: Helmsman on *Star Trek*'s *Enterprise* and representative Japanese character on the multi-racial bridge crew, best known for his hobbies, botany and fencing.

Surak: In *Star Trek,* the father of Vulcan philosophy of logical pacifism that governs all aspects of Vulcan culture. Also, the award given by the fan community to the amateur writers and artists of *Star Trek* fan fiction. Gene Roddenberry, series creator, was awarded (and accepted) a Surak award for lifetime achievement.

Tardis: Acronym for Time and Relative Dimension in Space, the space-time machine shaped like a British police call box in which the Doctor, title character of the BBC series *Doctor Who,* travels.

Tarrant, Del: In the series *Blake's 7,* a Federation pilot turned gunrunner who joins Avon in the third season of the series.

Travis: Blake's 7 villain, a Federation officer tracking the escaped convict Blake, whom he blames for the loss of his eye and arm, the latter of which has been replaced by cybernetic weaponry.

Trek: Short form for *Star Trek,* sometimes used as a referent to the series, but more often used generatively in the creation of series-specific terminology, such as: Trekdom (the constellation of interconnected commercial and fan cultures surrounding *Star Trek*);

Treklit (*Star Trek* fan fiction); Trekwriter (generally understood to be a fan writer of amateur *Star Trek* material, and not a writer who is paid for writing paperbacks or television scripts).

Trekker: The fan community's name for a *Star Trek* fan.

Trekkie: The term for a *Star Trek* fan most often used by news media, often with the connotation of silly, infantile behavior. Considered a derogatory term in the fan community.

Trexindex: Roberta Rogow's index of *Star Trek* fan fiction, the most comprehensive document of its kind in the fan community.

Tubbs, Ricardo: Sonny Crockett's partner from New York in the series *Miami Vice*. Went to Miami to find the drug dealers who murdered his brother, also a New York policeman, and stayed. Tubbs wears socks and drives a blue classic Cadillac convertible.

Uhura: The communications officer of the *Enterprise* in the television and movie series *Star Trek*. Most notable as one of the earliest black women portrayed in a command position on a military vessel.

Universe: The setting, characters, and assumptions under which a group of books, movies, television episodes, or amateur products are created. *Star Trek* as Gene Roddenberry wrote it is a universe, and the movies and second series, *S.T.:T.N.G.*, all fall within this universe. Fan stories in which certain characters in Roddenberry's universe marry and have wives and children, or exist in a harsh Empire, are examples of universes separate from but related to Roddenberry's creation.

Vader, Darth: The more visible villain of the *Star Wars* series of movies, he is the black-cloaked and masked right hand of the unseen (until the third movie) evil Emperor, and the father of both Luke Skywalker and Leia Organa.

Vincent: The leonine hero of *Beauty and the Beast,* he lives underground in the New York sewer system, with a civilization of refugees from the surface who dress in interesting bits and pieces and depend upon their helpers on the surface for supplies.

Vulcan: In *Star Trek*, the hot, dry planet on which live the Vulcans, a race with copper-based blood, greenish skin, and pointed ears. Vulcans are known for their logic and intelligence, for the fact that they suppress all display of emotion, and for the secrecy with which they guard their sex lives.

War of the Worlds: A short-lived syndicated series (1988–90) based on the 1953 movie of the same name. Notable for its obscure fandom in which a number of new fans made their first forays into fanzining, the show had a cast of characters balanced for gender and race, but particularly offensive special effects that many potential fans found offputting. In the second season, a new producer killed the fans' favorite character, American Indian career army officer Paul Ironhorse, and the show lost favor, barely making it through the season before it was cancelled.

Welcommittee: A fan organization created within the *Star Trek* fan community to act as a clearinghouse for newcomers interested in learning more about *Star Trek*, conventions, fanzines, or other fans in their neighborhoods.

Wiseguy: A police action series in which O.C.B. (Organized Crime Bureau of the FBI) agent Vinnie Terranova goes undercover in criminal organizations, ostensibly to find evidence to bring to trial, but often he undermines the organization from within. Many of his targets kill themselves to avoid capture, others go insane. Few go to jail.

Worf: In *S.T.:T.N.G.*, the Klingon security officer on the *Enterprise*.

Worldcon: World Science Fiction Convention, held every Labor Day weekend in a different city around the world. Early Worldcons attracted a few hundred hard-core science fiction fans, but today a Worldcon can attract up to ten thousand fans of a growing number of genres, subgenres, and media, who participate in a variety of fan activities throughout the five-day weekend convention.

Yar, Tasha: The former security officer on *S.T.:T.N.G.*'s *Enterprise*, killed by a slime monster when the actress decided to leave the series. Popular among fans for seducing the android Data.

Yoda: The oldest Jedi, a small, wrinkled, mystical Jim Henson puppet who trains Luke Skywalker in the way of the Force.

Zine: Short form of the term fanzine.

Note

1. Not all fans are comfortable with this status. A truthful and observant recorder of their culture is perceived by some as a greater threat than those who take away distorted views of the community. Lies are not as dangerous to secrets as the truth.

Appendix C. Who Are Fanziners?: Demographics

The earliest *Star Trek* fanzine publishers were already members of the science fiction community, and they carried into media fandom the idea of the nonprofit gathering place where fans and professional practitioners could meet. Media fans, particularly of electronic science fiction, who frequently share an interest in written science fiction, still gather at the literary conventions.

Of the many people performing various functions for the group's development and enrichment, some can be classified as core members of the community of media fanziners, while others of peripheral status can only be perceived as contributing members in the broadest sense. Core members, who must by definition both contribute in an immediate and direct way to the community and at the same time make their primary identification as community members, include the writers, artists, editors, and publishers of the fanzines. In the more esoteric fan groups, participants who produce difficult-to-find product—videotapes of source products and songtapes, and photocopies of privately circulated literature and art—are considered core. Members who organize fanziner conventions are core to this community, while members who organize conventions at which many interested groups attend are peripheral to the fanzine community to the extent of their convention activities, but may be considered core members by virtue of their primary identification with the group.

In 1985 I conducted a survey at a small media fanzine convention, More Eastly Con. I wanted to know two things about the fanziners: who they were, demographically, and what interests they had in addition to putting together and reading fanzines about television characters. I chose More Eastly Con for my survey for a number of reasons. The original Convention Committee, known for their Manhattan

UNIVERSITY of PENNSYLVANIA
PHILADELPHIA, PA. 19104

Faculty of Arts and Sciences

FOLKLORE AND FOLKLIFE
ROOM 415, LOGAN HALL CN

CAMILLE BACON-SMITH'S
<<< ETHNOGRAPHIC SURVEY AND TREKKER'S QUIZ >>>

--> Check off or number in order of preference

1. **Sex:** _Female   _Male   _Whenever I can

2. **Status:** _Single   _Divorced/Separated/Widowed
             _Married   _Semi-permanently attached

3. **Favorite fannish activity:**
_Writing fiction   _Hall costuming   _Art/Crafts
_Writing poems   _Masquerade costuming _Accosting
_Writing articles   _Editing fanzines   Howie & Bob
_Organizing cons   _Attending cons   Other_____

4. **Favorite Trek Genre (to read or write):**
_Mary Sue   _Other erotic   _Action-adventure
_K/S   _Hurt-Comfort   Other_____
_Lay Spock   _Satire

5. **Favorite Entertainment (Books, Movies, TV):**
_General SF   _Romance   _Comedy
_Fantasy   _Historical   _Non-fiction
_Sword & Sorcery _Classics   Other_____
_Mystery   _TV Soaps

6. **Educational Background:**
_High School   _BA/BS   _Post Masters
_Some College/AA   _MA/MS   _Ph.D.

7. **Age:** _18 to 30   _31 to 50   _over 50

8. **Would you like to talk more about your involvement in**
Trek? If yes, accost the ethnographer (Camille Bacon-
Smith) in the halls or write c/o above address. If no,

--> PLEASE STUFF THIS SURVEY <--
(IN THE BOXES MARKED PENN SURVEY AROUND THE CON)
LLP

Questionnaire completed by fans at More Eastly Con, 1985.

conventions each attended by as many as 17,000 people,[1] had organized the 1985 convention as a reunion party. They advertised the
convention, held at the LaGuardia Hilton over Labor Day weekend,
in a very limited way at other media conventions and at a few science
fiction conventions. Both the World Science Fiction Convention

(Worldcon), and the North American Science Fiction Convention (Nasfic), held in years such as 1985 when Worldcon falls outside the continental United States, are held on Labor Day weekend. This gave me a sampling of participants limited to community insiders who had access to information about the convention, and who also had a primary identification with the media fanzine community rather than the larger science fiction fandom. I could expect a high percentage of participants to be core members, and a statistically insignificant number of attendees to be drawn from outside the community. In follow-up interviews conducted at the convention, I found this assumption to be correct.

According to survey data and interview material, the members of the group are highly educated: many have a master's or higher degree, although many, like Roberta Rogow, returned to school in their thirties either to complete their bachelor's degrees or to earn an advanced degree. The majority of the community members are single, white, and heterosexual, although roughly 30 percent have been married and perhaps 10 percent have racial identities other than white.[2]

Through contacts in the Gaylaxians, a national gay and lesbian science fiction club, I have learned of one circle in Boston, just discovering the wider community of media fandom in 1989, in which half the members are gay. However, my sole lesbian informant, who supplied me with a list of friends in fandom that includes approximately 150 names from all parts of the United States, says that she has met only seven other lesbian women in fandom. I have seen only one fanzine, regularly published out of the U.K., which openly caters to a predominantly gay audience,[3] and this is the only place where I have ever seen stories or poetry depicting lesbian relationships written by women in media fandom. I have never heard the sexual orientation of a fan discussed in either a positive or a negative way in relation to a fan's writing or choice of reading material, nor have I ever seen it as an issue in the social interactions of the group.[4]

Race, perhaps because it is often so immediately visible, has been mentioned on occasion. One white fan from the Midwest, attending a *Star Trek* convention in the Baltimore area that featured Nichelle Nichols[5] as guest, mentioned to me how pleased she was to see so many (about 30 percent) participants of other races at the convention. She confessed that, believing as she did in the *Star Trek* concept of IDIC—a delight in the infinite diversity of the universe in infinite combinations—she had often been troubled that fandom had done so little to attract and make welcome black, Asian, and Hispanic women. In general, more women of color participate in media fandom than black and Hispanic men and women together attend science fiction functions. Of the two regions for which I have the most ethnographic evidence, the numbers are consistently higher for the Northeast than the Midwest, and include black men and women at the organizational, creative, and consumer levels.

While the overwhelming majority of the fanziner women identify themselves as middle-class, few are employed at their competence. level. Many work in service professions.

Over several years, Judith Gran and Dorothy Laoang have conducted a series of surveys using questionnaires inserted in a selected group of fanzines.[6] This readership group is limited to community members who read sexually explicit material, but is not limited to the group able to attend the More Eastly Con. Their analysis, like my own, indicates that most active fanziners are women, between the ages of 20 and 70, but with a high concentration of members who are unmarried and in their late thirties.

For statistical information about the product created within the community, I turned to Roberta Rogow's *Trexindex*.[7] Rogow, a children's librarian in northern New Jersey, has been indexing the writings and graphic arts that have appeared in the community's fanzines since 1977. The *Trexindex* has some limitations for our present purposes. By design it considers for inclusion only those items created on the *Star Trek* theme, or items created about other media sources that appear in fanzines highlighting *Star Trek* materials. The *Trexindex* does not include fanzines devoted to other source products, nor does it include material not printed in the fanzines, such as literature passed by photocopy, hanging art, or costume.

Given its limited goals, as of 1988, Rogow's *Trexindex* does list over thirty-four thousand items, produced by more than ten thousand community members from the United States and English-speaking countries, and from countries such as Japan, Germany, and Italy, where English is a second language. Some men do create for media fanzines, but they make up less than 10 percent (adjusted for male pseudonyms) of the writers listed in Rogow's *Trexindex*. Although fanzining itself is a traditional male activity in the science fiction community, there are no more than five male fanzine editors in this media community. The number of male participants drops to 0 percent in the most sexually explicit genres, although I know of several isolated examples of gay men who write homoerotic fiction in the fandom. The number of men writing fiction rises slightly for fanzines that concentrate more on action-adventure and humor.

Notes

1. Joan Winston, *The Making of the Trek Conventions* (New York: Playboy Press, 1979).
2. This latter figure is an estimate based on observation rather than survey data. Women of color participate at all levels of fandom, drawing for, writing in, and editing fanzines, performing filksongs and in plays and skits, and attending conventions and house gatherings. Co-editors Florence Butler and Lee Coleman, who run Black Coffee Press publication, are also national organizers in the Nichelle Nichols fan club that links their participation with other groups in the fan communities. In general, however, it is considered bad form in the community to call attention to a fan's physical characteristics, or to judge any work or participation by the color of a fan's skin.
3. That fanzine, like many others in the community, emphasized mutual support for its writers and audience. The most specifically gay political issue I saw in the ten fanzine issues I have read concerned a gay fan who was prohibited by law from buying the fanzine because he was not yet eighteen years old (he has since that time turned eighteen). Readers voted to accept the young man's subscription and his contributions to the fanzine, and the publisher explained the most frequent reason most fans gave for breaking the morals law: they felt that the youth, who expressed feelings of isolation and difference, needed the supportive environment of like-minded fans who openly discussed sexuality in a non-judgmental manner.
4. I have myself shared a room with my openly lesbian informant, a good friend, when we both attended a small convention. The arrangement roused only surprise that we knew each other, since we live at opposite ends of the continent. The fact we did know each other seemed to confirm once again for some fans that the community is indeed a small town spread very thinly across a large world.
5. Nichols played Uhura in the *Star Trek* television and movie series.
6. Judith Gran and Dorothy Laoang, "Kirk/Spock Survey Results—part 1," in *NTS*, undated.
7. Roberta Rogow, *Trexindex,* and Supplements 1–5 (Fairlawn, N.J.: Other World Books, 1977–88). While the index is a valuable tool for scholars of the *Star Trek* phenomenon, Roberta Rogow is the first to admit that the *Trexindex* is by no means complete. Roberta has collected data for her index from her own collection and those of friends, and from information volunteered by editors and publishers. Until recently, she only indexed material that appeared in *Star Trek* zines, excluding the creative output surrounding other source products. Her work, however, is the most comprehensive bibliographic source in the fan community.

Appendix D

KRAITH MASTER PLAN

EXPLANATION OF THE NUMBERING SYSTEM:

aI---------- stories that occur, according to internal chronology, before "Spock's Argument"
I---------- Main Stories. Eight planned, five written to date. All are titled "Spock's Something-or-other".
IA--------- Sub Stories occuring between the main stories. For example IA occurs between I and II, etc..
I(1) or IA(1)-- Sub-stories occuring as an epilog or a postscript to another story with no time break between.
AI or AIA---- Sub-stories occuring simultaneously with another story in the series describing events relating to
the other story, but not contained within the story.

Stories that appear in Kraith Collected volumes I-IV are marked KCI, KCII, KCIII, or KCIV.
Unless otherwise the author is Jacqueline Lichtenberg.

Kraith bI
Kraith aI
Kraith I   Spock's Affirmation KCI
Kraith IA   Shealku KCI
Kraith IB   Zyeto KCI
Kraith IC   Yehaena (unwritten)
Kraith ID   A Matter of Priority Anna Mary Hall KCI
Kraith E   The Lesson (outline only, see Kraith Creator's Manual I)
Kraith F   Ssarsun's Argument KCII
Kraith IG   The Way Home Anna Mary Hall

Kraith II   Spock's Mission KCI
Kraith II(1)   The Learning Experience Jean Sellar KCIII
Kraith IIA   T'Zorel KCI
Kraith IIB   The Disaffirmed Ruth Berman KCI
Kraith IIC   Operation Transplant Lori Dell
Kraith IID   ---------- (Ruth Berman, hypothetical sequel to The Disaffirmed)
Kraith IIE   Initiative KCIV
Kraith IIF   Ni Var Claire Gadzikowski
Kraith IIF(1)   ---------(unwritten sequel to Ni Var)
Kraith IIG   Diana Pat Osborne

Kraith AIII   The Tanya Entry Pat Zotti KCI
Kraith III   Spock's Argument
Kraith III(1)   The Obligation/Through Time and Tears Jacqueline Lichtenberg and Joan Winston KCIII
Kraith IIIA   Federation Centennial KCII
Kraith IIIB   Secret of Groskin KCIII
Kraith IIIC   Coup de Grace KCIII
Kraith IIIC(1) Coup de Partie Ruth Berman KCIII
Kraith IIID   Jh'nfreya   Debbie Goldstein and Carol Lynn
Kraith IIIE   Operating Manual, Anna Mary Hall KCIV

Kraith IV   Spock's Nemesis KCIII

Kraith V   Spock's Decision KCIV
Kraith VA ----------unwritten Ssarsun story
Kraith VB --------- unwritten Ssarsun story
Kraith VC --------- unwritten Ssarsun story
Kraith VD   Spock's Pilgrimage KCIV
Kraith VE   The Maze Joan Winston (unwritten)
Kraith VF   The Punis ment (outline only)
Kraith VG   T'Lel's Option (outlined only)
Kraith VH   Spock's Defection Sondra Marshak (outline approved)
Kraith VI   Kirk's Cure-All (outline only)
Kraith VJ   Beom Interlude (first draft)
Kraith VJ(1)   Kirk's Auction (outline only)
Kraith VK   Spock's Temper Tantrum Sondra Marshak (outline approved)
Kraith VL   ---------- (somehow we've got to end this line of developement)

Kraith VI   Spock's Command (outline only)
Kraith VIA   Ediface of Value (Outline only, may be scrapped soon)

Kraith VII   Spock's Challenge (story idea only)
Kraith VIIA T'Uriamne's Decision Jacqueline Lichtenberg and Sondra Marshak (outline only)

Kraith VIII   Spock's Memory (story idea only)

Bibliography

Abrahams, Roger. "Play in the Face of Death: Transgression and Inversion in a West Indian Wake." In *The Many Faces of Play*, edited by Kendall Blanchard. Champaign, Ill.: Human Kinetics Publisher, Inc.

Agar, Michael H. *The Professional Stranger: An Informal Introduction to Ethnography*. Orlando, Fla.: Academic Press, 1980.

Aker, Bawdrey, and Calory Vollage. "Stairs in his Eyes: A Phonographic Tail of the Spice Age." N.p., n.d. Photocopy.

Allen, Miriam. "Beau Mudd." *Masiform D #16*, edited by Devra Langsam. Brooklyn, N.Y.: Poison Pen Press, 1988. Fanzine

Allen, Robert C. "On Reading Soaps: A Semiotic Primer." In *Regarding Television*, edited by Ann Kaplan. Los Angeles: The American Film Institute, 1983.

Auerbach, Nina. *Communities of Women: An Idea in Fiction*. Cambridge, Mass.: Harvard University Press, 1978.

————. *Romantic Imprisonment: Women and Other Glorified Outcasts*. New York: Columbia University Press, 1985.

————. *Women and the Demon*. Cambridge, Mass.: Harvard University Press, 1982.

Bacon-Smith, Camille. "Breaking the Frame: Intrusion on a Costume Event." Annual Meeting of the American Folklore Society, Cincinnati, 1985.

————. "The Mary Sue Genre in Star Trek Fan Fiction." *Folklore Women's Communication*, 1984.

————. "Spock among the Women." *New York Times Book Review*, November 16, 1986.

Bainbridge, William Sims. *Dimensions of Science Fiction*. Cambridge, Mass.: Harvard University Press, 1986.

Bakhtin, Mikhail. *Rabelais and His World*. Bloomington: Indiana University Press, 1968.

Barthes, Roland. *Mythologies*. Translated by A. Lavers. New York: Hill and Wang, 1972 (1957).

————. *S/Z*. Translated by R. Miller. New York: Hill and Wang, 1974.

————. *Writing Degree Zero*. Translated by A. Lavers and C. Smith. New York: Hill and Wang, 1967 (1953).

Bascom, William. "The Forms of Folklore: Prose Narrative," *Journal of American Folklore* 78 (1965): 3–20.

Becker, Howard S. *Art Worlds*. Berkeley: University of California Press, 1982.

Bellman, Beryl L., and Bennetta Jules-Rosette. "Perception as Lived Experience: Do They See It Differently?" In *A Paradigm for Looking: Cross-Cultural Research with Visual Media.* Norwood, N.J.: Ablex, 1977.

Ben-Amos, Dan. "Analytic Categories and Ethnic Genres." *Genre* 2, no. 3 (1969): 275–301.

———. "Toward a Definition of Folklore in Context." *Journal of American Folklore* 84 (1971): 3–15.

Benjamin, Walter. *Illuminations.* Edited by Hannah Arendt and translated by Harry Zohn. New York: Schocken Books, 1969 (1923–50, posthumous).

Berger, John. *Ways of Seeing.* London: British Broadcasting Corporation and Penguin Books, 1972.

Berman, Ruth. "Visit to a Weird Planet Revisited." *Spockanalia,* edited by Devra Langsam and Sherna C. Burley, pp. 89–104. Brooklyn, N.Y., 1970. Fanzine.

Birdwhistell, Ray L. *Kinesics and Context.* Philadelphia: University of Pennsylvania Press, 1970.

Booker, D. "Preliminary Report on the Inscription on the *Kh'Marr Bowl.*" *Masiform D #13,* edited by Devra Langsam. Brooklyn, N.Y.: Poison Pen Press, 1983. Fanzine.

Bordwell, David. *Narration in the Fiction Film.* Madison: University of Wisconsin Press, 1985.

Brooke-Rose, Christine. *A Rhetoric of the Unreal.* Cambridge: Cambridge University Press, 1981.

Brower, Sue. "Criticism by Consensus: Viewers for Quality Television." Paper presented at the International Communication Association Conference, New Orleans, 1988.

Brunsdon, Charlotte. "Crossroads: Notes on Soap Opera." In *Regarding Television,* edited by Ann Kaplan. Los Angeles: The American Film Institute, 1983.

Calois, R. *Man, Play and Games.* New York: Schocken Books, 1979.

Cantor, Johanna T. "Rendezvous." *R & R XXII,* pp. 77–108. Bronx, N.Y.: Yeoman Press, Summer 1985. Fanzine.

Cantor, Muriel. "Audience Control." In *Television: The Critical View,* edited by H. Newcomb, pp. 311–34. New York: Oxford University Press, 1976.

Carey, Diane. *Dreadnought.* New York: Pocket Books, 1986.

Carraher, Lynda. "Prelude." *Masiform D #13,* edited by Devra Michele Langsam. Brooklyn, N.Y.: Poison Pen Press, 1983. Fanzine.

Caughey, John. "Imaginary Social Relationships in Modern America." *American Quarterly* 30, no. 1 (Spring 1978): 70–89.

———. *Imaginary Social Worlds: A Cultural Approach.* Lincoln: University of Nebraska Press, 1984.

Cawalti, J. "The Concept of Formula in the Study of Popular Literature." *Journal of Popular Culture* 3 (1969): 381–403.

Chambers, Ian. *Popular Culture: The Metropolitan Experience.* London: Methuen, 1986.

Chapman, Anthony, and Hugh C. Foot. *Humor and Laughter: Theory, Research, and Application.* London: John Wiley and Sons, 1976.

Chodorow, Nancy. *The Reproduction of Mothering: Psychoanalysis and the Sociology of Gender.* Berkeley: University of California Press, 1978.

Constitution of the World Science Fiction Society. June 1983. Article II, sections 2 and 3, published in the Program Book of *ConStellation.* The 41st World Science Fiction Convention, Baltimore, Md., 1983.

Crispin, A. C. *Yesterday's Son.* New York: Pocket Books, 1983.
Crites, Sue. "A Bitter God to Follow, A Beautiful God to Behold." *Masiform D #13*, edited by Devra Langsam. Brooklyn, N.Y.: Poison Pen Press, 1983. Fanzine.
Culler, Jonathan. *Structuralist Poetics.* Ithaca, N.Y.: Cornell University Press, 1975.
Czikszentmihalyi, Mihalyi. *Beyond Boredom and Anxiety.* San Francisco: Jossey-Bass, 1975.
deLauretis, Teresa. *Alice Doesn't.* Bloomington: Indiana University Press, 1982.
Derrida, Jacques. *Writing and Difference.* Translated by Alan Bass. Chicago: University of Chicago Press, 1978.
de Saussure, Ferdinand. *Course in General Linguistics.* Edited by C. Bally and A. Reidlinger, translated by Wade Baskin. New York: McGraw Hill, 1959 (1915).
Dick, Philip K. *The Man in the High Castle.* New York: Berkeley Medallion Books, 1962.
Dillard, J. M. *Demons.* New York: Pocket Books, 1986.
Duane, Diane. *The Wounded Sky.* New York: PocketBooks, 1983.
Eco, Umberto. *Semiotics and the Philosophy of Language.* Bloomington: Indiana University Press, 1986.
Farb, Peter. *Word Play.* New York: Alfred A. Knopf, 1974.
Ferguson, Brad. *Crisis on Centaurus.* New York: Pocket Books, 1986.
Fiedler, Leslie A. *Love and Death in the American Novel.* New York: Scarborough Books, 1966 (1960).
Fifth Season. Edited by Sheila Willis. Greenbelt, Md.: Spice Press, 1983. Fanzine.
Fine, Gary Alan. "Legendary Creatures and Small Group Culture: Medieval Lore in a Contemporary Role-Playing Game." *Keystone Folklore* 24, no. 1 (1984).
———. *Shared Fantasy: Role Playing Games as Social Worlds.* Chicago: University of Chicago Press, 1984.
Firth, Raymond. *Symbols, Public and Private.* Ithaca, N.Y.: Cornell University Press, 1973.
Fiske, John. *Television and Culture.* London: Methuen, 1987.
———. "Television, Polysemy and Popularity." *Critical Studies in Mass Communication* 3 (1986): 391–408.
Fiske, J., and J. Hartley. *Reading Television.* London: Methuen & Co., 1978.
Fox, Steven. "Theoretical Implications for the Study of Interrelationships Between Ritual and Play." In *Play and Culture*, edited by H. Schwartzman. New York: Leisure Press, 1980.
Friedrich, Paul. *The Meaning of Aphrodite.* Chicago: University of Chicago Press, 1978.
Fussell, Paul. *Poetic Meter and Poetic Form.* Rev. ed. New York: Random House, 1979.
Gabriel, Claire. *Quartet Plus Two.* Grosse Pointe Park, Mich.: Ceiling Press, 1987 (1975). Fanzine.
Gaines, Jane. "Women and Representation: Can We Enjoy Alternative Pleasure?" In *American Media and Mass Culture: Left Perspectives*, edited by Donald Lazere. Berkeley: University of California Press, 1987.
Geertz, Clifford. *The Interpretation of Cultures.* New York: Basic Books, 1973.

Gennep, Arnold van. *Rites of Passage*. London: Routledge and Kegan Paul, 1960 (1909).

Georges, Robert A., and Michael Owen Jones. *People Studying People*. Berkeley: University of California Press, 1980.

Gerrold, David. *The World of Star Trek*. New York: Ballantine Books, 1973.

Gilbert, Sandra M., and Susan Gubar. *The Madwoman in the Attic: The Woman Writer and the Nineteenth-Century Literary Imagination*. New Haven: Yale University Press, 1979.

Gilligan, Carol. *In a Different Voice*. Cambridge, Mass.: Harvard University Press, 1982.

Girard, René. *Violence and the Sacred*. Translated by Patrick Gregory. Baltimore, Md.: Johns Hopkins University Press, 1977.

Gitlin, Todd. *Inside Prime Time*. New York: Pantheon Books, 1985 (1983).

Goffman, Erving. *Frame Analysis*. New York: Harper Colophon Books, 1974.

———. *The Presentation of Self in Everyday Life*. Garden City, N.Y.: Doubleday Anchor Books, 1959.

———. *Relations in Public*. New York: Harper Colophon Books, 1971.

Goldstein, Kenneth S. *A Guide for Fieldworkers in Folklore*. Hatboro, Pa.: Folklore Associates, 1964.

Gombrich, E. H. "The Use of Art for the Study of Symbols." In *Psychology and the Visual Arts*, edited by James Hogg, pp. 149–70. Baltimore: Penguin Books, 1969.

———. "Visual Discovery Through Art." In *Psychology and the Visual Arts*, edited by James Hogg, pp. 215–38. Baltimore: Penguin Books, 1969.

Gossen, Gary. "Verbal Dueling in Chamula." In *Speech Play*, edited by Barbara Kirshenblatt-Gimblett, pp. 121–46. Philadelphia: University of Pennsylvania Press, 1976.

Gran, Judith, and Dorothy Laoang: "Kirk/Spock Survey Results—Part 1." In *NTS*. N.d. Letterzine.

Green, Rayna. "Magnolias Grow in Dirt: The Bawdy Lore of Women." *Southern Exposure* 4, no. 4 (1977): 29–33.

Grip. Edited by Roberta Rogow. Fairlawn, N.J.: Other World Press. Fanzine.

Gross, Larry. "Life Vs. Art: The Interpretation of Visual Narratives." Paper prepared for the U.S.-Hungarian Conference on Social Perception and Interpretation of Interaction in Literature, Budapest, 1983.

Gubar, Susan. "Representing Pornography: Feminism, Criticism, and Depictions of Female Violation." *Critical Inquiry* 13 (1987): 712–41.

Gumperz, John J., ed. *Language and Social Identity*. Cambridge: Cambridge University Press, 1982.

Haldeman, Laurie. "The Phone Call." *Zebra Three*, vol. 5, edited by Lorraine Bartlett. Rochester, N.Y.: Polaris Press, 1980. Fanzine.

Hall, Edward T. "Proxemics." *Current Anthropology* 9 (1968): 93–95.

Hall, Stephanie. "Reality is a Crutch for People Who Can't Deal with Science Fiction: Slogan-Buttons among Science Fiction Fans." *Keystone Folklore* (1989): 19–31.

Hall, Stuart. "Culture, the Media, and the Ideological Effect." In *Mass Communication and Society*, edited by James Curran, Michael Gurevitch, and Janet Woolcott. London: Edward Arnold, 1977, pp. 315–48.

———. "Subcultures, Cultures and Class, A Theoretical Overview." In *Resistance through Rituals: Youth Subcultures in Post-War Britain*, edited by Stuart Hall and Tony Jefferson. London: Hutchinson, 1976.

Hebdige, Dick. *Subculture: The Meaning of Style*. London: Methuen, 1979.

Heilbrun, Carolyn G. *Reinventing Womanhood.* New York: W. W. Norton, 1979.

Hesbois, Laure. *Les Jeux de Langage.* Ottawa: Editions de l'Université d'Ottawa, 1986.

Holland, Dorothy, and Naomi Quinn, eds. *Cultural Models in Language and Thought.* Cambridge: Cambridge University Press, 1987.

Horney, Karen. *Feminine Psychology.* Edited by Harold Kelman, M.D. New York: W. W. Norton, 1967.

Huizinga, John. *Homo Ludens.* Beacon Press, 1950.

Hymes, Dell. *Foundations in Sociolinguistics.* Philadelphia: University of Pennsylvania Press, 1974.

———. *"In Vain I Tried to Tell You."* Philadelphia: University of Pennsylvania Press, 1981.

———. *Language in Culture and Society.* New York: Harper and Row, 1964.

———. "Narrative Form as a 'Grammar of Experience.'" *Journal of Education* 164, no. 2 (1982): 121–42.

———, ed. *Reinventing Anthropology.* New York: Pantheon Books, 1972.

In the Public Interest. Edited by Laura Peck and TACS. Baltimore: Sunshine Press. Fanzine.

Interstat. Edited by Teri Meyer. June 1984. Fanzine.

Jenkins, Henry III. "*Star Trek* Rerun, Reread, Rewritten: Fan Writing as Textual Poaching." *Critical Studies in Mass Communication* 5, no. 2 (1988): 85–107.

Kadushin, C. "Networks and Circles in the Production of Culture." In *The Production of Culture*, edited by Richard A. Peterson, pp. 107–22. Beverly Hills: Sage Publications, 1976.

Kagen, Janet. *Uhura's Song.* New York: Pocket Books, 1985.

Kalčik, Susan. "'Like Ann's Gynecologist or the Time I was Almost Raped': Personal Narratives in Women's Rap Groups." In *Women and Folklore*, edited by Claire Farrer, pp. 3–11. Austin: University of Texas Press, 1975.

Kaplan, E. Ann. *Women and Film.* New York: Methuen, 1983.

Kirshenblatt-Gimblett, Barbara. "Speech Play and Verbal Art." In *Play and Learning*, edited by Brian Sutton-Smith, pp. 219–37. New York: Gardner Press Inc., 1979.

———, ed. *Speech Play.* Philadelphia: University of Pennsylvania Press, 1976.

Kraith Collected. Jacqueline Lichtenberg, originator and primary contributor; edited by Carol Lynn. Detroit, Mich.: Ceiling Press Publications, 1980 (1972). Fanzine.

Kramarae, Cheris, ed. *Technology and Women's Voices: Keeping in Touch.* New York: Routledge and Kegan Paul, 1988.

Kuhn, Annette. *Women's Pictures: Feminism and Cinema.* London: Routledge and Kegan Paul, 1982.

Kuhn, Thomas. *The Structure of Scientific Revolutions.* Chicago: University of Chicago Press, 1970 (1962).

Lakoff, George, and Mark Johnson. *Metaphors We Live By.* Chicago: University of Chicago Press, 1980.

Lamb, Patricia Frazer. "Romance, Eroticism, and/or Hurt-Comfort: What's Really Going On Here?" Paper delivered at the National Women's Studies Conference, Urbana, Ill., 1986.

Lamb, Patricia Frazer, and Diana Vieth. "Romantic Myth, Transcendence and *Star Trek* Zines." In *Erotic Universe*, edited by Donald Palumbo, pp. 235–89. New York: Greenwood Press, 1986.

Leerhsen, Charles. "Star Trek's Nine Lives." *Newsweek*, December 22, 1986.

LeGuin, Ursula K. *The Language of the Night.* Edited by Susan Wood. New York: Perigee Books, 1979.

Lévi-Strauss, Claude. *The Savage Mind.* Chicago: University of Chicago Press, 1973 (1962).

Lewis, Anthony. "A Calendar of *Analog* Upcoming Events," *Analog* (various issues) 1983.

Lichtenberg, Jacqueline, Sondra Marshak, and Joan Winston. *Star Trek Lives!* New York: Bantam Books, 1975.

Liebes, Tamar. "Ethnocriticism: Israelis of Moroccan Ethnicity Negotiate the Meaning of 'Dallas.'" *Studies in Visual Communication* 10, no. 3 (1984): 46–73.

Lorrah, Jean. *Epilogue,* and *Epilogue 2.* Originally published in fanzines *Tri-skelion #4 & #5,* and as *Sol Plus* special editions in 1977 and 1978. Reprints self-published by Lorrah, Murray, Ky.

———. *Full Moon Rising.* Bronx, N.Y.: Yeoman Press, 1976.

———. *NTM Collected.* Reprint. Murray, Ky.: Self-published, 1978.

———. *Trust, Like the Soul.* Murray, Ky.: Empire Books, 1988.

———. *The Vulcan Academy Murders.* New York: Pocket Books, 1984.

Lorrah, Jean, and Willard F. Hunt. "Visit to a Weird Planet." *Spockanalia,* edited by Devra Langsam and Sherna C. Burley, pp. 89–101 Brooklyn, N.Y.: Poison Pen Press (Garlic Press), 1968.

Luthi, Max. *The European Folktale: Form and Nature.* Translated by John D. Niles. Philadelphia: Institute for the Study of Human Issues, 1982 (1947).

McIntyre, Vonda N. *Star Trek: The Wrath of Kahn.* New York: Pocket Books, 1982.

Marks, Elaine, and Isabelle de Courtivon, eds. *New French Feminism.* New York: Schocken Books, 1980.

Mayne, Judith. "The Woman at the Keyhole: Women's Cinema and Feminist Criticism." *New German Critique,* no. 23 (1981): 27–43.

Miller, Nancy, ed. *Poetics of Gender.* New York: Columbia University Press, 1986.

Modleski, Tania. *Loving With a Vengeance: Mass Produced Fantasies for Women.* Hamden, Conn.: Archon Books, 1982.

———. "The Rhythms of Reception: Daytime Television and Women's Work." In *Regarding Television,* edited by E. Ann Kaplan, pp. 67–75. Los Angeles: The American Film Institute, 1975.

———, ed. *Studies in Entertainment: Critical Approaches to Mass Culture.* Bloomington: Indiana University Press, 1986.

Morgan, David. "Culture Work and Friendship Work: The Case of "Blooms-bury." *Media, Culture and Society* 4 (1982): 19–32.

Mukarovsky, Jan. *Structure, Sign and Function.* Translated by John Burbank and Peter Steiner. New Haven: Yale University Press, 1978.

Mulvey, Laura. "Visual Pleasure and Narrative Cinema." *Screen* 16, no. 3 (1975): 6–18.

Mussell, Kay. *Fantasy and Reconciliation.* Westport, Conn.: Greenwood Press, 1984.

Nichols, Bill. *Ideology and the Image.* Bloomington: Indiana University Press, 1981.

Nome. Edited by Victoria Clark and Barbara Storey. New York. Fanzine.

Ortner, Sherry B., and Harriet Whitehead, eds. *Sexual Meanings: The Cultural Construction of Gender and Sexuality.* Cambridge: Cambridge University Press, 1981.

Paulson, Ronald. *The Fictions of Satire.* Baltimore: Johns Hopkins University Press, 1967.

Pike, Kenneth L. "Towards a Theory of the Structure of Human Behavior." *Language in Culture and Society,* edited by Dell Hymes. New York: Harper and Row, 1964.

Porter, Andrew, ed. "Conventions, A Calendar of Upcoming Events." *Science Fiction Chronicle.* Various issues, 1986. Semi-professional science fiction news fanzine.

Powell, Chris, and George C. Paton: *Humour in Society.* New York: St. Martin's Press, 1988.

Pratt, Annis. *Archetypal Patterns in Women's Fiction.* Bloomington: Indiana University Press, 1981.

Propp, Vladimir. *Morphology of the Folktale.* Translated by Laurence Scott. Austin: University of Texas Press, 1968 (1928).

Radway, Janice. "Interpretive Communities and Variable Literacies: The Function of Romance Reading." *Anticipations. Proceedings of the American Academy of Arts and Sciences,* vol. 113, no. 3 (1984): 49–73.

———. *Reading the Romance.* Chapel Hill: University of North Carolina Press, 1984.

Redfern, Walter. *Puns.* Oxford: Basil Blackwell, 1984.

Rimmon-Kenan, Shlomith. *Narrative Fiction: Contemporary Poetics.* London: Methuen, 1983.

Roddenberry, Gene, and Stephen Whitfield. *The Making of Star Trek.* New York: Ballantine Books, 1968.

Rogow, Roberta. *Trexindex,* and Supplements 1–5. Fairlawn, N.J.: Other World Books, 1977–1988. Fanzine.

Roush, C. E. "Assignment Enterprise." *Maine(ly) Trek 4,* edited by Mary Ann Drach. Temple, Maine: Walking Carpet Press, 1985. Fanzine.

Russ, Joanna. *How to Suppress Women's Writing.* Austin: University of Texas Press, 1983.

———. *Magic Mammas, Trembling Sisters, Puritans and Perverts.* New York: Crossing Press, 1985.

Russell, W. M. S. "Folktales and Science Fiction." Presidential Address, *Folklore* 93 (1982).

———. "More about Folktales and Literature." Second Presidential Address, *Folklore* 94 (1983).

Sahlins, Marshall. *Culture and Practical Reason.* Chicago: University of Chicago Press, 1976.

Said, Edward: *The Word, The Text, and the Critic.* Cambridge, Mass.: Harvard University Press, 1983.

Salmond, Anne. "Theoretical Landscapes: On Cross-Cultural Conceptions of Knowledge." In *Semantic Anthropology,* edited by David Parkin, pp. 65–87. New York: Academic Press, 1982.

Sapir, Edward. *Language: An Introduction to the Study of Speech.* New York: Harcourt, Brace and Jovanovich, 1921.

Scarry, Elaine. *The Body in Pain.* New York: Oxford University Press, 1985.

Schwartzman, Helen. "Sociocultural Context of Play." In *Play and Learning,* edited by Brian Sutton-Smith. New York: Gardner Press, 1979.

————, ed. *Play and Culture.* New York: Leisure Press, 1980.

Sedgwick, Eva Kosofsky. *Between Men: English Literature and Male Homosocial Desire.* New York: Columbia University Press, 1985.

Selley, April. "'I Have Been, and Ever Shall Be, Your Friend': *Star Trek, The Deerslayer,* and the American Romance." *Journal of Popular Culture* (1987): 89–104.

Shiokawa, Kanako. "Between Here and There: Reinforcement of Expectations in Supernatural Experience Narratives of Japanese Speakers." Paper presented at the annual meeting of the American Folklore Society, Cambridge, Mass.: October 1988. Expanded January 31, 1989 (not published).

Showalter, Elaine. "Piecing and Writing." In *The Poetics of Gender,* edited by Nancy K. Miller, pp. 222–47. New York: Columbia University Press, 1986.

————, ed. *The New Feminist Criticism: Essays on Women, Literature, and Theory.* New York: Pantheon Books, 1985.

Singer, Jerome, and Dorothy Singer. "The Value of the Imagination." In *Play and Learning,* edited by Brian Sutton-Smith. New York: Gardner Press, 1979.

Smith, Barbara Herrnstein. *Poetic Closure: A Study of How Poems End.* Chicago: University of Chicago Press, 1968.

Smith, Paula. "A Trekkie's Tale." Reprinted in "Mary Sue: A Short Compendium." *Archives V* (Winter 1980), edited by Johanna Cantor. Bronx, N.Y.: Yeoman Press. Fanzine.

Smith-Rosenberg, Carroll. "The Female World of Love and Ritual: Relations between Women in Nineteenth Century America." *Signs* 1 (Autumn 1975): 1–29.

Spacks, Patricia Meyer. *The Adolescent Idea: Myths of Youth and the Adult Imagination.* New York: Basic Books, 1981.

————. *The Female Imagination.* New York: Alfred A. Knopf, 1975.

————. *Gossip.* New York: Alfred A. Knopf, 1985.

Spockanalia. Edited by Sherna (Comerford) Burley and Devra Michele Langsam. Brooklyn, N.Y.: Garlic Press Publication, 1967 (issue date). Reprint. Brooklyn: Poison Pen Press, 1979. Fanzine.

Spradley, James P. *Participant Observation.* New York: Holt, Rinehart and Winston, 1980.

Stern, Leslie. "The Body as Evidence: A Critical Review of The Pornography Problematic." *Screen* 23, no. 5 (1982): 39–62.

Stone, Kay. "The Misuses of Enchantment: Controversies on the Significance of Fairy Tales." In *Women's Folklore, Women's Culture,* edited by Rosan A. Jordan and Susan J. Kalčik, pp. 125–45. Philadelphia: University of Pennsylvania Press, 1985.

————. "Things Walt Disney Never Told Us." In *Women and Folklore,* edited by Claire Farrer, pp. 42–50. Austin: University of Texas Press, 1975.

Stotland, Ezra, Kenneth E. Mathews, Jr., Stanley E. Sherman, Robert O. Hansson, and Barbara Z. Richardson. *Empathy, Fantasy, and Helping.* Beverly Hills, Calif.: Sage Publications, 1978.

Strauss, Erwin S. "S.F. Convention Calendar." *Isaac Asimov's Science Fiction,* 1987 (13 issues).

Sutton-Smith, Brian. "Creativity and the Vicissitudes of Play." *Adolescent Psychiatry* 15 (1988): 307–18.

————. "Games of Order and Disorder." Paper presented at the annual meeting of the American Anthropological Association, Toronto, 1972.

————. "The Metaphor of Games in Social Science Research," *Play, Play Therapy, Play Research*. Paper presented at an international symposium, Amsterdam, 1985 (Berwyn: Swets North American, 1986), pp. 35–65.

————. "Reversible Childhood." *Play and Culture* 2 (1989): 52–63.

————. "In Search of the Imagination." In *Education and Imagination*, edited by D. Nadarer and K. Eagen. New York: T. C. Press, 1987.

————., ed. *Play and Learning*. New York: Gardner Press, Inc., 1979.

Sutton-Smith, Brian, and Diana Kelly-Bryne, eds. *The Masks of Play*. New York: Leisure Press, 1984.

Tedlock, Dennis. *The Spoken Word and the Work of Interpretation*. Philadelphia: University of Pennsylvania Press, 1983.

Thomas, Sari, ed. *Film/Culture: Explorations of Cinema in Its Social Context*. Metuchen, N.J.: Scarecrow Press, 1982.

Toelken, Barre. "Folklore, Worldview and Communication." In *Folklore: Performance and Communication*, edited by D. Ben-Amos and K. S. Goldstein. The Hague: Mouton, 1975.

Turnbull, Colin. "Learning Non-Aggression." In *Learning Non-Aggression*, edited by Ashley Montagu, pp. 161–221. New York: Oxford University Press, 1978.

Turner, Victor. *Dramas, Fields, and Metaphors: Symbolic Action in Human Society*. Ithaca, N.Y.: Cornell University Press, 1974.

————. *The Drums of Affliction*. Oxford: Clarendon Press, 1968.

————. *The Forest of Symbols*. Ithaca, N.Y.: Cornell University Press, 1967.

————. *Image and Pilgrimage in Christian Culture*. New York: Columbia University Press, 1978.

————. "Liminal to Liminoid, in Play, Flow, and Ritual: An Essay in Comparative Symbology." *The Anthropological Study of Human Play*. Rice University Studies, vol. 60, no. 3, pp. 53–92. Houston, 1974.

————. *Revelation and Divination in Ndembu Ritual*. Ithaca, N.Y.: Cornell University Press, 1975.

————. *The Ritual Process: Structure and Anti-Structure*. Ithaca, N.Y.: Cornell University Press, 1969.

Vance, Carole, ed. *Pleasure and Danger*. Boston: Routledge and Kegan Paul, 1984.

Van Hise, Della. *Killing Time*. New York: Pocket Books, 1985; later revised edition, n.d.

Weinstein, Howard. *The Covenant and the Crown*. New York: Pocket Books, 1981.

Welling, Lois. *The Displaced*. Champaign, Ill.: self-published, 1978.

Wenk, Barbara. *One Way Mirror. Masiform D special supplement # 2*. Brooklyn, N.Y.: Poison Pen Press, 1980. Fanzine.

West, Alan, Colin Martindale, and Brian Sutton-Smith. "Age Trends in the Content of Children's Spontaneous Fantasy Narratives." *Genetic, Social and Psychological Monographs* 111 (1984): 389–405.

Whorf, B. L. *Language, Thought, and Reality: Selected Writings of Benjamin Lee Whorf*. Cambridge, Mass.: MIT Press, 1954.

Whovian Times. Newsletter of the Dr. Who Fan Club of America, 1984.

Wicking, Christopher. "Conversation with Ray Menmiur and Gerry O'Hara." *Primetime* 1, no. 2 (Autumn 1981): 5–8.

Williams, Raymond. *Television, Technology, and Cultural Form*. New York: Schocken Books, 1975.

Williamson, Judith. *Consuming Passions: The Dynamics of Popular Culture.* New York: Marion Boyars Publisher, 1986 (1980).

Winston, Joan. *The Making of the Trek Conventions.* New York: Playboy Press, 1979.

Woolf, Virginia. *A Room of One's Own.* New York: Harcourt Brace Jovanovich, 1975 (1929).

Worth, Sol. *Studying Visual Communication.* Edited by Larry Gross. Philadelphia: University of Pennsylvania Press, 1981.

Worth, Sol, and John Adair. *Through Navajo Eyes: An Exploration in Film Communication and Anthropology.* Bloomington: Indiana University Press, 1972.

Wortham, Ann, and Leah Rosenthal, eds. *The Bizarro Zine # 2.* Brooklyn, N.Y.: Leah Rosenthal, 1989. Fanzine.

Wright, Will. *Six Guns and Society: A Structural Study of the Western.* Berkeley: University of California Press, 1975.

Index

Macrotexts, 52
Matthews, Susan, 62, 65, 130, 152
Mellanby, Dayna (*Blake's 7*), 142, 143, 146, 312
Menmuir, Ray, 183
Microflow, 133, 136–38, 157, 181, 184, 192
Modleski, Tania, 232
More Eastly Con, 64, 112, 115, 120, 121, 130, 159, 205, 242, 267, 268, 319
Mulvey, Laura, 186, 193, 195, 296
Myth, 274

Nasfic, 10, 312, 321
Nimoy, Leonard, 92, 186, 234

Olmos, Edward James, 190, 191

Parnes, Caren, 70, 73, 129, 131, 181, 190, 191, 235
Photocopying, 176, 210, 212
Polysemy, 232
Primetime, 180, 183
Prydonians of Prynceton, 313

Radway, Janice, 158
Rimmon-Kenan, Shlomith, 158
Ripley (*Alien*), 241
Robin of Sherwood, 28, 35, 314
Roddenberry, Gene, 82, 108, 155, 180, 186, 206, 284, 310, 316, 317
Rogow, Roberta, 93, 97, 153, 222, 317, 321, 322
Role-playing games
  gamers, 18, 120
  gaming, 18, 22, 41, 309
Romulan, 104, 106, 146, 237, 314
Rosenthal, Leah, 59, 60, 164
Roush, C. E., 151

Sahaj (*Star Trek*), 86
Said, Edward, 29, 32, 35, 38, 56, 58, 64, 82, 83, 88, 89, 91, 92, 96, 97, 99, 106, 124, 133, 154, 156, 159, 177, 184, 205, 206, 208, 209, 211, 212, 223, 235, 239, 241, 243, 256, 268, 286
Sapir, Edward, 302
Sarek (*Star Trek*), 58, 59, 64, 102, 103, 111, 112, 155, 156, 161, 261, 314, 315

Scarry, Elaine, 277–79
Scott, Montgomery "Scotty" (*Star Trek*), 95, 96, 101, 163, 176, 314
Sedgwick, Eva Kosofsky, 248
Selley, April, 145, 234, 241
Servalan (*Blake's 7*), 122, 131, 143, 160, 271, 314
Shatner, William 58, 155, 234
Showalter, Elaine, 56
Skywalker, Luke (*Star Wars*), 307, 311, 313, 314, 317, 318
Smith, Paula, 34, 94, 96, 286, 291
Songtape, 134, 175–81, 184, 194, 233, 312, 315
Soolin (*Blake's 7*), 143, 146, 315
Spock (*Star Trek*), 5, 33, 38, 39, 47, 53, 55, 58, 60, 64, 65, 91, 95–97, 101–8, 111, 112, 116, 117, 143, 145, 146, 150, 153–55, 157, 160, 161, 163, 166, 188, 189, 196, 220, 222–24, 229–31, 234–39, 250, 257, 261, 263, 264, 267, 276, 307, 308, 311, 312, 314, 315
Star Trek, 4, 5, 8, 9, 11, 12, 15–17, 22–25, 28–34, 37–40, 45, 53, 57, 58, 60, 62–65, 73, 75, 82–84, 86–94, 97, 98, 103, 107–9, 112, 115, 117, 120, 124, 128, 129, 131, 134, 136, 141–43, 146, 151, 154–56, 160, 163, 175–77, 180, 186, 189, 196, 197, 198, 203, 206, 208, 210, 215, 216, 222, 224, 228, 229, 234, 236, 237, 239–41, 244, 250, 257, 263, 267, 283, 299, 307–19, 321, 322
Starfleet, 23, 67, 94, 104, 105, 134, 151, 310, 315
Starsky, David (*Starsky and Hutch*), 310, 313, 314, 316
Starsky and Hutch, 25, 57, 60, 122, 134, 144, 196, 223, 233, 234, 257, 258, 266, 310, 313, 315
Steele, Remington (*Remington Steele*), 310, 313, 314, 316
Subtext, 196, 264
Sulu (*Star Trek*), 32, 153, 316
Surak (*Star Trek*), 60, 316
Sutton-Smith, Brian, 286, 291

Takai, George, 32, 33
Tardis, 58, 316

This book was set in Baskerville and Eras typefaces. Baskerville was designed by John Baskerville at his private press in Birmingham, England, in the eighteenth century. The first typeface to depart from oldstyle typeface design, Baskerville has more variation between thick and thin strokes. In an effort to ensure that the thick and thin strokes of his typeface reproduced well on paper, John Baskerville developed the first wove paper, the surface of which was much smoother than the laid paper of the time. The development of wove paper was partly responsible for the introduction of typefaces classified as modern, which have even more contrast between thick and thin strokes.

Eras was designed in 1969 by Studio Hollenstein in Paris for the Wagner Typefoundry. A contemporary script-like version of a sans-serif typeface, the letters of Eras have a monotone stroke and are slightly inclined.

Printed on acid-free paper.